TROLLOPE AND POLITICS

TROLLOPE
AND
POLITICS

A Study of the Pallisers and Others

JOHN HALPERIN

University of Southern California

BOOKS
10 East 53d St., New York 10022
(a division of Harper & Row Publishers, Inc.)

First published 1977 by
THE MACMILLAN PRESS LTD
London and Basingstoke

Published in the U.S.A. 1977 by
HARPER & ROW PUBLISHERS, INC.
BARNES & NOBLE IMPORT DIVISION

ISBN 0–06–492666–4

Printed in Great Britain

To
MY MOTHER AND FATHER
*whose devoted interest
helped keep this book going*

Contents

Preface

If Henry James chewed more than he bit off, Anthony Trollope, perhaps, chewed less. Especially in the Palliser novels, in which he is concerned primarily with the political system of Victorian England and its effects upon people, his subjects may seem to some larger than his treatment of them, ostensibly rather casual for so wide a view. This is both true and false. Trollope's political novels do not allegorize man's fate or prescribe theoretical alternative governments; but they do tell us much about the politics of the time, the role of individuals in politics and of politics in the lives of individuals, and the ways in which political and social systems interact and interdepend. They also tell us a good deal, should we care to know it, about Anthony Trollope himself — his political ideas, prejudices, aversions — and an understanding of these in turn helps to illuminate some previously dark corners of the novelist's mind, art, and life. That is a large claim; the reader of this book may decide for himself whether or not it is justified.

Trollope and Politics is divided into ten chapters. There is an introduction of sorts at each end of the book, though the one on the far side looks backward rather than forward. There is a chapter which discusses the grouping problem one has to face in dealing with Trollope's political novels, and explains the procedure upon which real political characters and events are brought to light throughout the discussion. Each of the six Palliser novels has a chapter devoted to it. And in the midst of these — because that is where it properly comes — is a chapter devoted to the only real political event of Trollope's life and the novel that resulted from it.

I make no claim that the subject has been exhaustively dealt with here. I have provided little detailed commentary on Trollope's developed convictions about many of the specific issues which so concerned his mid-Victorian contemporaries. I hope I have been able, at least, to define the political attitudes that come through in some of his books, to place these attitudes in the contexts of the man's life and work, and to show how closely his political novels are connected both to actual events and personages of his time and to his own evolving conception of Victorian society.

Grateful acknowledgment is made herewith to the Rockefeller Foundation; to the National Endowment for the Humanities; and to the College of Letters, Arts, and Sciences, and to the Department of English, of the University of Southern California for awards which helped to bring this book to completion earlier than possible otherwise; to Bill and Betsy Olson and the staff of the Villa Serbelloni, Bellagio, for providing such a marvellous place in which to work for five weeks; and to the Department of English and the Division of Humanities at USC for the granting of an early sabbatical without which, again, I should have been much longer at this task.

Sections of Chapters 1 and 8 appeared together in different form as "Politics, Palmerston, and Trollope's Prime Minister" in *Clio*, 3, No. 2 (February 1974), and I should like to thank the editors of *Clio* for permitting me to reprint this material here; a part of Chapter 9 appeared, also in different form, as "Trollope, James and the International Theme" in the *Yearbook of English Studies*, vol. 7 (January 1977), and I am grateful to the editors of the *Modern Language Review* for allowing it to be reprinted here.

I am also indebted to each of the following for graciously reading various sections of my manuscript as it grew and making many useful suggestions for its improvement: Alistair M. Duckworth, James H. Durbin, Jr., Donald Greene, N. John Hall, Barbara Hardy, Wendell V. Harris, A. Walton Litz, Hershel Parker, Andrew Wright. I am particularly grateful to Jack Hall for sound editorial advice, and also for various caches of information culled from some of Trollope's unpublished letters. I should like to thank Mr T. D. Rogers and his staff at the Bodleian Library, Oxford, Mr Lewis Tiffany, and Mrs Janet Kunert for their help in gathering materials needed to research this project. I wish also to acknowledge the kind assistance in various matters of Barry A. Bartrum, George Butte, and Andrew K. Platt.

I cannot resist mentioning the "help" of a precocious black and white cat of the American Alley variety named Lady Glencora Palliser, who at moments of inspiration (largely hers) has been fond of bounding over the keyboard of my electric typewriter, adding a few syllables here and there not entirely inappropriate to the language spoken by some of Trollope's politicians. These, I trust, have been found and purified.

I was introduced to Trollope as a graduate student by J. Hillis Miller. I remember well his advice to me to write a dissertation on Trollope, and my feeling at the time that Trollope did not bear much looking into. That I write on Trollope now is belated evidence among other things of the wisdom of dissertation directors.

J.H.

Los Angeles 1972 – London 1976

A Note on References

No standard or complete edition of Trollope's writings exists. Quotations from the novels and the *Autobiography* are taken from the Oxford World's Classics editions since these are more readily available than any others in most cases. Many of the World's Classics editions are double volumes in one cover; where this occurs (and it often does) my citations — appearing in parentheses just before or after quoted matter of substantive importance — are to volume and page-number. In double-volume editions the pagination begins a new sequence at the commencement of each "volume"; single-volume citations are to page-numbers only.

I have used the following abbreviations throughout notes for items cited in more than one chapter:

apRoberts   Ruth apRoberts, *The Moral Trollope* (Athens, Ohio, 1971)
Bartrum   Barry A. Bartrum, "A Victorian Political Hostess: The Engagement Book of Lady Stanley of Alderley," *Princeton University Library Chronicle*, 36, No. 2 (Winter 1975), 133–46
Blake   Robert Blake, *Disraeli* (London, 1966)
Booth   Bradford A. Booth, *Anthony Trollope: Aspects of His Life and Work* (Bloomington, Indiana, 1958)
Briggs   Asa Briggs, "Trollope, Bagehot, and the English Constitution," in *Victorian People* (Chicago, 1955), pp. 87–115
Burn   W. L. Burn, "Anthony Trollope's Politics," in *The Nineteenth Century and After*, 143 (March 1948), 161–71
Cicero   Anthony Trollope, *The Life of Cicero*, 2 vols. (New York, 1881)
Cockshut   A. O. J. Cockshut, *Anthony Trollope: A Critical Study* (London, 1955)
Critical Heritage *Anthony Trollope: The Critical Heritage*, ed. Donald Smalley (London and New York, 1969)
Curtis Brown   Beatrice Curtis Brown, *Trollope* (Denver, 1950)
Escott   T. H. S. Escott, *Anthony Trollope: His Public Services, Private Friends and Literary Originals* (London, 1913; repr. 1967)
Four Lectures   Anthony Trollope, *Four Lectures*, ed. Morris L. Parrish (London, 1938)
Greville   *The Greville Diary*, ed. Philip Whitwell Wilson (London, 1927)
James   Henry James, "Anthony Trollope," in *Century Magazine* (July

1883), repr. *Partial Portraits* (New York, 1888), pp. 97–133

Kenney   Blair G. Kenney, "Trollope's Ideal Statesmen: Plantagenet Palliser and Lord John Russell," *in NCF*, 20 (December 1965), 281–6

Letters   *The Letters of Anthony Trollope*, ed. Bradford A. Booth (London, 1951)

New Zealander   Anthony Trollope, *The New Zealander*, ed. N. John Hall (Oxford, 1972)

North America   Anthony Trollope, *North America*, ed. Robert Mason (Harmondsworth, England, 1968; abridged)

Palmerston   Anthony Trollope, *Lord Palmerston* (London, 1882)

Polhemus   Robert M. Polhemus, *The Changing World of Anthony Trollope* (Berkeley and Los Angeles, 1968)

Pollard   Arthur Pollard, "Trollope's Political Novels," Inaugural Lecture, University of Hull (April 1968), pp. 3–25

Pope-Hennessy   James Pope-Hennessy, *Anthony Trollope* (London and Boston, 1971)

Sadleir   Michael Sadleir, *Trollope: A Commentary* (London, 1927; repr. 1961)

Skilton   David Skilton, *Anthony Trollope and His Contemporaries* (London, 1972)

Snow   C. P. Snow, *Trollope* (London, 1975)

Speare   Morris E. Speare, *The Political Novel* (New York, 1924)

Stebbinses   Lucy Poate Stebbins and Richard Poate Stebbins, *The Trollopes: The Chronicle of A Writing Family* (New York, 1945)

Thackeray   Anthony Trollope, *Thackeray* (London, 1879)

Trevelyan   G. M. Trevelyan, *British History in the Nineteenth Century* (New York, 1922; repr. 1966)

Trollope Papers   Business Papers, Bodleian Library, Oxford

Walpole   Hugh Walpole, *Anthony Trollope* (New York, 1928)

Frequently cited Journals

NCF – *Nineteenth Century Fiction*
N & Q – *Notes & Queries*
PULC – *Princeton University Library Chronicle*
SEL – *Studies in English Literature*
TT – *The Trollopian*
VS – *Victorian Studies*

1 Fiction That Is True: Trollope and Politics

That it is a good thing to be well off, that it is well to act honorably, that it is about the best of all things to be a well-to-do English gentlemen, and that it is quite the best of all things to be at once a well-to-do English gentleman and a master of fox-hounds, are the sort of maxims which Mr. Trollope directly or indirectly presents for the acceptance of his admirers. The creed he holds is the fact that the life of an English gentleman is the most satisfactory kind of life which any man can spend.

The Nation, 12 March 1874

'I'm reading Trollope – the Palliser novels – and keep interrupting my wife to read her paragraphs that particularly strike me.'

Former Watergate Special Prosecutor Archibald Cox, quoted in *The New Yorker*, 20 January 1975

Of all his literary creations, Trollope loved the Pallisers most. In his *Autobiography* (written mostly 1875–6; published posthumously 1883) he describes the string of characters who inhabit the Palliser novels as "the best I ever made" and the novels in which they appear as "the best work of my life" (p. 155). He always had a special tenderness for these novels. And it is true that they represent the peak of his achievement – his widest canvas, his broadest range, his surest touch. The Barset novels, entertaining as they are, lean heavily upon caricature and farce. As tragedy is of higher seriousness than comedy, so the Palliser novels rather than the novels of Barchester represent Trollope's magnum opus.

No student of Trollope should be surprised by his interest in politics. Never satisfied to do just one thing at a time, he had a prodigious curiosity about people and places; this great vitality became channelled into many activities beyond the writing of fiction. Regularly he felt he must get out of his study and into the street – even into little-travelled corners of the world – to see life. Since he was always interested in the science of government, wherever he went on his travels – South Africa, Australia, New Zealand, the West Indies, North America, Italy, Iceland, the Sandwich Islands (Hawaii) – he observed carefully the political systems he saw,

1

and wrote about them in his travel books. Indeed, the many tedious passages in these books recounting with unrelenting detail how various peoples govern themselves betray Trollope's failure to understand how uninteresting to others this subject might be. His *Life of Cicero* (1881) and his edition of Caesar's *Commentaries* (1870) touch more than lightly upon the problems of political principle and expediency; the bulk of his contributions to the *Pall Mall Gazette, Fortnightly Review*, and *St. Paul's Magazine* between 1865 and 1869 are on political rather than literary matters. Always engaged by politics, Trollope was an informed political pundit and had opinions on a great many issues. From his earliest writings (articles on social and political conditions in Ireland; the *Dublin Review* asserted in 1869 that Trollope understood the Irish Tenant-Right question better than almost all Englishmen of his time) to his memoir of Lord Palmerston, almost the last thing he wrote, the novelist's fascination with politics is manifest. In the fifties he composed a series of essays on essentially political themes (written 1855—6; published for the first time in 1972 as *The New Zealander*); in the fifties and sixties he was a staunch defender of Palmerston and of Lord John Russell and his policies; also in the sixties he helped to found two politically progressive journals which characteristically supported the Liberal party (the *Fortnightly* and *St. Paul's* — he edited the latter); in the seventies he sided with Gladstone on the Eastern Question, speaking publicly on the issue and reading aloud to his family and some guests Gladstone's pamphlet on *The Bulgarian Horrors and the Question of the East* in 1876;[1] at the end of his life he broke explosively with Gladstone over matters essentially political. Trollope spoke no modern languages other than English, read little philosophy (nothing heavier than Bacon), knew no science; but on the subject of politics he was always well-informed.

Trollope says that "in that work of choosing his ruler does it most behove [one] to use all the care and all the skill that he can compass"; and also that "of all studies to which men and women can attach themselves, that of politics is the first and the finest."[2] A well-known section of his *Autobiography* declares:

> to sit in the British Parliament should be the highest object of ambition to every educated Englishman ... The man in Parliament has reached a higher position than the man out ... To serve one's country without pay is the grandest work that a man can do ... Of all studies the study of politics is the one in which a man may make himself most useful to his fellow-creatures ... of all lives, public political life is capable of the greatest efforts.

Trollope also tells us in *The Eustace Diamonds* (1871—73) that, "of all paths," public life is "the noblest and manliest" (p. 163); in *Can You Forgive Her?* (1864—5) he says it is "the highest and most legitimate pride of an Englishman to have the letters M.P. written after his name. No selection from the alphabet . . . confers so fair an honour" (II, 54); and in *Doctor Thorne* (1858) he declares that a seat in Parliament is a "prize . . . well worth any that can be paid for it short of wading through dirt and dishonour" (p. 200). This view — repeated again and again in various places, convinced as the novelist was that unpaid (as it was then) public service as a member of Parliament was the most disinterested and therefore the most patriotic activity for an educated man — led him to run for Parliament as a Liberal candidate in 1868. After "wading through" a great deal of "dirt and dishonour" in the borough of Beverley in Yorkshire — the voters of which were stunned by a bribeless campaign based on political principles clearly articulated — Trollope found his candidacy unequivocally rejected. He did not try again.

There can be no doubt that Trollope's frustrated political ambitions, both long before and long after Beverley, were sublimated in part into the writing of novels about politics. Having been "debarred from expressing my opinions in the House of Commons, I took this method of declaring myself," the novelist says of his political novels in the *Autobiography* (p. 262). Here the would-be politician spoke to the gallery of his readers; indeed, the Palliser novels, Trollope confesses, "served me as safety-valves by which to deliver my soul." These novels, which express so many of his political and social convictions, are in fact substitutes for political action; if Trollope could not air his political views in Parliament he could do so in his fiction. Yet they do not express merely one man's subjective view. Asa Briggs has said that "A more convincing impression of what everyday life was like in England in the middle Victorian years can be gathered from [Trollope's novels more readily] than from any other source"; pointing to the Palliser novels in particular, Briggs concluded that whoever reads Trollope may be enabled to "catch the flavour of his age more satisfactorily than anywhere else."[3]

In Trollope's day parliamentary White Papers were actually read by some laymen and portraits of leading politicians hung over the fireplaces of many homes. Like most of his contemporaries, Trollope believed instinctively in many of the institutions of his time (an attitude often satirized by Dickens; the two novelists have little in common). Unlike most of his fellow novelists, Trollope in his books expresses some of the normal qualities of these institutions and of those who believed in and peopled them (an employee of the Post Office for over thirty years, he was one of these people himself). It is unlikely that any other Victorian novelist could have put into the mouth of one of his heroes the following speech (from *The Claverings*, 1866–7): "No man has a right to be peculiar. Every man is bound to accept such usage as is customary in the world" (I, 282; the author of *Little Dorrit* could hardly have written *that*). Not surprisingly, then, Trollope's political novels introduce us to a great many ordinary politicians of middling stature whose convictions, abilities, and ambitions are equally ordinary. Bulging with detailed accounts of the everyday lives of such men and of the clubs and drawing-rooms they inhabit, these books have their settings in St Stephen's, Whitehall, Pall Mall, and the country houses where politicians and their hangers-on gather. As a sometime guest at political soirées and a constantly fascinated observer, Trollope knew how the powerful and great lived, and he is able to give an account of them in these novels. Yet it is the normal quality of everyday life that is most vividly recounted here.

It is not true that Trollope's political novels give merely a superficial picture of this segment of British life. Even unfriendly critics have admitted that these books articulate "a profound knowledge of the parliamentary system of England."[4] In them we can learn a great deal about partisanship, coalitions, the maintenance of parliamentary majorities, the procedures of dissolution. And we can see how political ambitions work on the sensibilities of professional politicians – some of whom struggle to maintain exemplary ethical standards, some of whom have long since abandoned the struggle. Critics have often commented on Trollope's "balance," his tendency to give both sides of a case, even to defend his own villains when no one else – not even his own characters – will do so. He typically saw politics as a continually shifting process of change and conciliation. And he typically saw personal life in political terms, unable as he was to imagine it as something separate from the life of the community. The theme of one of his last novels – *Dr. Wortle's School* (1881) – is that a bad life cannot be led in a good community without infecting that community, and he clearly believed the obverse of this too: a good life cannot be led in a bad community. In this novel Dr Wortle (often – but erroneously, despite the obvious sympathy with which he is drawn – assumed to be a self-portrait) tells Mr Peacocke that "no man [has] a right to regard his own moral life as isolated from the lives of others around him . . . a man cannot isolate the morals, the manners, the ways of his life from the morals of others. Men, if they live together, must live together by certain laws" (pp. 84 and 90). Politics and social life – and thus the public and the private lives – are seen by Trollope as inextricably connected, interdependent. His politicians often seek political power primarily as a social tool – as a means of making peers, giving Garters, and so forth, and of depriving enemies of these good things – and it is in order to do this that the political parties chiefly compete in the Palliser novels. "All political corruption resolves itself to this," Trollope says in *The New Zealander*. "Men . . . desire the power of distributing [loaves] to others, and the distinction with which such power will invest themselves. To keep or achieve this politicians have . . . for many ages descended to falsehood, intrigue, and Machiavellian crookedness. Such is political corruption."[5] Trollope understood that a politician must please both his own associates and the social Establishment if he is to succeed, and thus the political and social worlds are bound closely together in his novels. This has led some critics to think that Trollope's political novels, in the words of Bradford A. Booth, "are not really 'political' at all." Politics is "incidental" in these novels, Booth wrote; nor did he like them much as novels. His misleading and hostile account of them, coupled with the misreading of A. O. J. Cockshut and others (e.g., Leopold Amery: Trollope's political novels are political novels with the "politics left out"), has helped to keep the Palliser novels in relative obscurity for years. Though his subject was not Trollope's politics and he has little specifically to say on the subject, Robert M. Polhemus, writing in 1968, was one of the first to point out that Trollope's political novels are concerned with such important questions as "what politics should do and what motivates politicians . . . few other novelists give us such an acute sense of what it is like to live at the heart of a civilization's power elite." Exactly; the novelist's awareness of the ways in which politics and society interact makes his political novels that much more politically sophisticated and knowledgeable. His recognition that politics is not always concerned with large issues and important ideas makes his account of it more, not less, authentic.[6] Unlike Disraeli, Trollope was a story-teller, not a pamphleteer.

Trollope's "balance" — as well as a sort of creeping cynicism which increased as he grew older — also led the novelist to see the negative side of politics. If politics can be the grandest work that a man can put his hand to, it can also be the dirtiest. Trollope's judicious awareness of these contraries manifests itself in a curious sort of double vision which simultaneously admires and satirizes the profession of politics. So, despite his reverence, Trollope could also fill the Palliser novels with adventurers and opportunists who are never to be believed, men who regard politics as a huge game — "an affair of expediency" from which sincerity, principle, and patriotism are always absent.[7] This double vision runs through the Palliser novels and focuses on the abuses, tricks, and dishonesty of the average professional politician as well as on his rare virtues. Trollope saw politicians as buffoons as well as statesmen; indeed, no other English novelist — not even Disraeli — has left on record so many vivid and incisive portraits of political hacks or has written about them so mercilessly. Trollope saw that politics was often sham, mere theater, and settled nothing — that, in the words of *Phineas Finn* (1867–9), "The people can take care of themselves a great deal better than [politicians] can take care of them" (I, 31). His politicians frequently speak glowingly of the practical advantages of doing nothing while seeming to do much. Thus a typical leitmotif of these novels is that of the *game* of politics — politics as a series of tricks conducted by ambitious and greedy men who seek to camouflage their real, selfish objects in dissembling. The image of the party "game" recurs again and again throughout the political novels. For most of Trollope's politicians the game's the thing; party loyalty means choosing sides and sticking to one's friends. The comparison in *North America* of the Speaker of the U.S. House of Representatives to "a croupier at a gaming table who goes on dealing and explaining the results of the game" expresses a characteristic perspective. Indeed, politics in Trollope's novels often turns out to be what Fielding called "politricks" – a game the politician plays primarily for his own benefit, being a man on the make and acting, whether he knows it or not, for selfish ends.[8] In the *Autobiography* (pp. 253–4) the novelist declares that "A man who entertains in his mind any political doctrine, except as a means of improving the condition of his fellows, I regard as a political intriguer, a charlatan, and a conjurer." The epithet "conjurer" is applied throughout the Palliser novels to Trollope's most hated politicians, those who have taken the gamesmanship of politics beyond its usual bounds and turned it into a kind of sorcery whose selfish ends make it even more than ordinarily unwholesome and dangerous. It is only the exceptional individual in these novels who can remain aloof from the partisan contests over trivial issues which are seen to occupy so much time of political men. While Trollope reveres the occasional politician, his contempt for political *processes* and their paralyzing effects on individuals is manifest everywhere.

The only use of "any political doctrine," then, is to improve contemporary conditions. Unfortunately, "men with political views, and with so much of their future prospects in jeopardy also, are allowed to dress themselves differently for different scenes," Trollope reminds us (p. 14) in *The Belton Estate* (1865–6); and as a result most political activity is not conducted to improve the general condition of things. "In public life . . . who ever thinks of other interest than his own?" (*The Three Clerks*, 1858; p. 405).

Trollope's politicians often begin honestly, with good intentions; because of pressures brought to bear upon them by voters and colleagues, however, they gradually submerge their integrity in group action. Many have few real convictions to begin with – any real political creed being an impractical luxury for a professional politician. What is wanted is the ability to make oneself pleasant to others – the capacity for popularity. The political world, after all, is one of compromises; Trollope's politicians advocate political measures as others advocate health cures or racehorses. Convictions are a hindrance. For this the public – perversely driving politicians to commit themselves, insisting that a game be played – is largely responsible. Given man's natural greed, his desire for power, and his inherent contentiousness, the political process can turn an essentially decent person into part of the force which hampers rather than protects the public good. Trollope saw political evil as he typically saw other kinds – not so much Satanic and irredeemable, in the manner of Dickens, as simply the quotient of natural forces, less diabolical than accidental, the product of egoism, boredom, and a certain contingent arrangement of atoms. "In Downing Street and the Treasury Chambers our great men are . . . comparatively true," Trollope says in *The New Zealander*. "It is when they go down to the House and assume their guise as legislators that fallacy and intrigue are necessary or permitted. There they are both necessary and permitted."[9] Political men – like other men – misbehave themselves more easily in groups than as individuals; most troubles grow out of collective selfishness and stupidity rather than the spiritual corruption of individual men. After all, politicians can only achieve and retain influence and power by acting together. So for Trollope it is a question not so much of bad seeds and tragic flaws as of human weakness. He knew what effects political ambitions can have on the souls of weak men; the political process in his novels reveals and underlines these weaknesses.

Politics breeds various kinds of dishonesty. Trollope hated most the ceremony of lying. He liked words to mean what they were supposed to mean, and he heard political rhetoric with contempt. His novels teem with instances of insulting partisan rhetoric spoken hotly in the House of Commons, followed immediately by normal and even friendly discourse among the combatants after adjournment out of the vision of the public eye – that organ for whose benefit his parliamentary debates are largely staged. No man, he says, "can hold a high position in the government who finds himself unable to defend honest intentions by false excuses, or to repel undeserved accusations by disingenuous sophistry." Indeed, in the House of Commons "the aggregate of untruth is very large . . . truth is not even expected."[10] "You should not suppose that words always mean what they seem to mean," snarls a character in Trollope's late (1877–8) novel *Is He Popenjoy?* (I, 171).

So Trollope thought that politics brings out the worst in most men – most men being ordinarily susceptible to its subtle corruptions. Sir Thomas Underwood in *Ralph the Heir* (1870–1) – who is a much likelier self-portrait than Dr Wortle, as we shall see – articulates this belief unmistakably in a reference to his campaign for Parliament:

> 'In politics men skin each other without the slightest feeling. I do not doubt that Mr. Westmacott would ruin me with the most perfect satisfaction, if by doing so he could bring the seat within his own reach . . . and yet I believe Mr. Westmacott to be a kind-hearted, good sort of man. There is a theory among Englishmen that in politics no man need spare another. To wish that your opponent should fall dead among the hustings is not an uncharitable wish at an election.' (II, 43)

"In the battle of politics," says Trollope in his *Autobiography* (p. 254), "men are led further and further away from first causes, till at last a measure is opposed by one simply because it is advocated by another." The climactic political battles are fought over *who* is to do what is to be done – not *what* is to be done.

Most men, then, are not consciously dishonest from the first; through partisanship and contentiousness, they drift into insincerity. This is a lesson of *The Three Clerks*, in which many themes of the Palliser novels are given a dry run. Early on (p. 79) there is an interesting discussion between Harry Norman, the virtuous (but dull) hero, and Alaric Tudor, whose scruples succumb one after another to large ambitions. Justifying his scramble for place, Tudor remarks that "when a man comes home from a successful chase, with his bag well stuffed with game, the women do not quarrel with him because there is mud on his gaiters . . . Men become mere vegetables by being too scrupulous." A great man, he says, cannot afford to "pick his steps" so carefully. Norman replies: "Then I would not be great."

> 'But surely God intends that there shall be great men on the earth?'
> 'He certainly wishes that there should be good men,' said Harry.
> 'And cannot a man be good and great?'
> 'That is the problem for man to solve.'
> . . . 'It is all a quibble about a word,' said Alaric.

But it is not just a quibble about a word. It is one of the questions to which the Palliser novels, one after another and in various ways, address themselves. Can a scrupulous man become a strong political leader? Is scrupulousness a weakness in politics? Can a great man also be a good man? Must a man become base in order to become "great"? Tudor, who decides not "to be impeded by small scruples," finds that as long as his villainy is both successful and undetected he can be lionized in society: "a man may wallow in the mire . . . besmear himself from head to foot in the blackest, foulest mud, and yet be received as an honoured guest by ladies gay and noble lords" if he is sufficiently adroit (p. 191). Hostesses do not ask the man at the top how he got there; they are much more likely to ask him to dinner. Realizing this, Alaric debates with himself the novel's central issue: do "men of the world, the great and best men whom he saw around him, really [endeavour] to be honest, or . . . only to seem so [?] Honesty was preached to him on every side; but did he, in his intercourse with the world, find men to be honest? Or did it behove him, a practical man . . . determined to battle with the world . . . to be more honest than his neighbours?" (p. 287). This question too is asked by the Palliser novels; the answer is sufficiently plain at the end of them.

Also interesting about *The Three Clerks* is the way it anticipates *The Way We Live Now* (1874–5) and the later Palliser novels in seeing the moral corruption of modern life as infecting all the professions with equal virulence. Political dishonesty in such circumstances becomes simply another expression of what Chaffanbrass in *Phineas Redux* (1873) calls the doctrine of "*caveat lex*":

It has now become the doctrine of a large class of politicians that political honesty is unnecessary, slow, subversive of a man's interests, and incompatible with quick onward movements. Such a doctrine in politics is to be deplored; but alas! who can confine it to politics? It creeps with gradual, but still with sure and quick motion, into all the doings of our daily life. How shall the man who has taught himself that he may be false in the House of Commons, how shall he be true in the Treasury Chambers? or if false there, how true in the Exchange? and if false there, how shall he longer have any truth within him?

(The Three Clerks, p. 357)

Trollope's model of a modern politician in *The Three Clerks* is Undecimus Scott — the Augustus Melmotte of the early fiction. Scott understands instinctively "that though he should be a model of purity before the public, it did not behove him to be very strait-laced with his own party." He is a Tory, but has no political opinions to speak of. What he does have "at his fingers' ends" is "the cant phraseology of ministerial subordinates" (p. 88) and the ability to make himself useful and agreeable to others. But he must be particularly careful in the choice of friends: "He could not afford to associate with his fellow-men on any other terms than those of making capital out of them . . . how could such a one live, if he did not turn to some profit even the convivialities of existence?" (p. 90). Scott is never trusted by his own party; but in the world of the latter Palliser novels — fifteen and more years later — he would have been an angel. Trollope's slow progress to pessimism — accelerated mightily by his experience as a candidate for Parliament in 1868 — accounts for many differences of emphasis and perspective between his early and late novels. His general subjects of interest, however, never varied much.

It may seem from all this that Trollope's "balance" in politics is decidedly toward cynicism. This is true; but his idealism died hard. As late as the writing of the *Autobiography* he revered the profession of M.P., as we have seen. He also had great faith in the capacity of the unusual individual to withstand the immoralizing processes of the system and retain his integrity in the face of them all. Such a man may be forced out of the political Establishment; but the mere fact of his existence is cause for hope, even when things are at their worst.

As Trollope's reverence dimmed, so did his partisan loyalties. In his last novels real differences between the parties are few indeed. While they are finally seen to differ, as always, in terms of *personnel*, they are not seen to differ in terms of *doctrine* — except, as we shall see, on the question of helping or not helping to bring the social classes closer together, diminishing the "distances" (a favorite word) between them. This is a small area of difference, after all. Throughout much of his writing life, Trollope's partisan stance was not balanced — despite his description of himself in the *Autobiography* as "an advanced conservative liberal." Until his last years he was an outspoken Liberal and an instinctive foe of the Conservative

party and of what he conceived its few principles to be. This does not
mean that Trollope, in today's terminology, could be described accurately
as "liberal." On the contrary – though he was certainly "advanced" on
some issues, his was essentially a conservative temperament. The Liberal
party of the time was no more "liberal" than the Conservative party.
Indeed, the oldest great landowning families in mid-Victorian England
were Whigs; and the most radical measures of the nineteenth century were
enacted by Tory ministries.

Trollope's usual partisan prejudice is at work almost everywhere in his
political novels. When, in *The Duke's Children* (1879–80), young Lord
Silverbridge for no particular reason decides to desert the Palliser family
tradition for the Tory cause, his father, the nominal leading man of these
novels, is distressed. Palliser may respect his political opponents, but he
would no sooner expect to find a Conservative in his family circle than a
plumber. "I suppose it's as respectable to be a Conservative as a Liberal,"
suggests his daughter. "I don't know that at all," snaps Trollope's hero.
But it is important to distinguish Trollope's partisan feelings from his
characteristic way of thinking about things – and to remember how little
party labels meant, then as now. Victorian Liberalism included much that
was conservative.

Trollope detested the Conservative party all of his life. Even when
angry with the Liberals he refused to turn to their opponents. There is not
much political theory in the Palliser novels, certainly, but there is a series
of attacks on the Tories. One of the things Trollope disliked most about
them was their tendency, as he saw it, to promote revolutionary measures
for reasons of political expediency while in their hearts yearning for a
return to past forms and values. Speaking in *The Bertrams* (1858) of the
late forties and early fifties, Trollope comments bitterly:

> At that time men had not learnt by experience, as they now have, that
> no reform, no innovation, – experience almost justifies in saying, no
> revolution, strikes so foully in the nostrils of an English Tory as to be
> absolutely unreconcilable. When taken in the refreshing waters of
> office, any such pill can be swallowed. This is a fact now recognized in
> politics; and it is a great point in favour of that party that their power
> of deglutition should be so recognized. Let the people want what they
> will, Jew senators, cheap corn, vote by ballot, no property qualifi-
> cations, or anything else, the Tories will carry it for them if the Whigs
> cannot. A poor Whig premier has none but the Liberals to back him;
> but a reforming Tory will be backed by all the world – except those
> few whom his own dishonesty will personally have disgusted.

Unlike many of his literary contemporaries, Trollope had not been
brought up in Liberal circles (Dickens and Thackeray, who had been, both
ultimately attacked the Whig aristocracy – though Thackeray stood for

Parliament as a Liberal). Trollope always revered the great Whig families and saw the Tory leaders as upstart con-men. As we shall see, he came especially to hate Disraeli. Indeed, the Conservative *volte-face* which helped to bring about the Second Reform Bill (1867; one of many instances in the Victorian period when Tories and Radicals worked together, a phenomenon alluded to in the passage quoted above) broadened his contempt for official Toryism and for Disraeli personally[11] — and led him to make his Conservative Prime Minister in *Phineas Redux* bring in a bill for Disestablishment (Trollope in 1868 publicly accused Disraeli of being willing to disestablish anything for political ends). Similarly, in *The Three Clerks* — written more or less contemporaneously with *The Bertrams* — Trollope attacks Peel's repeal of the Corn Laws as an example of Conservative untrustworthiness. The virulence of the assault (pp. 355–7) is remarkable.

> Who has given so great a blow to political honesty, has done so much to banish from men's minds the idea of a life-ruling principle, as Sir Robert Peel? . . . He has taught us a great lesson, that a man who has before him a mighty object may dispense with those old-fashioned rules of truth to his neighbours and honesty to his own principles, which should guide us in ordinary life . . . Thrice in his political life did Sir Robert Peel change his political creed, and carry, or assist to carry . . . the measures of his adversaries. Thrice by doing so he kept to himself that political power which he had fairly forfeited by previous opposition to the requirements of his country . . . Posterity will point at him as a politician without policy, as a statesman without a principle, as a worshipper at the altar of expediency, to whom neither vows sworn to friends, nor declarations made to his country, were in any way binding . . . Had Sir Robert Peel lived, and did the people now resolutely declare that the Church of England should be abandoned, that Lords and Commons should bow the neck, that the Crown should fall, who can believe that Sir Robert Peel would not be ready to carry out their views? . . . That Sir Robert Peel should be a worshipper of expediency might be a matter of small moment . . . were it not that we are so prone to copy the example of those whose names are ever in our mouths.

It is true that Peel changed his mind about the Corn Laws several times. The issue, however, was a difficult one, and most historians feel now that in ultimately supporting Repeal he acted for the best. Indeed, posterity has generally admired rather than reviled Peel. In the *Autobiography* — written nearly twenty years after *The Three Clerks* — Trollope during a discussion of political virtue refers to "the glorious time when some great self-action shall be possible, and shall even be demanded, as when Peel gave up the Corn Laws" (p. 308); by then he had come to see that politics makes many demands upon one's integrity and that an honest change of

heart may stand as a beacon-light of truth amidst the murk of dishonesty
and cross-purposes. When he wrote the passage about Peel in *The Three
Clerks*, Trollope was also thinking of Peel's support of Catholic Emancipation and the reform of Parliament after initial opposition to both
measures; on these issues too posterity has treated Peel kindly — giving
him credit for leading unimaginative men to enact enlightened legislation.
In all that he did in the forties, Peel had been opposed in Parliament by
the ambitious young Disraeli, a fellow Tory miffed at not being taken into
the government — who in the sixties was to support, for personal and
party advantage, an equal number of "radical" measures. Peel began to
look better and better to Trollope the more he heard and saw of the new
Tory leader — another personification of "expediency," and one of the
"Jew senators" whose advent is mentioned so contemptuously in *The
Bertrams*.

In his official election address to the voters of Beverley in 1868,
Trollope declared that "Every Session during which a Conservative or Tory
Government is in power, the political progress and improvement of the
nation is impeded instead of furthered"; and he added that this feeling was
"a principal article of my political creed." In a speech a few days later he
said that "to be Conservatives politically speaking seems to me to be
unnatural." Trollope had to take a partisan stand in the campaign, but he
did not have to say these things. He believed that by definition "A
Conservative in Parliament is . . . obliged to promote a great many things
of which he does not really approve . . . You can't have tests and
qualifications, rotten boroughs and divine right of kings back again."[12]
The Conservative by his very nature is a sort of political dinosaur when he
is not being a political chameleon, treacherous and dishonest. There is a
long and whimsical aside in *The Eustace Diamonds* on the reactionary
nature of Conservatives:

> [Such men] feel among themselves that everything that is being done is
> bad, — even though that everything is done by their own party. It was
> bad to interfere with Charles, bad to endure Cromwell, bad to banish
> James, bad to put up with William. The House of Hanover was bad. All
> interference with prerogative was bad. The Reform Bill was very bad.
> Encroachments on the estates of the bishops was bad. Emancipation of
> Roman Catholics was the worst of all. Abolition of corn-laws, church-
> rates, and oaths and tests were all bad. The meddling with the
> Universities has been grievous. The treatment of the Irish Church has
> been Satanic. The over-hauling of schools is most injurious to English
> education. Education bills and Irish land bills were all bad. Every step
> taken has been bad. (p. 33)

Despite the fact that everything is bad and getting worse, to the Tory mind
"old England is of all countries in the world the best to live in, and is not

at all the less comfortable because of the changes that have been made." Is there a contradiction, a paradox here? Not really: "A huge, living, daily increasing grievance that does one no palpable harm, is the happiest possession that a man can have." The Tories, if "pressed hard ... will almost own that their so-called convictions are prejudices. But not for worlds would they be rid of them" (pp. 32–3). Thus Trollope on the Tory character.

This does not mean that Trollope did not have genuinely progressive, even "liberal," views on some issues. Again and again we encounter the novelist's feeling that while the stratification of society is inevitable, one should still do what one can to assist those at the bottom to help themselves upwards – and he saw the Conservatives as opposing such efforts, the Liberals as cooperating in them. He did not believe in "equality," either absolute or otherwise; on the contrary, "equality" is pronounced in several places to be a dream. But Trollope says that we must all believe in and help to defend "liberty," especially the freedom of all people to create their own opportunities and to take advantage of those they find. While he accepted the existence of privileged classes, Trollope also felt that at least a theoretical entry into them by others should be possible. Thus he could believe simultaneously in aristocracy and "Liberalism." He favored universal free public education before the Forster Act of 1870 (W. E. Forster was a close friend) came along, as statements in *North America* in 1862 and on the hustings at Beverley in 1868 make clear. He attacked the Irish Church Establishment because, he said, it was anti-democratic, uncharitable, and unpopular. At Beverley he also declared his opposition to temperance legislation; and the position he took there on the ballot was actually a Radical one at the time (he opposed it because he wished workers to be able to vote for whom they liked *openly*, without fear of reprisals by employers). He criticized forced conscription. He sympathized with Garibaldi's cause in Italy against the attack by Napoleon III in 1867,[13] and with Turkey against the attack of Russia in 1877. He advocated the separation of "power" and "grandeur," approving of a constitutional monarch without real power and of a civil leadership which – like Palliser's in *The Prime Minister* (1875–6) – eschews personal grandeur in the exercise of real power. He generally supported moderately progressive politicians, and helped to found – and wrote for – several progressive journals, as we have seen. And he was one of the few prominent Englishmen of his time to support the North in the American Civil War. Indeed, he wrote *North America* in part to defend the North (at least its mission to preserve the Union, a cause he thought virtuous but lost) – and to mitigate the obvious Toryism of his mother's famous best-seller in 1832, *Domestic Manners of the Americans*. Frances Trollope's book had openly disparaged life in a democracy at a time when the Great Reform Bill was being hotly debated in England; of course the Tory press praised the book and the Whig press attacked it. Though in the preface to her *Belgium and Western Germany in 1833* (1833) Mrs Trollope denied having any "strong party feeling" one way or the other, her satire of democratic life and American customs was carried on in *The Barnabys in America* (1843) and two later novels. In a sense Trollope was trying in *North America* to "balance" the family's treatment of America – a fact which he readily admits in his preface to the book (though he too found much to dislike in America).

One critic has written that Trollope "was a Liberal primarily because he was an optimist."[14] It might be said instead that he was a Liberal primarily because he was a conservative – the Conservatives seeming to him to be nothing at all. He became less optimistic as he got older, and certainly his preference for the Liberal party grew less energetic as the years went by. Finally, late in life, he broke explosively with Gladstone over Irish policy – in which, having lived in Ireland for so many years, he was greatly interested; and but for his friendship with Forster he might have publicly repudiated the Liberal party. He preferred it to the Conservative party, yes; but his attachment was less philosophical than social and temperamental. He knew many of the leading Liberal statesmen of the day and was invited to some of their homes. He disliked the unprincipled adventurers who seemed to have seized control of the Tory party. And he was a man who liked to belong to things in any case – the clubs, the Church, the hunts, the party – more for the sake of convenience than out of carefully developed conviction. He describes his own un-theoretical nature in that of Sir Thomas Underwood in *Ralph the Heir*.

Trollope's essential conservatism is deep-rooted and consistent – much more consistent than his vague and spasmodic liberalism, and indeed the most consistent aspect of his thought from the beginning to the end of his life.

He always favored political rule by an oligarchy of aristocrats: "all forms and manners of government . . . do and must . . . resolve themselves into oligarchies" of some sort, he says in *The New Zealander*; and indeed, "The few best men of a people are always those who should rule." Power is a "privilege . . . of some few who are specially chosen" to govern; "the best few" are always "looked for, and in some sort found. And so the government goes on and is conducted, in the one and only way in which the government of a great people can be managed." Elsewhere in *The New Zealander* he says, simply: "The aristocrat is . . . of all men the best able to rule."[15] This is certainly plain enough. It is an argument of each of the Palliser novels – in *Can You Forgive Her?*, for example, which asserts that a country is better off when its politicians have "a personal stake" in it; in *Phineas Redux* (II, 443), which declares that the rulers of England should be "looked for among the sons of Earls and Dukes . . . as [they] . . . may be educated for such work almost from their infancy"; in the procla-mation of the same novel that "some men . . . seem to have been born to be Cabinet Ministers, – dukes mostly, or earls, or the younger sons of such, — who have been trained to it from their very cradles and of whom we may imagine that they are subject to no special awe when they first enter into that august assembly, and feel but little personal elevation" (I, 373–4); in *The Duke's Children* (I, 213), where Palliser argues eloquently that maintenance of the aristocracy is "second only in importance to the maintenance of the crown." Put simply: "the England which we know could not be the England that she is but for the maintenance of a high-minded, proud, and self-denying nobility" (*Phineas Redux*, II, 188). In *The New Zealander* Trollope speaks to the "danger" of aristocratic rule — so often a fact of nineteenth-century English life:

> We now hear much to the prejudice of the English aristocracy, and are told daily of our danger because the rule of the country is altogether in aristocratic hands. Would that it were! In what other hands can the rule of any country be safely placed? For what purpose have we an aristocracy here among us, if it be not that they may rule and guide us rightly?
>
> The main duty of all aristocrats, and we may say their only duty, is to govern; and the highest duty of any aristocrat is to govern the state.

Critics have usually failed to comprehend this aspect of Trollope's thought — assuming, perhaps, that a man intelligent enough to write novels must also be a democrat. Thus Morris E. Speare declared — in capital letters — that Trollope had great "faith in the COMMONER as a coming benign influence in English public affairs" — a misreading in which he was enthusiastically joined by Booth.[16]

Trollope's preference for aristocrats as political leaders has a partisan slant. The Pallisers have always been Whigs; and the great families which Trollope most admired were the old Whig familes, the conservative progenitors of Victorian Liberalism. His prejudices are discernible everywhere — even when, as in *Phineas Redux*, he is contemptuous of the political process; they testify to his belief that the two parties, in one respect at least, are not at all like one another.

> 'I do believe in the patriotism of certain families. I believe that the Mildmays, FitzHowards, and Pallisers have for some centuries brought up their children to regard the well-being of their country as their highest personal interest, and that such teaching has been generally efficacious. Of course, there have been failures. Every child won't learn its lesson however well it may be taught. But the school in which good training is most practised will, as a rule, turn out the best scholars. In this way I believe in families.' (*Phineas Redux*, I, 216)

In this eloquent speech, Barrington Erle — though not always an admirable figure in these novels — articulates both a cardinal point of Trollope's political faith and the *donnée*, as it turns out, of one of his greatest novels: *The Duke's Children*.

The Mildmays, FitzHowards, and Pallisers — like Erle — are Liberals. While the days of the great Whig families are more or less over, Trollope acknowledges, some vestiges of their beneficent heritage yet remain.

> In former days, when there were Whigs instead of Liberals, it was almost a rule of political life that all leading Whigs should be uncles, brothers-in-law, or cousins to each other. This was pleasant and gave great consistency to the party; but the system has now gone out of vogue. There remains of it, however, some traces, so that among the nobler born Liberals of the day there is still a good deal of agreeable family connection. (*Phineas Redux*, I, 137–8)

Trollope's complacent picture of government-by-family[17] expresses an obvious prejudice. Indeed, in a long passage later in *Phineas Redux* he pauses to discuss the superiority of Whig-Liberal governments to Tory governments specifically in terms of their usual aristocratic components:

> There is probably more of the flavour of political aristocracy to be found still remaining among our Liberal leading statesmen than among their opponents. A Conservative Cabinet is, doubtless, never deficient in dukes and lords, and the sons of such; but conservative dukes and lords are recruited here and there, and as recruits, are new to the business, whereas among the old Whigs a halo of statecraft has, for ages past, so strongly pervaded and enveloped certain great familes, that the power in the world of politics thus produced still remains .... With them something of the feeling of high blood, of rank, of living in a park with deer about it, remains. They still entertain a pride in their Cabinets, and have, at any rate, not as yet submitted themselves to a conjuror. The Charles James Fox element of liberality still holds its own, and the fragrance of Cavendish is essential. (I, 432–3)

This is a crucial statement. Trollope at one stroke underscores his preference for the Liberals (in this respect not at all like the Conservatives, whose "great" families are only the most recent *nouveaux riches* of the political arena), his admiration for the old families generally, and his approval of their exclusiveness. The passage demonstrates how Trollope's political Liberalism and temperamental conservatism are in perfect accord: he likes the Liberals better than the Tories because the aristocracy of the former is purer and older. The two admired Whigs evoked with such tenderness at the end of this passage are founding fathers of the Liberal party, not contemporary politicians. His preference for the Liberals has nothing to do with modern "liberalism." Indeed, as historian Donald Southgate has pointed out, mid-nineteenth-century Whiggery, being aristocratic in terms of "personnel" and oligarchic in terms of "influence," was "the most ostentatious and self-conscious constituent of . . . 'the Establishment' " of the time.[18] And a most telling phrase is the one about the conjuror – a reference, as subsequent chapters will make clear, specifically to Disraeli; the Liberals have never submitted themselves to such a leader, and Trollope hopes they never will. Certainly his hatred of Disraeli helped to color his view of the parties. Here the Conservatives and their leader are seen as upstart magicians and outsiders – while the Liberal leaders are portrayed as statesmen, products of an historical continuity which has eluded the Tories and which they can only ape. (This also goes far toward explaining why Trollope's anger with the Liberals was often so quick to kindle in later years – they were once favorite nephews, and he hated to see them lowering themselves to the level of their opponents.)

Trollope's preference for the privileged classes is made manifest in myriad other ways. *Lady Anna* (1874) and *The American Senator* (1877) both emphasize the "superiority" (Trollope's word) of the upper classes and how much pleasanter it is to be with the rich than with the poor. In *Can You Forgive Her?* the heroine's father tells her that "Rank and wealth are advantages . . . Take them as a whole, the nobility of England are pleasant acquaintances to have . . . if I had a choice of acquaintance . . . I should prefer the peer" (I, 266). There is this from Trollope's *Thackeray* (1879): "A peer taken at random as a companion would be preferable to a clerk from a counting-house, – taken at random: the clerk might turn out to be a scholar on your hands, but the chances are the other way."[19] In *Is He Popenjoy?* (written just before *Thackeray*) virtually the same sentiments are articulated by the wise Mrs Montacute Jones: "I like having lords in my drawing-room. They look handsome, and talk better, than other men. That's my experience. And you are pretty nearly sure with them that you won't find you have got somebody quite wrong" (II, 80).

Trollope was by no means the Victorian Barry Goldwater; in terms of what most Victorians thought, his own thinking was less reactionary than simply normal. As Briggs has demonstrated[20] so well, Trollope believed heartily in Walter Bagehot's concepts of the "old deference" and "dignity" of the English constitution as safeguards against the barbarisms of rude democracy. "Deference" meant habitual respect for social superiors and contempt for urban radicalism. Gladstone, no Radical, in the fifties was fond of referring to "the strong prejudices in favour of the aristocracy which pervade all ranks and classes of the community." The framers of the Second Reform Bill were no less aware in the sixties that the prestige of the aristocracy must not be tampered with. The best government – that most likely to bring social peace and political tranquility – was, in the opinion of Bagehot, Trollope, and many of their contemporaries, government by select few: upper-class members of Parliament who were alone sufficiently educated and experienced in life, as well as removed from the temptations of material greed, to undertake the work. Bagehot's

The English Constitution appeared serially in 1867 in the *Fortnightly*,
with which Trollope was closely connected; we may be sure that he read
it. He accepted Bagehot's concept of the "select few" and stressed the
contrast between the elite classes and the demos. The poor people in
Trollope's novels often make themselves ridiculous in one way or
another — Dickens's sometime equation of poverty with virtue could not
be farther from Trollope's views on the matter (it is interesting that
Bagehot attacked Dickens on the ground that poor people are "poor
people to read about . . . unfit for prolonged delineation"). Like Bagehot,
Trollope had little sympathy for the poor, cared little about them, and
knew even less about the social problems caused by extreme poverty.
Needless to say, he wished for no transfer of political power from rich to
poor, no redistribution of wealth (there are no Marxist studies of
Trollope). In his novels the working-class voter is portrayed as either
greedy and unprincipled, or cretinous. Nor do the middle classes offer an
alternative repository of faith. Indeed, they are seen by the novelist as
especially unsuited to hold or exercise political power — being so
vulnerable to the temptations of material speculation. Some of Trollope's
harshest satire is directed against manipulative capitalists who are also
would-be statesmen. Only a few members of the middle classes are able in
these novels to resist temptation and work honestly for worthwhile
political ends. A virtue of aristocratic rule in the eyes of Trollope and
Bagehot was that it staved off the rule of mere wealth — "the religion of
gold," in Bagehot's phrase: both he and Trollope feared that the "select
few" might eventually be overwhelmed by the merely rich (a fear
memorably articulated in *The Way We Live Now*). The upper middle
classes were seen by Trollope as hopelessly enmeshed in speculation,
stock-jobbing, and other commercial activities incompatible with honest
political rule. He was afraid that the ruling classes might not escape such
entanglements; the fact that the villains of his political novels are often
middle-class businessmen with political aspirations expresses this fear. As
Briggs noted, the growing new "world of wealth was making it difficult to
distinguish between fortune-hunting and real industry, between social
aspiration and legitimate self-help." Trollope never condemned the
acquisitive instinct, feeling as he did that "mercenary tendencies" enable a
talented man to make himself useful to many others. Wanting money for
its own sake of course is bad; and in the face of his occasional uncertainty,
his sometime failure to perceive when the mercenary tendency was selfish
and when it was not, Trollope took frequent refuge in his concept of the
"gentleman" — a phenomenon hard to define, he admitted, but always
immediately recognizable. He knew, at any rate, what he meant: he
preferred the effortless grace of the man of good manners to the rougher
individualism of the pushing bourgeois. "Deference" and "dignity" were
always important to him, and so he put his "select few" above the
multitude. It should not surprise us, then, to discover in the political

novels that the process by which even good men get into Parliament is a
sordid and corrupt exercise in bribery, propaganda and violence, during
which the would-be legislator has to crawl through the mud to get to
Westminster. Whenever the select few touch the unselect many, the few
are dirtied. It is also no wonder, then, that in *Phineas Finn, The American
Senator*, and elsewhere Trollope defends pocket boroughs as being more
likely than boroughs in which really "democratic" elections are held to
send enlightened representatives to Parliament. The novelist had nothing
against the old system of aristocratic patronage and influence.

Trollope's elitism goes beyond his love of aristocracy.

> There are places in life which can hardly be well filled except by
> 'Gentlemen' ... It may be that the son of the butcher of the village
> shall become as well fitted for employment requiring gentle culture as
> the son of the parson ... When such is the case, no one has been more
> prone to give the butcher's son all the welcome he has merited than I
> myself; but the chances are greatly in favour of the parson's son. The
> gates of the one class should be open to the other; but neither to the
> one class nor to the other can good be done by declaring that there are
> no gates, no barriers, no differences.

This is also the social outlook of Palmerston — one of Trollope's chief
political heroes — who wrote in 1850:

> We have shown the example of a nation in which every class of society
> accepts with cheerfulness the lot which Providence has assigned to it;
> while at the same time each individual of each class is constantly trying
> to raise himself in the social scale — not by injustice and wrong, not by
> violence and illegality — but by persevering good conduct, and by the
> steady and energetic exertion of the moral and intellectual faculties
> with which his creator has endowed him.

Both men believed in equality of opportunity — Trollope less than
Palmerston, though the novelist was perhaps more inclined to believe in
equal right to pursue such opportunities as did exist. But Trollope's
published statements do not suggest any belief in absolute equality of
opportunity itself — or in any kind of "equality," as we have seen. "The
theory of equality ... is one to which all human efforts should ... tend
... But could you establish absolute equality in England tomorrow ... the
inequality of men's minds and character would re-establish an aristocracy
within twenty years," declares the astute Sir William Patterson in *Lady
Anna* (pp. 365–6). In the same novel it is said by one character that "God
Almighty has chosen that there should be different ranks to carry out his
purposes" (p. 244) and by another that without class distinctions
"everything would get mingled, and there would soon be no difference. If

there are to be differences, there should be differences. That is the meaning of being a gentleman, – or a lady" (p. 171). So one does not picture Trollope standing with open arms in Downing Street waiting to welcome there "the son of the butcher." "There is no reason why that which suits Lord Palmerston should not suit Mr. Jones," says Trollope in *The New Zealander*, in his essay on "Society," "but let Mr. Jones be studious to adopt no custom as his own which is recommended by its suitableness to Lord Palmerston, and not at all by its suitableness to himself." And he adds here, in case the point be missed: "No man can be made happy by the fact of walking into a . . . drawing-room with a better coat on his back than that usually worn by him."[21] Like a good conservative, Trollope had grave doubts about the ability of the working classes to do much for themselves, though he felt they ought to be allowed to try. He favored individual progress and advancement – but not at the cost of altering or destroying the social fabric. "It is well that some respect should be maintained from the low in station towards those who are high, even when no respect has been deserved," he states unequivocally in *The Claverings* (II, 225). He held the door open, but expected no visitors.

Trollope's loud opposition to competitive examinations as part of the screening of applicants for the Civil Service is in keeping with these attitudes. He felt that such examinations were blindly inhumane; worse, they did not, as he thought they should, guarantee that appointments would be made whenever possible to "gentlemen," men of good family rather than men of mere education who might come from nowhere and no one. Some "places in life" should not depend only on intellect and learning; Trollope kept on saying this (in the fiction most notably in *The Three Clerks*, and *The Last Chronicle of Barset*, 1867).

The novelist accepted as a necessary fact of existence the stratification of society. "I dislike universal suffrage; I dislike vote by ballot; I dislike above all things the tyranny of democracy," he proclaims in *North America*.[22] All his life Trollope hated the Radicals; those who appear in his novels are drawn unsympathetically. George Vavasor in *Can You Forgive Her?* is a criminal, Bott in the same novel is a toady, Turnbull in *Phineas Finn* is a demagogue, Moggs in *Ralph the Heir* is a fool, and Daniel Caldigate in *John Caldigate* (1879) is cold, humorless, and unappealing. Thomas Thwaite, the "good" Radical tailor in *Lady Anna*, can be treated gently because "no rational scheme of governance . . . had ever entered his mind, and of pure politics he knew [nothing]" (pp. 25–6). Rich, landed aristocrats are the proper rulers; they *must* serve or breach the trust between themselves and the country, out of which they have willingly been given so much. In order to perpetuate their ability to rule, they must also work to preserve their own order; Trollope's conscientious aristocrats do this.

In *North America* the novelist declares that "no form of existing government – no form of government that ever did exist, gives or has given so large a measure of individual freedom to all who live under it as a constitutional monarchy." And he suggests that Queen Victoria send one of her sons across the sea to become King of Canada. It has been said that, for Trollope, "To proclaim oneself a republican . . . simply means high treason."[23] This is an exaggeration — but not an outrageous one. The few republicans who turn up in his novels — there is an odious collection of them in *Ralph the Heir*, and some plain silly ones in *He Knew He Was Right* (1868–9) — are treated with contempt, and often satirized.

Also like a true conservative, the novelist preferred the executive to the legislative branch of government; and in a bicameral system he trusted the upper house more completely than the lower. He felt it was the function of an upper chamber to protect the country against excessively radical measures proposed by the lower; and he always looked with repugnance upon periodical attempts by the Commons to abolish the Lords — efforts which he associated with the most extreme and dangerous elements of democracy. In *The New Zealander* he describes the peerage's loss of political power since the Reform Bill of 1832 as "A tendency much to be lamented." Readers of *Australia and New Zealand* (1873) and *The Fixed Period* (1882; a novel), to take just two more examples, can find these opinions clearly stated.[24]

Such things being understood, a number of Trollope's other characteristic attitudes may be seen as complementary. Consider his discussion in *North America* of the American Negro. We should not expect him in 1862 to sound like an officer of the NAACP. Yet years after Wilberforce's eloquence and the abolitionists' success, what Trollope says here is ungenerous. It is inconceivable to him "that the Negro can be made equal to the white man." After all, "the Negro is the white man's inferior through laws of nature . . . He is not mentally fit to cope with white men." And again: "the Negro is not the white man's equal by nature." Not surprisingly, the novelist also supported the Empire — even though, in the sixties and seventies, Empire was a concept closely identified with Disraeli and the Tories. In *North America* he refers to England's willingness "to spread civilization across the ocean!" and to the acquisition of colonies in the interest of "carrying out the duty . . . of extending civilization, freedom, and well-being through the new uprising nations of the world." And he adds: "the national ambition [understands that] . . . there can be no glory to the people so great or so readily recognizable by mankind at large as that of spreading civilization from East to West, and from North to South."[25] From the English government, Trollope wrote two years later in *Can You Forgive Her?*, "flow the waters of the world's progress, — the fullest fountain of advancing civilisation" (II, 54).

The novelist was equally unambiguous on other matters involving class. He complains bitterly in *North America* about classless American train carriages, the "free admixture of different classes" in American hotels, the "coarse attire and unsophisticated manners" of Westerners, the roughness

of the American lower classes generally — and he describes himself here as
pining away for the "civility ... of a well-ordered servant"[26] (well — he
wanted to see the country). On the question of marriage and class he
sounds like a conservative novelist of a later time:

> a man from the ordinary ranks of the upper classes, who has had the
> nurture of a gentleman, prepares for himself a hell on earth in taking a
> wife from any rank below his own — a hell on earth, and, alas! too
> often another hell elsewhere also. He must either leave her or loathe her
> ... he will have to endure habits, manners, and ideas, which the close
> contiguity of married life will force upon his disgusted palate, and
> which will banish all love. (*The Three Clerks*, p. 383)

Gissing was four years old when this was published.

On questions of the day such as the status of women and the rights of
Jews, Trollope was unflinchingly reactionary: he hated the new feminism
and shared many of the usual prejudices against Jews — attitudes clearly
expressed in the Palliser novels. On the sticky question of Irish
Tenant-Right he is not altogether clear; but what he does say on the
subject — e.g., *Castle Richmond* (1860), p. 60 — suggests that he disliked
the system's injustices but not the system itself (he always opposed any
attempt to tamper with free enterprise). Though he had little to say of
them directly, throughout his life he detested the Evangelicals — favoring
High Churchmen, as the Barset novels make clear (Disraeli, remember, was
the great patron of the Low Church, while Gladstone appointed only High
Churchmen — men like Archdeacon Grantly). In one of his election
addresses at Beverley, Trollope declared that he "would never be a
member of any Church which is mixed up with and looks upon the state
as its support" — not so much advocacy of separation of church and state
as an assertion that the church ought to seal itself off from the impurities
of the civil power. He had said more or less the same thing in articles
published in 1865 and 1866.[27]

Trollope, then, was a political pundit all his life, though not always a
political sage. Some of *The New Zealander* is simply silly; the political
·sections of the travel books are often incredibly tedious. And the novelist's
prognostications in *North America* are, many of them, amusingly inept. He
says here that the South will defeat the North, after which "the West" will
also secede and form a third nation; that the Washington Monument will
never be completed, and indeed that the city of Washington itself will
never be rebuilt; that Lincoln, a mediocrity who should never have been
elected, was wrong to relieve General McClellan, has conducted the war
incompetently, and cannot possibly be re-nominated or re-elected: "no
man in the Union would be so improbable a candidate for the Presidency
in 1864 as Lincoln."[28] The leading politicians of Trollope's day did not
seek him out for advice.

Trollope's interest in politics naturally spilled over into some of his novels. His critics have been fond of saying that his knowledge of the subject is so superficial that politics in these novels is really unimportant. How explain, then, the political issues they raise, the political characters who populate them, the extended commentaries in them on political questions? Trollope, remember, says in the *Autobiography* (p. 184) that in his political novels he expressed his political convictions, that in them he had been able to have a "fling at the political doings of the day" — "I took this method of declaring myself." His two most purely political tales, *Phineas Finn* and *Phineas Redux*, treat issues actually being debated in the House of Commons as they appeared (e.g., parliamentary reform, the ballot, Irish land and church questions). And, as we shall see, Trollope based some of his political characters on actual politicians of the day — though he says he did not do so. In the *Autobiography* the novelist draws a very fine distinction by proclaiming that his political portraits are those "not of living men, but of living political characters" (p. 307). He wants us to view them, he says, as illustrations of political types, which they certainly are, but not as real people, which some of them certainly are. As Henry James said in his memorial essay, Trollope's love of "the real" led him to want "to tell us what certain people were and what they did in consequence of being so."[29] Trollope always denied specificity; regardless of his mendacity in this, it is true that the nature of the man himself, not his particular political philosophy, usually interests him most. His originality is in characterization rather than in ideas. So while there exist certain resemblances between Trollope's characters and real politicians of the day, it remains less important to make these identifications than to see these characters as illustrations of the interaction between certain types of men and certain social and political situations — a subject treated much more than superficially in the political novels. Since in several of the novels' leading politicians elements of more than one historical personage are embodied, such identifications in any case are often difficult to make. But it is possible to make some; and the skepticism on this issue of much previous Trollope criticism makes it especially important to do so.

Trollope's habit of using real politicians as models for some of his fictional ones is yet another demonstration, should it be needed, of the closeness with which he followed politics. While his political novels stress and express a great many other themes — some of which, admittedly, have little to do with politics — it is hard to see how novels about Victorian politics and politicians could tell us much more about these subjects. Arthur Pollard has said that Trollope's political novels are "historical as a faithful reflection of the life of their time."[30] If it is true that Trollope, more than any other Victorian writer, gives us a "convincing impression of what everyday life was like in England," it is primarily the Palliser novels — focused as they so often are on real toads in real gardens — that make this so.

2 The Political Novels: Which, Who, and What

His political novels are distinctly dull, and I confess I have not been able to read them.

> Henry James, in "Anthony Trollope" (1883)

His political novels are the best political novels in the English language.

> Hugh Walpole, in a preface (1924) to
> *The Golden Lion of Granpere*

And apologetic statesmen of a compromising kind,
Such as — what d'ye call him — Thing'em bob, and likewise — Never
    mind,
And 'St — 'st — 'st — and What's-his-name, and also You-know-
    who —
The task of filling up the blanks I'd rather leave to *you*.
But it really doesn't matter whom you put upon the list,
For they'd none of 'em be missed — they'd none of 'em be missed!

> *The Mikado* (1885)

It has been usual for some years now to group together *Can You Forgive Her?* (1864–5), *Phineas Finn* (1867–9), *The Eustace Diamonds* (1871–3), *Phineas Redux* (1873), *The Prime Minister* (1875–6), and *The Duke's Children* (1879–80) under the heading of the Political or Parliamentary Novels — or, more recently, the Palliser Novels. And yet Trollope never made this grouping himself. Indeed, the promotion of the six into a separate category occurred long after his death. In *Anthony Trollope: A Commentary* (1927), Michael Sadleir listed the six together as the Political Novels. Although the division of the novels was largely his own, it derived in part from a compilation by Spencer Nichols in *The Significance of Anthony Trollope* (1925). Nichols, in turn, had accepted the classification made by Speare, who discussed the six novels together in his book on *The Political Novel* (1924). Speare, however, refused to accept *Can You Forgive Her?* as a genuine part of the series.[1] He referred his reader to T. H. S. Escott, who dealt with the novels together as political in tone and focus but never actually gave them any subsuming collective name. Nevertheless Dodd, Mead & Company reissued the six novels in various editions between 1893 and 1928 with the words "The Parliamentary Novels" on the spine. More recently, in an Introduction to *Can You Forgive Her?* Sadleir proposed that "Palliser Novels" would be a more appropriate term than any of the others; the term gained acceptance, so that when in 1950 the Oxford University Press began publishing its "Illustrated Trollope" edition it substituted the term "Palliser Novels" for the more usual "Parliamentary Novels." The six have recently (1973) been reissued in paperback by Oxford once again as "The Palliser Novels."

Whatever they are called, it is clear that the six are not so easily grouped together as the novels of Barsetshire, in which geography and a particular cast of characters provide, through repetition and variation, some unity and coherence. Even here, however, Trollope is equivocal, suggesting in his *Autobiography* that *The Small House at Allington* (1862–4) might not, after all, belong properly to the Barset series. Said Trollope (p. 239): "I have sometimes wished to see during my lifetime a combined republication of those tales which are occupied with the fictitious county of Barsetshire. These would be *The Warden, Barchester Towers, Doctor Thorne, Framley Parsonage*, and *The Last Chronicle*." Accordingly, a few years after writing this passage – on 12 March 1878, to be exact – he signed with Chapman & Hall an agreement to bring out a series called "Chronicles of Barset" consisting of those five novels.[2]

Trollope was particular about the categorization of his novels – so much so, indeed, that after a great deal of self-contradiction he wound up making very few groupings. Nowhere, for example, does he describe the books we have come to call the Palliser novels as belonging together as part of a series, and nowhere does he use the term "Parliamentary Novels" (though he does refer often to "The Pallisers" as the continuing focus of a group of "semi-political" novels). He discusses the grouping question explicitly in two places in the *Autobiography*. In the first instance: "Who will read *Can You Forgive Her?, Phineas Finn, Phineas Redux*, and *The Prime Minister* consecutively, in order that he may understand the character of the Duke of Omnium, of Plantagenet Palliser, and Lady Glencora? Who will ever know that they should be so read?" (p. 159). Trollope wrote this before *The Duke's Children* was finished; but what about *The Eustace Diamonds*, which had already appeared? Clearly he did want his readers to encounter sequentially the four novels he mentions. Elsewhere in the *Autobiography* he points to *Phineas Finn* as the novel which "commenced a series of semi-political tales" – thus leaving out *Can You Forgive Her?*. Following his lead, Escott described *Phineas Finn* as "the earliest" of the political stories; later, contradicting himself, he said that *Can You Forgive Her?* "became very dear to the author as the first of a series that continued with *Phineas Finn, Phineas Redux*, and *The Prime Minister*"[3] – leaving off the list this time both *The Eustace Diamonds* and *The Duke's Children*.

Trollope also says that he considered the two *Phineas* novels to be one continuous and uninterrupted story despite the years and the books that separated them. He declares in the *Autobiography* (pp. 274–5) that "They were, in fact, but one novel, though they were brought out at a considerable interval of time and in different forms"; their separation was due to "much bad management," he adds, "as I had no right to expect that novel-readers would remember the characters." These comments suggest that though he considered the two *Phineas* novels parts of a close-knit whole, he did not so consider *The Eustace Diamonds*, which comes between them. Further evidence of this may be found in an unpublished letter to Henry Howard, then Governor of Rhode Island, written less than two years before the novelist's death. Here Trollope lists the volumes of the Palliser series for Governor Howard, again leaving out *The Eustace Diamonds*.[4] As late as 1964 a blurb on the front flap of the Oxford World's Classics edition of *Phineas Redux* described the novel as a sequel to *Phineas Finn* and "the second in Trollope's series of political novels" – thus leaving out *Can You Forgive Her?* and *The Eustace Diamonds*.

Undoubtedly *Can You Forgive Her?*, *The Eustace Diamonds*, and *The Duke's Children* are the least political of the six, and of these *The Eustace Diamonds* would seem, at first glance, to have the weakest claim to inclusion. There is little more political action *per se* in it than there is in *Rachel Ray* (1863) or *The Way We Live Now*, and certainly much less than in *Ralph the Heir*, which recounts the story of Trollope's unsuccessful run for Parliament. The novelist himself considered the popular success of *The Eustace Diamonds*, which gave a needed lift to his declining reputation in the early seventies, due primarily to its account "of a cunning little woman of pseudo-fashion, to whom, in her cunning, there comes a series of adventures, unpleasant enough in themselves, but pleasant to the reader" (*Autobiography*, pp. 295–6). Neither politics nor the Pallisers – who are seen, it is true, only intermittently in the novel – are mentioned here. Even Sadleir thought the novel belonged to the political series only because Lady Glencora, Lord Fawn, and others who appeared in *Phineas Finn* play a part in it; he said nothing about politics in it.[5] Indeed, no one has.

What reasons are there, then, for accepting Sadleir's grouping and considering the Palliser novels, including *The Eustace Diamonds*, as a group, a sequence? Well, there are many.

In the first place, *none* of the "political novels" is exclusively about politics. Trollope's interest, in each of these novels, is in part the social milieu of politicians. In *The Prime Minister*, for example, we see Plantagenet Palliser at home more often than at the office even though he is the current Premier; indeed, his story takes up only half of the novel. Even in the *Phineas* novels, the most political of the six, almost as much attention is given to Phineas Finn's social peregrinations and love entanglements as to his political career, and there are several other love stories thrown into *Phineas Finn* as well. *Can You Forgive Her?* and *The Duke's Children* have less politics in them than either of the *Phineas* novels; the former focuses mainly on the emotional vacillations of Alice Vavasor, the latter on Palliser in political retirement — as father rather than as statesman. If there is as much social as political philosophy in these novels it is because Trollope's interest in politicians, as in clergymen, embraces their social as well as their professional lives. In the famous apologia which concludes *The Last Chronicle of Barset*, again and again in *Barchester Towers* (1857), and elsewhere throughout the other novels in the Barset series, Trollope emphasizes his interest in clergymen as men rather than as ministers. And so in the *Autobiography* he says that readers of his political novels would have been bored by stories purely political in interest; he realized that he "could not make a tale pleasing chiefly, or perhaps in any part, by politics. If I wrote politics for my own sake, I must put in love and intrigue, social incidents, with perhaps a dash of sport, for the sake of my readers" (p. 272). "Love and intrigue" account for half the pages of the Palliser novels — with the possible exception of *Phineas Redux* — and in some of them (*Can You Forgive Her?*, *The Eustace Diamonds*, *The Duke's Children*) substantially more than half. Unlike Disraeli, a professional politician who wrote what is often political propaganda under the guise of fiction in order to promulgate or elucidate a particular political creed (and attack some political enemies along the way), Trollope was a professional novelist who in some of his books dealt with politics, and with politicians in society. This does not mean that he had no political creed of his own — only that his primary concern as novelist was less with political theses than with those human beings who are politicians. It is in this sense that all of his political novels are political. They simply present, as he says in the *Autobiography*, "political characters" rather than other kinds (p. 307). While he was interested in the nature of political processes, he was even more interested in the nature of man-as-politician.

To keep up interest, his political novels must range far beyond politics; Trollope knew this. *The Eustace Diamonds* is therefore no exception among the Palliser novels in this respect. If it is the weakest link in the political chain, that fact shows how strong the chain really is.

All six novels deal in part with politics, in part with Parliament, and in part with Pallisers. Even in *The Eustace Diamonds*, the novel's two leading male characters, Lord Fawn and Frank Greystock, are politicians. Lizzie Eustace and her diamonds eventually become, comically enough, a hot political issue. Fawn is a member of the government. Greystock is an M.P. with higher political aspirations, and we are given glimpses into his parliamentary career. We also see Parliament faced with the necessity of settling some colonial problems and of responding to Palliser's currency reform measure. The Pallisers, while they have not much to do in the novel, are most certainly present and accounted for – in the Duke's fascination with the Eustace affair, in Lady Glencora's entrance into the controversy, and of course in Palliser's heroic efforts on behalf of his decimal coinage bill.

Indeed, a number of substantial connections link *The Eustace Diamonds* with the Palliser novels that precede and follow it. One of these is its unflattering and cynical picture of party politics – a picture we shall examine in its proper place.

Were we to exclude *The Eustace Diamonds* from the Palliser series we would be confronted, on moving from *Phineas Finn* to *Phineas Redux*, with some unanswerable questions and bewildering developments (despite Trollope's assertion that the two *Phineas* novels represent one uninterrupted story). *The Eustace Diamonds* carries forward the stories of many of the characters who are important to the plots of the other novels. Palliser, who becomes Liberal Chancellor of the Exchequer in *Phineas Finn*, has served in this capacity for more than two years when *The Eustace Diamonds* opens. Glencora, unfortunately not at her best in this novel, does little more than interfere, briefly and irrationally, in the questions of the diamonds and Lizzie's suitors. The old Duke of Omnium, who has some importance in *Phineas Finn* and whose death in *Phineas Redux* takes Palliser out of the House of Commons and helps to make him Prime Minister in *The Prime Minister*, is seen in *The Eustace Diamonds* as a querulous invalid living on scandal. Emilius, introduced at the end of *The Eustace Diamonds* in time to marry Lizzie, is essential to the plot of *Phineas Redux*. There his machinations to restore himself to his wife's good graces cause a murder to be committed for which Phineas is tried. Fawn, who first appears as a minor character in *Phineas Finn* courting Violet Effingham and then Madame Max Goesler, reappears in *Phineas Redux* as a bumbling witness at the trial, and in *The Prime Minister* as a bumbling orator in the House of Lords. He is again a minor figure in these novels, having occupied so many pages of *The Eustace Diamonds*. It is Violet Effingham's marriage to Lord Chiltern at the end of *Phineas Finn* that causes Fawn to court Lizzie Eustace in *The Eustace Diamonds*. Finn, who is in Ireland during the action of *The Eustace Diamonds*, returns in *Phineas Redux* to marry Madame Goesler. Lizzie, a minor character in *Phineas Redux*, also reappears briefly in *The Prime Minister*. Many of the characters in *The Eustace Diamonds* are also of importance in the two *Phineas* novels, and much of what happens in *Phineas Redux* would be inexplicable without reference to *The Eustace Diamonds*. Indeed, the extinction of any of these lights would seriously hamper the coherence of the series as a whole. We must therefore treat them as if they were meant to be treated together. For whatever Trollope thought, these novels together tell a story.

II

Some mention should be made here of the strategy employed throughout to connect characters, events, and some of the political opinions expressed in the novels with real characters and events and with Trollope's actual political opinions.

The last first. In the preceding chapter some generalizations about Trollope's political feelings were made; and yet much was also omitted there because a number of political questions will be dealt with as they present themselves for consideration in the novels themselves. To have discussed these questions apart from the novels in which they are embedded would have been to anticipate needlessly — and to reduce the interest with which we might otherwise approach the political issues each of the novels takes up.

The question of how much Trollope drew on contemporary politics and politicians in writing these novels has been considered briefly by a few critics, but there is no sustained investigation or discussion of it anywhere. One of the prevailing views over the years has been that Trollope's disclaimers ought to be accepted and his political novels regarded as wholly "fictional" as his other novels. Others have expressed contrary suspicions — but little more. In some instances Trollope's politicians and "fictional" political events were inspired by contemporary persons and events, and the present discussion will be the first real attempt to prove this. A separate chapter could have been devoted to the "who's who" and "what's what" questions; again, however, such issues are best taken up as they relate to particular novels. Since each novel tells a different story, several cases, and not just one, have to be argued — and thus the old idea that Trollope's political novels are pure fiction and his political characters and events purely autonomous creations have to be refuted in different ways in different chapters. Each story presents its own case; to attempt to match up in one place every politician and event in the political novels with real-life counterparts would have been tedious, it would have reduced the interest we might otherwise find in the novels themselves as we examine them, and in any case it would have been difficult — not to say misleading — given Trollope's tendency often to stick together into one creation various bits and pieces culled from different sources. Yes, Trollope put such people as Disraeli, Gladstone, Russell, Palmerston, Bright, and Derby, among others, into his novels; and yes, such real issues as the Second Reform Bill, Disestablishment, parliamentary reform, the ballot, and Tenant-Right provide background and context for the stories some of the novels tell. These things are taken up in connection with the novels. The reader may therefore decide for himself how "political" each novel really is, how strong are its ties with specific political realities, to what extent it expresses private feelings of the novelist. One may say that these novels are very "political" indeed; but such an assertion becomes persuasive and significant only when it is tested against the stories themselves.

Trollope's political experiment at Beverley — and the resulting novel, *Ralph the Heir* — are discussed at the point where, chronologically, they occurred. This means the Palliser novels are not treated consecutively; it also means, however, that some of the events in the novelist's life which bear directly on his political novels — being placed where they belong — may properly help to illuminate the works which came after them.

3   The Birth of the Pallisers: *Can You Forgive Her?*

Doodle has found that he must throw himself upon the country, chiefly in the form of sovereigns and beer. In this metamorphosed state he is available in a good many places simultaneously and can throw himself upon a considerable portion of the country at one time. Britannia being much occupied in pocketing Doodle in the form of sovereigns, and swallowing Doodle in the form of beer, and in swearing herself black in the face that she does neither — plainly to the advancement of her glory and morality — the London season comes to a sudden end, through all the Doodleites and Coodleites dispersing to assist Britannia in those religious rites.

> Dickens, *Bleak House* (1852)

We want practical results rather than truth.

> *Phineas Redux*

'The proper place for a woman is behind the veil.'

> Arnold Bennett, in the
> *Clayhanger* trilogy

"Can we forgive Miss Vavasor? Of course we can, and forget her, too," said Henry James. His attitude is similar to that of the *Spectator*'s reviewer: "Can we forgive her? . . . Certainly, if it were worth while, but we scarcely care enough." Though the *Saturday Review*, like almost all other contemporary journals, found a great deal to like in the novel, it pronounced Alice "tedious."[1] They disliked Alice ("uninteresting and unintelligible," added the *Spectator*); but they loved Lady Glencora Palliser, found her and George Vavasor brilliant, unforgettable creations, and proclaimed that Trollope in *Can You Forgive Her?* had surpassed himself in the art of domestic realism. The Greenow-Cheesacre-Bellfield story was dismissed by the *Athenaeum* as "coarse caricature," but on the whole critics of the 1860s rated the novel one of Trollope's best to date (he had already published five of the six Barset novels and *Orley Farm*, among others). *Can You Forgive Her?* appeared serially between January 1864 and August 1865 and was published in book form in two volumes, the first in October 1864 and the second in June 1865 (in the

Autobiography, p. 149, Trollope says the novel appeared in 1863–4, but his memory is at fault here).

A perusal of that infamous accounting of income from his novels which Trollope appended to his *Autobiography* reveals that *Can You Forgive Her?* brought him more money than any other book he published.[2] And yet the novel has never been a favorite of twentieth-century readers, many of whom would seem to concur in James's conclusion that in it Trollope "presents no feature more remarkable than the inveteracy with which he just eludes being really serious; unless it is the almost equal success with which he frequently escapes being really humorous." Figures from the Oxford University Press, publishers of the World's Classics series, indicate that *Can You Forgive Her?* is not even among the top twelve Trollopian best-sellers of this century despite its distinguished place in the novelist's list of earnings — nor, for that matter, are any of the Palliser novels, which in general have been less popular with modern readers than the chronicles of Barset.[3] With the exception of *The Eustace Diamonds*, least political of the six, the later Palliser novels were not popular with the Victorian audience, which in general also preferred Barchester — an exact reversal of the fate of the two series, it may be worth noting, in nineteenth-century America.

Can You Forgive Her?, paradoxically, has been at the same time one of the least systematically discussed and most controversial of the Palliser novels. Trollope himself agreed with many of the critics of his time that he had never done better work, though he admitted that he was not terribly fond of Alice. Escott felt that *Can You Forgive Her?* represented an advance over the Barset novels. Sadleir called it "awkward, sententious and discordantly episodic," and for the most part ignored it. Hugh Walpole found all the characters "revolting" and Alice herself "the stickiest and most stupid" of Trollope's heroines. The Stebbinses, in an otherwise unsympathetic study, gave the novel high praise, as did Beatrice Curtis Brown and Sir Edward Marsh, who rated Alice one of Trollope's most successful heroines.[4] More recent full-length studies are alike in having virtually nothing to say about *Can You Forgive Her?*. Several essays published in the last decade do suggest some revival of critical interest in the novel.[5]

When viewed simply as the history of Alice Vavasor, it is easy to see why *Can You Forgive Her?* should have been so easily passed over by so many for so long. Whatever its general literary merits, however, the novel is of crucial importance as the introductory volume of the Palliser series — that is, as a political novel in its own right — and in this role it has been utterly neglected. Alice fades more or less away with the last pages of *Can You Forgive Her?* (she is mentioned briefly in *The Prime Minister* as — still — a tedious lecturer on morality to Lady Glencora; soon afterwards, perhaps not coincidentally, her husband is appointed by Palliser ambassador to Persia), but the Pallisers, introduced here, linger on.

There is no doubt that the novel occupied for Trollope a special and important place. He makes explicit his particular fondness for it in the *Autobiography* (p. 150), where he discusses together the two novels in which Plantagenet Palliser made his initial appearances: *The Small House at Allington* and *Can You Forgive Her?* — written virtually back to back, with only *Miss Mackenzie* (1865) in between. In an oft-quoted passage (pp. 155—9, *passim.*) Trollope identifies the origins of his lifelong tenderness for the book:

> Of *Can You Forgive Her?* I cannot speak with too great affection . . . that which endears the book to me is the first presentation which I made in it of Plantagenet Palliser, with his wife, Lady Glencora. By no amount of description or asseveration could I succeed in making any reader understand how much these characters with their belongings have been to me in my later life; or how frequently I have used them for the expression of my political and social convictions. They have been as real to me as free trade was to Mr. Cobden, or the dominion of party to Mr. Disraeli; and as I have not been able to speak from the benches of the House of Commons . . . they have served me as a safety-valve by which to deliver my soul.

Speare, as we know, refused to consider *Can You Forgive Her?* a genuine part of Trollope's political series, while Cockshut, Curtis Brown, and others have always seen the novel and its successors as only incidentally concerned with politics rather than as *political novels*. To persist in this attitude in light of Trollope's statement — or of the most casual reading of the novels themselves, for that matter — seems patently absurd.

The main plot of *Can You Forgive Her?*, it is true, has politics only at its periphery. Trollope got it from his own never-produced 1850 drama *The Noble Jilt* (there is some carry-over in the novels: John Grey actually calls Alice "The noblest jilt that yet halted between two minds!"; and in *The Eustace Diamonds* Trollope sends a group of characters to the Haymarket Theatre to see a play called *The Noble Jilt*, during the performance of which the diamonds are stolen again). The play itself is more a combined adaptation of Sir Henry Taylor's play *Philip van Artevelde* (1834) and Frances Trollope's novel *The Widow Barnaby* (1839) than a wholly original piece of work (there are also some resemblances to Thackeray's *The Newcomes*, 1853—55).[6] However, the Palliser sections of *Can You Forgive Her?*, and the story of George Vavasor, are both completely original and genuinely political; while the less ostensibly political story of Alice and her friends demonstrates the many ways in which social and political action are connected — an important theme throughout the Palliser series.

Can You Forgive Her? marks the first actual appearance of Lady Glencora, of whom we have heard before (in *The Small House at*

Allington) but never as yet seen. Palliser himself, however, had appeared briefly as an uncharacteristically flirtatious, would-be adulterer in *The Small House*, where he sighs after the married daughter of Archdeacon Grantly, Lady Dumbello. In this novel he is described unpromisingly as "a thin-minded, plodding, respectable man, willing to devote all his youth to work, in order that in old age he might be allowed to sit among the Councillors of the State" and by George de Courcy as "one of the slowest fellows I ever came across" (I, 319 and 329). Palliser has his moments of folly in *Can You Forgive Her?* as well, but we see him growing in the Palliser novels toward political and social maturity — very much along lines, incidentally, prescribed for politicians in general by Sir Henry Taylor, the author of *Philip van Artevelde*, in his study *The Statesman, an Ironical Treatise on the Art of Succeeding* (1836).[7]

To the extent that the Palliser novels represent an advance in technique over the Barset novels, as Escott and some earlier critics suggested, they do so in the gradual development of their ongoing characters, in whom we are able to detect the processes of growth. Archdeacon Grantly and Mrs Proudie, delightful and unforgettable as they may be, do not grow significantly in the series of novels in which they appear. Palliser in *The Duke's Children* seems light-years away from the Palliser of *The Small House at Allington* or even *Can You Forgive Her?* — and yet in some ways very much the same man. This is the genius of his portrait, strung out through seven novels and 18 years. Palliser moves in these novels, in the political sphere, from would-be politician to Prime Minister of England (he does not have to wait until "old age" to "sit among the Councillors of the State," becoming Chancellor of the Exchequer at 29), and in the social from "thin-minded" spoony to an austere Duke of Omnium, a bereaved middle-aged widower with children to raise. One might go so far as to say that the premiership is ultimately only a preparation for fatherhood. For since social and political action in the Palliser novels are so closely intertwined, Palliser's progress in the two spheres is neither separable nor unrelated.

It is *Can You Forgive Her?* which introduces us to the world of the Pallisers, Trollope's favorite world — to the society of politicians, and to the politics of social behavior.

II

Yet the title takes us to the heroine. Alice Vavasor is of course connected, through her interests, her friends, and her relatives, to politics and politicians, but her contribution to the novel's political commentary is less crucial than that of other characters in *Can You Forgive Her?*. Her story illustrates among other things some of the ways in which political and social considerations may interact, but Alice herself is neither a Palliser nor a politician. In another light, however, she is very important indeed: as a predecessor of, and perhaps an inspiration for, some more celebrated literary heroines – and, in the same connection, as an expression of Trollope's feelings about "independent" women. Since comparatively little will be said subsequently about the heroine of *Can You Forgive Her?*, she will be considered – briefly, now – in this light.

James's uncharitable remark about Trollope's Palliser novels – "His political novels are distinctly dull, and I confess I have not been able to read them" – has often been dredged up by modern critics of Trollope equally uncharitable. We know that the second part (at least) of James's statement is untrue – that he was an avid reader of Trollope, that he published an unsigned review of *Can You Forgive Her?* in 1865 and that he discussed *The Duke's Children* in his memorial essay (1883) on the novelist. He may indeed have forgiven Miss Vavasor, but he did not forget her; in fact he was so far from forgetting her that when, some years later, he came to write *The Portrait of A Lady* (1880–1), he put some of Alice into Isabel Archer, with the result that the two heroines bear many striking resemblances. Since James was often either defensive or misleading about the influence upon him of other writers, this particular case of obfuscation, while interesting and long unrecognized, is not anomalous.[8]

Isabel, we may recall, is always being told that she has too many ideas; indeed, James himself tells us that she is over-loaded with theories, that she thinks too much about herself for her own good.[9] Alice Vavasor, as Trollope makes clear, also thinks too much: "That Alice . . . had thought too much about [marriage], I feel quite sure. She had gone on thinking of it till she had filled herself with a cloud of doubts . . . She thought too much . . . and was . . . over-prudent in calculating the chances of her happiness" (I, 134 and 137). Beyond this, the two heroines share a common failing: a proud ambition to do something extraordinary with their lives despite the ordinariness of their worlds and of their own mental equipment. It should not be necessary here to prove again what every reader of *The Portrait* must already know: that Isabel, with her buoyant expectations and her high opinion of her own capabilities, becomes "ground in the very mill of the conventional" (p. 470). James asks: "Who was she, what was she, that she should hold herself superior? What view of life, what design upon fate, what conception of happiness, had she that pretended to be larger than these large . . . occasions?" (p. 101). Of Alice, Trollope says:

> What should a woman do with her life? . . . Alice . . . was ever asking herself that question, and had by degrees filled herself with a vague idea that there was a something to be done . . . if only she knew what it was. She had filled herself . . . with an undefined ambition that made her restless without giving her any real food for her mind . . . How might she best make herself useful . . . in some sort that might gratify her ambition . . . was . . . the question which seemed to her to be of most importance. (I, 134–5 and 401)

The similarity of Alice's "ambition" to Isabel's is surely clear. Moreover, both Isabel and Alice are too fond of having their own way – too self-willed for their own good. Isabel "doesn't take suggestions"; Alice, says Trollope, "was independent . . . and . . . not inclined to give up that independence to any one." And when, finally, each heroine becomes aware of her folly, each comes to the same realization: her own pride, her own self-will, her own self-confident but nonetheless faulty perception of things have caused her to make mistakes. There is no one else to blame. Alice, discovering how little she wants to marry her cousin George Vavasor after rejecting John Grey's suit in order to re-engage herself to George, realizes that "she had gloried in her independence, and this had come of it! . . . All her troubles and sorrows in life had come from an overfed craving for independence" (I, 473 and II, 38). Further:

> She was sure that she had acted on her own convictions of what was right and wrong; and now . . . she had begun to feel that she had been wrong . . . She had been weak, foolish, irresolute – and had finally acted with false judgment . . . and there must now, she acknowledged, be an end to . . . that pride which had hitherto taught her to think that she could more wisely follow her own guidance than that of any other . . . She had taken her fling at having her own will, and she and all her friends had seen what had come of it . . . She had made a fool of herself in her vain attempt to be greater and grander than other girls. (II, 299, 368, 473, and 500, *passim*.)

Again the similarity to Isabel Archer – "It was impossible to pretend that she had not acted with her eyes open; if ever a girl was a free agent she had been," and " 'I was perfectly free; it was impossible to do anything more deliberate' " (pp. 333 and 400; Isabel here of course is speaking of her fatal marriage) – is striking. Both act with "false judgment" after conscious deliberation. What is perhaps the most interesting connection between them lies in the most morally damning aspect of each: the egoism, the arrogance, of thinking oneself special, superior. Alice had wanted "to be greater and grander than other girls"; "all her misery," Trollope goes on to say, "had been brought about by this scornful superiority to the ordinary pursuits of the world – this looking down upon humanity" (II, 285). Isabel, in the later novel, had sought "the high places of happiness, from which the world would seem to lie below one, so that one could look down with a sense of exaltation and advantage, and judge and choose and pity" (p. 349). The failing in each instance – the feeling of superiority, the desire to be able to "look down" upon others – is the result of an inflated estimation of one's own powers and abilities, an inflation bred by arrogance and its partner self-indulgence. Trollope throughout *Can You Forgive Her?* accuses Alice of "self-devotion" (e.g., II, 364); and Isabel too suffers mightily from the same disease:

Isabel was . . . liable to the sin of self-esteem; she often surveyed with complacency the field of her own nature; she was in the habit of taking for granted, on scanty evidence, that she was right; she treated herself to occasions of homage . . . She thought too much about herself; you could have made her colour, any day in the year, by calling her a rank egoist. She was always planning out her development, desiring her perfection, observing her progress. (pp. 53 and 55)

Both Isabel and Alice consistently ignore the good advice tendered by relatives and friends who predict, accurately enough, that their romantic notions (in a practical age) will get them into trouble. And both use their independent means foolishly. Indeed, the failure of both is largely the result of their having money of their own, which makes them willing prey to fortune-hunters. Isabel ultimately realizes that she married partly "in order to do something finely appreciable with her money." Alice tells her father that she cannot find fault with George Vavasor simply because he wishes "to get that for which every man is struggling." Both hope, and fail, to make great men of little men with their money. John Vavasor's reply to his daughter on the money question recalls what Isabel's friends say to her of Osmond: "He will drain you of every shilling . . . He's going to marry [you] for [your] money; then . . . he'll ill-treat [you]" (I, 440 and 466). Neither heroine pays any attention to this warning. Alice's father concludes that this is what "comes of leaving money at a young woman's disposal" — the very question (what will she do with her money?) that had led Ralph Touchett, out of selfish curiosity, to persuade his father to make Isabel an heiress. And the scenes in *Can You Forgive Her?* in which George Vavasor and his sister Kate plot to take advantage of Alice and her money are not unlike those in *The Portrait of A Lady* in which Osmond and Madame Merle plot to take advantage of Isabel and *her* money.

John Grey's terse defense of Alice to her father — "She has meant to do right" — is equally applicable to Isabel; intentions, however, are less important than the results of them in these novels. After sketching the pitfalls and penalties of feminine independence, the two novels depart from one another in the fate of their heroines. Alice, temporarily choosing the wrong man (a cousin), finds her way back to the right one just in time; while Isabel, who had turned down three suitors (one of them a cousin) any one of whom probably would have made her happier than she is with Osmond, finds that it is too late to separate herself from her destiny — she must lie in the bed she has made for herself. The novels go their own ways, yes; but then Trollope writes novels in which people usually do learn from their mistakes in time, while James typically writes novels in which people realize their mistakes too late for such enlightenment to be of practical use. It is the difference between comedy and tragedy. Alice only needs to understand in time that "if [a woman] shall have recognized the necessity of truth and honesty for the purposes of her life . . . she need [not] ask

herself many questions as to what she will do with it" (I, 135). The
marriage question does not require to be solved by metaphysics. And so at
the end of *Can You Forgive Her?* Alice comes to a realization — not unlike
Isabel's — that "nobody has ever been so stupid as I have" (Lady Macleod
charitably amends the adjective to "self-willed"). Alice has done nothing
immoral; she has simply gotten her priorities scrambled. Isabel, however,
inhabits a different universe, and must suffer.

In creating one of literature's most perverse heroines who is not also
immoral, Trollope was expressing his distaste both for independent women
and the more general evil of self-indulgence; both of these traits are
exhaustively traced in Alice's story. Lady Glencora Palliser, the novel's
other leading woman, may seem at first glance to be even more self-
sufficient and self-indulgent, but ultimately she does not strike out an
independent path in *Can You Forgive Her?*, nor does she find it possible
for long to please only herself; her part of the story is about what she does
not do (she does not leave her husband). Her wit, her irreverence, her
unstuffiness, and her dread of prudery — traits Alice patently lacks — form
her special appeal and of course make the novel's nominal heroine even
more drab, if possible, by contrast. But Glencora is not an independent
woman as Alice is, and that is why at the end of the novel we have much
less to "forgive" her for.
    It is typical of Trollope's attitude toward women that he advocated
their education through programs of reading not in order to help them
become productive citizens but rather to help them find a way to exorcise
boredom and loneliness.[10] His unsubtle attack on organized feminism
through the "Rights of Women Institute, Established for the Relief of the
Disabilities of Females" — abbreviated, ironically, to the "Female Disabilities" — is an unforgettable element of *Is He Popenjoy?*. Here the
Rights of Women movement is said by one character to have its origin in
"old maids who have gone crazy . . . because nobody has married them . . .
the whole thing is disgraceful, and always was," while another expresses
the opinion that "Women are quite able to hold their own without such
trash as that." Any list of Trollope's own favorite female characters would
certainly have to include Glencora and Lily Dale, both of whom are often
perversely stubborn; neither, however, is by any stretch of the imagination
"emancipated," a state Trollope seems to have associated with self-
proclamation, theft, hypocrisy, perspiration, grunting, and a moustache
(the Baroness Banmann in *Is He Popenjoy?* — who belittles her feminist
rival Olivia Q. Fleabody by calling her a female). Indeed, Lily Dale's
unshakable love for the worthless Adolphus Crosbie and her equally
untiring resistance to the deserving John Eames throughout hundreds of
pages of the later Barset novels — written more or less contemporaneously
with *Can You Forgive Her?* — are as far from Alice Vavasor's brand of
vacillating self-indulgence as possible. Lily needs others to an extent

unknown to Alice, and Trollope always preferred his Lilys to his Alices. Perhaps his mother's abrasive self-sufficiency imbued him with a tenderness for dependent women and made him more sensitive to hardness in women than he might otherwise have been. In any case, his feeling about women's rights is articulated explicitly in *Is He Popenjoy?* when the worldly-wise Mrs Montacute Jones speaks of them to Lady George, the novel's heroine: "That's what comes, my dear, of meddling with disabilities. I know my own disabilities, but I never think of interfering with Providence. Mr. Jones was made a man, and I was made a woman. So I put up with it, and I hope you will do the same" (II, 248). Lady George's conclusion: "I'll never have anything more to do with disabilities." And Olivia Q. Fleabody herself has by the end of the novel — Trollope's wording is significant — "settled down into a good mother of a family" (II, 311), thus coming to her senses.

In *He Knew He Was Right* a decade earlier appears "the republican Browning," the women's-rights enthusiast Wallachia Petrie. A poet and a bore, Miss Petrie believes she can "get on very well without male assistance"; and she is able to believe she is right, Trollope concludes, "because the chivalry of men had given to her sex that protection against which her life was one continued protest" (p. 717). In *North America* he had addressed himself specifically to this question. "The happy privileges with which women are at present blessed," Trollope wrote, "have come to them from the spirit of chivalry. That spirit has taught men to endure in order that women may be at their ease." American women, he complained, have "acquired a sufficient perception of the privileges which chivalry gives them, but no perception of that return which chivalry demands from them."[11] About Wallachia Petrie he pointedly adds: "The hope in regard to all such women, — the hope entertained not by themselves, but by those who are solicitous for them, — is that they will be cured at last by a husband and half-a-dozen children" (p. 720). One "cures" a disease. Also in *He Knew He Was Right* — for one of only two times among Trollope's many novels — John Stuart Mill's writings on women are mentioned. Charles Glascock, portrayed throughout the novel as a sensible and kindly man, declares to a "republican" who asks him what he thinks of Mill that he has never read him; and being pressed on the question of Mill's contention that "women must at last be put upon an equality with men," Glascock replies with his own question: "Can he manage that men shall have half the babies?" (p. 521). Mill is also mentioned twice in *Phineas Finn* (II, 145 and 243); in both instances he is referred to humorously by women who have no use for his feminist theories.

Trollope's own knowledge of Mill is doubtful, since Mill's *Logic* is the only volume by him known to have been in Trollope's library;[12] Glascock, perhaps, was speaking directly for the novelist. These references to Mill are nevertheless revealing. Mill's attempt to popularize the idea of the equality of the sexes profoundly affected social thought and even some customs as early as the 1860s; and well before he died (1873) the laws regarding women's property and personal rights were beginning to be reviewed. The influential Society for Promoting the Employment of Women had come into existence in the fifties; and the Married Woman's Property Act, though not passed into law until 1882, had been introduced in Parliament as early as 1856. Queen's College was founded in 1848, Bedford College in 1849 (and Girton later on, in 1872). But into the sixties and seventies Trollope's barren feminists and vulgar meddling female careerists betray only his contempt for the feminist movement. Social historian J. A. Banks is certainly right when he suggests that Trollope may be read less for information about the feminist movement than "for deep insights into the nature of the opposition which [it] had to face." The novelist's own lecture "On the Higher Education of Women" (1868; delivered as *He Knew He Was Right* was appearing), which characterizes the modern too-"thoughtful" woman as vague, purposeless, excited, and generally ineffectual, reiterates the views of Mrs Montacute Jones :

> As we cannot turn a man into a woman . . . so neither can we give to her the gift of persistent energy by which he does perform, and has been intended to perform, the work of the world. There is no doubt a very strong movement now on foot in favour of such assimilation, arising chiefly, as I think, from a certain noble jealousy and high-minded ambition on the part of a certain class of ladies who grudge the other sex the superior privilege of manhood.[13]

Complaining that American women "talk loudly together, having a theory that modesty has been put out of Court by women's rights," Trollope in *North America* mounts a savage attack on the hard, sharp ladies who "know so much more than they ought to know," are "tyrants to their parents, and never practice the virtue of obedience till they have half-grown-up daughters of their own." They have a delusion, he says, "that destiny is to be worked out by the spirit and talent of the young women." And he concludes with a bald assertion of his feelings in the matter: "I confess for me Eve would have had no charms had she not recognized Adam as her lord." Mill had written in *The Subjection of Women* (1869) that "All the moralities tell them that it is the duty of women and all the current sentimentalities that it is their nature, to live for others; to make complete abnegation of themselves, and to have no life but in their affections."[14]

It has been noted that Trollope's antipathy to the women's-rights movement stems in large part from his conviction that women did and should wield great social power without resorting to the streets. A woman, he felt, could live a life both domestic and "full"; indeed, she was most a force for good when presiding over the hearth and making its goodness radiate outward beyond the life of the home. "As soon as the woman began to have great public ambitions of her own . . . and . . . to over-reach herself by interfering with those things the intricacies of which she knew little or nothing," said Speare, paraphrasing very accurately indeed what he took to be Trollope's feelings on the matter, "she became not a constructive force but a destructive influence."[15] If this point of view reminds us of the creator of Mrs Pardiggle and Mrs Jellyby, Mrs Clennam and Madame de Farge — and it should — it is because Dickens, who in so many ways was so less Radical than has been thought, was making some of the same complaints, and indeed making them long before Trollope. In 1851 he attacked the new proselytizing fervor of the early feminists in an article published in *Household Words*. Entitled "Sucking Pigs," its argument comes down heavily upon the modern woman who feels the need to "agitate, agitate":

> She must take to the little table and the water bottle. She must be a public character. She must work away at the Mission. It is not enough to do right for right's sake. There can be no satisfaction . . . in satisfying her mind . . . that the thing she contemplates is right, and therefore ought to be done, and so in calmly and quietly doing it, conscious that therein she sets a righteous example which never in the nature of things can be lost or taken away.[16]

Women who want to become "independent" are portrayed by Trollope and Dickens as neurotic, confused, wavering, and unhappy — unfeminine in their aggressive hardness and, ultimately, embittered failures.

It seems clear now that both Trollope and James — and between them George Eliot in *Middlemarch* (1871–2) — were concerned not only with questions of personal egoism and misplaced idealism but also with the foolishness, as they saw it, of the new feminism — especially when it took the form of the "thoughtful" woman: the modern woman who is stirred up by the startling new ideas of the time to find out what she should "do" with her life. Alice Vavasor, that is to say, is one of the first of a type the most spectacular reappearance of which occurs in the novels of George Eliot and James and which seems to have been created in response to a particular topical question — the "woman" question. In its notice of *Can You Forgive Her?* the *Westminster Review* commented that Alice "has, half-consciously, become deeply infected with the nineteenth-century idea that there was something important to do with her life." Trollope was reading *Emma* in 1864 as he was writing *Can You Forgive Her?* and commented admiringly on the way in which Jane Austen exposes the "folly," "vanity," and "ignorance" of "the female character"[17] — clearly his own subject as well at the time. A few years later, in *The Vicar of Bullhampton* (1869–70; written just after *He Knew He Was Right*), Trollope reintroduces the "woman" question when the restless Mary Lowther debates with herself the issue of the day:

When a girl asks herself that question, — what shall she do with her life? — it is so natural that she should answer it by saying that she will get married, and give her life to somebody else. It is a woman's one career — let women rebel against the edict as they may; and though there may be word-rebellion here and there, women learn the truth early in their lives . . . That our girls are in quest of husbands, and know well in what way their lines of life should be laid, is a fact which none can dispute. Let men be taught to recognise the same truth as regards themselves, and we shall cease to hear of the necessity of a new career for women. (pp. 259–60)

And Trollope goes on here to condemn the "mock modesty" demanded of marriageable women, calling it "a remnant of the tawdry sentimentality of an age in which the mawkish insipidity of the women was a reaction from the vice of that preceding it." A girl's desire to be married, he concludes, is natural, ubiquitous, and reasonable; and "the whole theory of creation requires it" (p. 260). As one critic has said, "that special angle from which Trollope sees with cynical warmth reduces reality for any woman to marrying and having two children and being honest with an honest husband." It is this view of women against which Bella Wilfer in Dickens's *Our Mutual Friend* (1864–5) is reacting when she proclaims her unwillingness to be merely "the doll in the doll's house," the famous phrase which gave Ibsen his title; indeed, it was often the nature of this world "to see the intelligent woman as a threat and to try to keep her in a doll's house."[18]

A lot of silly sentimental nonsense has been written about Trollope's supposed sympathy for the economically and vocationally helpless Victorian woman; thus it may be worth demonstrating that the attitudes alluded to here are by no means anomalous in the spread of his work. As early as 1848, Fanny Wyndham in *The Kellys and the O'Kellys* is made to declare: "Thank Heaven, I'm not a queen, to be driven to have other feelings than those of my sex" (p. 358); she is in love and wants to marry — unlike the cold cousin she is speaking to here, Lady Selina Cashel, who "had vainly and foolishly built up for herself a pedestal, and there she had placed herself," unhappily above all men and marriage. In *The Three Clerks*, written a decade later, Trollope attacks the permissiveness with which Mrs Woodward brings up her three adolescent daughters — and, five years before he began to write *Can You Forgive Her?*, draws on *Philip van Artevelde* in his argument: "The assertion made by Clara van Artevelde, that women 'grow upon the sunny side of the wall,' is doubtless true; but young ladies, gifted as they are with such advantages, may perhaps be thought to require some counsel, some advice, in those first tender years in which they so often have to make or mar their fortunes" (p. 27). Young ladies should not be allowed to decide a great many things for themselves. In *Phineas Finn*, written mostly in 1866, an instructive contrast is offered between Violet Effingham and Laura Standish — as between Fanny Wyndham and Selina Cashel in the earlier novel. By this time, however, public affairs have entered the picture. Violet's energies are devoted not to "the sterile wastes of Women's Rights," to which at one time she facetiously suggested she might devote herself, but rather, happily for her, into wifehood and motherhood, the usual Trollopian prescription for feminine happiness; while Lady Laura, who believes a woman's life is only half a life because she cannot have a seat in Parliament, represents the woman who takes politics so seriously as to endanger her own happiness. Indeed, rather than live "half a life" with a man she loves, Laura marries a man she does not love in an attempt to extend her political influence; and her ardent desire to use politics to resolve her emotional frustrations destroys both her life and her husband's.[19] Violet eschews public affairs and is happy; Laura does not do this and is destroyed. In *Sir Harry Hotspur of Humblethwaite* (1870), Trollope speaks ambiguously of his conception of the "genus girl": "We know that [girls] will, sooner or later, [fall in love]; and probably as . . . [soon] as opportunity may offer. That is our experience of the genus girl in the general; and we quite approve of her for her readiness to do so. It is, indeed, her nature; and the propensity has been planted in her for wise purposes" (p. 69). Emily Hotspur, the novel's heroine, believes that "a woman should not marry . . . unless she could so love a man as to acknowledge to herself that she was imperatively required to sacrifice all that belonged to her for his welfare and good" (p. 164). This is certainly clear enough; and Trollope went on saying more or less the same things throughout the 1870s, as the women's-rights movement gathered steam. "It is certainly God's intention that men and women should live together, and therefore let the leap in the dark be made," he tells us, a year after *Sir Harry Hotspur*, in *Ralph the Heir* (II, 329–30), spiritedly defending the institution of marriage. "Wicked as men and women are it is . . . evidently intended that they should marry and multiply" (p. 141), he declares in his late novel *John Caldigate*, which is not prevented by having one of fiction's stupidest heroes from arguing that a woman's first and only duty is to cleave to her husband and child no matter what emergency may seem to weaken those ties. Indeed, for over thirty years Trollope said the same things to women: marry and have children - that is what you should "do."

When, therefore, John Grey in *Can You Forgive Her?* resolves "to treat all that [Alice] might say as the hallucination of a sickened imagination" (I, 143), we are meant to see her political ambitions as mere fictions, the stuff and substance of romance, idle and unhealthy daydreaming, a neurotic craving for excitement. Alice's "hallucination" is that she must fulfill herself by "doing something with her life" instead of "burying herself" as a wife — so she denies her genuine love for Grey and becomes instead subject to visions. Alice must learn to yield self-indulgence to propriety and good sense; it is this side of *Can You Forgive Her?* — the fate-of-the-"thoughtful"-woman side — that has prompted some critics to describe it as a pioneering modern-problem novel of sorts. The anti-feminist theme is embellished by the presence in the novel of the two Miss Pallisers — suffragette types, stuffy, ineffectual, and in general unsympathetically drawn. Polhemus's assertion — characteristic of his frequently odd slant on Trollope's heroines — that *Can You Forgive Her?* shows women to be members of an oppressed second sex is utter nonsense.[20]

There are resemblances between the too-thoughtful women of Trollope and James who want to lead extraordinary lives despite ordinary capabilities and George Eliot's Dorothea Brooke, whose ambitions are not unlike those of the heroines of *Can You Forgive Her?* and *The Portrait*. This should be clear to any reader of the three novels. It is worth remembering that at the end of *Middlemarch* Dorothea still feels vaguely "that there was . . . something better which she might have done" than marry Ladislaw and raise his children, and that George Eliot pointedly denies this: "Many who knew her, thought it a pity that so substantive and rare a creature should have been absorbed into the life of another, and be only known in a certain circle as a wife and mother. But no one stated exactly what else that was in her power she ought rather to have done." There *is* nothing else "she ought rather to have done." Since "great feelings will often take the aspect of error, and great faith the aspect of illusion," what is good in the world comes primarily from "unhistoric acts" committed by those who live "faithfully a hidden life." George Eliot says it another way in *The Mill on the Floss* (1860): "the happiest women, like the happiest nations, have no history."[21] There is no encouragement here, even from the great lady novelist herself, for a woman to do anything other than, as Trollope says in *The Vicar of Bullhampton*, "get married, and give her life to somebody else."

The influence of George Eliot upon James, and specifically of *Middlemarch* upon *The Portrait*, has been fully documented[22] and requires no further elaboration here. What has not been sufficiently recognized, however, is the debt both James and George Eliot owe to *Can You Forgive Her?*. George Eliot told Mrs Lynn Linton that, if it had not been for Trollope, she was not sure she could have written *Middlemarch* as in fact it was written; and certainly such phrases in *Can You Forgive Her?* as "she [Alice] would have liked to have around her ardent spirits" (I, 111) must have caught George Eliot's fancy and stuck in her memory.[23] What James took from *Middlemarch* is well-known, but what he took from Trollope's novel — either directly, or through George Eliot's version of its theme, or both — is not well-known. If Isabel resembles Dorothea, both resemble Alice; the "What should a woman do with her life?" question is central in all three novels. Each writer, in his or her own way, deals with the modern "thoughtful" woman — Trollope for the most part disparagingly, ironically, George Eliot more thoughtfully, perhaps, and certainly in part autobiographically, and James less polemically or subjectively than psychologically and sociologically.

It is by no means certain that among the three novelists the youngest of them — James — did all of the taking, But surely he took more than he thought.

Let us remember Trollope's dictum in *Can You Forgive Her?*: "if [a woman] shall have recognized the necessity of truth and honesty for the purposes of her life, I do not know that she need ask herself many questions as to what she will do with it." Alice's interests go beyond "truth and honesty," as we have seen; she is also, in fact, enamored of politics, and this is one of the things that draws her initially to her cousin George. Such an interest can only be emotionally compromising for this particular woman, especially since she is a dilettante in these matters. It is certainly no accident that George Vavasor is one of the novel's two leading politicians, and that it is he who is so instrumental in bringing about Alice's moral confusion. That politics and political interests can have social consequences, and vice versa, and that politics can be a dirty and corrupting business, are two paramount themes of the Palliser novels from beginning to end. And so it is not altogether surprising to discover early in *Can You Forgive Her?* (I, 136) that the novel's abrasive and foolish heroine, among her other follies, "had undoubtedly a hankering after some second-hand political manoeuvring."

III

Two of Trollope's most repulsive villains — George Vavasor, and Ferdinand Lopez in *The Prime Minister* — are unsuccessful politicians. Both are businessmen of sorts, stockbrokers who swindle, cheat, and lie in an attempt to get into Parliament; both ultimately fail. Lopez finally throws himself in front of a train, while Vavasor goes off to America — punishments almost equivalent for a Trollope character.

That neither is a Tory (Vavasor is a Radical, Lopez, a Liberal) is interesting but not especially significant. For the novel's "good" politician, Plantagenet Palliser, isn't a Tory either; like Trollope himself, he is a conservative Liberal. In tracing the incipient careers of two Liberal/Radical politicians — Palliser at the outset of his career is described as "a Radical in public life," but one who does not "want to be called a Radical . . . or to be called anything at all" and as a man who "would not for worlds transgress the social laws of his [Whig] ancestors" (I, 290 and II, 490) — Trollope is less interested in partisan than in moral distinctions. The novel's political theme concerns itself with different kinds of political behavior and the extent to which such behavior is conditioned by the nature of the political process and by the interconnections between political action and social influences. In addressing these questions, *Can You Forgive Her?* provides a worthy introduction to the Palliser series.

It is no accident that both Lopez and George Vavasor — the "bad" politician of *Can You Forgive Her?* — are middle-class commercial entrepreneurs. Lopez, like Undecimus Scott in *The Three Clerks*, attempts to manipulate the stock market for his own profit; and one of Trollope's most constant and bitter complaints is against those who pursue parliamentary careers to protect and enhance their own social and financial positions rather than to serve their country without ulterior motive. For George Vavasor "politics was business, as well as beer, and omnibus-horses, and foreign wines" (I, 154). And when he ruminates on the "pickings in the way of a Member of Parliament" —

> Companies, — mercantile companies, — would be glad to have him as a director, paying him a guinea a day, or perhaps more, for his hour's attendance. Railways in want of vice-chairmen might bid for his services; and in the City he might turn that 'M.P.' which belonged to him to good account in various ways. With such a knowledge of the City world as he possessed, he thought that he could pick up a living in London, if only he could retain his seat in Parliament. (II, 368)

— he defines himself as the would-be political type most abhorrent to Trollope. The novelist believed that men without private means should stay out of party politics. Parliamentary life is expensive; men without money are inevitably subject to corruption both political and social and to a humiliating loss of personal independence.

The consistency of Trollope's feeling about the disastrous mix of politics and business is striking in many of his pronouncements on public affairs. Aristocrats have relatively few corrupting material temptations; but such men as stockbrokers — and lawyers and doctors and journalists — are often so tempted. Just as such men, as he says in *The New Zealander* (the essay on "Society"), will ostentatiously spend twice as much as aristocrats "on their costly pleasures . . . in vainly looking for social joys," so will they try to buy their way into public splendor.[24]

Perhaps the two novels outside of the Palliser series in which we may best see some of this — one late, the other early — are *The Way We Live Now* and *The Three Clerks*. Trollope, as we know, feared the advent of a new aristocracy built on money alone; the most spectacular result of this fear is Melmotte in *The Way We Live Now*. What Trollope disliked most about the new commercial giants growing up was that they should want to go into Parliament to get into "Society" and to protect their interests as directors of and stockholders in City companies. The novelist felt that Parliament deserved better — and Melmotte appropriately makes a fool of himself when he attempts to speak in the House of Commons. Yet he is elected (defeating an equally unscrupulous hack journalist); the novel was written in large part to combat the idea growing fashionable in the seventies that "success was wealth and wealth was God."[25]

Almost two decades earlier Trollope had felt the same way; *The Three Clerks* — less well-known but no less explicit — amply shows this.

> He had used the Honourable before his name, and the M.P. which . . . followed after it, to acquire for himself a seat as director at a bank board. He was a Vice-President of the Caledonian, English, Irish, and General European and American Fire and Life Assurance Society . . . He was a director also of one or two minor railways, dabbled in mining shares, and, altogether, did a good deal of business in the private stock-jobbing line . . . The one strong passion of his life was the desire of a good income at the cost of the public. (pp. 87–8 and 90)

The Hon. Undecimus Scott, M.P., desires only "a good income at the cost of the public" — a perfect inversion of what an ideal public servant should want. The novel goes on to show Scott (who, reversing Melmotte's career, goes in for politics as a way into business rather than vice versa), a member of a parliamentary committee looking into the building of a bridge between Limehouse and Rotherhithe, attempting to manipulate the rise in value of the bridge shares long enough to sell those he owns for a quick profit — knowing all the time, of course, that the bridge will not be built. Scott himself is never reticent about the advantages of this sort of career:

> 'Why are members of Parliament asked to be directors, and vice-governors, and presidents, and guardians, of all the joint-stock societies that are now set going? Not because of their capital, for they generally have none; not for their votes, because one vote can be but of little use in any emergency. It is because the names of men of note are worth money. Men of note understand this, and enjoy the fat of the land accordingly.' (p. 103)

The distinguished Board of Melmotte's railway in *The Way We Live Now* belongs to the *genre* Scott is talking about here. Such men go into politics to help themselves rather than others. "Men in general . . . go into Parliament for the sake of getting places of £1,200 a year," Sir Gregory Hardlines tells Alaric Tudor in *The Three Clerks*; "An obscure man . . . [has] nothing to sell," says Undecimus Scott. Better be the "managing director of a bankrupt swindle" than a nobody — if you want to succeed in politics. A man "can do anything if he is in the House, and he can do nothing if he is not," says Scott. "It is not only what a man may do himself for himself, but . . . what others will do for him when he is in a position to help them." And he adds — being at the time temporarily between seats: "let me get [in] again, and they'll do for me just anything I ask them" (p. 288). This perfectly defines a consistent object of Trollope's most inveterate contempt.

Thus from the outset we should be aware that George Vavasor, in addition to the heavy load he already carries as official villain of *Can You Forgive Her?*, must also be seen as the vivid illustration of a type of commercial politician — a would-be "man of note" — most hateful in the eyes of his creator. Although he ultimately becomes an unscrupulous, selfish, vindictive, and even vicious man, George does not begin as one. His indigenous greed and hard-heartedness help turn him into what he becomes, but so do the political aspirations by which he is haunted. For him, a parliamentary career is an immoralizing process; his political failure finally turns him into a would-be murderer, a real criminal. Since his political motives are always opportunistic he is never a figure of pathos.

George's political career is inseparable from questions of money. Later, in the two *Phineas* novels and in the characters of Frank Greystock in *The Eustace Diamonds* and Ferdinand Lopez in *The Prime Minister*, Trollope was to make an extended examination of the moral perils of parliamentary aspirations in a man without independent means. Here the problem is neither as subtle nor as complicated, and it is finally resolved in melodrama. The lessons, however, are always the same: patriotism, honesty, courage, eloquence — these qualities are no doubt pleasant for a public man to possess, but they are superfluous in one who has not the means to buy a seat or the political allies who will find him a safe one; and such qualities are not sufficient of themselves to preserve the spirit of independence in an ambitious man without means.

The member sitting in the Chelsea seat which George covets spent £6,000 getting himself there at the last election. Mr Scruby, George's election agent, is blunt enough on the question of money: "I could tell you such tales! I've had Members of Parliament, past, present, and future, almost down on their knees to me in this little room . . . There is so much you see, Mr. Vavasor, for which a gentleman must pay ready money" (I, 455). "Ready money" means bribery; the side that bribes the most wins the most in Trollope's elections. Mr Grimes, the publican who helps George in his campaign, believes "that the possession of a vote had always meant hard cash." Grimes is the basic Trollopian democrat, the ancestor of Pile and company of *Ralph the Heir* and of all the greedy electors of the later political novels who define the context in which the would-be politician must succeed if he is ever to be visible in Parliament. Grimes's major interest in elections is in what he calls "the game," a reference to the exchange of money for votes. A candidate, Grimes feels, must not be allowed to have his run without paying for that privilege: "Anybody'd go and get his self elected if we was to let the game go by!" says the fastidious Mr Grimes (I, 155). George is thus asked for £3,000 — and this for the chance to sit in Parliament for a few months, the end of a rump session; he is aware that, win or lose, the whole business will have to be repeated again six months hence.

As is so often the case in the Palliser novels, the subsequent election is itself characterized as a great "game," the progression of which reveals the insincerity and cynicism of players and participants alike. George talks of playing "the game out" and, while he is briefly in Parliament, of its being his "game to support the ministry." In a long aside at the beginning of the second volume, Trollope's own cynicism on the subject is expressed clearly:

> in this Olympus partners are changed, the divine bosom, now rabid with hatred against some opposing deity, suddenly becomes replete with love towards its late enemy, and exciting changes occur which give to the whole thing all the keen interest of a sensational novel ... Members of Parliament ... are apt to teach themselves that it means nothing; that Lord This does not hate Mr. That, or think him a traitor to his country, or wish to crucify him; and that Sir John of the Treasury is not much in earnest when he speaks of his noble friend at the 'Foreign Office' as a god to whom no other god was ever comparable ... But the outside Briton ... should not be desirous of peeping behind the scenes. No beholder at any theatre should do so. It is good to believe in these friendships and these enmities, and very pleasant to watch their changes. (II, 12)

Here Parliament is described in mock-heroic language as a dramatic production, a scene from a novel, a fake, a game, a sham. People, being "not much in earnest," do not say what they mean, and vice versa; the legal tender of Parliament is rhetorical counterfeit, its inhabitants actors in a theater who behave differently on the two sides of the curtain. An "irate gentleman" makes a speech: "in spite of his assumed fury, the gentleman was not irate. He intended to communicate his look of anger to the newspaper reports of his speech"; meanwhile "enemies [were] shaking hands with enemies, – in a way that showed an entire absence of all good, honest hatred among them" (II, 15–16). Real hatred, at least, would be honest; everything here is made up for the gallery.

It is not surprising, then, that the process by which this Elysium is attained is also viewed as a vast joke by Trollope. Vavasor, who is later to lose his seat when his money and his credit run out, gets himself admitted to the parliamentary game for a few months by learning to play the electioneering game, another exercise in sham. Its major ingredient is a "cry," a slogan; George's is "Vote for Vavasor and the River Bank," a bogus scheme – "perfectly unintelligible" to the district's voters – for pouring millions of pounds into local construction projects. (That such a pork-barrel ultimately made good politics for someone may be seen today in the Chelsea Embankment.) George complains to Scruby that the River Bank project is impossible of fulfillment. But an aspiring M.P. needs an issue, and Scruby's reply is indicative:

'What matters that? ... You should work it up ... Get the figures by heart ... so ... nobody can put you down. Of course it won't be done. If it were done, that would be an end of it, and your bread would be taken out of your mouth. But you can always promise it at the hustings, and can always demand it in the House. I've known men who've walked into as much as two thousand a year, permanent place, on the strength of a worse subject than that!' (II, 46)

"Of course it won't be done" — do things for your constituents and you cease to have issues to run on; leave them undone and complain long enough about their not being done and you may get yourself a secure position. This program of opportunism and mendaciousness is adopted by Vavasor, who learns well to play his part: "He was able even to work himself into an apparent heat when he was told the thing was out of the question; and soon found that he had disciples who believed in him ... He worked hard, and spoke vehemently" (II, 47–8). George becomes another "irate gentleman"; he perseveres, and is elected. *The Prime Minister* tells us that "a good cry is a very good thing" (II, 179); here it elects a man almost by itself, and is thus seen to be a very good thing indeed.

George has had to make moral compromises because it is only by doing so that he may be admitted into the sacred club. After all, as Trollope says in his *Life of Cicero*, "a scrupulous man is impractical in politics."[26] Palliser remarks to Alice Vavasor that the metropolitan seats "should be left to rich commercial men who can afford to spend money on them." He understands what such elections are like and why such districts are not promising ones for men without means. But George has had, temporarily at least, such means at his disposal.

We know about Alice's "hankering after some second-hand political manoeuvring"; we also know that she has her own money and that she wishes to do something useful with it. For George, who according to his own sister does not "understand what it is to be honest," Alice's money is always the chief interest in his relation with her: "he would have made no ... offer had she been penniless, or ... had his own need been less pressing" (I, 448). That Alice knows this pretty accurately suggests that she must share the blame for the unpleasant results of their engagement, but it does not make George more virtuous. He admits that he is "very fond of money and ... not particularly squeamish. I would do anything that a man can do to secure it" (II, 1).

George Vavasor is the man as beast, and the beast as politician. Trollope shows in him the bad ends to which selfish political ambition can lead, just as he shows the other side of the political coin in Palliser. Political aspiration, unless it is patriotic and unselfish, can become diabolical. For George ultimately becomes much more than selfish; he becomes criminal, and largely through frustrated political ambition. For a man who lacks both patriotism and money, politics is the temptation of the Devil; George is ultimately compared by Trollope to Cain — and, later, is seen as a Satanic figure (e.g., II, 49). George himself says: "I'm not . . . sure that I have not been wrong in making this attempt to get into Parliament, — that I'm not struggling to pick fruit which is above my reach . . . I am ready to risk anything. . . . I would toss up to-morrow . . . between the gallows and a seat in the House" (I, 488). There is apparently little difference between the two for such a man.

Disillusioned by his closer view of parliamentary life, "beginning to hate his seat . . . What good had it done for him, or was it likely to do for him?" (II, 152), discovering that he must find at least another £2,000 if he wished to sit in Parliament longer than three months, George nevertheless vows that he will stick at nothing to perpetuate his political career. His thoughts become at last those of the villain of a stage melodrama: "He would get it; — as long as Alice had a pound over which he could obtain mastery by any act or violence within his compass . . . He would get it; though in doing so he might destroy his cousin Alice and ruin his sister Kate. He had gone too far to stick at any scruples" (II, 153). When Alice makes it plain that she does not wish to marry him after all, and when on top of this his grandfather very sensibly leaves the family estate away from his grandson, for all intents and purposes George is finally robbed of his last hope to remain in Parliament. His response is to curse everyone he knows as well as "the House of Commons, which had cost him so much, and the greedy electors who would not send him there without his paying for it" (II, 218). Like Lopez later, he thinks "of an express train rushing along . . . and of the instant annihilation which it would produce" (II, 219); but he rejects suicide and thinks of murder instead, contemplating successively the doing in of Alice, his grandfather (were it still possible), his sister Kate — but "Nothing was to be got by killing his sister" (II, 215), so he breaks her arm instead — Scruby, and, ultimately, "The City" itself. He attempts to murder Grey, and failing goes off to America to escape prosecution. Thus the career of George Vavasor.

Phineas Finn is warned by his friend Mr Low in the next Palliser novel to establish himself professionally before going into Parliament so as to remain independent of pecuniary considerations once there. Ignoring this good advice, Phineas as a politician without means is forced to choose between moral compromise and the termination of his political career. Such a one always finds himself in an equivocal position eventually: "There is, probably, no man who becomes naturally so hard in regard to money," says Trollope in *The Eustace Diamonds* (p. 75). As George learns how important it is for would-be statesmen to be rich, we in turn begin to discover the moral perils of the political process.

Trollope's point is underlined in various other ways. Burgo Fitzgerald also pursues money, but he is neither heartless nor a politician, and his degradation is never as morally acute as George's. Of Burgo, Trollope says: "there was always about him a certain kindliness which made him pleasant to those around him ... I think the secret of it was chiefly ... that he seemed to think so little of himself" (I, 376). Burgo is irresponsible but never vicious; his aspirations are amorous rather than political. He refuses to take a handout from Palliser late in the novel when he is in most desperate need of money, declining as he says to take Glencora's money "when she would not give me herself!" (Mrs Greenow, in a different context to be sure, says more or less the same thing: "[Living] on his wife ... I look upon as about the meanest thing a man can do. By George, I'd sooner break stones than that" – I, 503. The other George, of course, takes what he supposes to be Alice's money without Alice. The man Mrs Greenow ultimately marries, though also in pursuit of money all his life, has no ambition other than to be comfortable, and therefore, according to Trollope, Captain Bellfield is "simply an idle scamp ... moderate in his greediness.") Trollope explicitly compares Burgo with George at one point. Burgo's "curses," he says, "had none of the bitterness of those which George Vavasor was always uttering. Through it all there remained about Burgo [an] honest feeling ... that it all served him right. ... If he loved no one sincerely, neither did he hate any one; and whenever he made any self-inquiry into his own circumstances, he always told himself that it was all his own fault ... George Vavasor would have ground his victims up to powder ... but Burgo ... desired to hurt no one" (II, 323). Burgo is not a politician – either professionally or morally: "it was not in him deceit, – or what men call acting" (II, 114). Clearly, the larger the ambition in some men the greater the opportunity for moral corruption.

The peculiar vulnerability of the impecunious politician is emphasized indirectly in another way. Glencora is also prey to temptations, but she does not succumb to immorality – in part, certainly, because she is insulated by financial security. There have been moments in her life, she says, "when I almost made up my mind to go headlong to the devil. ... A man can [do it] ... All he wants is money, and he goes away and has his fling. Now I have plenty of money ... and I never got my fling yet" (II, 354). Glencora, of course, is not in Parliament; but here she makes the point that it is always easier to be virtuous when one is well-heeled. Yet she is no Becky Sharp. George, by contrast, had longed "for money all his life ... till the Devil ... hardened his heart" (II, 213 and 298).

It makes a difference, having money or not – as the career of the novel's other leading politician also makes clear. But Palliser's part of the story in *Can You Forgive Her?* suggests too that political leaders are more wisely taken from a social class other than that of George Vavasor.

IV

Grey, telling the story of Vavasor's moral collapse to Palliser, concludes with a lesson: "The end of it all is ... that public men in England should be rich like you, and not poor like that miserable wretch, who has now lost everything that the Fates had given him" (II, 411–12).

Here, as elsewhere in Trollope's work, the novelist's feeling that men of Palliser's position – rich aristocrats – are most fit for political leadership in England becomes patent. In *Can You Forgive Her?* we perceive in Palliser, though at this time he is still under 30, many of the traits that Trollope admired in men of his rank. Despite Glencora's whimsical, hilarious version of how the Pallisers got started (I, 278–9) and her equally entertaining account of the uselessness of the ducal seat at Gatherum Castle (II, 508–9), Trollope's political sympathies are plainly on the side of the wellborn. It is important to the novelist that such men do not have personal vanity of rank, but rather look upon their position as a trust, a tool with which to be useful to their country. Trollope hated snobbery and pretension. Throughout the political series Palliser's class pride is based on national rather than on personal grounds: he is a modest and unassuming man whose one great goal in life is to be useful to his country, thus justifying in the only way possible the existence of the great family to which he belongs. "Such a one . . . justifies to the nation the seeming anomaly of an hereditary peerage and of primogeniture," Trollope declares in the *Autobiography*. In *Can You Forgive Her?* Palliser tells Grey: "I don't think a man is a bit better because he is rich, or because he has a title; nor do I think he is likely to be in any degree the happier. I am quite sure that he has no right to be in the slightest degree proud of that which he has had no hand in doing for himself . . . I don't think I'm proud because chance has made me my uncle's heir" (II, 418–19). Trollope makes it clear that Palliser's interest in wealth is based on political and patriotic ambitions rather than on personal ones: "He wanted great wealth for that position at which he aimed . . . [which would do] less than nothing . . . for his own personal comfort . . . but [rather give] to him at once that rock-like solidity which is so necessary to our great aristocratic politicians" (I, 305; this is to become one of the great lessons Palliser labors to pass on to the next generation in *The Duke's Children*, at the other end of the political series). Unlike George Vavasor's pursuit of Alice, Palliser's of Glencora M'Cluskie, the richest heiress of her time, results from his desire to give rather than get.

Palliser's great ambition might be folly in a lazy or selfish or unprincipled man, or in a dilettante. But this man, who need never do a day's work in his life, works hard at being a politician so that some day he may be a statesman knowledgeable and efficient. "He seldom gives over work till after one, and sometimes goes on till three," says Glencora. "It's the only thing he likes" (I, 302). Trollope adds: "He . . . worked much harder than Cabinet Ministers generally work." Palliser believes in doing his duty by his class and his country: "He had learned to comprehend that the world's progress depends on the way in which men do their duty by each other, – that the progress of one generation depends on the discharge of such duties by that which preceded it" (I, 377; this too he strives to teach his children in the last of the Palliser novels). Why does he work so hard? Why does he eschew the usual pursuits and pleasures of nineteenth-century gentlemen of leisure? "To all men unmitigated unrelenting labour is in itself grievous; nay more, to all men such labour is impossible, unless the inward spirit be sustained by ambition. Yet it is by labour such as this, and by such labour only, that the duties of a great statesman can be performed," says Trollope in *The New Zealander*.[27] In *Can You Forgive Her?* Palliser tells Grey: "The chief gratification comes from feeling that you are of use" (II, 463). This is one of Palliser's constant preoccupations, as it was one of Trollope's. To work hard and to be of use, thus justifying over and over again each day one's place in the world and the respect of others — these motivating forces in Palliser are surely projections of the novelist himself. "There is no bread so sweet as that which is eaten in the sweat of a man's brow," Trollope declares in *North America*; it is a cardinal principle, articulated everywhere. "Work never palls on us, whereas pleasure always does" (I, 101), is the way it is put in *The Claverings*. "There is no human bliss equal to twelve hours of work with only six hours in which to do it," Trollope says in the *Autobiography*. The "happiest man" is he who has the most work to do and feels that his "hours are filled to overflowing," so that he "can hardly steal minutes enough for sleep," he declares in *The Duke's Children*. And he adds here: "hard work, and hard work alone," can create "self-contentment" (I, 238—9). In *Ralph the Heir* he speaks at some length of "work" as of a narcotic: "there are men who love work, who revel in that, who attack it daily with renewed energy, almost wallowing in it, greedy of work, who go to it almost as the drunkard goes to his bottle, or the gambler to his gaming-table. These are not unhappy men" (II, 277; Trollope's personal involvement here is patent). There is nothing wrong with political ambition in this kind of man; indeed, Palliser's desire in *Can You Forgive Her?* to become Chancellor of the Exchequer is pointedly characterized by the Duke of St Bungay as "about the finest ambition by which a man can be moved." As long as rich and powerful men are not self-serving, wealth and ambition are virtues; fortunately, "from the ranks of the nobility are taken the greater proportion of hard-working servants of the state" (*Lady Anna*, p. 223). These are among Trollope's most ubiquitous themes.

Palliser, in conversation with his languid cousin Jeffrey, says this in *Can You Forgive Her?*: "There is no . . . error so vulgar . . . as that by which men have been taught to say that mercenary tendencies are bad. A desire for wealth is the source of all progress. Civilization comes from what men call greed. Let your mercenary tendencies be combined with honesty and they cannot take you astray" (I, 323). The novelist speaks more bluntly in *Lady Anna*: "The man who is insensible to the power which money brings with it must be a dolt" (p. 27). Trollope's novels never condemn worldliness, and one reason for this is his belief that if "mercenary tendencies" were the sole property of dishonest men such men would eventually hold sway over honest men. Civilization comes in part from greed, and so does progress — good Victorian philosophy. It is not surprising, then, to find two of Trollope's most appealing clerics accepting this thesis. Archdeacon Grantly says: "If honest men did not squabble for money, in this wicked world of ours, the dishonest men would get it all; and I do not see that the cause of virtue would be much improved" (*Barchester Towers*, p. 130). In *Is He Popenjoy?* the Dean of Brotherton says virtually the same thing, though more eloquently:

> 'It is a grand thing to rise in the world. The ambition to do so is the very salt of the earth. It is the parent of all enterprise, and the cause of all improvement. They who know no such ambition are savages and remain savage. As far as I can see, among us Englishmen such ambition is, healthily and happily, almost universal, and on that account we stand high among the citizens of the world. But, owing to false teaching, men are afraid to own aloud a truth which is known to their own hearts.' (II, 286)

Money, or its absence, corrupts bad men, like George Vavasor; but it is also a useful tool, a civilizing tool, in the right hands (Trollope, remember, approved of the concept of Empire). Thus it is important that good men be "mercenary"; were they simply passive we would all suffer. "I think every man is bound to do the best he can for himself — that is, honestly," says Gertrude Woodward in *The Three Clerks*; "there is something spoony in one man allowing another to get before him, as long as he can manage to be first himself" (p. 139). The good must fight all the harder because the bad have so many natural advantages: "Let two unknown men be competitors for any place, with nothing to guide the judges but their own words and . . . looks, and who can doubt but the dishonest man would be chosen . . . Honesty goes about with a hang-dog look . . . Dishonesty carries his eyes high" (*The Eustace Diamonds*, pp. 480–1). "You shall meet two men of whom you shall know the one to be endowed with the brilliancy of true genius, and the other to be possessed of moderate parts, and shall find the former never able to hold his own against the latter" (*The Duke's Children*, I, 244). Let the "mercenary tendency" be unashamedly admitted, then: "While rank, wealth, and money are held to be good things by all around us, let them be acknowledged as such" (*He Knew He Was Right*, p. 863). In politics the abdication of good men in favor of unprincipled men can be especially catastrophic. And so in *The Prime Minister* (II, 180) the Duke of St Bungay speaks contemptuously of "the honest men [who] . . . desert their country in order that the dishonest men may have everything their own way." And so too, discussing in his *Life of Cicero* Cicero's condemnation of Caesarism, Trollope condemns passivity, silent acquiescence in immorality, as "a great social evil."[28] A man should stand up — especially a good man.

Thus a healthy respect for money is not a sin, despite the story of George Vavasor. This theme echoes throughout *Can You Forgive Her?*. The shrewd Mrs Greenow knows that "Money's never dirty"; Glencora, though not herself a mercenary woman, understands this principle just as well: "Diamonds are diamonds, and garnets are garnets; and I am not so romantic but what I know the difference" (II, 477 and 502).

For Palliser, who according to Trollope would rather be a Cabinet minister than an angel (II, 276), "the British House of Commons is everything, everything. That and the Constitution are everything . . . The man who is counted by his colleagues as number one on the Treasury Bench . . . is the first of living men" (II, 510).

What sort of man is this? What personal traits does Trollope give to this manifestation of his ideal politician? He is a man, first of all, to whom pretension, surfaces, and labels are abhorrent. Tall, thin, looking like a gentleman, there is "nothing in his appearance that was remarkable. It was a face that you might see and forget . . . Mr. Palliser was a man who had never thought of assisting his position in the world by his outward appearance" (I, 281). He is "a man not apt to new friendships . . . not a man with whom it was easy to open an acquaintance" (II, 374–5). These things at once separate him from the general run of politicians, those specialists in popularity. He is a genuine person despite his wealth and rank — honest, plain, and literal. It is this genuineness, this realness, that appeals most to the novelist, who so hated sham. In a long essay mid-way through the first volume of *Can You Forgive Her?*, Trollope defines the qualities of the man that most set him apart from his political colleagues.

Mr. Palliser was one of those politicians in possessing whom England has perhaps more reason to be proud than any other of her resources, and who, as a body, give to her that exquisite combination of conservatism and progress which is her present strength and best security for the future. He could afford to learn to be a statesman, and had the industry wanted for such training. He was born in the purple . . . surrounded by all the temptations of luxury and pleasure; and yet he devoted himself to work with the grinding energy of a young penniless barrister labouring for a penniless wife, and did so without any motive more selfish than that of being counted in the roll of the public servants of England . . . He rather prided himself on being dull, and on conquering in spite of his dullness. He never allowed himself a joke in his speeches, nor attempted even the smallest flourish of rhetoric. He was very careful in his language, labouring night and day to learn to express himself with accuracy. . . . He had taught himself to believe that oratory, as oratory, was a sin against that honesty in politics by which he strove to guide himself. He desired to use words for the purpose of teaching things which he knew and which others did not know; and he desired to be honoured for his knowledge. But he had no desire to be honoured for the language in which his knowledge was conveyed. He was an upright, thin, laborious man ... whose parts were sufficient to make his education, integrity, and industry useful in the highest degree. It is that trust which such men inspire which makes them so serviceable; — trust not only in their labour ... nor yet simply in their honesty and patriotism. The confidence is given to their labour, honesty, and patriotism joined to such a personal stake in the country as gives them a weight and ballast which no politician in England can possess without it. (I, 302–3)

To have "a personal stake in the country" is the best guarantee a statesman can offer to skeptical colleagues. Indeed, the "trust" and "confidence" Palliser inspires — the "exquisite combination of conservatism and progress" (a phrase which nicely articulates Trollope's attraction to the Liberal party of the time) he represents — alone make it possible in *The Prime Minister* for England, during a difficult political period, to have a respected government of three years' standing.

The attitude expressed here toward political oratory is also typical of Trollope — who, like his hero, hated the rhetorical flourish and all kinds of dissembling; feeling that words should mean what they express, he too strove to use them so as to communicate rather than obfuscate. The novelist detested the rhetorical style of Disraeli (pilloried in *Phineas Redux*), and Palliser's plainness (he refuses "to give words a stronger significance than they should bear" — II, 242) is in part an answer to it. George Vavasor as a political orator craftily speaks for effect; like most of his colleagues in the House of Commons, he regards political talk as an end in itself. Most of the parliamentary speeches Trollope gives us in these novels are of this latter variety; *Can You Forgive Her?* provides ample exposure to the negative example of political speech, as we shall see.

There is one other comment in *Can You Forgive Her?* on the virtues and duties of Palliser's class, and this concerns the birth of Palliser's heir — the Lord Silverbridge who is to become so important a figure in *The Duke's Children*. On the occasion of this birth of a future Duke of Omnium, Trollope waxes sentimental and prophetic, attributing to the child's existence an importance reminiscent, perhaps, of that attributed to the young Prince Hal in another political saga. Trollope says:

Wondrous little baby, — purpureo-genitus! What have the gods not done for thee. ... Better than royal rank will be thine, with influence more than royal, and power of action fettered by no royalty. Royal wealth which will be really thine own, to do with it as it beseemeth thee. Thou wilt be at the top of an aristocracy in a country where aristocrats need gird themselves with no buckram. All that the world will give will be thine; and yet ... thy chances of happiness are no better ... than

are those of thine infant neighbour just born, in that farmyard cradle.
(II, 506–7)

The political importance, the national seriousness, of such a birth is
expressed plainly here, and without irony. The child's family is the
political royalty of England – the only kind of royalty that matters.

V

Palliser and Vavasor are alike in one crucial way. Their activities as
politicians are tempered and even at times directed by their social or
private lives. We have seen how Vavasor's lack of means affected his
political life and how his political failure corrupted his private life. In *Can
You Forgive Her?* the connections between social and political action are
emphasized everywhere. Vavasor, for example, "did not become a Radical
till he had quarrelled with his grandfather" (I, 136). Palliser's domestic
troubles result in part from his political activities, and finally his political
career is affected – even brought to a halt – by domestic considerations.
This chicken-and-egg interconnectedness begins with the story of how
Lady Glencora does *not* run off with her former lover.

Early in the novel Palliser's inattentiveness as a husband is seen as a
direct consequence of his Herculean political labors; deep in Blue Books,
he does not see the gathering storm. "To lose his influence with his party
would be worse to him than to lose his wife, and public disgrace would hit
him harder than private dishonour . . . He could thus afford to put up with
the small everyday calamity of having a wife who loved another man
better than she loved him" (I, 307). Glencora wonders "whether he
understands what it is for people to love each other; – whether he has ever
thought about it . . . Would it not . . . be better to be beaten by . . .
[Burgo] than to have politics explained to her at one o'clock at night by
such a husband as Plantagenet Palliser?" (I, 352 and II, 25). This is his odd
way of making love to her: Trollope's political characters frequently get
tangled up in their failure to separate love and politics. Palliser remains
blind to his wife's restlessness, and to her temptation. Glencora tells Alice:
"though they all say that Plantagenet is one of the wisest men in London,
I sometimes think that he is one of the greatest fools . . . I don't
understand Parliament and the British Constitution, but I know more of
them than he does about a woman" (II, 102 and 104). Palliser's blind
side – the domestic side – is soon to play havoc with his political career as
his political career has been playing havoc with his domestic life. The two
lives are the same life.

Glencora's near-elopement with Burgo finally brings Palliser to domestic focus, and from that point onward the relationship between the
two sides of his life is altered – the domestic begins to govern the political
rather than vice versa. Coming at last to an understanding with his wife,
Palliser decides that he will take her abroad for a year even though

Parliament is in mid-session and he has high hopes of being asked to join the current Liberal ministry. It is precisely at this moment that the Duke of St Bungay arrives bearing an invitation to Palliser from the Prime Minister to become Chancellor of the Exchequer. The *rapprochement* and the offer come in consecutive chapters; Palliser is made to choose between a long-time political ambition and a recently understood private duty. The Cabinet post of course is declined now, Palliser admitting to the Duke that "This thing you have offered me . . . is the only thing I have ever coveted" (II, 240–1). The political choice is made because of domestic considerations – Palliser discovers at last that he loves his wife, that her happiness must be his most important consideration. He now feels "that he could not bear to part with her, even if there were no question of public scandal, or of disgrace. He had been torn inwardly by that assertion that she loved another man. She had got at his heart-strings at last" (II, 243). He has come full circle since believing that loss of party influence would be worse than private dishonor. Now "his wife's safety was his first duty." The Duke of St Bungay ponders what is not to be "because a woman has been foolish!" Glencora herself contemplates with awe the magnitude of her husband's sacrifice: "If you could know how he has longed for this office; – how he has worked for it day and night, wearing his eyes out. . . . He has been a slave to it for years, – all his life, I believe, – in order that he might sit in the Cabinet. . . . He has hoped and feared, and has been . . . sometimes half-mad with expectation" (II, 271).

Political and social action are never separable in these novels. Palliser is even said to be changed physically by his choice: "His descent from an expectant . . . Chancellor of the Exchequer, down to a simple, attentive husband, seemed to affect his gait, his voice, and all his demeanour" (II, 332). His habits and interests are altered: "At this special crisis of his life he hated his papers and figures and statistics, and could not apply himself to them. He, whose application had been so unremitting, could apply himself now to nothing" (II, 336). Palliser's premature political retirement causes him great anxiety: "how was he to live for twelve months out of the House of Commons? What was he to do with himself, with his intellect and his energy, during all these coming dreary days?" (II, 349). The fear of having nothing to do, we know, was also a recurring fear of the novelist's. Glencora's pregnancy offers another example of how the political life can be subordinated to the domestic in a man who has learned the importance of the latter. Suddenly finding himself the expectant father of an embryo duke, Palliser becomes "so confused . . . that he could no longer calculate the blunders of the present Chancellor of the Exchequer . . . The one thing in the world which he had lacked; the one joy he had wanted so much . . . was coming to him." And he muses: "What good was all the world to him if he had nothing of his own to come after him? . . . It would be better to him, this, than being Chancellor of the Exchequer. He would rather have [this] . . . than make half a dozen consecutive annual speeches in Parliament" (II, 414–17, *passim.*).

It has been noted[29] that while Palliser is exclusively a politician he is
without an heir, that it is only when he compromises between the public
and the private sectors by giving up politics for a while that the heir
appears. Just as women such as Alice and Glencora must learn to
compromise between the ideal and the real, so, apparently, men must learn
to compromise between the public and the private lives. The compromise
is not an easy one, however, and only the exceptionally trustworthy
succeed in making it. Political and social interests are not only inextricably
mixed; they also must be recognized as interdependent or one will destroy
the other. Palliser and his wife learn "that there could be no chance of
happiness between them, unless each could strive to lean towards the
other" (II, 373). The "trustworthy" men in *Can You Forgive Her?* do
compromise (Grey ultimately gives up his sequestered existence to enter
politics, thus reversing and complementing Palliser's action), while those
who are unwilling to compromise between the public and the private life,
such as George Vavasor (public) and Burgo Fitzgerald (private), are
"untrustworthy" and ultimately fail altogether. Even the relatively
independent Mrs Greenow acknowledges the virtue of compromising
between what she calls "bread and cheese" and "rocks and mountains" –
and prescribes a little of each for everyone.

The theme of political and social connection is emphasized in several
other ways in *Can You Forgive Her?*. Mrs Greenow is a brilliant social
politician, one who somehow always gets what she wants. In good political
fashion she turns "every seeming disadvantage to some special profit"; her
greatest diplomatic feat is the treaty she negotiates between Cheesacre
(not Cheeseacre, as George Levine spells it) and Charley Fairstairs late in
the novel. An accomplished tactician, Mrs Greenow undoubtedly is the
sort who could manage a controversial bill through the House of
Commons. Another resourceful social politician is Lady Monk – more
unscrupulous than Mrs Greenow, and also less successful. She certainly
fails in her various schemes to get her nephew Burgo to run off with
Glencora. She is, however, the political hostess incarnate – not that her
parties are exclusively political in nature, but rather her social pre-
eminence is maintained by tactics which can only be called political. The
"giving of parties was her business, and she had learned it thoroughly."
People think it a good thing to be seen at Lady Monk's parties; invitations
are carefully given and subject to much advance strategy. The Duchess of
St Bungay, a dull, stupid woman, is asked to one of the parties "in the
same way as the Lord Mayor invites a Cabinet Minister . . . even though
the one man might believe the other to be a thief." There are many
aspiring social and political figures who make "strong interest to obtain
admittance within her ladyship's house, – who struggled and fought . . . to
get invitations. Against these people Lady Monk carried on an internecine
war" (II, 95–7, *passim.*).

VI

Another characteristic Trollopian theme is the ease with which political alliances are made and unmade, their essential insincerity and meaninglessness. Palliser makes an ally of Sir Cosmo Monk by going to Monkshade for three days and sitting with him "at dinner . . . at the same table, [drinking] a glass of wine or two out of the same decanters, and [dropping] a chance word now and again about the next session of Paliament" (I, 429). Social connection is the glue of political connection. In the same way, Palliser's political alliance with Mr Bott begins to become unglued when the latter makes the mistake of whispering suspicions to his mentor about Glencora's conduct, and it completely collapses when Palliser learns that Bott behaved unpleasantly to Alice at Matching: "Mr. Palliser . . . felt himself constrained to abandon his political ally" (II, 370), even though there is no political disagreement between them.

There is another such lesson in the story of Lord Brock's relations with Mr Finespun, Palliser's predecessor as Chancellor of the Exchequer. It seems certain (as we shall see later on) that Brock is Palmerston. Finespun is an early version of Gladstone. An excellent administrator, a man who really understands the economy of his country, Finespun is described in these words by the Duke of St Bungay:

> 'I admire his character and his genius, but I think him the most dangerous man in England as a statesman. He has high principles, – the very highest; but they are so high as to be out of sight to ordinary eyes. They are too exalted to be of any use for everyday purposes. He is honest as the sun, I'm sure; but it's just like the sun's honesty, – of a kind which we men below can't quite understand or appreciate. He has no instinct in politics, but reaches his conclusions by philosophical deduction. Now, in politics, I would a deal sooner trust to instinct than to calculation. I think he may probably know how England ought to be governed three centuries hence better than any man living, but of the proper way to govern it now, I think he knows less. Brock half likes him and half fears him.' (II, 236–7).

The resemblances to Gladstone are unmistakable (as are the early indications of Trollope's eventual disillusionment in him). Gladstone served as Chancellor of the Exchequer throughout most of Palmerston's second ministry (1859–65) – as Trollope was writing *Can You Forgive Her?* – and ultimately had to resign the Chancellorship because his Cabinet colleagues could not approve many of the sweeping economic measures he wanted to enact, especially the further lowering of import tariffs after the Cobden Treaty of 1860. Indeed, Gladstone's drastic reduction of duties on French and other wines in the early sixties while Chancellor earned them the nickname of "Gladstone wines" – a fact to which Trollope himself had referred in *North America*. Greville, an astute

observer of the scene, felt that Palmerston finally came to detest
Gladstone so intensely as to desire secretly the defeat of measures in the
House introduced by his own Chancellor;[30] and this also describes the
relationship between Brock and Finespun in *Can You Forgive Her?*. Brock
ultimately uses the pretext of a disagreement with Finespun over "French
wines" to throw him out of the Cabinet (II, 440). It is true that there are
also elements of Palmerston (and of Lord John Russell as well) in Palliser
himself, and of Gladstone in another Trollopian Prime Minister, Mr.
Gresham (these questions are examined in some detail in Chapters 4 and
8). But what is articulated in the relationship between Brock and
Finespun, itself only incidental in the novel, is not so much the story of
Palmerston's stormy relations with Gladstone as the precarious nature of
expedient political alliances in general, whose fate depends less on
philosophical considerations than on personal ones. Brock decides to get
rid of Finespun because he doesn't like him any more. He offers the post
to Palliser – with the results we have seen. Brock must not let the
shakiness of his political coalition become visible, so immediately after
offering Finespun's job to another man he gets up in the House of
Commons and makes a strong speech in praise and defense of his revered
colleague Finespun. Little do his hearers suspect that this political
association stays intact only because of Glencora's conduct. As it turns
out, shortly thereafter Palliser becomes available – and Brock immediately
jettisons Finespun.

Brock's speech in defense of Finespun – not a word of which is
sincere – reintroduces us to another theme. We have encountered the
Trollope-Palliser theory of parliamentary language: words should mean
what they express. But partisan rhetoric almost by definition must be
insincere and self-aggrandizing; George Vavasor's Chelsea speeches represent what the candidate on the stump often sinks to. He and Brock are not
the only politicians in *Can You Forgive Her?* to speak empty phrases; and
indeed the novel, after offering us a positive example of parliamentary
language-theory and practice in Palliser, includes as part of its commentary
on opportunism and expediency in politics an extended scrutiny of the
negative example. What is chiefly required of a successful parliamentary
orator is good lungs and the capacities to avoid "eloquence" wherever
possible, absorb abuse with equanimity, and feign anger and disgust when
such emotions are called for. The "irate gentleman" we encountered
earlier has the attention of his colleagues as long as he speaks abusively of
others; let him attempt to go beyond partisanship and wax eloquent,
however, and he is lost. Consider the case of Mr Fitzhoward, who rises to
second a totally inaudible and fumbling speech by Lord Cinquebars (a
name borrowed from Thackeray):

Every word fell from Mr. Fitzhoward with the elaborate accuracy of a
separate pistol-shot; and as he became pleased with himself in his

progress, and warm with his work, he accented his words sharply, made rhetorical pauses, even moved his hands about in action, and quite disgusted his own party, who had been very well satisfied with Lord Cinquebars. There are many rocks which a young speaker in Parliament should avoid, but no rock which requires such careful avoiding as the rock of eloquence. Whatever may be his faults, let him at least avoid eloquence. (II, 13—14).

The parliamentary speaker ought to eschew patent inaccuracy or inordinate length or genuine ill-temper; "but none of these faults are [sic] so damnable as eloquence" (II, 14), Trollope concludes. This lesson is well-known to most of the accomplished politicians in his novels. Gotobed in *The American Senator* observes an opening of Parliament and comments on the speeches he hears there: "There was no touch of eloquence, — no attempt at it ... [the speakers were] afraid to attempt the idiosyncrasy of passionate expression" (p. 268). Great eloquence betrays an independent spirit — anathema to a political party.

Who, then, is listened to with satisfaction in Parliament? Palliser, as we have seen, does not play games of partisanship; he never jokes, he never attacks. He does get up his facts and presents them with clarity. This undeniably achieves the respect of his colleagues, but it does not achieve their attention. Whenever he speaks — and this is true of his parliamentary addresses throughout the Palliser novels — everyone either leaves or falls asleep. On the other hand Mr Farringcourt — "a man to whom no one would lend a shilling, whom the privilege of that House kept out of gaol, whose word no man believed" (II, 61) — is listened to because he plays the game so skilfully. Even George Vavasor, during his brief parliamentary tenure, is quickly disillusioned:

This art of speaking in Parliament, which had appeared to him to be so grand, seemed already to be a humdrum, lonely, dull affair. No one seemed to listen to what was said. To such as himself, — Members without an acquired name, — men did not seem to listen at all. Mr. Palliser had once, in his hearing, spoken for two hours together, and all the House had treated his speech with respect, — had declared that it was useful, solid, conscientious, and what not; but more than half the House had been asleep more than half the time that he was on his legs. (II, 152—53)

The theme is underlined, finally, by the tragedy of poor Lord Middlesex, a sincere and patriotic man who has studied carefully the problem of church reform. As he begins to speak — the culmination of much laborious dedication — "the Members were swarming away through the doors like a flock of sheep" (II, 59). Lord Middlesex can have but little consolation.

He knew that the papers would not report one sentence in twenty of
those he uttered. He knew that no one would listen to him willingly. He
knew that he had worked for weeks and months to get up his facts, and
he was beginning to know that he had worked in vain ... He had given
heart and soul to this affair. His cry was not as Vavasor's cry. ... He
believed in his own subject with a great faith, thinking that he could
make men happier and better, and bring them nearer to their God ...
He had been all his life at this work ... He was an earnest man,
meaning to do well, seeking no other reward for his work than the
appreciation of those whom he desired to serve. But this was never to
be his. For him there was in store nothing but disappointment ...
Finding that [the House] contained but twenty-three Members, [the
Speaker] put an end to his own labours and to those of poor Lord
Middlesex. With what feelings that noble lord must have taken himself
home ... can we not all imagine? (II, 60—1)

Lord Middlesex is one of Trollope's idealized politicians — a man who is
genuinely interested in "improving the condition of his fellows," but
whose honesty and sincertiy are impotent to move men; his subject bores,
and his colleagues dislike earnestness, which can be dangerous (the leaders
of Lord Middlesex's own party "escaped out of the House, as boys might
escape from school"). Middlesex's lordship is mentioned several times; like
Lord Earlybird in *The Prime Minister*, he belongs to that class of
hard-working, conscientious, disinterested, and independent noblemen so
distrusted by party professionals and so revered by Anthony Trollope.
Failing at last, Middlesex goes home envying Farringcourt, who had kept
the House and the gallery full as he spoke: "The reporters [worked] their
fingers wearily ... And as the Premier was attacked with some special
impetus of redoubled irony, men declared that he would be driven to enrol
the speaker among his colleagues, in spite of the dishonoured bills and evil
reports. A man who could shake the thunderbolts like that must be paid to
shake them on the right side" (II, 62). Trollope touches here upon another
favorite theme: the opportunism of those who attack governments in the
hope of being asked to join them and the cynicism of governments which
employ this method of silencing their critics. On each side we can see what
sort of man is preferred.

The twin themes of opportunism and expediency are carried on in a
number of other ways in *Can You Forgive Her?*. Vavasor clearly belongs to
the political school most detested by Trollope. So does Bott, the Radical
member for Manchester. His political creed is clearly stated: "We must give
and take, you know ... nothing can be done if we don't give and take ...
it's a fair system of give and take" (I, 331—2). Trollope later expands his
portrait: "Mr. Bott had been born small ... He was a tuft-hunter and a
toady ... He was both mean and vain, both a bully and a coward, and in
politics ... quite unscrupulous in spite of his grand dogmas; but he

believed he was progressing in public life by the proper and usual means"
(II, 55). Usual, certainly, if not always proper. Bott supports Palliser in
Parliament because "Mr. Palliser was a rising man. ... If he came into
power ... then they who had acknowledged the new light before its
brightness had been declared, might expect their reward" (II, 56). We have
seen how and why this political alliance ultimately ceases to exist. As it
turns out, Bott, like Vavasor, loses his seat in the general election. Both are
Radicals, both are opportunists, and both lose. He was never sympathetic
to the Radicals; but Trollope's hatred of the political hack — a *genre*
ubiquitous in his novels, and of which Bott is a prime example —
transcends mere party lines. The hack may belong to any party; but, never
independent, he will certainly belong to one of them. In unmistakable
language, Trollope sums up in *The New Zealander* his feelings about such
types. The vast majority of professional politicians, he says, are men
"whose whole political lives have been passed in doing the work of a
weathercock, turning ever which way the breezes of patronage may blow,
men who have always been up for sale, like some old screw well known at
Tattersals; men who in every phase of their political career have ridiculed
the very idea of purity, men by whom scuples have been regarded as follies
and public truth as at best a political dream."[31]

Politics possesses an infinite potential for moral corruption of the
individual. Even a man such as Palliser is forced at times to touch pitch, as
it were, in the course of his advancement. He dines with the amoral Sir
Cosmo Monk, as we have seen, because he needs supporters: "He was, in a
manner, canvassing for the support of the Liberal party, and it would not
have suited him to show any indifference to the invitation of so influential
a man. ... Sir Cosmo had a little party of his own in the House, consisting
of four or five country gentlemen, who troubled themselves little with
thinking. ... Sir Cosmo was a man with whom it was quite necessary that
such an aspirant as Mr. Palliser should stand well" (I, 425–6). The
equivocal, to say the least, nature of politics is emphasized also by various
choric voices. Commenting on the possibility of his entering public life,
Grey says that he would "as soon be called on to choose a Prime Minister
for the country, as ... a cook for a club." John Vavasor replies: "Of
course you would. ... There may be as many as a dozen cooks about
London to be looked up, but there are never more than two possible Prime
Ministers about. And as one of them must be going out when the other is
coming in ... there can be [no] difficulty. Moreover, nowadays, people
do their politics for themselves, but they expect to have their dinner
cooked for them" (II, 287). During one of those innumerable col-
loquies — half gossip, half politics — between Alice and Glencora, the
latter recounts a conversation between her husband and his uncle, the
present Duke of Omnium. Palliser, in charity, had suggested that his cousin
Jeffrey be given the Silverbridge seat. The Duke, however, vetoed this;
"Jeffrey had no fortune," and besides Palliser should "put in" a friend

who would be an effective parliamentary ally (II, 495). Glencora thinks it
will be the diffident Grey (it will be); and she takes the occasion to reveal
to Grey's fiancée an uncomplicated view of political life: "He'll be . . . a
lord of something, or an under-somebody of State; and then some day
he'll go mad, either because he does or because he doesn't get into the
Cabinet" (II, 495–6).

VII

Despite the comic spectacle that politics can often be, the novelist's
essential ambivalence is also clear in *Can You Forgive Her?*. A man who
could draw such a character as Plantagenet Palliser obviously has feelings
about politics other than those demonstrated in the tale of George
Vavasor. *Can You Forgive Her?* also introduces us to a strain of Trollopian
political thought as characteristic in its way as any other.

We may recall that it is Palliser's great goal to be "useful"; his rank and
his money are only important to him so far as they may be made
nationally useful through public service, and it is this usefulness that
constitutes his identity in his own eyes. In one place the question of public
usefulness is explicitly debated between Palliser and Grey. Echoing
Trollope's earlier pronouncement that, in the social sphere, "if [a woman]
shall have recognized the necessity of truth and honesty for the purposes
of her life" she has done enough, Grey tells Palliser that "if a man can so
train himself that he may live honestly and die fearlessly," he has done
enough. Palliser disagrees, and Trollope takes his hero's side:

> 'He has done a great deal, certainly,' said Mr. Palliser. . . . He knew very
> well that he himself was working for others, and not for himself; and he
> was aware, though he had not analysed his own convictions on the
> matter, that good men struggle as they do in order that others, besides
> themselves, may live honestly, and, if possible, die fearlessly. [Grey]
> had thought more about all this than the rising star of the House of
> Commons; but the philosophy of the rising star was the better
> philosophy of the two. . . . 'I don't see why a man should not live
> honestly and be a Member of Parliament as well,' continued Mr.
> Palliser. (II, 425)

Grey himself is not considered a complete husband by Alice until he has
taken the political plunge. But this is no cause for regret; Grey is honest,
mature, and wealthy, the right sort to enter politics. As Alice (sounding
like Trollope) says, "Of all positions which a man may attain that . . . is
the grandest" (I, 419) – and again: "There's no position in the world so
glorious!" (II, 511 – the last page of the novel).

In fact the glories of parliamentary life are summed up explicitly in a
remarkable passage early in the second volume. Here Trollope, as he so

often does, drops the thread of his story momentarily and speaks directly to the reader. His subject is Parliament, and he begins at the entrance:

> Between those lamps is the entrance to the House of Commons, and none but Members may go that way! It is the only gate before which I have ever stood filled with envy, — sorrowing to think that my steps might never pass under it. There are many portals forbidden to me . . . but my lips have watered after no other fruit but that which grows so high. . . . Hast thou never confessed . . . that Fate has been unkind . . . in denying thee the one thing that thou hast wanted? I have done so . . . I have told myself . . . that to die and not to have won that right of way . . . not to have passed by the narrow entrance through those lamps . . . is to die and not to have done that which it most becomes an Englishman to have achieved.
>
> There are, doubtless, some who come out by that road, the loss of whose society is not to be regretted. England does not always choose her six hundred and fifty-four best men . . . Dishonesty, ignorance, and vulgarity do not close the gates of that heaven against aspirants; and it is a consolation to the ambition of the poor to know that the ambition of the rich can attain that glory by the strength of its riches alone. But though England does not send thither none but her best men, the best of her Commoners do find their way there. It is the highest and most legitimate pride of an Englishman to have the letters M.P. written after his name. No selection from the alphabet . . . confers so fair an honour . . . This country is governed from between the walls of that House . . . from thence flow the waters of the world's progress, — the fullest fountain of advancing civilisation. (II, 53—4)

That the Vavasors, the Botts, and the Farringcourts may share in it from time to time does not diminish the parliamentary glory. Trollope's enthusiasm was dimmed a few years later when he attempted to pluck that fruit his lips so watered after; his campaign for a seat was unsuccessful and he did not enjoy his confrontation in the flesh with the English democracy, as his *Autobiography, Ralph the Heir*, and *Phineas Redux* so memorably demonstrate. The later political novels, inevitably, take a less optimistic view of the political system. Nevertheless, the famous passage in the *Autobiography* on parliamentary service quoted in Chapter 1 ("to sit in the British Parliament should be the highest object of ambition to every educated Englishman") was written in the mid-1870s, some years after his run for Parliament (1868), and it demonstrates that Trollope never wholly lost his veneration of parliamentary life. In his essay on "The House of Commons" in *The New Zealander*, he declares that "England sends thither her wisest and best of her citizens"[32] — which shows that he believed this at least from the mid-fifties on. His reverence for a particular parliamentary type is given expression throughout the later Palliser novels in the character of Palliser himself, whose idealism and selflessness are tested in various ways during his career. He suffers political failures but few if any moral ones, reaffirming Trollope's faith that a good man is more trustworthy than any system, even if the system is stronger. He hoped that good men could make the system better, and he wanted others to believe that this was possible. "If I can teach politicians that they can do their business better by truth than by falsehood," he says in the *Auto-biography*, "I do a great service" (pp. 192–3). And yet we also know what was Trollope's opinion of those who professed to have "any political doctrine." Since politics, as it is so often practiced, is only an empty game, unfamiliar to those who are sincere and therefore difficult for them to master, the moral qualities of the would-be public servant must be as interesting to the observer as political success or failure. For England does not always choose her best men.

4 Parliament Lost: *Phineas Finn*

'But you have not imparted to me,' remarks Veneering, 'what you think of my entering the House of Commons?'

'I think,' rejoins Twemlow feelingly, 'that it is the best club in London.'

Dickens, Our Mutual Friend (1864–5)

Parliament was a club so eligible in its nature that all Englishmen wished to belong to it.

The Duke's Children

'They say the House is a comfortable club.'

Phineas Finn

While *Phineas Finn* may not be the best of the Palliser novels (indeed, I reserve that distinction for *The Duke's Children*), it is undoubtedly one of the three more purely *political* novels of the six — less melodramatic and contrived than *Phineas Redux*, more single-mindedly focused on politicians and political processes than *The Prime Minister*. It may well be the best political novel in English. "There is nothing much like *Phineas Finn* in English fiction," one critic has written; it is a political novel "of extraordinary range." Even Booth, no friend of the Pallisers, called *Phineas Finn* "the best of the Palliser novels [and] still good reading." Trollope himself, though stating clearly his preference for *Orley Farm* and *The Last Chronicle of Barset* (always two favorites of his and the public), remarks in the *Autobiography* that "*Phineas Finn* . . . was successful from first to last" (p. 275). He presumably means "successful" as a novel, and with some of the general public — for the fact is that contemporary reviewers, perhaps regretting that *The Last Chronicle of Barset* really was the last, found little to like in the book.[1] For Trollope, it was sufficient that "the men who would have lived with Phineas Finn read the book, and the women who would have lived with Lady Laura Standish read it also" — for, he says, "As this was what I had intended, I was contented" (*Autobiography*, p. 273). *Phineas Finn* was the first serial in Trollope's unsuccessful *St. Paul's Magazine*; the novelist collected £3,200 for it from the publishers (it is thus tied for second place in earnings behind *Can You*

Forgive Her? with *He Knew He Was Right*, written just after *Phineas Finn*), so he was more than satisfied. Indeed, since *Phineas Finn* was his first full-length novel to appear after the immensely popular *Last Chronicle* (two long stories, *Nina Balatka* and *Linda Tressel*, appeared between *The Last Chronicle* and *Phineas Finn*), it could hardly have been a financial failure. Such things were important to him. *Phineas Finn* ran in *St. Paul's* from October 1867 until May 1869 and was published in two volumes in March 1869.

The book was fairly widely noticed. The *Spectator's* unsigned review — probably written by R. H. Hutton — made a common complaint of contemporary critics when it argued that the novel was superficial, shallow. We never *see* any "deep moral struggle" going on in anyone, the reviewer complained, though we are told that it is there; and Phineas himself is the shallowest of the shallow. Lord Chiltern, Madame Max Goesler, and Robert Kennedy are skilful portraits — Kennedy in particular. Lady Laura is unconvincing, the rest are dull. The novel is not one of Trollope's best. Far below *The Last Chronicle*, it is inferior even to *Can You Forgive Her?*. Thus the *Spectator*. The unsigned notice in the *Saturday Review* was patronizing and disdainful. Trollope is a master of drawing clergymen, "and he is perhaps the most trustworthy male lecturer living on the mental anatomy of young ladies," but he is neither versatile nor brilliant enough to write meaningfully about political life. In this respect he is Disraeli's inferior as a novelist (how Trollope must have writhed over *that*!). Trollope's usual method of "light castigation" coupled with "implied reverence" is inappropriate to his subject here. Political stories should be less chivalrous, more biting. The novelist is too tolerant; his portraits are "inoffensive and colourless." Phineas is an entertaining hero of romance but utterly unbelievable as a politician (the reviewer astutely noted that *Phineas Finn* is one of only a few novels by Trollope *with* a real hero).[2]

The only unqualified praise for *Phineas Finn* among the journals was to be found in the pages of the *Dublin Review* (Trollope's novels were always relatively popular in Ireland; he was known there, having lived in Ireland from 1841 to 1859, and it was also felt that he was more understanding of and sympathetic to Irish conditions than most Englishmen of his time — as indeed he was). Trollope was lauded for *not* caricaturing the Irish and for portraying Irish "social relations" with a rare exactitude. (There is actually little of Ireland in *Phineas Finn*; Irish readers were starved for any serious treatment of Ireland by popular English writers. Trollope himself, though undoubtedly pleased by praise given his earliest writings on Ireland,[3] later regretted that he had brought Ireland or Irish characters into the political novels at all, as we shall see.) The reviewer concluded with a plea — in which Trollope must have delighted — that "some Irish constituency should do itself the honour of gratifying Mr. Trollope's unaccountable desire to enter Parliament"[4] (the review appeared just a year after the novelist's unsuccessful campaign at Beverley).

No one through the years has liked Phineas very much. Walpole called him "a hollow drum" — a phrase translated by Booth, who more or less agreed, to mean "full of sound and [signifying] nothing." Both said the political characters were not alive; Booth added: "the aggressive warfare of politics shows itself [here] only as a species of shadowboxing." Like a number of later critics, Booth found Lady Laura and Kennedy the novel's most interesting characters. Speare also pronounced the politicians "unconvincing *as* political characters: [they] are men whose minds he shrewdly infers from their manners, and not because he knows them intimately."[5] Escott did no special pleading for *Phineas Finn*, nor did Sadleir. Cockshut and R. W. Chapman argued questions of name, place, and identity and did little else in their brief discussions of the Palliser novels. Lately Trollope scholars — with the notable exception of Polhemus, who has been Trollope's most astute critic in recent years — have said little about *Phineas Finn*. The early objections to Phineas as a character have rarely if ever been refuted; he has suffered by being one of the few conventional Victorian heroes (by which I mean, briefly, consistently passive, one to whom things happen) in Trollope's fiction, so peopled with convincing protagonists. Phineas is conceived more in the tradition of Oliver Twist than in that of Josiah Crawley.

In the *Autobiography* Trollope tells us how he prepared himself to write *Phineas Finn*:

> as I could not take my seat on those benches where I might have been shone upon by the Speaker's eye, I had humbly to crave his permission for a seat in the gallery, so that I might thus become conversant with the ways and doings of the house in which some of my scenes were to be placed. The Speaker was very gracious, and gave me a running order for . . . a couple of months. It was enough, at any rate, to enable me to be very tired, — and, as I have been assured by members, to talk of the proceedings almost as well as though Fortune had enabled me to fall asleep within the House itself. (p. 272)

Trollope spent much time in the Strangers' Gallery of the House of Commons in 1866 in preparation for his task (and presumably his experience also helped whet his desire "to fall asleep within the House itself," for he attempted to join the club just two years later). Having, as he did, an extraordinary "sense of fact," "a real gusto for what was," Trollope's cautious studiousness paid off. Booth, Speare, and company notwithstanding, Trollope's political sketches, according to some of the shrewdest parliamentarians of the present day, are "right both in tone and detail" (so says Harold Macmillan, for one).[6] The novelist, however, did make some mistakes, mostly of a strategic nature. He goes on in this section of the *Autobiography* to lament the "blunder" of having used an

Irish hero: "There was nothing to be gained . . . and there was an added
difficulty in obtaining sympathy and affection for a politician belonging to
a nationality whose politics are not respected in England" (p. 272). It was
purely accidental – he had mapped out the scheme of the book during a
visit to Ireland. In spite of the book's Irishness, however, he felt it was a
success; yet it was not one of his great public favorites largely because,
says Trollope, people "not conversant with political matters could not care
much for a hero who spent so much of his time either in the House of
Commons or in a public office" (pp. 272–3). Thus there is a good deal of
what he calls "love and intrigue" dished up – though less than in any of
the other Palliser novels except *Phineas Redux*. Trollope concludes by
reporting that he himself liked the book except for the ending – "as to
which till I got to it I had made no provision." Suspecting as he did that
Phineas would return to politics in a future volume or two, the marriage
with Mary only created for Trollope the "unpleasant and awkward
necessity" of having to do away with her later. Eventually he returned to
Phineas because, as he says, he found himself "so frequently allured
back to my old friends. So much of my inner life was passed in their company." The old friends are identified as the Duke of Omnium, his
nephew Plantagenet Palliser, and Lady Glencora Palliser. He started
Phineas Finn with them in mind but got sidetracked, Trollope admits.
He adds that Lady Laura is the best character in both *Phineas Finn* and its
sequel.

                                   II

Despite the claim of some reviewers that *Phineas Finn* contained little to
teach the reader about contemporary politics, Trollope was immediately
attacked by the *Daily Telegraph* (31 March 1869) for "ungentlemanly
conduct" in drawing portraits of living politicians such as Disraeli,
Gladstone, Derby, Russell, and Bright. It was widely assumed at least that
the demagogue Turnbull was an unflattering likeness of Bright. In
his reply to the newspaper Trollope declared that it is neither "gentle-
manlike" nor "right" to paint, malignantly, public men as they may
appear in private, and that he had not done this in *Phineas Finn*. On the
question of Turnbull and Bright he said this:

> In the character of Mr. Turnbull . . . I depicted Mr. Bright neither in his
> private or public character; and I cannot imagine how any likeness
> justifying such a charge against me can be found. The character that I
> have drawn has no resemblance to [him] . . . in person, in manners, in
> character, in mode of life, or even in the mode of expressing political
> opinion. It was my object to depict a turbulent demagogue; – but it
> was also my object so to draw the character that no likeness should be
> found in our own political circles for the character so drawn. I have
> been unlucky . . . but I protest that the ill-luck has not been the result

of fault on my part. I intended neither portrait nor caricature, and most assuredly I have produced neither.[7]

As we shall see, Trollope was being considerably less than candid. While it is not true that Trollope ever admitted that Turnbull was Bright, as Sadleir erroneously reported, the novelist in his letter to the *Telegraph* does not, significantly, deny the paper's other identifications, which were that de Terrier was Derby, Daubeny was Disraeli, Mildmay was Russell, and Gresham was Gladstone. Indeed, in a letter written to Mary Holmes some years later (15 June 1876) in answer to questions she raised about some of the characters in *The Prime Minister*, Trollope takes a stand significantly less militant: "though in former novels certain well-known political characters, such as Disraeli and Gladstone, have been taken as models for such fictitious personages as Daubeny and Gresham, it has only been as to their particular tenets. There is nothing of personal characteristic here. When that has been attempted by me, — as in the Palliser people . . . there has been no distinct idea in my own mind of any living person. They are pure creations; and (as I think) the best I have ever made."[8] In the same year he wrote in his *Autobiography*: "As to the incidents of [*Phineas Finn*], the circumstances by which these personages were to be affected, I knew nothing [in advance]. They were created for the most part as they were described. I never could arrange a set of events before me" (p. 274).

Some scholars, naively asserting that a man so ferociously truthful as Trollope must always be believed, have accepted his denials. Chief among these has been A. O. J. Cockshut, whose work on Trollope is still widely cited. Trollope was "a man who in his life was a byword for frankness," said Cockshut; he cannot bring himself to believe that in the letter to the *Telegraph* the novelist "was a liar." And he concluded, with marvelous bathos: "now, if Turnbull really was drawn from Bright, then Trollope cannot have thought very highly of the latter." Less important than Cockshut's — but nonetheless indicative — is the work of Beatrice Curtis Brown, who stated flatly that all of Trollope's statesmen were "unidentifiable" and that any supposed likenesses to real politicians were "far-fetched." Booth referred to "the absence of current political issues" in Trollope's political novels; and he cited Avery's comment about the novelist's "complete incapacity to be interested in, or understand, political issues." Even Sadleir insisted that on the subject of politics Trollope was utterly untheoretical.[9]

Undoubtedly many of Trollope's political characters are either made up or composites of several politicians known to him; others are simply illustrations of types. It is time to lay to rest once and for all, however, the silly notion that the Palliser novels deal with imaginary politicians and imaginary political events. Even without the substantial existing evidence connecting people and events in Trollope's political novels with contemporary politicians and events, one may question the assertion that Trollope must always be believed. Why so? His letter to the *Daily*

Telegraph is, pure and simple, full of lies, as we shall see; and his other denials over the years may be equally distrusted. Trollope's chief occupation was making things up; what he made up he published. A letter, a newspaper article, a paragraph in the *Autobiography* represented to him pieces of publishable work like any others, and he was little more specially zealous about "truth" in them than he would have been during his morning stint of fiction-writing. He tells us in the *Autobiography*, for instance, that he wrote nothing while living and working in London in the 1830s and that the first time he ever "put pen to paper" was in September 1843. He would then have been 28. These statements are false; he kept both a diary and a commonplace book during these early years. And then there is the evidence of his own Charley Tudor in *The Three Clerks* – an obvious self-portrait – who scribbles away for magazine editors in his spare time while a young clerk in London. Of *The Macdermots of Bally-cloran* (1847), his first novel, he says in the *Autobiography* (pp. 62–3) that he expected nothing but failure, never heard of anyone reading it or saw any critical notices of it, but nevertheless was neither disappointed nor hurt and never complained about it. But *The Macdermots* was praised by both the *Spectator* and the *Athenaeum*, and Trollope must have known this; and no writer can release his progeny into the world without some hopes for them: "Unless Trollope was different . . . from any writer who has ever lived, or . . . from any young man who has made any kind of effort whatever, almost none of [what he says about *The Macdermots*] can conceivably be true: and where it can be checked some of it appears to be untrue," C. P. Snow has written. Trollope is less than frank on other subjects. In the *Autobiography* (p. 306) he says of *The Way We Live Now*: "I by no means look upon the book as one of my failures; nor was it taken as a failure by the public or the press." The latter part of this statement is simply not true, as Trollope knew very well; the book was reviled by press (except *The Times*) and public alike. In 1875 no one had a good word to say for this great novel. And then there is the *Little Dorrit* affair. When *The Way We Live Now* was published in 1874–5, Trollope was accused of deriving Melmotte from Dickens's Merdle. Trollope told Escott – and Escott repeated this in his memoir as gospel truth – that he read *Little Dorrit* for the first time in 1878 while travelling to Germany. But in fact he had not only read it upon publication two decades earlier but had written an article on it. Such a deliberately misleading denial may seem surprising; but Trollope, remember, was also fond of saying that he had never met any clergymen before writing the Barset novels. He was always a very secretive man. There is no particular reason to believe everything he says about his novels.[10]

In *Phineas Finn*, at least, it is absolutely clear that Trollope is drawing upon contemporary politicians and political situations. Critics of the 1860s understood this. Indeed, the two major reviews of *Phineas Finn* commented specifically upon the obvious similarities of Turnbull to

Bright, for one. The *Spectator* said simply that Turnbull embodies the "worst parts" of Bright. The *Saturday Review* went much farther and claimed there was no doubt whatever as to who Turnbull was: Trollope "is cruelly careful the veriest child shall not fail to recognize his pet aversion under the *alias* he has given him." Even Bright's clothes are accurately described: "The future historian may refer to [*Phineas Finn*] to discover what was the material of which Mr. Bright's waistcoats were made."[11] But the reviewer objected that Trollope's portrait contained a "curiously inaccurate estimate ... of that gentleman's character" — "the contemplation of Mr. Bright ... [acting] upon Mr. Trollope as a red rag upon a bull." Several incidents in *Phineas Redux* help confirm the conclusion that Turnbull is Bright; we shall come to them in their place. *Phineas Finn*, indeed, provides sufficient evidence. Turnbull, like Bright, is a Radical; like Bright he is a manufacturer; like Bright he is rich, with a great many servants and thousands of acres of property; like Bright he is a fierce, loud, rough, overbearing man in public; and his cry, "free trade in everything except malt," sounds very much like Bright, a Quaker and a temperance reformer.[12] Beyond the careful description of Turnbull's invariable public dress (*Phineas Finn*, I, 196), Trollope's picture of the man himself, coupled with the other evidence, would have left the reader of the 1860s in no doubt as to who was meant: "He was one of the most popular [politicians] in the country. Poor men believed in him, thinking that he was their most honest public friend. . . . It could hardly be said that he was a great orator. He was gifted with a powerful voice, with strong ... convictions, with perfect self-reliance, with almost unlimited powers of endurance, with hot ambition, with no keen scruples, and with a moral skin of great thickness" (I, 197). In the growing debate over the ballot question in *Phineas Finn* Turnbull and Daubeny behave very much as Bright and Disraeli did in 1866 (as Trollope was writing the novel) during the agitation over household suffrage that was to lead directly to the Second Reform Bill. This occurred during Russell's second ministry (1865–6) and helped bring about its downfall. Bright favored household suffrage and led a great franchise agitation which aroused much feeling in 1866. Disraeli and the Conservatives cared little for Bright's bill, but when Russell's Liberal government opposed it as being too liberal they joined with Bright on the chance of throwing out the ministry. In June 1866 a combination of Conservatives and 40 Whigs voted together to defeat the Russell government's counter-proposals on extending the franchise, and the Prime Minister resigned. Derby took over for the third time, and the Tories were in. The agitation in the country, presided over by Bright, went on through the autumn of 1866 — "In vain the country houses were filled that Christmas with ladies and gentlemen abusing Bright"[13] — and in January 1867 Disraeli, always an opportunist on Reform and now convinced that Reform was coming one way or another, privately consulted Bright as to what measures of Reform could lay the question to rest. The reader of *Phineas Finn* (which began to appear serially in October 1867) will immediately see the similarity between this account and Trollope's description of the collusion between Turnbull and Daubeny — on such issues as the disfranchisement of rotten boroughs and extension of the suffrage — for personal political ends (i.e., to confound and defeat the Liberals), despite the fact that they themselves agree on little. Here is part of Trollope's account of this:

> With great dignity Mr. Daubeny had kept aloof from Mr. Turnbull and from Mr. Turnbull's tactics; but he was not the less alive to the fact that Mr. Turnbull, with his mob and his big petition, might be of considerable assistance to him in the present duel between himself and Mr. Mildmay. I think Mr. Daubeny was in the habit of looking at these contests as duels between himself and the leader on the other side of the House, — in which assistance from any quarter might be accepted if offered. (I, 283—4)

Bright constantly criticized Russell's measures on electoral reform as not going far enough and helped get up a "big petition" in support of his cause. Disraeli aided and abetted Bright in the House of Commons for his own purposes. The machinations of Daubeny and Turnbull along these lines in *Phineas Finn* weaken Mildmay as Disraeli's and Bright's weakened Russell (and Mildmay unmistakably resembles Russell, as we shall see). In *The English Constitution* — running, remember, in the *Fortnightly* throughout 1867 — Bagehot refers to "those unnatural alliances of Radicals and Conservatives by which each [seeks] power at the expense of principle." The novel's political events reflect a tangible historical reality, here and elsewhere.

Trollope was fond of satirizing the Radicals, and this was not his last word on Bright. In *The Fixed Period* there is a gunboat called *H.M.S. John Bright*, in which is mounted a huge gun, a "250-ton swiveller"[14] — a sort of ultimate weapon so powerful it can destroy a city with a single shot, and so devastating it need never — in theory — be used. However, the *John Bright* has to be called out at one point to help quell a Commonwealth rebellion at Gladstonopulis, Brittanula. The gun, Trollope comments, "has been prepared by the ingenuity of men, able to dominate matter though altogether powerless over mind" (II, 91).[15] Clearly this is a comment on Bright's rhetoric — capable by its volume of stunning the senses but otherwise ineffectual and unimportant. Nor is this all. An unpublished letter in the Parrish Collection at Princeton University dated 22 September 1882 (less than three months before Trollope's death), addressed "My dear Collins" (presumably William Lucas Collins), refers in its second paragraph to Gladstone and Bright thus: "I for one cannot forgive him the injustice which he has done in Ireland at the behest of Mr. Bright." This certainly supports the contention of the *Daily Telegraph* that *Phineas Finn* was written in part out of Trollope's hatred of Bright, a hatred which obviously never abated. True, in one of his campaign speeches at Beverley Trollope referred to Gladstone and Bright together as "great men . . . dear to your hearts . . . dear to mine," but the context shows plainly that the novelist was appealing along strictly partisan lines for his own candidacy; and the speech in question, one of Trollope's most Radical, was delivered before the Working Men's Liberal Association of Beverley, which was very likely indeed to have Radical sympathies.[16]

Daubeny — not Daubeney, as Ruth apRoberts spells it throughout — becomes a major character in *Phineas Redux*, where the identification with Disraeli is clear enough. In *Phineas Finn* it is also patent. We see Daubeny working with Turnbull to bring down Mildmay, as Disraeli worked with Bright to bring down Russell. "To crush the Whigs by combining with the Radicals was the first and last maxim of Mr. Disraeli's tactics," Lord Robert Cecil, younger son of the second Marquis of Salisbury (a Tory colleague of Disraeli's), wrote in 1860; "he made any Government while he was in opposition next to an impossibility." His tactics — "so various, so flexible, so shameless" — were always effective: "so long as his party backed him, no Government was strong enough to hold out against his attacks."[17] Lord Blake says :

> Disraeli was perhaps the first statesman systematically to uphold the doctrine that it is the duty of the Opposition to oppose. Indeed, he might be said by this practice to have established the precedent on which all subsequent Opposition leaders have acted. Whatever proposal the Government put forward, whatever its merits, you could always find something wrong with it, some reason for attack. In the end, if you went on long enough, you would beat them in the House, or at the very least put yourself in position to beat them at the next general election . . . Disraeli's first instinct was to oppose, and, if he did not always do so, it was for reasons of expediency or because Derby overruled him. To Disraeli the object of politics was power and he never forgot it.

We should have no trouble recognizing Disraeli in the Daubeny of *Phineas Finn* — a man who will accept "assistance from any quarter" in order to bring down his Liberal enemies. It is well known that Disraeli and Bright were unconventional but nonetheless effective political allies in the Commons between 1848 and 1868;[18] and Daubeny's unholy alliance with Turnbull on the issue of Reform is Trollope's version of the real thing. Daubeny's attitude toward Reform, like Disraeli's, is essentially opportunistic; and, like Disraeli, he sees his duels with the Liberals as personal contests to be won at all costs. As in the case of the Second Reform Bill of 1866–7, in *Phineas Finn*, despite the fact that the initiatives for Reform do not come from the Tory side of the House, the Conservatives are the chief beneficiaries of such initiatives as emanate from the divided other side and take maximum partisan advantage of the situation. Having a bill of some sort forced upon them once the Liberals have managed to defeat themselves by intraparty squabbling, the Tory leaders of 1866–7 were determined to pass a bill – any bill – in order to stay in office. "The reform bills of ministers" in this period "were less triumphant vindications of principle than useful political manoeuvres," Briggs has written; and we see in *Phineas Finn* an accurate distillation of the historical reality. Derby and Disraeli, that is, behaved at this juncture pretty much as de Terrier and Daubeny behave in *Phineas Finn*, the political action of which is set at the time of the Second Reform Bill. Later, in *Phineas Redux* (I, 53), Gresham says that before becoming the Tory leader Daubeny was aided in his audacious policies and private ambitions by serving for years under "a leader who, though thoroughly trusted, was very idle." Contemporary readers must have seen the similarity here to the relation between Disraeli and Derby before the latter stepped down.

There is more evidence even than this. Daubeny's name is shortened by friends and enemies alike to "Dubby," which of course recalls Disraeli's nickname of "Dizzy." When in *Phineas Finn* Laurence Fitzgibbon tells Phineas that "Dubby would give his toes and fingers to remain in" – and we learn immediately that "Dubby was the ordinary name by which . . . Mr. Daubeny was known: Mr. Daubeny, who at that time was the leader of the Conservative party in the House of Commons" (I, 30–1) – every Victorian reader would have known who was being referred to. Daubeny is also described here as knowing "exactly the rules of [parliamentary] combat" and as "a gladiator thoroughly well-trained for the arena in which he had descended to the combat" (I, 72), which also accurately describes Disraeli as a party leader. Daubeny's hilarious and outrageous attempt at one point to speak before an important division for hours late at night in the hope that some of the ancient Liberals trundled in to vote against him will either go to bed or die is something worthy only of a Disraeli. We may also note that in *Phineas Finn* there is a party hack named Barrington Erle whose chief activity is partisanship, and that Ralph Earle was the name of the man who headed Disraeli's notorious spy system in the Foreign Office in the late 1850s.

Lord de Terrier certainly seems to be Derby. Lord de Terrier is the Conservative leader in *Phineas Finn*; by the time of *Phineas Redux* he has given way to Daubeny. Derby resigned in 1868 and died in 1869 – between the writing of the two novels. He was Prime Minister three times: February–December 1852, February 1858–June 1859, and June 1866–February 1868. *Phineas Finn* opens with de Terrier as Prime Minister, faced with Liberal majorities against him, dissolving the House and calling new elections. Certainly Derby's various short spurts of office-holding were largely due to continued Liberal majorities against him. Trollope tells us at the beginning of *Phineas Finn* that de Terrier "had now been in office for the almost unprecedentedly long period of fifteen months"; no other Conservative Prime Minister — indeed, no other Victorian politician — could have been twitted in this way. The tenure of Derby's last ministry, which went on for almost two years, would have been unknown to Trollope in 1866 when he wrote the opening chapter of *Phineas Finn* (of course he could have revised it for the 1869 edition, but Trollope is known to have revised rarely); as he was writing it, however, Derby was certainly Prime Minister. The fifteen months in office mentioned by Trollope corresponds exactly to the length of Derby's second ministry, during which Disraeli was Tory leader in the Commons, as Daubeny is during de Terrier's tenure as party chief. The relationship between Daubeny and de Terrier, as we have seen, is not unlike that of Disraeli and Derby in the early sixties. Finally, de Terrier — "thoroughly trusted" yet "very idle," aloof and detached — presents an accurate picture of Derby even during his years in office.

The list goes on. Mr Mildmay clearly is a version of Lord John Russell. He is, as we have seen, a victim of collusion between Daubeny and Turnbull on the ballot question as Russell was a victim of Disraeli and Bright in 1866, over a year before *Phineas Finn* began to appear. Like Russell, Mildmay is related to all the great Whig families of the time. Mildmay is Prime Minister between Lord Brock and Mr Gresham. There is some of Palmerston in Brock and of Gladstone in Gresham, as we shall also see; Russell's second ministry (1865–6) came after Palmerston's death and before Gladstone's first ministry in the progression of Liberal Cabinets in the sixties. Palmerston died in 1865. In *Can You Forgive Her?*, which appeared in 1864–5, Brock is still the Liberal leader. In *Phineas Finn* he has been replaced by Mildmay, as Palmerston was replaced by Russell in the mid-sixties before Gladstone took over. Mildmay himself is an old man who is rumored to be near retirement. Russell, whose first ministry was back in 1846–52, had been around for a long time by the mid-sixties and was also close to retirement. In *Phineas Finn* it is said that Mildmay's "love of reform is an inherited passion for an old-world liberalism" (I, 330), which sounds very much like Russell's brand of old-fashioned (conservative) liberalism. It is also worth noting that the reference in *Phineas Finn* to a quarrel and subsequent reconciliation between Brock and Mildmay recalls the bitter feud between Palmerston and Russell in the early fifties, healed after the Crimean War when Russell served in Palmerston's Cabinet. (There are also a number of resemblances between Palliser and Russell[19] and between Palliser and Palmerston, as we shall see in Chapter 8; Trollope often used bits and pieces of different men to make up his fictional politicians, as I have said.)

There are obvious elements of Palmerston in Brock. Brock has quarreled with Mildmay and made it up, as Palmerston did with Russell. Brock is the Liberal leader in the early sixties in *Can You Forgive Her?*; Palmerston's last ministry was from 1859 to 1865 and he was succeeded by Russell, as Mildmay replaces Brock as Liberal leader between *Can You*

Forgive Her? and *Phineas Finn.* (Trollope may have been working on his memoir of Palmerston while he was writing *Phineas Finn* in 1866; despite the belief of most critics that this is the case, evidence recently unearthed by the present writer suggests rather that *Lord Palmerston* does not date from this period.[20]) In any case, Trollope began *Phineas Finn* just 13 months after the death of Palmerston — one of his great political heroes. Brock's Cabinet includes Gresham and Mildmay; Gladstone and Russell served in Palmerston's. More to the point, Brock is said to have brought the Crimean War successfully to a close and then, as Prime Minister, has excellent luck in an Indian mutiny episode. These resemblances to Palmerston are unmistakable. In *Phineas Redux* (II, 339) Monk says of Brock that he had "a thick skin, an equable temper, and perfect self-confidence"; and in *The Prime Minister* (I, 102—3) Mrs Finn says of him: "He loved his country dearly, and wished her to be, as he believed her to be, first among nations. But he had no belief in perpetuating his greatness by any grand improvements. Let things take their way naturally, — with a slight direction hither or thither as things might require. That was his method of ruling." Both of these characterizations could easily fit Palmerston.[21] And it is also said of Brock in *The Prime Minister* (I, 265) that he used "drawing-room influences" to help himself in politics — something for which Palmerston was perhaps more notorious than any other British statesman of the nineteenth century.

Trollope, as we saw, did not deny that Daubeny was Disraeli or Gresham Gladstone. Gresham's hallmarks in the Palliser novels are intellect, eloquence — "the greatest orator in Europe" (*Phineas Finn*, I, 329) — arrogance, and temper, all of which point clearly to Gladstone[22] (his being pictured briefly in *Can You Forgive Her?* as Finespun does not negate this — we simply see him there in a different role, as Chancellor of the Exchequer; Gladstone served Palmerston and Russell in that capacity). Gresham is described in *Phineas Finn* as wishing to "fashion [the future] anew out of the vigour of his own brain" (I, 330); this too sounds very much like Gladstone. It is said in *Phineas Finn* that, in all probability, it is on Mr Gresham's "shoulders ... that the mantle of Mr. Mildmay would fall" (I, 329) — which in fact is what happens in the second half of *Phineas Finn*, just as Russell finally retired to make way for Gladstone. Gresham favors Disestablishment of the Irish Church, as Gladstone did (this becomes a major issue in *Phineas Redux*). Gladstone in the late sixties, and particularly in 1868, met fierce opposition in both parties to his policy on Irish Tenant-Right. Now Trollope tells us in the *Autobiography* (p. 275) that he finished writing *Phineas Finn* in May 1867. But it was probably finished earlier than that; and as the novel ran serially until March 1869 in a journal of which he himself was editor, Trollope would have had ample opportunity and time to make Tenant-Right the paramount issue for Phineas in the novel's concluding chapters. Gladstone persisted in his Irish

policy despite the great opposition within Liberal ranks, and this is what
Gresham does — causing Phineas to resign at the end of *Phineas Finn*. The
time element here, in other words, does not rule out the issue's relevance
for the novel, though at first glance it might appear to be so ruled out.
Sadleir suggested that in Gresham Trollope blended Peel's character and
Gladstone's views,[23] but there is more of Gladstone in Gresham than that.
Only the *Spectator* among contemporary voices remained skeptical about
the Gresham-Gladstone connection, basing its opinion on the tenuous
ground that Gresham pays too little attention to "the past" to be
Gladstone.

Escott and Speare both thought that Monk vaguely resembled Gladstone and the *Spectator* said he contained a few characteristics of Cobden.
While the latter surmise has some plausibility, it is more likely that Monk
is an original creation of Trollope's. Monk's brand of selfless patriotism,
however, takes a direction which may remind us of a famous politician of
an earlier era. One of Monk's greatest moments in *Phineas Finn* comes as
he lectures Phineas on the necessity of devoting oneself to causes, even if
they are lost or unpopular ones, if they seem truly worthwhile. If you
argue persuasively enough for a measure, says Monk, you will at least force
men to think of it; and "Many who before regarded [it] . . . as chimerical,
will now fancy that it is only dangerous, or perhaps not more than
difficult. And so in time it will come to be looked on as among the things
possible, then among the things probable; — and so at last it will be ranged
in the list of those few measures which the country requires. . . . That is
the way in which public opinion is made" (II, 421). Surely this is similar
to Burke's well-known feeling that a good speech in the Commons which
may not immediately change any votes is worth making in order to
provoke members to think of the subject, thus preparing the ground for a
more successful *sortie* on a future occasion.[24] There is no justification for
going any further than this.

Trollope's contemporaries supposed that Lord Chiltern was a portrait
of Lord Hartington, later the eighth Duke of Devonshire; and Escott,
Sadleir, and Pope-Hennessy have since agreed with this identification. The
fact is, however, that Chiltern and Hartington have almost nothing in
common, and in all likelihood the traditional idea is simply wrong.
Chiltern's name, not to mention his life and habits, would make his being
modelled on a political activist (the Duke served briefly as Prime Minister)
very unlikely, not to say ludicrous; Barry A. Bartrum's surmise that
Chiltern is probably a likeness of the Marquess of Waterford or one of his
horsey set is probably correct.[25]

Surely the icing on the political cake is provided by the names Trollope
chooses. Daubeny and Gresham are obvious both in their first letters and
in the number of their syllables. Lord de Terrier is not that far from Lord
Derby; and Derby and Disraeli is a combination close in sound, certainly,
to de Terrier and Daubeny. Brock is a sort of pun; it suggests a badger, a

tenacious animal with sharp teeth — which evokes Trollope's conception of
Palmerston (in *Lord Palmerston*, 1882, as we shall see). Indeed, in *The Three
Clerks* Trollope plays around with this pun a good deal. He uses the
word "brock" for badger in the sentence "Such a brock has not for years
been seen in the country-side" (he is talking about badger-baiting); and
later he uses the word "badger" to signify the head of a political party in
the phrase, "recommended . . . to the confidence of successive badgers."
And he takes the pun to its farthest extreme by naming the current Prime
Minister Badger: "Poor Badger, how much he has to bear!" (pp. 394, 414
and 430, *passim*.; Palmerston at the time — 1858 — was out, but he had
just been in and was about to come in again). To return to the others.
Mildmay sounds like a gentle old man, such as the diminutive Russell at
the end of his career. Turnbull suggests the unpredictability and bellicose
roughness of a Bright. Julius Monk and Edmund Burke are names of
equivalent length and sound, though that is more tenuous.[26]

Let us not forget Phineas Finn himself. Escott said he physically
resembled Colonel King-Harman, a friend of Trollope's whom the novelist
sometimes met at the Arts Club. Sadleir nominated Joe Parkinson, an
English journalist who married a millionaire's daughter and became a
wealthy director of companies. Later he changed his mind and put forward
John Pope-Hennessy (James's gradfather). Needless to say, the grandson
enthusiastically endorsed this idea; and recently a number of other critics
have agreed with the identification — which, despite the fact that it is as
erroneous as the others, has come to be the accepted one. There are some
superficial political and circumstantial resemblances. John Pope-Hennessy,
a young politician from Cork whose origin was the same sort of
unpromising middle-class background as Phineas Finn's, also made a
success of himself in London society — becoming a protégé of Disraeli
(Pope-Hennessy was a Tory; but this alone need not disqualify him, since
Trollope often made such changes to hinder identification) and ultimately
marrying a daughter of Sir Hugh Low. Lord Snow has suggested as a model
for Finn Sir William Gregory of Coole, a Harrow schoolfellow of
Trollope's and a lifelong friend. Like Finn, Gregory opposed his own
party's Irish policy (Gregory was a Tory) and supported Tenant-Right as
an M.P. He finished his career as governor of Ceylon. Since, however,
Gregory himself called Trollope's Irish member "a libel upon the Irish
gentleman," it is unlikely that he would have thought much of Snow's
suggestion.[27]

Bartrum's candidate is Chichester Parkinson-Fortescue, later Lord
Carlingford. Actually taken by some contemporaries as the model for
Finn, Fortescue was a young, handsome, Irish M.P. who served both as
Under Secretary of State for the Colonies and Chief Secretary for Ireland
(offices held by Finn in, respectively, *Phineas Finn* and *The Prime
Minister*) and worked diligently for Irish land reform (as Finn wishes to do
at the end of *Phineas Finn*). Fortescue did all of these things before

Trollope began to write his political novels, so the chronology is all right; and an equally convincing part of the argument is that he ultimately became the fourth husband of Frances, Dowager Countess Waldegrave, in all likelihood the original of Madame Max Goesler – whose second husband, of course, turns out (in *Phineas Redux*) to be Phineas Finn. Finn is probably Carlingford.[28]

Surely, however, there is also a good deal of Trollope himself in his hero. Phineas's political career is in part sheer Trollopian wish-fulfillment. The account of Phineas's financial embarrassments, especially the twenty-first chapter ("Do Be Punctual"), is a light-hearted personal reminiscence of Trollope's "out-at-elbows Post Office days"[29] (told in the third chapter of the *Autobiography*; Trollope's chief fictional version of himself as a young clerk is Charley Tudor in *The Three Clerks*, also constantly in debt and asked to "be punctual"). The seventieth chapter ("The Prime Minister's House"), an account of a huge party hosted by Mrs Gresham, while modelled on the sort of bash Lady Palmerston was famous for giving, is probably drawn first-hand from Trollope's own experiences at political parties thrown by Lady Stanley of Alderley, in whose house he was a frequent guest from 1863 on. Her husband was Postmaster-General during the years 1860–6, and it is known that he was fond of the novelist. His wife's house was a social center for Whig-Liberal politicians, especially after the death of Palmerston in 1865. Phineas's feeling of pride at being one of the few guests invited by Lady Glencora Palliser to dinner *before* one of her receptions (II, 23) may well reflect Trollope's similar sentiments on the occasion of such invitations from Lady Stanley.[30] There is more. Finn, like Trollope himself, comes over from Ireland to find success in England, moves into the fashionable world, becomes disillusioned, yet keeps some of the passive detachment of an outsider.[31] Also relevant is the fact that Trollope was always saying – in his novels, in his *Autobiography*, in his letters and lectures – that a man should never be rewarded too early in life, before he has had a chance to know what he wants, work for it, and properly appreciate getting it. It took Trollope a long time to get where he wanted to be, both as a writer and at the Post Office. He had no literary success until the late 1850s, by which time he was in his early forties; indeed, he had to wait for it longer than any other Victorian novelist (Dickens, for example, was famous at 24). The Post Office did not promote him to Surveyor until he was 39 (in 1854); and the fact that he wrote of his promotion, late as it was, proudly to his mother proves that, protestations of his to the contrary notwithstanding, Trollope had been worried and mortified at being so often and pointedly passed over. "No work can be done, no pleasure received, no content obtained without an effort," he wrote a year later in *The New Zealander*.[32] So it is not surprising to find that people in his novels who get good things handed to them too early, before they have had a chance to earn and deserve them, almost always suffer on account of it. (Trollope's early feelings of deprivation may help to explain his, as they help to explain Dickens's, acknowledged ability to describe so vividly some of life's most ordinary pleasures – that "complete appreciation of the usual" Henry James talks about in connection with Trollope.) Early in *Phineas Finn* Phineas paints for himself "a not untrue picture of the probable miseries of a man who begins life too high up on the ladder, – who succeeds in mounting before he has learned how to hold on when he is aloft. . . . If he did this thing [run for Parliament] . . . he might become utterly a castaway. . . . He had heard of penniless men who had got into Parliament and to whom had come such a fate" (I, 9). Mr Low preaches the waiting lesson to Phineas throughout the novel – warning him that anyone who is not financially independent when he enters Parliament cannot be his own man there and must come to either political or moral perdition. This is indeed one of the major lessons Phineas is to learn. Getting to Parliament too quickly and easily and tripped up by his own premature success, Phineas personifies a point of view Trollope came involuntarily to adopt as a result of his own unhappy and frustrated early years.

Beyond his possible autobiographical connections, Phineas's overall situation is believable enough – despite the skepticism of some of his critical enemies over the years. A product of a mixed marriage (Catholic father, Protestant mother), Phineas is brought up a Catholic and his sisters as Protestants, which was common practice in such circumstances in nineteenth-century Ireland. Before the Fenian outrages which commenced in 1867, Irish members of Parliament did still attach themselves to one of the major English parties, as Phineas does, instead of sitting in a bloc by themselves, as they were to do later. The positions he takes once there border closely on Trollope's own commitment to what might be called ecumenicism (*Autobiography*, p. 62). His support of Monk's Irish Tenant-Right measure in *Phineas Finn* – as well as his later approval of Disestablishment in *Phineas Redux* – is certainly credible given his biography. Trollope himself, both as a former resident of Ireland and as a student of contemporary politics, followed and understood the Irish questions which plagued English politics during his lifetime; as a result Phineas Finn, whatever his merits as the hero of a novel, is an authentic Irish politician of the 1860s. Regardless of his opinions on Irish Tenant-Right questions, Trollope sought always to give a true account of such matters in his novels.[33] In a lecture "On English Prose Fiction as a Rational Amusement," delivered in 1869 (as *Phineas Finn* was winding to a close in the pages of *St. Paul's*), Trollope declared:

A novelist is false who, in dealing with this or that phase of life, bolsters up a theory of his own with pictures that are in themselves untrue. There is at this moment a great question forward as to the tenure of land in Ireland. I may have my ideas upon it and may desire to promulgate them in a novel. But if for the sake of promoting my theory, I draw a picture of Irish landlords which is not a true picture, — which I have no ground for believing to be true, — in which I make them out to be cruel, idle, and God-abandoned reprobates, because I have a theory of my own to support in my novel, then my book is a false book, and I am a liar.[34]

"There is at this moment a great question forward as to the tenure of land in Ireland. I may have my ideas upon it, and may desire to promulgate them in a novel." Trollope refers here to the final chapters of *Phineas Finn* — in which the question actually is raised to be debated among party politicians and to cause a crisis of conscience in the hero.

In the 1860s Trollope helped found both *St. Paul's* and the *Fortnightly*, each a progressive voice devoted primarily to Liberal interests. Between 1865 and 1868, contemporaneously with the writing and appearance of *Phineas Finn*, he published in the *Pall Mall Gazette* — besides reviews of new books — articles on such politically sensitive topics as Lord Brougham, Lord Westbury, Lord John Russell, American conditions, Prévost-Paradol, the St Albans Raiders, church endowments, and clerks and usurers. In 1868 he ran for Parliament. It is not surprising, then, that *Phineas Finn* deals with the real political problems of a real political system instead of creating a romantic world of its own. The party structures and changes of leadership — which both *Phineas* novels describe in some detail — resemble those of the later 1860s, with the Conservative minority facing a disunited combination of Whigs, Liberals, and Radicals.[35] Written in 1866–7, when public opinion was causing the Second Reform Bill to be passed, it is not astonishing that *Phineas Finn* should be narrated against this background and that its hero should succeed initially as a Liberal who supports the party of Reform. The reviewers, whatever they might think of the *Phineas* novels as novels, certainly recognized their own world portrayed in them. The *Saturday Review* commented that *Phineas Finn* shows "what was the bearing of the . . . Liberal leaders of the time in society"; and the *Dublin Review* observed that despite its ostensible focus on the recent past, in telling the story of the disruption of a Liberal ministry over the Irish land question the novel was turning out to be prophetic.

Phineas Finn demonstrates another kind of knowledge hardly surprising to anyone acquainted with the novelist's biography: knowledge of the Civil Service. Like his political heroes Palmerston and Russell, Trollope felt that competitive examinations for the service were likely to reduce rather than enhance the prospects for "government on principles of the strictest purity" — a pathetic ideal of the moment. Perhaps arising in part out of a conviction that if "gentlemen" had been required to take examinations in his day he could never have been a public servant,[36] in his novel of the Civil Service, *The Three Clerks*, Trollope shows not the "best" but rather the most cunning and unscrupulous men winning jobs through examinations — and while he suggests that there are incompetents in the service, he has more sympathy for them than for the hard men who wish to hound them out of office to increase efficiency. And yet a great many nasty things are said in *Phineas Finn* about civil servants and the system of patronage which found jobs for them. Many of the negative comments are made by Phineas's voluble landlord Bunce, and some of the abuses are figured in characters like Laurence Fitzgibbon and in such issues as the great potted-peas controversy (of which more shortly). Before 1870, certainly, Whitehall had been the happy hunting-ground of political hacks — the Taper and Tadpole of Disraeli's fiction, the Roby and Ratler of Trollope's. Ministers of all parties regarded the patronage system as a legitimate means of keeping their political supporters in good humor. The Civil Service generally was filled with nominees of peers and those of commoners who were in Parliament or had other means of influence. Gorged with incompetent and impecunious younger (and often illegitimate) sons of influential men, Whitehall's reputation for laziness and incompetence was proverbial; and Bunce's picture of it as a place where people sit drinking tea with their feet up on the desk is not far removed from the historian's allusion to the "heavy swells with long whiskers [who] lounged in late and left early." The civil servant's usual office hours in these days were 10.00 a.m. to 4.30 p.m. Trollope himself used to come to work, when he came at all (he was allowed for years by his superiors at the Post Office to hunt two days a week), at around 11.30 a.m.; though he enjoyed his position he never liked administrative work — and did very little.[37] In *The Three Clerks* there is a great deal of lounging around, time-wasting, and absenteeism among civil servants.

Still, civil service "jobbing," as it was called, was regarded by most politicians as an indispensable tool of their trade; indeed, after Peel discontinued the distribution of honors and peerages on which Pitt had relied, the Civil Service was "the only field even of modified corruption left to Victorian statesmen."[38] Competitive examinations, recommended in 1853 by the Northcote-Trevelyan report on the Civil Service, did help to reduce jobbery after 1855, and in 1870 Gladstone managed to abolish patronage in almost all public offices and substitute competitive examinations in its place. In *Phineas Finn*, a novel of the sixties, jobbing is still very much part of the life of an aspiring politician, and indeed is the last resource of young M.P.s like Phineas, who, without an independent income, must depend on government patronage for survival. How this affects the political system itself is a major concern of *Phineas Finn*.

Let those who think the characters and events in the Palliser novels are wholly original creations look about themselves more carefully, then. *Phineas Finn*, for one, is a political novel whose people and issues reflect and revise various historical realities of the 1860s, and no amount of Trollopian denial and outrage, no amount of critical emphasis on the novelist's propensity to "daydream" and on his brilliantly "real" characters, can erase this fact. *Phineas Finn* could not have been written in any other time or place — period. Trollope, after all, was a man whose profession was fiction, itself a kind of lying. Why then should he not lie a little in a letter or two, or even in his *Autobiography* — when these, like his novels, were written for publication?

III

It should be apparent that *Phineas Finn* is about politics and politicians, whether real or imaginary; what has led some otherwise intelligent people to think that it is not "really" a political novel is a mystery. And moreover it is a pivotal novel in the Palliser series. It both develops themes more mutely present in *Can You Forgive Her?* and introduces us, in its examination of the beginnings of a political career, to a number of motifs that are to be threaded throughout its successors.

A number of angry choric voices in *Phineas Finn* declaim upon politics. Lord Chiltern calls it "the meanest trade going . . . and . . . the most dishonest . . . I don't believe that [most politicians] . . . work at all" (I, 93). Bunce, while not actually insisting that "no honest man can be a member of the Government," thinks of such men that "honesty's a deal easier away from 'em" (II, 61). Madame Max Goesler on contemporary politics: "the only thing disgraceful is to admit a failure" (II, 175). And Mr Monk: "I am inclined to think that Ministers of Government require almost as much education in their trade as shoemakers or tallowchandlers" (II, 310). All of these people are sympathetic characters; we may take some of what they say to heart while acknowledging the special prejudice of each.

What is it, in the main, that gives politics in this novel its special odor? *Phineas Finn*, far more than *Can You Forgive Her?*, portrays the world of partisan politics and examines the stranglehold of the political hack upon the parliamentary doings of the day. Narrow partisanship pervades almost every political issue and almost every parliamentary mind; this is seen by Trollope as especailly pernicious because it destroys not only the pretense of democratic and free government but the moral hygiene of public men.

In his initial interview with Barrington Erle, the Whig private secretary, Phineas is told that being a member of a party means voting with its leader; what is wanted is "a safe man" — a man, that is, without "views of his own." Admitting that he has views of his own, Phineas tells Erle that these, together with the feelings of his constituents, will guide his conduct in Parliament if he is elected. Erle, the novel's chief spokesman for the hard party line and the virtues of discipline and unity, reacts unequivocally to Phineas's moderate declaration of independence:

Such language was to him simply disgusting. It fell upon his ears as false

maudlin sentiment. . . . he hated the very name of independence in
Parliament, and when he was told of any man, that that man intended
to look to measures and not to men, he regarded that man as being
both unstable . . . and dishonest. . . . No good could possibly come
from such a one, and much evil . . . probably would come . . .
Parliamentary hermits were distasteful to him, and dwellers in political
caves . . . According to his theory of parliamentary government, the
House of Commons should be divided by a marked line, and every
member . . . required to stand on one side of it or on the other . . . He
thought that debates were good, because of the people outside, —
because they served to create that public opinion which was hereafter
to be used in creating some future House of Commons; but he did not
think it possible that any vote should be given on a great question,
either this way or that, as the result of a debate; and he was certainly
assured . . . that any such changing of votes would be dangerous,
revolutionary, and almost unparliamentary. A member's vote . . . was
due to the leader of that member's party. Such was Mr. Erle's idea of
the English system of Parliament. (I, 17–19, *passim.*)

Hating "independence" as something "unstable" and "dishonest," considering debates good only for public relations and shocked that any
member should be swayed by one ("almost unparliamentary"), Barrington
Erle, in the almost comic inversion of his values, represents the worst
aspects of the English party system as Trollope sees it. The worst aspects,
unfortunately, are those most visibly shared among his fellow professionals. Remembering "the careers of other men" who have come and
gone, Erle pronounces Phineas fit to run despite his expression of
independence: "By the end of the first session the thong will be cracked
over his head, as he patiently assists in pulling the coach up the hill,
without producing from him even a flick of his tail," he tells a colleague
(I, 19); the image of the M.P. as a carriage-horse in drag aptly articulates
the party ideal.

Phineas Finn poses the question, Can Phineas Beat the System and
become a Great Man despite his Humble Origins, while at the same time
remaining Free and Independent — or must he submit to "slavery and
degradation" in order to achieve political survival? If the latter, will he
submit or get out? The answer, of course, is that since he won't submit he
must get out, not being a rich man. Phineas may begin as a sort of cross
between Oliver Twist with the world all before him and Cinderella with
her three wishes, but ultimately the authorities will neither find him a rich
grandfather nor let him try on a fancy slipper, and so he must eventually
return to the humble hearth in his pumpkin. There is some suspense — for
a time. Can Phineas avoid falling "into the regular groove"? His friend Low
is skeptical: "You will be the creature of some minister. . . . You are to
make your way up the ladder by pretending to agree whenever agreement

is demanded from you, and by voting whether you agree or do not ... It is at best slavery and degradation" in order to get "some few precious hundreds a year, lasting just so long as [the] party may remain in power" and Phineas can retain his seat (I, 56).

One may well ask what such a system makes of its leaders and their followers. Erle puts it this way: "A political leader is so sure of support and so sure of attack, that it is hardly necessary for him to be even anxious to be right" (I, 64). He need not even be *anxious* to be right, much less *be* right! Politics is simply a contest between two teams in which might makes right; each man is expected to do his duty and not to go over to the other side, even if it means sacrificing convictions he is not supposed to have anyway. Violet Effingham thinks that all M.P.s are by definition types of sheep: " If one jumps at a gap, all go after him, – and then you are penned into lobbies, and then you are fed, and then you are fleeced" (I, 142). That her view is an incisive one is suggested by the remarks of Mr Ratler, another Liberal hack: "A man who can vote hard ... and who will speak a few words now and then as they're wanted, without any ambition that way, may always have his price" (I, 157). Adds Erle: "Heart should never have anything to do with politics" (I, 258). Phineas learns that Erle simply "was born on that side ... and has been receiving Whig wages all his life. That is the history of his politics" (I, 290). Lady Laura Kennedy, though more sensitive and probing, is no less partisan. Told that some Liberals might not support the party position during the Turnbull agitations, she snaps: "Every one of them ought to lose his seat." Though she is thoughtful on many subjects and considers herself "a strong Radical Reformer" on some of them, she too, having been "born on that side," detests the Liberal who will not support his team during interparty warfare.

A perfect examplar of the Erle-Ratler prescription for usefulness is Sir Marmaduke Morecombe, the Chancellor of the Duchy of Lancaster in Mildmay's Cabinet. He is there, and has been there during the last three Liberal Cabinets, because he has "the virtue of being true to Mr. Mildmay, and of being duly submissive." This, indeed, is his only virtue, for Sir Marmaduke "has nothing to do, – and were there anything, he would not do it. He rarely speaks in the House, and then does not speak well" (I, 328). Later, having spent a great deal of time being "a serviceable stick who can be made to go in and out [of Cabinets] as occasion may require," Sir Marmaduke (since "the stick will expect some reward when he is made to go out") is given a peerage. As Lord Mount Thistle he thinks of the next promotion open to him and dreams of "a viscount's coronet, when he was once more summoned to the august councils of Ministers" (I, 343–4). And so it goes. Such a man is a moral cipher; and yet, Trollope tells us, "A Prime Minister sometimes finds great relief in the possession of" such men. In the same spirit, Phineas's Irish colleague Laurence Fitzgibbon, though incompetent to do work of any kind, is made a colonial under-secretary by

Mildmay as a reward for voting properly. "It seems to be all a matter of favour and convenience . . . without any reference to the service" (II, 54), Phineas notes — and then sulks because no appointment has been given to him. He has voted consistently with his party; as yet no issue has come along to test his loyalty.

When Fitzgibbon loses his seat and Phineas takes his place at the Colonial Office he soon becomes aware that as his importance in the party expands so do the assumptions and expectations of others about his partisan zeal. Drawing a substantial salary now, Phineas's views on issues should presumably be not only more orthodox but more aggressively articulated. When a vote looms on the question of disfranchising some rotten boroughs — one of which, belonging to old Lord Brentford, Phineas is sitting for at the time — questions of loyalty and conscience suddenly cease to be academic.

> He could no longer be a free agent, or even a free thinker. He had . . . taught himself to understand that members . . . in the direct service of the Government were absolved from the necessity of free-thinking. Individual free-thinking was incompatible with the position of a member of the Government, and unless such abnegation were practised, no government would be possible . . . He knew that it would be his duty as a subaltern to vote as he was directed. It would trouble his conscience less to sit for Loughton and vote for an objectionable clause as a member of the Government, than it would have done to give such a vote as an independent member. (II, 57–58)

Government is not "possible" where "free-thinking" prevails; party discipline must have a demoralizing effect upon those of its victims who have any energy of mind. To vote to defeat disfranchisement is less embarrassing to Phineas as a member of the Government than as an independent member because everyone will assume as a matter of course that a man in the pay of the Liberals and who sits for one of the tainted boroughs would never vote to deprive himself of all he has. And yet were he tied to no party Phineas would have wished to vote the other way, the rotten-borough system being distasteful to him. Here is a crucial distinction. Men who can afford not to be in the employ of a party can retain their self-respect and honesty; others, forced to consider party before merit, cannot. Young men — any men — without independent incomes are foolish to make the attempt — exactly what Low has been telling him.

Seeking advice on the rotten-borough question, Phineas finds there is plenty available. Brentford, described at one point as a "thorough reformer," nevertheless understands well enough the "use of a little borough of his own" — especially as "there were so very few noblemen left who had such property belonging to them" (I, 363); it is "a convenience to a great peer." And so, vociferously supported by his "Reforming" daughter, he denounces to Phineas the attempt to disfranchise Loughton and the other boroughs. Regarding pocket boroughs as "abominations," Phineas desires "in his very heart of hearts – to extinguish all such Parliamentary influence, to root out for ever the last vestige of close borough nominations" (I, 355). Certainly he is more of a Radical than Lady Laura, despite all her posturing. Nevertheless he understand that he "would be bound to vote against the clause, knowing the clause to be right, because he was a servant of the Government" (II, 92). Even Monk advises Phineas to vote with his friends: "if you want to be useful, you must submit yourself in such matters to those with whom you act" (II, 97). That so honest a man as Monk gives such advice in friendship is an indication of the system's irredeemable nature. Phineas takes this advice – knowing now the humiliation of the politician with nothing but his convictions to fall back upon. As it turns out the clause is carried anyway. Trollope pauses here to tell us that right and wrong in such instances, far from being exclusively on one side or the other, are usually matters of expediency and thus relative: "Loughton and the [others] ... were anathematized, exorcised, and finally got rid of ... by the voices of the gentlemen who had been proclaiming the beauty of such pleasant vices all their lives, and who in their hearts hated all changes that tended towards popular representation" (II, 98). So the Tories, hating the measure, vote for it because they must try to beat the Liberals on any issue; while Phineas and doubtless others who approve the measure vote against it.[39] Here is an excellent illustration of how meaningless are studies of the voting patterns of politicians.

On the question of pocket boroughs Trollope himself was much more tolerant than his hero. He explicitly defends the system in a number of places – perhaps most elaborately in *The American Senator*. Here he tells the story of the pleasant political relationship between a great Whig marquis, Lord Rufford, and his borough, called Quinborough. The Marquis is "driven ... by his conscience to make some return to the country for the favour shown to his family" by always sending to Parliament from his pocket borough "some useful and distinguished man, who without such patronage might have been unable to serve his country." Rufford's more opportunistic political opponents, on the other hand, characteristically put up for election "a friend of the people, – so called, – an unlettered demagogue, such as is in England in truth distasteful to all classes." Fortunately the borough "in spite of household suffrage and the ballot had always returned the member favoured by the marquis," and thus – and perhaps only thus – it is always well-represented in Parliament (p. 264). Since men of rank and wealth are often most suited either to lead or to choose those who lead, the pocket-borough system has the advantage of producing election results more satisfactory than usual while also providing an efficient and untroublesome means of achieving them. In addition to its other virtues, the system spares the uninformed electors the necessity of having to decide whom to vote for. In *Can You Forgive Her?*, remember, Palliser as a member of a great Whig family has a pocket borough (Silverbridge) at his disposal after he vacates it himself and thinks nothing of simply giving it to Grey after Grey has been accepted in marriage by his wife's cousin. Indeed, he speaks on this occasion "with disdain in his voice as to the possibility of anybody [standing] with a chance of success against him" or his chosen successor "in his own family borough ... That that seat should be seriously disputed hardly suggested itself as possible to the mind of any Palliser" (II, 368–9). Later, in *The Duke's Children*, Palliser "gives" the borough to his son and heir. Trollope has no objections to make; the Whig families instrumental in carrying the great Reform Bill, he says, after all "have been right ... [to] have kept in their hands, as rewards for their own services to the country, no more than the country is manifestly willing to give them" (*Can You Forgive Her?*, II, 369). At the time of *Can You Forgive Her?* the pocket-borough system was still widespread. By the time of *The Prime Minister*, written a decade later, Palliser — as Premier — thinks somewhat differently; he scrupulously avoids any interference in the Silverbridge election, which on that occasion is won by a Tory.

Trollope never objected to peers controlling more than their share of votes in Parliament; better they, he felt, than manufacturers, entrepreneurs, and financial and social opportunists of all shades. And so, though he wants us to see the party system diluting Phineas's political integrity, he still spares a moment to defend the old system of influence. After all, he argues in *Phineas Finn* (I, 355), such favors bestowed by peers upon needy and deserving statesmen have had their national benefits; they have "prevailed from time out of mind ... between the most respectable of the great land magnates, and young rising liberal politicians. Burke, Fox, and Canning all had been placed in Parliament by similar influence." When Phineas decides to avoid being impractical and "overscrupulous" on this issue, Trollope never wholly condemns him: "You must take the world as you find it, with a struggle to be something more honest than those around you ... they who attempted more than this flew too high in the clouds to be of service to men and women upon earth" (I, 356). If you are too inflexible you can do no one any good; be flexible and you can work much of the time for things you believe in. Cockshut's assertion that "Trollope saw the rotten borough system as absurd"[40] is carelessly inaccurate, surely. The novelist's view of political processes, though stern, is often worldly to the point of complacency. Yet he never blinks away the moral damage that can be done to some men even by a system that works. It is all part of his political double vision.

As Phineas's parliamentary career lengthens he finds himself more and more "constrained to adopt the views of others, let them be what they might. Men spoke to him as though his parliamentary career were wholly at the disposal of the Government, — as though he were like a proxy in

[the] pocket" of Gresham (who has taken over the leadership from Mildmay); "when directed to get up and speak on a subject he was bound to do so" (II, 201). So Phineas begins to perceive the answer to the question Trollope wrote *Phineas Finn* largely to answer: "as he had made up his mind to be a servant of the public in Parliament, he must abandon all idea of independent action . . . unless he did so he would be neither successful as regarded himself, or useful to the public he served" (II, 221–2). You cannot be both independent and in office; but you can be "useful to the public" if you eschew independent thought. Phineas lays the issue directly at Monk's feet (II, 222): "Could a man be honest in Parliament, and yet abandon all idea of independence?" Monk is a beacon-light of honesty in the moral murkiness of this world; yet even he says: "You have taken up the trade now, and seem to be fit for success in it. You had better give up thinking about its special honesty." Do your job, be useful, and stop worrying about metaphysical questions of honesty and truth. Trollope adds: "Perhaps there is no question more difficult to a man's mind than that of the expediency or inexpediency of scruples in political life. Whether would a candidate for office be more liable to rejection from a leader because he was known to be scrupulous, or because he was known to be the reverse?" Scruples may be expedient for one's peace of mind, but they are inexpedient as far as political place is concerned – this is the answer. The political leaders of Trollope's world prefer unscrupulous men to scrupulous ones – the former will do as they are told in all emergencies, which is how parties survive. As Erle says: at least a Tory can be expected to be your enemy if you are a Liberal; you know where he stands. But an independent member of Parliament can drive you crazy with hesitations, discriminations, fastidiousness. Give me an enemy over a fair-weather friend any day, says Erle. Normal values and judgments are often reversed in this world; and many of its inhabitants ultimately cease being able to tell the difference between honesty and dishonesty anyway. Bunce tells Phineas: "a man gets so thick into the mud that he don't know whether he's dirty or clean. You'll have to wote as you're told, and of course you'll think it's right enough" (II, 61).

Though he had advised Phineas to postpone his parliamentary career, and though he is a loyal Tory, Low nevertheless sides with Lady Laura, Monk, Erle, and all of the others who urge Phineas not to break with his party, now that he is in office, over some fancied matter of conscience. "You have put yourself into a boat with these men," Low solemnly declares, "and you must remain in the boat." But Phineas is finding "sitting still in the boat . . . irksome" (II, 283). Integrity and loyalty are difficult partners in this situation. "The truth is," Phineas says later, "that a man in office must be a slave, and that slavery is distasteful" (II, 312). The first issue threatening to separate Phineas's conscience from his vote also threatens to separate him from his job. He begins to envy the truly independent members who can "say almost whatever they please"; he sees the vulnerability of his position in the government as that part of "the system which made it impossible . . . to entertain an opinion of his own." He resolves to resign his office and his seat "if he found that his independence as a man required him to do so." Meanwhile, he is told even by Lord Cantrip — one of the few consistently admirable politicians in the Palliser novels — that Monk is "a dangerous friend" for him. Why? Because the germ of independence may be contagious, and Phineas cannot afford to catch the disease. Honesty here is literally dangerous: this is the considered view of a sane and sensible man.

When the issue of Irish Tenant-Right arises — brought forward by Monk himself — Phineas sees that the Tories "will all vote for the bill en masse, — hating it in their hearts all the time." Daubeny is bidding for office — "and of course those who want office with him will vote as he votes." To be in office is better than anything — indeed, it is the *only* thing — in politics. The Liberals oppose Monk's measure not, characteristically, because they dislike it, but because the party management does not wish Tenant-Right to become an issue in the present session — it prefers to introduce its own measure later on. As over the issue of Disestablishment in *Phineas Redux*, the members of both parties line up here in accordance with partisan requirements absolutely at variance with convictions they hold (when they hold any). Phineas, unwilling now to support mere factionalism against what he thinks are the best interests of those he has been sent to Parliament to represent (he is again sitting for an Irish constituency now), signifies to his friends that, as an Irish member, he is called upon to have views of his own — which in this instance are not in accord with those of the Liberal party. In a chapter entitled "Job's Comforters" — suggesting that Phineas is being tested by hostile forces — he receives more advice on the matter. "I can only advise you . . . to forget [it]. . . . If you will do so, nobody else will remember it," says Lord Cantrip (II, 334). "All that Irish stump balderdash will never be thrown in your teeth by us, if you will just go on as though it had never been uttered," says Erle. Vote with us; no one will remember for long, or care. Vote against us and "you'll sacrifice yourself and do no good to the cause. I never knew a man break away in this fashion, and not feel afterward that he had done it all for nothing" (II, 338 and 336). The ensuing conversation between Phineas and Erle defines the issue clearly enough.

'But what is a man to do, Barrington? He can't smother his convictions.'

'Convictions! There is nothing on earth that I'm so much afraid of in a young member of Parliament as convictions. There are ever so many rocks against which men get broken. One man can't keep his temper. Another can't hold his tongue. A third can't say a word unless he has been priming himself half a session. A fourth is always thinking of himself, and wanting more than he can get. A fifth is idle, and won't be

there when he's wanted. A sixth is always in the way. A seventh lies so
that you never can trust him. I've had to do with them all, but a fellow
with convictions is the worst of all.'

'I don't see how a fellow is to help himself. . . . When a fellow begins
to meddle with politics they will come.'

'. . . It ought to be enough for any man . . . to know that he's a
Liberal.' (II, 336–7)

To a loyal party man "convictions" are more dangerous than (1) bad
temper, (2) loquaciousness, (3) timidity, (4) self-aggrandizement, (5)
idleness, (6) clumsiness, and (7) mendaciousness. "I've had to do with
them all, but a fellow with convictions is the worst of all." Most of
Trollope's professional politicians believe something like this.

The party line is laid down for Phineas by a number of his friends.
Perhaps the most straightforward is Lord Cantrip (II, 350): "A man in
office . . . [is] dispensed from the necessity of a conscience with reference
to" matters beyond his work. Independence, the succinct Mr Bonteen tells
Phineas, is "d––d useless." Even Gresham himself condescends to advise
Phineas: "a great party [must] act together, if it is to do any service in this
country" (II, 365 and 407). Just before the vote on Tenant-Right, Monk
uses the image employed earlier by Violet Effingham to characterize his
colleagues – they are "purblind sheep"; nevertheless, he says, they "enable
a leader to be a leader," and thus "in that way they are useful." Most of
them "have no idea of any kind on any bill." They "simply follow the
bell. . . . Argument never touches them. They do not even look to the
result of a division on their own interests, as the making of any calculation
would be laborious to them. Their party leader is to them a Pope whom
they would not dream of doubting" (II, 412).

In the end, once again, those who hate the idea of Tenant-Right vote
for it for political reasons, while the incumbent government and its
supporters, most of whom favor it, vote against it *en masse*. This time,
however, Phineas votes in accordance with his convictions and against his
party. Since this means he must resign his place at the Colonial Office, he
resolves also to resign his seat – he cannot afford to remain an M.P. any
longer without an income. His vote deprives him of nearly everything he
values in London – his job, his income, his seat, and some of his friends. It
may cost a man much to be honest in politics. For once, however, Phineas
will enjoy speaking in the House; what he says will not be canned. "He had
given up his place in order that he might be able to speak his mind, and
had become aware that many intended to listen to him as he spoke"
(II, 419). There is a causal connection here; he gives up his place *in order
that* he may speak his mind. Because he has done so an unusual number of
M.P.s – used to hearing only the party line – will listen to him with
interest. Much earlier (I, 158–9) Monk had told him – and the theme is
repeated again and again – that "the delight of political life is altogether in

opposition. Why, it is freedom against slavery, fire against clay, movement against stagnation!" There is a charm in opposition, Monk had said, "worth more than all the patronage and all the prestige of ministerial power." In opposition one needs "to care for no one . . . [except] those who sent [him] there!" Monk can afford to be independent. Phineas discovers that one cannot be independent politically unless he is also independent financially — and that a politician who is not rich must either succeed at the expense of his integrity or fail to succeed altogether. The novel poses a moral problem of high seriousness. When Low tells Phineas that his "temptation has come in the shape of this accursed seat in Parliament," we should not discount the pointedness of the language.

There is no problem discerning Trollope's attitude in *Phineas Finn* toward party politics — Phineas's fate defines it clearly enough. In a review written in 1865 — just before he began work on *Phineas Finn* — of Charles Buxton's *Ideas of the Day on Policy* (1865), Trollope comments that, for an independent M.P., sticking to one's beliefs, "though full of trouble for [oneself], is ultimately very beneficial to the country." And he adds: "The man must rid himself of his scruples and undertake the exigencies of public life . . . with a mind indifferent to its impurities and complexities; or else he must work forever in opposition, and must be fighting on small points against things which he knows to be good in the main." Politics breeds moral compromise. Some years later, in his *Life of Cicero* (written between 1877 and 1880), Trollope expresses his admiration for Cicero as a man who always acted — at times inconsistently — for what he thought was the public good. "When the politician takes the office offered to him — and the pay . . . he must vote with his party," Trollope says here; yet Cicero never became the partisan of any system or school: "He was too honest, too wise, too civilised, too modern for that."[41]

IV

Party politics is also connected to a number of residual themes. Elections, as in *Can You Forgive Her?* and succeeding volumes, are occasions for bribery and other kinds of dishonesty. Erle tells Phineas before his first canvass that Loughshane will not be an expensive contest since the electors "were so ignorant of the world's good things that they knew nothing about bribery." Lord Tulla, contesting Phineas's proposed candidacy at the next election, resolves "to fight the borough . . . to the last shilling." Fitzgibbon is convinced that the results of elections are "accidents which fell out sometimes one way and sometimes another, and were altogether independent of any merit or demerit on the part of the candidate himself" (I, 29). When Phineas switches over to Lord Brentford's borough of Loughton (he later goes back to Loughshane; Mr Kennedy's seat is Loughlinter, and surely Trollope is having some fun with these names, suggesting that one electoral district is pretty much like another), he finds that even though suffrage and the ballot are raging issues of the day, the electors there think it "rather a fine thing to be . . . held in the hand by an English nobleman" and regularly vote in accordance with the Earl's instructions. Indeed, Phineas discovers that even the middle-class voters of Loughton "liked being bound hand and foot, and being kept as tools in the political pocket of a rich man. [Each] . . . was proud of his own personal subjection" (I, 362). Phineas is elected there "without any trouble to him or . . . to any one else. He made one speech . . . and that was all he was called upon to do" (I, 379). Nevertheless, there is a hefty bill to pay for the privilege of becoming "Lord Brentford's member," the Loughton voters apparently being unwilling to abrogate *all* of the cherished rights of British electors. It seems to Phineas that no "political feeling" of any kind exists in the place.

Once in, the M.P. has several devices at his command to ensure his longevity. The major one is loyalty to his colleagues, as we have seen. And, as in *Can You Forgive Her?*, there is also the stratagem of doing as little as possible once "in." The only people who "do things," Fitzgibbon explains to Phineas, are those who are out and want to get in: "I never knew a government yet that wanted to do anything. Give a government a real strong majority . . . and as a matter of course it will do nothing." As Brentford tells Lady Glencora, "It has been the great fault of our politicians that they have all wanted to do something," and he says a word in defense of *fainéant* governments. Another member of Mildmay's Cabinet feels strongly that "No man ought ever to pledge himself to anything."

After all, then, perhaps no great talent is required to become a successful politician (as distinct from statesman; there are few of these around). To succeed one "must learn to have words at command when he is on his legs . . . in the same way as he would if he were talking to his own servants. He must keep his temper; and he must be very patient . . . Cabinet Ministers . . . are not more clever than other people," says Lady Laura (I, 64), despite her other failings an acute observer of English politics. Her description might apply equally well to a senior domestic servant or a master of hounds. Phineas himself comes to decide that nothing "very wonderful is required in the way of genius" of one who might wish to lead his party; he must only "be commonly honest, and more than commonly popular" (I, 88). The latter is more important; therefore he who wishes to be a popular leader must, like Turnbull, have "a moral skin of great thickness." As Kennedy observes, such a man must also use patronage skilfully and "answer every man's question so as to give no information to any one." The legislation he puts forward should be designed less to benefit the nation than to confound the opposition – to "defy hole-picking," as Trollope puts it (II, 165).

Phineas Finn also continues the investigation into political rhetoric begun in *Can You Forgive Her?*. One of the first things we learn about Phineas himself, for example, is that he prepared for his parliamentary

career by debating with others "night after night ... some ponderous
subject without any idea that one would ever persuade another, or that
their talking would ever conduce to any ... result. But each of these
combatants had felt ... that the present arena was only a trial-ground for
some possible greater amphitheatre" (I, 8). Again, it is talk as an end in
itself — rhetoric that is empty and debate that resembles a gladiatorial
game in which there is a winner and a loser. Early in the novel Daubeny
makes a speech of "studied bitterness" in which he attacks Mildmay and
his followers on grounds both personal and general, touching upon
"personalities," "accusations of political dishonesty and ... cowardice and
falsehood," attributing to his political enemies "mean motives" and
"unscrupulous conduct" (I, 72). Mildmay, however, pays little attention
to such accusations — indeed, he "was quite ready to take Mr. Daubeny by
the hand the next time they met." Just rhetoric, Daubeny's speech was
expected of him by friend and foe alike and taken seriously only by the
gallery, for whose benefit it was made. The defeat of Lord de Terrier's
government provides a similar lesson. The Tories, says Daubeny, will
never — copying "the factious opposition of their adversaries" —
recriminate; on the contrary, they will be quietly wise, even meek: which
"was generally felt by gentlemen on both sides ... to be 'leather and
prunella' ... very little attention was paid to it" (I, 99). As always an
enemy of words without meaning, Trollope expands upon this episode of
changing ministries :

> The Queen had sent for Mr. Mildmay in compliance with advice given
> her by Lord de Terrier. And yet Lord de Terrier and his first lieutenant
> [Daubeny] had used all the most practised efforts of their eloquence
> for the last three days in endeavouring to make their countrymen
> believe that no more unfitting Minister than Mr. Mildmay ever at-
> tempted to hold the reins of office! Nothing had been too bad for them
> to say of Mr. Mildmay, — and yet, in the very first moment in which
> they found themselves unable to carry on the Government themselves,
> they advised the Queen to send for that most incompetent and baneful
> statesman! (I, 99—100)

Despite the public hatred, in "private life Mr. Daubeny almost adulated his
elder rival, — and Mr. Mildmay never omitted an opportunity of taking Mr.
Daubeny by the hand ... I doubt whether Mr. Daubeny would have
injured a hair of Mr. Mildmay's venerable head, even for an assurance of
six continued months in office." As a member of the opposition Daubeny
immediately makes several "waspish attacks" which are "felt by both
parties to mean nothing" (I, 130), and then subsides. Trollope goes on
here to compare the British political system with that of America, where
political leaders, he says, "are in earnest" and "really mean what they
say"; "in the eyes of strangers our practice must be very singular. There is
nothing like it in any other country" (I, 100).

The Daubeny-Mildmay business is not exceptional. When Monk joins Mildmay's Cabinet he is attacked by Turnbull, his old Radical ally. Indeed, "one would have thought, from Mr. Turnbull's words, that they had been the bitterest of enemies. Mr. Monk was taunted with his office, taunted with his desertion . . . taunted with his ambition, – and taunted with his lack of ambition" (I, 223). "As to what Turnbull says about me in the House," Monk laughingly tells Phineas, "he and I understand each other perfectly." Despite the "violent words" spoken, Monk and Turnbull are "able to walk away from the House arm-in-arm, and not fly at each other's throat by the way" (I, 322). At one point Turnbull is given some comeuppance by Gresham, who calls him "a recreant to the people"; but no one pays any attention to the apparent seriousness of this charge either, least of all Turnbull himself. Words mean nothing inside this world; they are spoken for the press and the voters outside. This cavalier dishonesty Trollope always abhorred; it goes, to the root of what he most detested about politics – the habit of verbal dissembling, which he saw as an emblem of rottenness. He says of parliamentary rhetoric in *The New Zealander*: "Things must be spoken of to the public ear as being too base even for human infection, which are looked on among the speakers as peccadilloes not worth a reproach. Faults which when patent to the public are held too heinous for pardon are matters only for easy joke when discussed in private circles."[42] Such lying makes a mockery of statesmanship. An example is the debate in *Phineas Finn* on Reform. It is felt to be necessary only because "the press and the orators were too strong to be ignored." Convictions, as usual, go for little: "That Reform was in itself odious to many of those who spoke of it freely, who offered themselves willingly to be its promoters, was acknowledged" (I, 404–5). The members of Mildmay's Cabinet are lukewarm on the issue but wish to appear to be warmer. Their feelings on Reform are summed up by Trollope: "something must be conceded. Let us be generous in our concession . . . Let us at any rate seem to be generous. Let us give with an open hand, – but still with a hand which, though open, shall not bestow too much" (I, 405). Above all, let us not say what we are thinking. Bunce has no difficulty seeing how politicians use words to their own advantage: "They're for promising everything . . . but not one in twenty of 'em is as good as his word." Forensic skill, then, is not an exceptional talent for a politician; it is merely another clever trick in the arsenal of deceit. As Violet says: "I don't think that it is very much of an accomplishment for a gentleman to speak well. Mr. Turnbull, I suppose, speaks well; and they say that horrid man, Mr. Bonteen, can talk by the hour together" (I, 306). In a world in which words are weapons rather than tools, to be able to use them well can be a danger rather than a boon. In *Can You Forgive Her?* Palliser's preference for literalness was explained to us. Trollope's own ferociously literal style is sufficient testament to what he thought of verbal embroidery.

The sham nature of what goes on in Parliament is emphasized in other ways. Part of the rhetorical game played there is in acting the part as well as speaking it. Thus Mildmay is proficient at displaying timely emotion: "His voice faltered on two or three occasions, and faltered through real feeling; but this sort of feeling, though it be real, is at the command of orators on certain occasions, and does them yeoman's service" (I, 282). As in *Can You Forgive Her?*, it is suggested that words may also be used by some to club their way into the nation's inner councils. To such men "office is offered ... with one view only, — that of clipping their wings." It is blackmail on one side, bribery on the other. Madame Max understands how the system operates: "aspirants to office succeed chiefly by making themselves uncommonly unpleasant to those who are in power. If a man can hit hard enough he is sure to be taken into the [Government] ... not that he may hit others, but that he may cease to hit those who are there." You get on by abusing the other side. She adds, in poignant understatement: "I don't think men are chosen because they are useful" (II, 34).

In his essay in *The New Zealander* on the House of Commons, Trollope discusses the lying patterns of members. One passage in particular is interesting for its connections with *Phineas Finn*: "If Mr. Smith out of the House states that Black is White he will lose his credit for veracity, and men will gradually know him for a liar. But if he merely votes Black to be White within the House, no one on that account accuses him of untruth. Did he not do so, he would be as a public man impracticable, unmanageable, useless, and utterly unfit for any public service." In *Phineas Finn* the theme is manifest everywhere. Indeed, in several places Trollope's wording is similar. Bunce identifies lords of the Treasury simply as those who "wotes; that's what they do! They wotes hard; black or white, white or black." Phineas swears to Low that he will resign before becoming such a man: "A man who is ready to vote black white because somebody tells him, is dishonest" (this is after Phineas's vote on the rotten boroughs but before his vote on Tenant-Right). When Phineas acquaints Mary with the moral dilemma he faces and she laments the possibility of his being out of Parliament, he replies: "what is a man to do? Would you recommend me to say that black is white?" Madame Max, "coming ... to understand the mysteries of an English cabinet," advises Phineas to get out of politics: "what — you are to be in Parliament and say that this black thing is white, or that this white thing is black, because you like to take your salary! That cannot be honest!" (II, 334). Trollope concludes the *New Zealander* essay by declaring that "each honourable member who is induced by any circumstances to vote that Black is White does whatever in him lies to destroy the honour of England. ... And unfortunately every honourable member that does so vote has it in his power to do much."[43] No matter what the circumstances, lies are destructive. In *The Claverings* the novelist refers to "the permanent utility of all truth, and the permanent injury of all falsehood" (II, 257); honesty is the best policy — even in politics.

Politics in *Phineas Finn* is frequently compared to different kinds of games and politicians to players of games. Badger-baiting, which is to be an important metaphor in *The Prime Minister*, is mentioned twice in *Phineas Finn*. Aspasia Fitzgibbon refers to members who spend "Sunday in arranging how ... most effectively [to] badger each other on Monday"; while Phineas explains to Mary that his position at the Colonial Office "simply means that if any member wants to badger some one in the House about the Colonies, I am the man to be badgered." There are two references to soccer. In the first Madame Max tells Phineas that she knows "no one so young who has got the ball at his feet so well. I call it nothing to have the ball at your feet if you are born with it there"; while Erle, urging Phineas not to give up what he has so successfully gained, puts it this way: "You've hit the thing off, and have got the ball at your foot ... for God's sake, don't go and destroy it all by such mad perversity as this."[44] Politics is also likened to horse-racing — a theme taken up more elaborately in *The Duke's Children* — when Chiltern tells Phineas: "They talk of legs on the turf, and of course there are legs; but what are they to the legs in the House?" Other equestrian images connect politicians with horses in harness: "I've always had a sort of fear ... that you would go over the traces some day," says Ratler to Phineas at the end of the novel; while Bonteen adds that Irishmen "are the grandest horses in the world to look at out on a prairie, but ... don't like the slavery of harness." "And the sound of a whip over our shoulders sets us kicking," replies Phineas (II, 365). When Erle approved Phineas's candidacy, remember, he felt that despite the young man's professed independence soon "the thong will be cracked over his head, as he patiently assists in pulling the coach up the hill, without producing from him a flick of his tail." Duels between Daubeny and Mildmay on the floor of the House are described in another vein, as gladiatorial contests and prize-fights. "Mr. Daubeny ... showed himself to be a gladiator thoroughly well-trained for the arena in which he had descended to the combat. His arrows were poisoned, and his lance was barbed, and his shot was heated red, — because such things are allowed. He did not poison his enemies' wells or use Greek fire, because those things are not allowed. He knew exactly the rules of combat" (I, 72). After this elaborate image comes one in which Trollope refers to the "good-humoured, affectionate, prize-fighting ferocity in politics" and to the party leaders as "the two champions of the ring who knock each other about for the belt and for five hundred pounds a side once in every two years. How they fly at each other, striking as though each blow should carry death if it were but possible!" And yet, he adds, reverting to the old theme, "there is no one whom the Birmingham Bantam respects so highly as he does Bill Burns the Brighton Bully, or with whom he has so much delight in discussing the merits of a pot of half-and-half. And so it was with Mr. Daubeny and Mr. Mildmay" (I, 100). Phineas, remember, prepared for the House of Commons as if it were an "amphitheatre." Finally, there are several references to politics simply as a "game." Being in office and being in opposition are compared by Fitzgibbon, who tells Phineas that men of independent means usually "prefer the [latter] game, and if you don't care about money, upon my word it's the pleasanter game of the two." It seems to Phineas at one point that "He was playing a great game, but hitherto he had played it with so much success, — with such wonderful luck! that it seemed to him that all things were within his reach." A little later his mood is different: "All that he had done had been part of a game which he had been playing throughout, and now he had been beaten in his game."

Trollope's dour perspective sometimes leads him into some unsubtle satire of a different sort. His description of Mildmay's Cabinet (I, 327—30) is a case in point. There is our friend Sir Marmaduke Morecombe, with whose accomplishments and future prospects we are already familiar; there is the Lord Chancellor, Lord Weazeling, "who made a hundred thousand pounds as Attorney-General"; there is the Home Secretary, Sir Harry Coldfoot, so fond of inaction that he is "willing to give up to some political enemy the control of the police, and the onerous duty of judging in all criminal appeals"; there is Viscount Thrift, First Lord of the Admiralty, who has "the whole weight of a new iron-clad fleet upon his shoulders," and whose great aspirations are to translate Homer and wear the Garter; there is Lord Plinlimmon, the Comptroller of India, who is "very good at taking chairs at dinners, and making becoming speeches at the shortest notice"; and so on. It is the mock-heroic treatment, a strain of satire which becomes more emphatic in the later Palliser novels. In *Phineas Finn* it figures in the great potted-peas question.

As a most junior M.P., Phineas is placed on a committee to study the use of potted peas in the armed forces. The committee's investigation is described at some length.

> The potters ... wanted to sell their article to the Crown, [and] declared that an extensive, — perhaps ... an unlimited, — use of the article would save the whole army and navy from ... scurvy, dyspepsia, and rheumatism ... typhus and other fevers, and would be an invaluable aid in all other maladies. ... The peas in question were grown ... in Holstein ... and it ... seemed to many that the officials of the Horse Guards and the Admiralty had been actuated by some fiendish desire to deprive their men of salutary fresh vegetables, simply because they were of foreign growth. But the ... War Office and the Admiralty declared that the potted peas in question were hardly fit for swine ... [The] witnesses examined ... only proved the production of peas in Holstein, — a fact as to which Phineas had no doubt. The proof was naturally slow, as the evidence was given in German, and had to be translated. (I, 238—40, *passim.*)

This is humorous enough; and yet how easily time is wasted on silly issues by men who are supposed to be serving the public interest. Inevitably the potted-peas isue, like the controversy over the Limehouse-Rotherhithe bridge in *The Three Clerks* and that over the Eustace diamonds in the next Palliser novel, is taken up along party lines. Since Lord de Terrier's government is in at the time, Phineas as a Liberal feels called upon to be an aggressive member of the potted-peas committee, asking commissariat officers hard "questions respecting cabbages and potatoes, and ... whether the officers on board a certain ship did not always eat preserved asparagus while the men had not even a bean" — and so on. Eventually potted peas are debated in the full House. By this time Phineas has become an enthusiastic enemy of potted peas; and the Liberals, in opposition, latch onto the issue as an extra stick with which to beat the government. Trollope concludes: "To attack is so easy, when a complete refutation barely suffices to save the Minister attacked, — does not suffice to save him from future dim memories of something having been wrong, — and brings down no disgrace whatsoever on the promoter of the false charge ... [who is sufficiently gratified] ... that out of all the mud which he has thrown, some will probably stick!" (I, 350—1). The debate rages. Potted peas, in this particular amphitheatre, are as critical as war and peace, for there is partisan ground to be gained or lost. "Let any man conversant with the politics of the day see the names of a [parliamentary] committee, and be made acquainted with the subject of inquiry," says Trollope in *The New Zealander*, "and he will be able to place the ayes and no's on every subject on which the Committee may divide, without any reference whatsoever to the evidence." Debate will change no man's mind. Such work is "mummery."[4][5] When the potted-peas committee's work is over presumably another "huge blue volume" will be published, as at the end of the parliamentary investigation of the Limehouse-Rotherhithe bridge. In that business the committee's expenses were £60 per day, "but it never occurred to any one ... to get up and declare ... that such a waste of money and time on so palpably absurd a scheme was degrading" (*The Three Clerks*, p. 401). Indeed, since the committee's attention to the matter inflates the value of the bridge shares, which are owned mostly by M.P.s, the parliamentary interest is rather on the side of extending the inquiry. No one in *Phineas Finn* makes money on potted peas; but that so trivial an issue can polarize and convulse the nation's chief legislative body must make us wonder if anyone is legitimately and effectively dedicated to the public interest.

V

As in the other Palliser novels, Trollope emphasizes in *Phineas Finn* the connections between political activity and one's social and/or financial status. Indeed, as in *Can You Forgive Her?* there seems to be no real separation between political and social life, nor between success in either sphere and solvency. From the moment Phineas's father, at the insistence of the ladies of the family, agrees to increase his son's allowance so that he can run for Parliament, the relationships between social life and political life are intertwined and inseparable from the theme of money and financial security. The impecunious Phineas's first seat (Loughshane) comes to him as a result of a peer's quarrel with his brother, his second (Loughton) is the product of a rich woman's influence, and – after another stint on behalf of the constituents of Loughshane – his third seat (Tankerville, in *Phineas Redux*) is secured by the discovery of his opponent's bribery.[46]

In a novel in which politics, society, and money are all so closely connected it is not surprising to discover that women are of tremendous importance, that the hero himself is a better model for a Lothario than for a promising politician, and that his political success is largely due to his popularity with women. As Trollope was interested in the Barset novels in placing the clergy socially, so too in the Palliser novels there is emphasis on the social backgrounds of Parliament – and especially on the great influence of women over political ambition and success, their large share of the political game. Political success anywhere depends in part on charming the social elite of the Establishment – on, that is, approval social as well as political. If in these novels politics sometimes seems "frivolous and amateurish – women whispering to powerful politicians on behalf of handsome, pleasant young men, important political decisions being made at dinner parties, personal likes and dislikes shaping public policy" – this picture nevertheless is as true for the nineteenth century as for any other, including our own. An ambitious politician must always please a peer constituency of social fashion and power.[47] It is interesting to note that a generous amount of feminine whispering and intriguing on behalf of handsome young men at dinner parties and other places also occupies many pages of Disraeli's novels – indeed, he himself refers in one of them to "those social influences which in a public career are not less important than political ones."[48] This is one thing the two greatest political novelists of their time – who disagreed on so many things – did not dispute.

Consider Madame Max Goesler. A social politician, like many of the politicians in the novel she has a "game" to play, and she plays "with great skill and caution." A chapter in *Phineas Finn* is actually called "Madame Goesler's Politics" (LX), and in it the "politics" of everyday life in society is detailed – in a spirit, once again, which Disraeli may have found congenial.[49] As in politics, "success in this world is everything"; and because thinking leads to doubting, and doubt leads to error, "The safest way in the world is to do nothing." Madame Max's social career parallels Phineas's political career until his resignation. While she is currying favor with the old Duke of Omnium and attempting to store up a supply of social good will, Phineas is voting against his convictions, toadying to important people in his party, and bouncing amorously around from one

(Liberal) society woman to another.[50] About the time Madame Max decides to turn down the foolish old Duke — despite the commanding social position such a marriage would give her — Phineas decides to vote his convictions and to marry Mary Flood Jones, thus giving up a promising political position. The two themes intersect when Madame Max proposes to Phineas to help save his political career with her money — and because she loves him — and he turns her down. Both have become rebels — Phineas abandoning his party and his career, she giving up the preeminent social status of an English duchess. (Appropriately, then, they are mated in *Phineas Redux*.)

Lady Laura, who feels that "a woman's life is only half a life, as she cannot have a seat in Parliament" (I, 70), sublimates both her political yearnings and her passionate attachment to Phineas into political maneuverings in his behalf (indeed, he owes almost all of his early political successes to her backing), even to the point of driving her husband insane with jealousy. Feeling that "The curse is to be a woman at all" in a man's world, Laura "from her earliest years of girlish womanhood had resolved that she would use the world as men use it, and not as women do" (II, 143 and 13). Like Alice Vavasor's, however, Laura's resolution to be independent ends badly — in this case in frustrated love, an impossible marriage, widowhood and isolation. When we take leave of her in *Phineas Finn* she is alone in the world except for her father, and the brother whom she rarely sees; she has no children and no family life, and when her father dies (in *Phineas Redux*) she is utterly alone. Her political ambitions make her a rebel against her sex, and she pays the ultimate price. Like Alice, she is not allowed to defy the conventional nineteenth-century view of woman's proper place and role and get away with it; she ought to be a mother and have a family. Her social isolation is largely the result of her political ambitions; the two worlds are never far apart in her story, as in Madame Max's. Laura's final fate, decided (in *Phineas Redux*) nearly a decade later than Alice's, is more harsh; for here there is no second (or third, or fourth) chance. But the lessons are the same.

Trollope clearly means us to perceive the many resemblances between the political world of men and the feminine world of Society. To put it bluntly: Society is the politics of women; they pursue social prestige as intently as their husbands pursue political power. Thus it is no accident that the various maneuvers — defeats, victories, alliances, rivalries, and so on — of the ladies remind us of those of their parliamentary husbands. For Trollope, the search for social status and that for political power spring from similar motives and desires and thus are objectified in many of the same ways.[51] If Society is the politics of women, politics is the Society of men; the two worlds are complementary parts of one whole.

This theme is demonstrated in yet other ways in *Phineas Finn*. Understanding that a wealthy wife would enable him to become an independent member of Parliament and give him status in society, Phineas

manages to fall in love with several eligible women in succession — Lady
Laura, Violet Effingham, and Madame Max — while betrothed to Mary.
Each of these women has close connections to the Liberal party hierarchy.
Phineas understands readily enough that "Simply as an introduction into
official life nothing could be more conducive to chances of success than a
matrimonial alliance with Lady Laura" (I, 47), who knows the leading
Liberal politicians of the day and is related to several of them. Indeed, she
helps him a good deal simply by talking to her friends. Generated by the
support of his mother and sisters, Phineas's political career is extended
through the help of Laura and ultimately is cemented in the marriage with
Madame Max; at every stage it is a by-product of feminine influences.
Laura herself preaches to Phineas the lessons of advance-through-marriage.
She justifies her union with Kennedy on the ground that his wealth will
give her political influence in the drawing-room — the only kind of
political influence available to her, since she cannot stand for Parliament.
She marries a rich man, then, "in order that she might be able to do
something in the world" — but we know the fate Trollope accorded to
women who wish to "do something." Laura bluntly tells Phineas that he
must marry a woman with money if he is to succeed politically. Later she
protects him from the political consequences of his romantic blundering
(the duel with Chiltern). Political success so often depends on the goodwill
of influential people. The career of Kennedy, who is put into the Cabinet
only because of his great wealth and his wife's family, offers another
instructive lesson. His political failure demonstrates among other things
that while money and family may get you there they cannot keep you
there if you are socially inept, which Kennedy is; so much of politics is in
fact conducted in the drawing-room. And yet, conversely, a rich man with
little else to offer may obviously go far.

After Laura, Phineas's next amorous adventure is with Violet; and she
becomes so hopelessly intertwined with his political hopes that even he
cannot distinguish between them. When his run after Violet ends in failure,
however, he knows well enough what it is he has lost: "the weight of his
sorrow was occasioned by the fact that he had lost an heiress . . . everything
had seemed so suitable. Had Miss Effingham become his wife, the mouths
of the Lows and of the Bunces would have been stopped altogether. Mr.
Monk would have come to his house as a familiar guest, and he would have
been connected with half a score of peers. A seat in Parliament would be
simply his proper place, and even Under-Secretaryships of State might
soon come to be below him" (II, 161–2). An aspiring politician must
charm the constituency of fashion and power to which he belongs; to do
this he needs money. When Madame Max's little dinner party, which
includes Phineas and Lord Fawn — both of whom at the time are pursuing
Violet — turns out a dismal failure, she puts it down to having at the same
table two men who are in office together; but the astute Mrs Bonteen
comments that her mistake was to invite "two claimants for the same

young lady," each of whom is poor and politically ambitious. Madame Max's misreading is a logical one, since Phineas and Fawn spend the evening contradicting each other on various political subjects. Again, the private life and the public life are the same life.

Men such as Monk and Turnbull can be politically independent because they can afford to refuse office. Low lectures Phineas on this theme when the Irish land question begins to loom on the parliamentary horizon: "When a man has means of his own he can please himself. Do you marry a wife with money, and then you may kick up your heels, and do as you like about the Colonial Office. When a man hasn't money, of course he must fit himself to the circumstances of a profession" (II, 284). Monk says exactly the same thing: a poor man who chooses to "make Parliament a profession . . . can have no right even to think of independence" (II, 202). The system has "made it impossible for [Phineas] . . . to entertain an opinion of his own" (II, 327). Thus he is tempted by Madame Max's proposal, tempted to betray Mary (II, 341–2): "Half a dozen people who knew him or her might think ill of him . . . but the world would not condemn him! And when he thundered forth his liberal eloquence . . . as an independent member, having the fortune of his charming wife to back him, giving excellent dinners . . . would not the world praise him very loudly?" The "world" here is of course the fashionable world of political society – which could hardly condemn a man for employing unsavory strategy to gain a political and social objective. Despite her passionate attachment to him, Laura urges Phineas to save his political career by accepting Madame Max's offer – her love for him having always depended upon his political aspirations. "Make her your wife, and you may resign or remain in office just as you choose. Office will be much easier to you than it is now, because it will not be a necessity," says Laura. Phineas dreams what he might "not do with an independent seat in the House of Commons, and as a joint owner of the little house in Park Lane . . . How would the Ratlers and the Bonteens envy him. . . . The Cantrips and the Greshams would feel that he was a friend doubly valuable . . . and Mr. Monk would greet him as a fitting ally, – an ally strong with the strength which he had before wanted. With whom would he not be equal? Whom need he fear? Who would not praise him?" (II, 359–61, *passim.*). Who indeed, since men at the top are never asked how they got there. But he cannot do it.

At the end of the novel Phineas sums up for himself the meaning of his experience – and Trollope's message touches, characteristically, on political, social, and economic considerations as if they were one:

It is almost imperative . . . that they who devote themselves to [politics] . . . should be men of fortune. When he had commenced his work . . . he had had no thought of mending his deficiency . . . by a rich marriage. Nor had it ever occurred to him that he would seek a marriage

for that purpose. Such an idea would have been thoroughly distasteful
to him. There had been no stain of premeditated mercenary arrangement upon him at any time. But circumstances had so fallen out with
him, that as he won his spurs in Parliament . . . and was placed . . . in
office . . . prospects of love and money together were opened to him,
and he ventured on . . . because these prospects were so alluring.
(II, 408)

Politics and society have worked together to seduce the innocence of
Phineas Finn and substitute in its place a cynical materialism capable for
the moment of almost any moral compromise. But, being the hero of a
Victorian novel — and being the hero as well, Trollope suspected, of a
forthcoming Victorian novel — Phineas could not very conveniently be
made to give in to all of his temptations. His political failure is instructive.
Defying popular opinion and the cynicism of popular morality, Phineas
finally puts honesty and loyalty above mere "success" — which indeed is
incompatible with honesty and loyalty — and so he cannot succeed where
success is all that matters. Phineas will have another day — but only after
waiting and working and acquiring means.

Certain other leitmotifs demonstrate how politics and society become
one. There is subtle but consistent emphasis on Phineas's physical good
looks and appeal to women (e.g., II, 61–2) and how important this is to
his career. A number of gatherings in *Phineas Finn* are equally political and
convivial in their intent and their results — a case in point being the
Pallisers' party at Matching, at which "there was not a guest who had
voted for Mr. Turnbull's [rotten-borough] clause, or the wife or daughter,
or sister of any one who had so voted." Lest we have missed the point,
Trollope adds: "in these days politics ran so high that among politicians all
social gatherings were brought together with some reference to the state of
parties" (I, 100). And there is the pairing of the "season," which reaches
its height during the sitting of Parliament each year, with the economic
and social well-being of a great many people. So that, for example, when
Parliament disbands one year in June — earlier than usual — this causes
"the great dismay of London tradesmen and of young ladies who had not
been entirely successful in the early season"; "Mr. Mildmay, by his short
session, had half ruined the London tradesmen, and had changed the
summer mode of life of all those who account themselves to be anybody"
(I, 240–1 and 384). Nor is Phineas, we learn, the only M.P. who is brought
into debt by the "season," a parliamentary career, and an insufficient
income. Mr Clarkson, the moneylender, informs him that he has "known
Parliament gents this thirty years and more. Would you believe it, — I've
had a Prime Minister's name in that portfolio . . . and a Lord Chancellor's
. . . and an Archbishop's too. I know what Parliament is" (I, 237).

When the *Spectator*'s reviewer remarked of *Phineas Finn* that politics,
in it, is shown "too completely from the social side," clearly he missed a

main point of the novel. But others have consistently made the same mistake. Booth complained that while there is much social philosophy in *Phineas Finn* there is little political philosophy. Of course the two are inseparable; who, indeed, is to say where political philosophy ends and social philosophy begins? Even so current and perceptive a reader of Trollope as Bartrum has written that the parties people give in the Palliser novels are really social rather than political affairs — as if there could be a difference[52] (there is certainly nothing exclusively social about the Pallisers' party at Matching).

Trollope could have selected as his hero a zealot touched by a great cause or an idealistic youth hungering to right injustice. This is what Disraeli, the most popular political novelist of the day, usually did. Instead Trollope wrote a political novel that was in effect a novel of manners, a domestic tragedy, rather than a tract. Unlike Disraeli, he was more interested in verisimilitude than in propaganda; his politicians, like real ones of the time, loll around the House of Commons with crossed legs, hats tilted forward, eyes half closed,[53] instead of having assignations with exquisite maidens in moonlit ruins or passionate conversations with swarthy billionaires during thunderstorms. Thus *Phineas Finn* is a better political novel than any of Disraeli's, and thus it tells us less about the novelist and his fantasies than about the real nature of the social and political milieux surrounding Parliament. Disraeli's novels generally set forth a program or satirize political opponents or do both; the great problem in *Phineas Finn* is how to reconcile the demands of the inner world with those of the outer world[54] — if indeed it is possible to do so without acknowledging them to be one world.

VI

Things are not all black. The system is pernicious, yes, but not all men are corrupted or defeated by it; and the existence of a few good men is cause for hope. Phineas, of course, resists temptation, but in doing so ruins his political career — or seems to — and this leaves him in no position to advance the cause of virtue. There are, however, others.

Among these is Monk, whose chief importance lies not in who he may be but rather in what he thinks. We have already heard him on the duties of legislators and why they should espouse unpopular causes worth espousing. Monk takes over from the almost invisible Palliser the other side of politics in this novel — the good side, the side Trollope revered and wished to become part of. "Mr. Monk had great ideas of his own which he intended to hold, whether by holding them he might remain in office or be forced out . . . and he was indifferent as to the direction which things in this respect might take with him" (II, 201). This is ideal, if you can afford it; Monk can. Having enough not to be dependent upon office, he helps express Trollope's feeling that men of substance rather than adventurous entrepreneurs should populate the benches of Parliament. When Monk speaks to Phineas of Reform he speaks solely of what will serve the country — and he is the only one in the novel to do so: "The necessity for remodelling [the system] is imperative, and we shall be cowards if we decline the work ... [We must be] faithfully representative of our nation ... [and] I think that we should endeavour to keep our seats as long as we honestly believe ourselves to be more capable of passing a good measure than are our opponents" (I, 409 and 407, *passim.*). This is very un-"political" (Barrington Erle undoubtedly would call it "unparliamentary") and helps to explain why Monk — who preaches loyalty to causes rather than to leaders — is regarded by almost everyone as a dangerous maverick. Yet even Monk — virtuous as he is — has a fairly cynical, certainly practical, understanding of party politics. Despite his own high principles, he advises Phineas to toe the partisan line and stay where he is long enough to do some good. This is kindly pragmatism rather than hypocrisy.

Palliser himself does not have much to do or say in *Phineas Finn*, but he is a presence in the novel and serves, like Monk, as an example of the untainted side of politics. Remarkably enough, he is concerned less with any possible threat (from Madame Max) to his heirship as the next Duke of Omnium than with his budget, which he works on prodigiously (he is Mildmay's, and later Gresham's, Chancellor of the Exchequer). His feelings about his uncle and Madame Max are simple enough. " 'We can't prevent him if he chooses to do it,' said [Mr Palliser to his wife; he] had his budget to bring forward that very night, and ... in truth cared more for ... [it] than he did for his heirship at that moment" (II, 218). Madame Max's comment: "He likes the House of Commons better than the strawberry leaves, I fancy. There is not a man in England less in a hurry than he is" (II, 249). Thinking more of his budget than of his dukedom, Palliser in *Phineas Finn* again represents — fleetingly, to be sure — the Trollopian ideal of the hard-working, selfless, patriotic aristocrat, the kind of man who indeed *should* be Chancellor of the Exchequer. Surely the system that chooses him to fill that position cannot be entirely misguided. Palliser says almost nothing in the novel, but at one point he does say something striking — at least in the world of *Phineas Finn*. Hearing the restless Phineas declare that it does no harm to have "advanced ideas" since "one is never called upon to act upon them practically," Palliser snaps back: "That is a very dangerous doctrine. . . . I always am really anxious to carry into practice all those doctrines of policy which I advocate in theory" (II, 33–4). Trollope's verdict on these early years of Palliser's political career is prophetic: "If industry, rectitude of purpose, and a certain clearness of intellect may prevail, Planty Pall . . . may become a great Minister" (I, 329).

The reverent side of Trollope, then, is in evidence in this novel, as it was in *Can You Forgive Her?*. Monk and Palliser are good men, and both are members of a reigning government.

In the *Autobiography*, as we know, the novelist speaks of the duty and privilege of political service as the highest a man can attain. That feeling, expressed too in *Can You Forgive Her?*, is less pronounced in *Phineas Finn* — but it is still there. Phineas regards the profession of M.P. as "of all things in the world the most honourable"; and he says to Laura what Trollope himself felt: "I think it's a man's duty to make his way into the House; — that is, if he ever means to be anybody" (I, 41). And Phineas tells Low: "I . . . regard legislation as the finest profession going" (I, 75). Nothing like this can possibly be said without irony in *Phineas Redux* — or even in *Ralph the Heir*, which followed so closely upon Trollope's run for Parliament. *Phineas Finn* is the last of the pre-lapsarian political novels — the novels written before Beverley.

Honesty may not be a cardinal virtue in the world Phineas wishes to live in, and it certainly comes easier to a man who can afford it than to a man who cannot. But as Bunce tells Phineas at the end of the novel, "It takes a deal to ruin a man if he's got the right sperrit." Finding himself part of a spiritual minority and therefore a political loser in the world of *Phineas Finn*, Phineas, like many political losers in that world, nevertheless escapes being a moral loser as well; and virtue being so often rewarded in the Victorian novel, we may be reasonably sure that he will return another day to try his luck at "the finest profession going."

5 The Real Thing: Beverley and *Ralph the Heir*

In *Ralph the Heir* the story appears to be all underplot and all vulgar people.

Henry James

Ralph the Heir contains the best election episodes in English fiction.

Asa Briggs

The election at Percycross, in *Ralph the Heir*, is probably the best election in Victorian fiction.

W. L. Burn

No episode of Mr. Trollope's ever surpassed it in ability.

Spectator (15 April 1871)

This book contains election episodes unsurpassed in English fiction.

Michael Sadleir

One day when Trollope was in his early twenties, his uncle, Henry Milton, a clerk in the War Office, asked him what he wanted to be. Trollope said that his greatest ambition was to become a member of Parliament. Uncle Henry replied, with more than a touch of sarcasm, that few clerks in the Post Office became Members of Parliament. "It was the remembrance of this jeer which stirred me up to look for a seat as soon as I had made myself capable of holding one by leaving public service," Trollope writes in the *Autobiography* (p. 250). Uncle Henry by then was long dead, and clearly Trollope's motivation was not so frivolous. His passion to stand well in his own eyes — to be more than people, especially relatives, thought him — never deserted him. But much more important was his feeling — as we know, but it will bear repeating — that a seat in Parliament "should be the highest object of ambition to every educated Englishman."

The Stebbinses said that Trollope really "was not actuated by any strong wish to serve his country" and that he would have been "bored by his duties" had he gotten in; since he had no "important measure to propose" and "preferred keeping his money to spending it," they are baffled by his decision to run. Equally irrationally, Sadleir referred to the

Autobiography passage quoted above as making a "quaint declaration" and to Trollope's decision to run at Beverley as an instance of "obstinacy," of his unwillingness to "admit that the chicanery of a political caucus could cheat an Anthony Trollope of his ambition." In the same spirit Lance O. Tingay has written that "Trollope's bid to represent the Liberal party in the House of Commons was made from motives of social ambition rather than otherwise" — motives which the novelist attacked again and again in his books. Even Escott said of Trollope that his "Westminster ambitions implied no more idea of being useful than does entrance into any first-class club." But Trollope's "declaration" — though none of these critics takes it seriously — is at the heart of what he believed most of his life. It is "in keeping with the whole of Trollope's attitude toward politics and society" — "not a casual opinion but the bedrock foundation of his concept of useful citizenship."[1] Trollope had waited and watched and thought and planned for thirty years before finding himself able to take the parliamentary plunge. At last, at age 53, he took it.

The story of the connections, or rather in most cases the would-be connections, of the earlier Victorian novelists and men of letters with the House of Commons is an interesting one. Disraeli's search for a constituency began as early as 1832 and was successful (at Maidstone, Kent) only several attempts and five years later — and then because of the sponsorship of the patron of a pocket borough. On the other side of the House, Macaulay also sat for a pocket borough (Lord Lansdowne's family seat, Calne). Disraeli's friend Bulwer-Lytton sat in Parliament first as a Radical for the constituency of St Ives (Cornwall), later as a Conservative; his son, the first Earl of Lytton — the novelist "Owen Meredith" — finished off his political career by occupying, disastrously, the position of Viceroy of India in Disraeli's second ministry (surely never before or since have two romantic novelists served so prominently, or otherwise, in the same government). In 1841 Dickens was asked by the Liberals to stand for Reading (Berkshire); he declined. Trollope's idol Thackeray stood as a Liberal for the city of Oxford in 1857 and was beaten by the Tory candidate (Cardwell) by 53 votes, then a sizeable spread. Bagehot, meanwhile, tried four times unsuccessfully to get into Parliament as a Liberal. And in the same 1868 election in which Trollope ran, Kinglake stood for the borough of Bridgwater in Somerset (the author of *Eothen* was returned but promptly unseated on petition, and the borough was later disfranchised). Trollope understood well enough the political ambitions that could reside in the breast of a man of letters. Thackeray, Trollope says in his monograph, "had his moment of political ambition, like others" — "and paid a thousand pounds for the attempt."[2] Trollope's "moment" came in 1868.

"Anthony's ambition to become a candidate . . . is inscrutable to me," Dickens wrote to Tom Trollope, the novelist's elder brother. "Still, it is the ambition of many men, and the honester the man who entertains it, the better for us, I suppose."[3] Writing later in the *Autobiography* (p. 256), Trollope himself, with the benefit of hindsight, says he knew he "could do no good by going into Parliament" – it was too late for him to be embarking on a new career: "But still I had an almost insane desire to sit there, and to be able to assure myself that my uncle's scorn had not been deserved." (Again the passion for self-justification, even late in life; Henry Milton, it may be worth noting, was his mother's brother.) Dickens from his early years saw the electoral process as utterly corrupt and government as hopelessly incompetent; he never wanted any part of it. But Trollope began to feel that way only late in life, and after Beverley. Beforehand, to serve in Parliament had seemed to him something worthwhile; equally important to a man so governed by what others thought was the ample precedent (though much of it was unencouraging) for what he wanted to do. The political tradition had been sufficiently confirmed and adorned by some of the novelist's leading fellow-craftsmen by 1868; and his life-long interest in political processes made his desire to belong to the chief legislative body of the land no inexplicable vagary. The Post Office did not offer the prestige available to a member of Parliament. Despite his success as a public servant, Trollope realized "that, in Bagehot's famous phrase, 'a clerk in the public service is "nobody"; and you could not make a common Englishman see why he should be anybody.' "[4]

In 1867 Trollope had been invited by his good friend Charles Buxton to stand for a seat in Essex in order to relieve Buxton's family county (and Trollope's adopted one) from "the thraldom of Toryism," as Trollope says in the *Autobiography*; he promised – "rashly" – to do so in case of a dissolution. However, there was none; Disraeli put through the Second Reform Bill and took over the Conservative party leadership upon Derby's retirement. A reapportionment clause in the Bill rearranged the Essex constituencies. In 1868, when Disraeli finally dissolved, Trollope tried to get himself nominated for what would have been a safe seat in Essex. Sadleir unaccountably says that Trollope was "defrauded" of the seat,[5] but in fact previous claims of other men prevented the novelist from getting the nomination there (the two Liberals who ran for the new Essex divisions were both elected without a contest – though both were unseated in the Tory landslide of 1874). Knowing, as Trollope puts it in the *Autobiography* (p. 257), "the weakness of my ambition" and therefore not allowing him to "escape ... being put forward for some impossible borough as to which the Liberal party would not choose that it should go to the Conservatives without a struggle," his political friends looked around for another seat for him. "At last, after one or two others, Beverley was proposed to me, and to Beverley I went."

In Beverley, the capital of the East Riding section of Yorkshire with a population of 14,000, corrupt election practices had long survived the First Reform Bill, as they had in most boroughs; but Beverley, which first returned members to Parliament in the year 1295, had a particularly long-standing record of corruption, which emerged with some fanfare after the election of 1868. There had been bribery petitions challenging the announced election results in 1837, 1857, and 1860. A royal commission later uncovered corruption in all of the six elections preceding the 1868 election except that of 1854 – when, said *The Times*, "there really was a pure election, but it was quite an accident." In the course of the investigation an account book for the election of 1807 was produced which showed that among the 1,010 electors who had voted for one of the candidates, only 78 had taken no money for doing so. This was the borough – "the doubtfully virtuous borough," as the *Manchester Examiner* called it – Trollope stood for.[6]

Thackeray, when he ran at Oxford eleven years earlier, enjoyed some advantages entirely denied to Trollope when he stood for Beverley. Thackeray had the backing of the powerful Reform Club, of which he was a member; and then he had been invited to stand by his good friend Charles Neate, a Fellow of Oriel College, locally respected and well-known. Neate took Thackeray around Oxford and generally helped him as much as he could; and having previously sat for the borough himself, Neate knew his way around. And yet Thackeray made a poor fight of it. He discovered immediately, as he wrote to Dickens (this was before the Garrick Club quarrel), that "Not more than 4 per cent of the people here . . . ever heard of my writings. Perhaps as many as 6 per cent know yours, so it will be a great help to me if you will come and speak for me." After his defeat Thackeray was philosophical; "It is what I expected, and I take it as the British schoolboy takes his floggings, sullenly and in silence."[7]

Trollope had neither Thackeray's few advantages nor many illusions about the probable result of his venture (though it undoubtedly taught him a few unpleasant lessons). He had no particular sponsor at Beverley – indeed, despite his friendships with various Liberal politicians he got his nomination only in return for a contribution to the Liberal election fund – and he was not a member of the Reform Club. He was almost totally unknown in the borough, which had been represented for the past ten years by two popular Tories, Sir Henry Edwards and Christopher Sykes. Edwards, considered unbeatable even by the Liberal agents, was chairman of the Beverley Waggon Company, manufacturers of railway cars and agricultural machinery. He had spent a good deal of money over the years on local charities, and the voters were used to taking his money.[8] In the *Autobiography* (p. 258), Trollope describes him as a man who "had contracted a close intimacy with [the borough] for the sake of the seat," and comments that through the town's long history of petitions and voided elections – "through it all," as he says – Sir Henry kept his seat "with a fixity of tenure next door to permanence."

When Trollope first went to Beverley on 30 October 1868 the Liberal agent there – W. S. Hind, a local solicitor – told him he would spend a lot of money and lose the election; he would petition the result and spend more; there would be a commission and the borough would be disfranchised (*Autobiography*, pp. 257–8; these things turned out in the main to be true, though Trollope got off rather cheaply at Beverley and did not bring about nor pay for the petition). As he says himself, the novelist "persisted" stubbornly "in the teeth of this" warning and handed over the £300 his agent asked for. Later an additional £100 was requested, and paid. This was the full cost of Trollope's campaign — not the "nearly £2,000" figure pulled out of the air by Sadleir.[9] Beverley had two members. In 1868 four candidates went to the hustings — two Liberals and two Conservatives. The two latter were the strongest of the four — not only because of Sir Henry Edwards's influence and popularity, but also because, Sykes having retired, Edwards had paired himself with a wealthy young candidate (Captain Edward Hegan Kennard) who had started his campaign early and spent a lot of money in the town to ingratiate himself. Trollope's running-mate was Marmaduke Maxwell of Everingham, the eldest son and heir of Lord Herries (a local Scots Catholic peer) and subsequently father-in-law of the Duke of Norfolk. Maxwell had read Trollope's novels and was delighted to be associated with him; the two Liberal candidates got on very well with one another[10] (better than with the voters, as it turned out).

Trollope had described elections in *Doctor Thorne, Rachel Ray, Can You Forgive Her?*, and *Phineas Finn*. Now at last he saw one at firsthand. His experiences as a candidate were not pleasant. He began by knowing, actually, little more about elections than the average newspaper-reader; he learned quickly, to his own discomfiture. Worst of all was the publicity of his resounding defeat by the party of Disraeli in a year in which, ironically, the Gladstonian landslide brought the Liberal party emphatically back to power (its majority in the Commons was 112 after the election). It is not surprising, then, that the political themes of the novels written after Beverley tend to be articulated with less tolerance, less patience.

The novelist describes in the *Autobiography* (p. 259) the awful drudgery of campaigning for office. The time spent canvassing was "the most wretched fortnight of my manhood . . . I was subject to a bitter tyranny from grinding vulgar tyrants." These were his agents and supporters (on some of whom, as we shall see, he wreaked his vengeance in *Ralph the Heir*) — principally some local journalists, a Baptist minister (William Carey Upton), a local employer of labor (Colonel Hodgson), and very few other "gentlemen." The county families were supporting Edwards, as usual; and the Church party was so strong in the Tory interest that Trollope was absolutely told not to go to church at Beverley: "No Church of England church in Beverley would on such an occasion have welcomed a Liberal candidate. I felt myself to be a kind of pariah in the borough." At one time he heard a local Church of England minister "speaking of us as the foes of the Protestant Church."[11] (Trollope took his revenge on the clergy of Beverley in the figure of Mr Pabsby in *Ralph the Heir*.) "From morning to evening every day," Trollope goes on to complain, "I was taken round the lanes and by-ways of that uninteresting town, canvassing every voter, exposed to the rain, up to my knees in slush, and utterly unable to assume that air of triumphant joy with which a jolly, successful candidate should be invested." The novelist found it difficult to remain patient and diplomatic with the fools and bores he met at Beverley; and he became furious when he was told (by a Liberal publican) that if he took any time out during the campaign for hunting, as he had proposed to do, "all Beverley would desert us." But the hunting season was in full swing; defying his advisors, Trollope disappeared briefly from meetings of his committee in order to indulge his annual passion. How much this "queer frivolity" (Sadleir's phrase) may have hurt him politically is problematical; it could not have helped him much, though according to Escott "Trollope . . . did himself no harm by letting the householders see him in his top boots and pink riding through the streets on the way to a famous meet." "His sportsmanship formed a real point in his favour," Escott added — somewhat naively — because "Yorkshiremen love a horse, and are instinctively attracted to a bold rider to hounds." Unfortunately, Trollope chose to treat himself to a little diversion precisely at a time when his beleaguered committee was working night and day on his behalf and his own presence was required at both public meetings and private strategy sessions; yet on several occasions he cancelled speeches and conferences rather than miss a meet.[12]

There has been some question about Trollope's effectiveness as a speaker on the hustings. He himself complains that he had to speak somewhere every night, "which was bad; and to listen to the speaking of others, — which was much worse." He says in the *Autobiography* (pp. 255—6) that he was not a good speaker: "with infinite labour, I could learn a few sentences by heart, and deliver them, monotonously, indeed, but clearly." He found that he could say things in a "commonplace fashion" but that he frequently spoke too quickly in his hurry to get it over with. Further, he says, he "had no power of combining, as a public speaker should always do, that which I had studied and that which occurred to me at the moment." He could speak only from memory or only impromptu, but in no combination of the two — "which was very bad indeed, unless I had something special on my mind." Usually he did not. The Stebbinses, predictably enough, supported this view of Trollope's forensic failures. As he was writing his memoir Escott apparently talked to some men who had witnessed and remembered the 1868 election at Beverley; his picture is quite different from Trollope's self-deprecating one. Though he lost the election, Escott reported, contemporary witnesses declared that the "balance of speaking talent was undoubtedly on Trollope's side." So successful was he that the Tories in mid-campaign offered to withdraw Kennard if the Liberals would withdraw Trollope, thus giving the seats to Edwards and Maxwell. The Liberals — "deeply impressed by Trollope's unconventional treatment of familiar subjects and the sense of intellectual power of all he said," according to Escott — refused the bargain. (He also said they invited Trollope to try the borough again at the next election; this is probably true if one can judge from several comments the defeated candidate made after the election, as we shall see. But by then Beverley's political existence had been extinguished.) Escott concluded: Trollope was "at least a respectable figure"; as a speaker "he delighted without exception, and on both sides . . . clothing in clear and terse phrase thoughts that were the condensed essence of practical wisdom and shrewd insight." Clearly this version is distorted by prejudice; such a virtuoso — delighting "both sides" — could not have finished at the bottom of the poll, as Trollope did. Booth said of Escott, quite rightly, that he was "carried away" in his account by partiality to the novelist. But he himself relied on published texts of Trollope's speeches to conclude that there is "not the slightest evidence" of the novelist's having been "anything but a most indifferent campaigner"; and he was obviously astonished to discover in some of these speeches a patronizing attitude toward the workmen who comprised the bulk of the Beverley electorate. Surely little of *manner* can be deduced from cold print over a century later; nor should Booth have been surprised if the novelist sometimes patronized his working-class audiences (and yet some of the political positions Trollope took at Beverley were decidedly Radical ones, as we shall see). Gladstone, Lord Shaftesbury, Lord Bryce, and Thomas Hardy among others heard Trollope speak in 1876 at a public meeting on the Eastern Question (apparently the Duke of Westminster, who was in the chair, tugged in vain on Trollope's coattails after he had exceeded his allotted time); and Bryce's disinterested verdict was that the novelist, "a direct and forcible speaker," "would have made his way had he entered Parliament."[13] The truth in the matter of Trollope's effectiveness as a speaker and political campaigner probably lies closer to Escott's account, obviously inflated as it is, than to Trollope's "unduly modest" (Pollard's phrase) version of his own performance or to those of Booth and the Stebbinses, which are exaggeratedly uncomplimentary.

We come now to the matter of substance — the issues of the campaign and what Trollope said about them.

Trollope made his first public speech — described by the (Liberal) *Beverley Recorder* as "one of the ablest and most fluent addresses ever heard in Beverley" — on the first evening of his arrival in the borough, but in this speech he did not touch specifically on the issues. Instead he made a strictly partisan statement. He told his listeners that "to be Conservatives politically speaking seems to me to be unnatural"; and he concluded: "I do not think any man has a right to go into the House, and call himself what is popularly termed an 'Independent' member. A man going into the House is bound to make himself useful to the party to which he adheres

... You must work in bodies, in drilled regiments, to do any political good, or any other large work in the world. You must work shoulder to shoulder, and move step by step."[14] This may sound like a denial of Trollope's faith in the moral advantages of political independence; but in fact he is addressing himself here specifically to the Liberal party's notorious lack of discipline in the Commons between 1866 and 1868 which had allowed the Tories to remain in office without a majority and deprived Gladstone of the Premiership.

The novelist's official election address, dated from Waltham House, Waltham Cross, 28 October 1868, and published in Beverley three days later, devotes about half of its space, along the same lines, to a strictly partisan appeal:

> the chief duty of a Liberal member in the House of Commons will be to give a firm and continued support to the Leader of the Liberal party. No Liberal can doubt that during the last two Sessions of Parliament there was great fault on the part of gentlemen sitting on the Liberal side of the House, from whom such support was to have been expected. By deviations on their part from the straight line of Parliamentary tactics, the power of the Government has been thrown into the hands of the Tories; and as the result, the Reform Bill which the country demanded has been carried under the auspices of Mr. Disraeli, in whom, certainly, the nation has no confidence, instead of under those of Mr. Gladstone, on whom the whole Liberal Party in England places an active reliance.
>
> Every Session during which a Conservative or Tory Government is in power, the political progress and improvement of the nation is impeded instead of furthered. Holding this as a principal article of my political creed, I beg to assure you of this above all things, — that, should you do me the honour of sending me to Parliament as one of your representatives, it will be my purpose to give an active, constant, and unwearied support to Mr. Gladstone. (*Beverley Recorder*, 31 October 1868)

This portion of the address certainly seems to bear out the contention of the Stebbinses that at Beverley Trollope only "affirmed that he stood where he had been standing for thirty years," and that of Booth that the novelist's speeches were "general and pedestrian," "full of the platitudes of electioneering," generally "cold and uninspiring," and indicative of "little more than that Trollope was a staunch Liberal [and] a loyal follower of Gladstone." In a speech delivered toward the end of the campaign (16 November), Trollope proclaimed boldly: "If you do me the honour of sending me to Parliament I shall consider it to be my greatest and highest duty to serve my country by voting in the Liberal ranks."[15]

Booth, the Stebbinses, and others who have condemned Trollope for taking at Beverley a purely partisan or "pedestrian" stance have simply ignored, however, the rest of what he said there. Nothing could be more unfair than the contention that during his campaign the novelist only followed the party line and refused otherwise to commit himself.

Certainly on Irish Church Disestablishment Trollope was in agreement with Gladstone, though his election address is neither as conciliatory nor as ambiguous on the issue as Gladstone himself was in 1868. The election address continues: "The great question of the coming ... Session will be the Disestablishment and Disendowment of the Irish Church" (the chief political controversy of *Phineas Redux* — set principally in 1868, when the general election centered precisely on this issue); "for many years I have been one of those who have denounced the gross injustice and absurd uselessness of the Irish Church Establishment." Defending Gladstone's position and attacking Disraeli's (later in the campaign he charged that Disraeli would disestablish the Church of England itself if it served his purposes to do so; as the rhetoric heated up, Sir Henry Edwards accused Gladstone of being a Roman Catholic), Trollope goes on to complain of the Irish Church that it supports the ascendancy of rich over poor, lacks charity toward the latter, and is generally hated by the people anyway. "That the Irish Protestant Church will speedily be Disendowed and Disestablished," the address sums up, "no intelligent politician in England or Ireland now doubts." Trollope, of course, was right — though he was not in Parliament to cast his vote for Gladstone. Nor was this his last word on the issue. On 12 November he spoke to a meeting of about 4,000 persons and referred to "the disendowment and disestablishment of that monstrous anomaly the Irish Church" as a "great work."[16]

Though Trollope favored the Liberal party and endorsed (perhaps more strongly than necessary) its position on Disestablishment, it is important to note that he either ignored, embellished, or totally disagreed with the party line on a number of other issues. He was in no sense as pro-clerical as Gladstone and the Tractarians generally, in the first place. Second, his election address makes a strong statement on education and takes a position which in the 1868 election was needlessly provocative, though certainly in line with the novelist's feelings on the subject as expressed so often elsewhere (e.g., in *North America*). Trollope says in the election address: "The question which will next [that is, after Disestablishment] press upon Parliament will probably be that of the Education of the People. I am of opinion that every poor man should have brought within his reach the means of educating his children, and that those means should be provided by the State." In our time this may seem tame; in 1868, two years before Forster's Education Act became law, Trollope's position must have seemed gratuitously Radical to the publican, the Baptist minister and the retired colonel. In a speech to the Beverley Working Men's Liberal Association on 9 November Trollope is even more inflammatory on the issue: "The education of the people in this country is not equal to the education of the people of America, where every adult can read and write. I do not desire to Americanise our English institutions; but I do want to see a system of education established by which every man, woman, and child, and the poorest of the land, may be benefited by it."[17]

In the third and fourth places, Trollope loudly opposed his Liberal supporters on the only two issues which really interested them in 1868 – the ballot, and temperance legislation. Feeling that bribes rather than issues decided most elections, he denounced the secret ballot – which was supported at this time by most of the Liberal party – on the ground that it was "unmanly"; he argued instead for extended electoral divisions and "independent feeling" as the proper weapons against political intimidation and corruption. In his speech to the Working Men's Liberal Association, Trollope was unequivocal: "I will not like to see any working man coerced as to the manner in which he gives his vote, but will much rather see him discharging his noblest duty openly and independently. The time is coming . . . when all employers of labour cannot dream of asking their workmen for whom they are going to tender their votes."[18] And on the question of the Permissive Drink Bill – strongly favored by the Liberal party – Trollope again took an independent line, declaring his opposition to legislation such as this and suggesting instead that "the evil results of vicious conduct" could not be cured by "unmanly restraints" and that, as he says in the *Autobiography* (p. 260), "the gradual effect of moral teaching and education" would be a more effective collar upon excessive drinking than any parliamentary act.

This proves how inaccurate it is to accuse Trollope of docilely following the party line at Beverley. He himself says in the *Autobiography* (p. 255) that a good Liberal "should have been able to swallow such gnats" as the ballot and the temperance bill to do himself any real good at Beverley – but "I would swallow nothing" and was therefore "altogether the wrong man." He freely admits that he could never have been a "practical" party man ("I should never be satisfied with a soft word from the Chancellor . . . but would always be flinging my over-taxed catchup in his face"); and even Booth acknowledged, albeit grudgingly, that the novelist's "sense of obedience to the interest of [party] policy" was so inadequate as to have prevented him from ever becoming "a good party man."[19] In his *Life of Cicero*, remember, Trollope expressed his admiration for Cicero as a man too "honest," "wise," "civilized," and "modern" to become a blind partisan; he himself never became one. The charge that he condemned party politics in his novels while toeing the line as a candidate must be dismissed as unenlightened gossip. The novelist's major complaint in the aftermath of Beverley, as a matter of fact, was that no one paid any attention to what he actually did say. He saw that he had been brought to Beverley only to defeat Sir Henry Edwards, "or to cause him the greatest possible amount of trouble, inconvenience, and expense," and that no one cared what he thought about anything. Few if any of his supporters supposed that he would be successful, and none of them – according to Trollope – paid the least attention to his views: "my strongest sense of discomfort [at Beverley] arose from the conviction that my political ideas were all leather and prunella to the men whose votes I was soliciting. They cared nothing for my doctrines, and could not even be made to understand that I should have any" (*Autobiography*, p. 259). These are not the sentiments of a party hack who wishes to shroud in platitudinous vagueness any possibly controversial views he may hold. But they are the words of a man who believed that the voters were rarely better than the candidates who courted them. So he patronized them.

Trollope says in the *Autobiography* that he knew all along how the affair at Beverley would turn out. His agent had warned him; he should have listened. "It was wrong that one so innocent in such ways as I, so utterly unable to fight such a battle, should be carried down into Yorkshire merely to spend money and to be annoyed," he admits. "I suffered for my obstinacy. Of course I was not elected" (p. 260). He finished at the bottom of the poll — though with a fairly respectable (for a neophyte) 19.7% of the vote. He had 740 votes. His colleague Maxwell finished just above him with 895 votes. Edwards and Kennard, the two Conservatives, were elected with 1132 and 986 votes, respectively. The last few hours of the election campaign had been eventful; there had been rowdyism in the streets and even a Watergate-like raid on Conservative headquarters by some Liberal sympathizers who, according to the *Hull News*, "forced an entrance into [the] Tory committee room, and took possession of a money bag and some documents."[20] And there was a great continuous shouting out of party slogans and broadsides — among which, on the Tory side, were the following:

ELECTORAL TIP FOR BEVERLEY
Ho! rhubarb, magnesia, ho! bismuth and jalap!
   Ho! Jenkins and Robinson, Walker and Brown;
'Tis said that our worthy friend Anthony Trollope
   Would like to be Member for Beverley town.
Oh! do not elect him, 'twould be such a pity,
   For really with work he is getting quite thin;
Just fancy him stuck on a Draining Committee,
   Or bored like his own Mr. Phineas Finn!
Say no to him sweetly without any fighting,
   And leave not the Tories you have, in the lurch;
Friend Anthony Trollope is wanted for writing
   And not, sirs, for wronging poor Pat and the Church!
So all ye good Yorkshiremen, cunning as Reynard,
   And able, they say, to bite living or dead,
Cheer Maxwell and Trollope, but put Mr. Kennard
   Up on the poll second with Edwards as head!

And:

ADVICE TO BEVERLEY ELECTORS
Ye good men of Beverley, stick fast and hard,
To Sir Henry Edwards and Captain Kennard.
Be true to yourselves, and you'll certainly 'wallop'
Mr. Constable Maxwell and Anthony Trollope!

The Liberals replied by denouncing Edwards for having voted in the late session to reduce Beverley's parliamentary representation from two to one; and their election poster concluded with this ungalvanizing refrain:

Sir Henry Edwards sat on the Government wall;
Sir Henry Edwards obeyed the Government call;
Sir Henry Edwards will have a great fall,
And all Sir Henry's shufflings, and all his Men,
Can't lift Sir Henry on the wall again.

ELECTORS! Vote for
MAXWELL AND TROLLOPE,
who won't deceive you.[21]

Beverley stayed in the news long after the election was over. There was a petition (from the town, not from Trollope himself); Edwards and Kennard were the respondents. As at Sudbury, which had been disfranchised in a celebrated case in 1844, spectacular revelations of corruption of every kind emerged. Beverley elections, it turned out, had provided for years an ūnrivalled opportunity for voting citizens to make money, eat free food, drink free beer. The party spirit, it was discovered, was devoted during elections less to the articulation of policy than to a contest between the voters to determine which of them could make the most money. The judge who examined the case on 9 March 1869 discovered that over a hundred persons had been guilty of offering or taking bribes of different kinds, and the election was declared void. Chief corruptor was a local draper, the agent of Sir Henry Edwards. His method had been to buy up as many voters as he could on the occasion of the municipal elections for town council which had been held prior to the general election. His theory — and a good one it had been — was that this was both less obtrusive and more effective than the old practice of bribing during the more carefully scrutinized parliamentary elections, and that the voters would remember their commitments when the important moment came. He had not been subtle about it, however. On the day of the town elections this Tory agent drew £800 from the bank. He installed various assistants at strategic points around the town and then settled himself at the Golden Ball tavern with a bag of gold coins on the table in front of him. The voters entered singly and in small groups; the agent paid them from fifteen to twenty shillings apiece and wrote down in his notebook the name of each bribed adherent and the amount paid. He told each voter as he paid him that the money was for two votes – for, that is, both the municipal election held that day and the parliamentary election to be held two weeks later. In this way he bought somewhere between 800 and 1,000 votes.[22] The *Hull & Eastern Counties Herald*, in a special *Election Supplement* published on 3 November 1868, unabashedly printed the following description of what happened that day: "When the poll opened money was lavishly expended, and it soon became evident that the Conservatives had boasted truly when they affirmed that any amount of money would be used to ensure success. . . . As a result of the very extensive buying of the candidates there was a good deal of drinking, and quite early in the day several disgraceful street fights took place. . . . Last night a brass band paraded the streets in celebration of the Tory victory." The Conservatives carried all six town council seats in the municipal election; and so the handwriting was on the wall for the general election to follow.

Having unearthed this much, the judge gave way to a royal commission, which in the summer of 1869 thoroughly examined the state of the borough. Bribery was proven, the voiding of the election was upheld, and the two Tories lost their seats. Ultimately, in 1870, Beverley was disfranchised altogether. Trollope's agent was proved a prophet. Sir Henry Edwards, tried for bribery, was acquitted. Called to testify by the royal commissioners, Trollope, like his own Sir Thomas Underwood in *Ralph the Heir*, declared to one and all: "If any of my money was spent [to bribe] . . . it was without my knowledge or instruction. To my knowledge none of the money" he gave his agent "was used to corrupt the electors, either by money or beer, or any other way"; and he reminded the court that he "stood at the bottom of the poll." The commissioners later reported that the evidence given by Trollope and Maxwell had convinced them that the two candidates "had not been parties either directly or indirectly to the bribery."[23]

In the *Autobiography* (p. 261), Trollope sums up: "In this way Beverley's privileges as a borough and my Parliamentary ambition were brought to an end at the same time." His feelings in the mid-1870s, when he was writing the memoir, were bitter. "I did not get in, yet I was in at the death; for the effort of my defeat involved Beverley's own parliamentary demise . . . I at least had the satisfaction of seeing those who had walked over me faring worse than myself, inasmuch as they not only lost their seats but their money too." And so he did not "altogether regret" having run. Without his "fortnight of misery" Sir Henry Edwards might not have been unseated or the borough disfranchised.

It . . . seemed to me that nothing could be worse, nothing more unpatriotic, nothing more absolutely opposed to the system of representative government, than the time-honoured practices of the borough of Beverley. It had come to pass that political cleanliness was odious to the citizens. There was something grand in the scorn with which a leading Liberal there turned up his nose at me when I told him that there should be no bribing, no treating, not even a pot of beer on our side ... To have assisted in putting an end to this, even in one town, was to a certain extent a satisfaction.

(*Autobiography*, pp. 261–2)

In this way Trollope learned at first hand that the Liberals were about as bad as the Tories, and the later political novels reflect this knowledge. If "political cleanliness was odious to the citizens," it was equally odious to both sides. Trollope never forgot the "scorn" he mentions here. Nor did he ever forget the "misery" of campaigning or the various ways in which a candidate is dirtied – in both senses of the word – when he aspires to office. The composition of *The Duke's Children* dates from the same period as that of the *Autobiography*, and into this last of the Palliser novels Trollope put a very personal statement:

Parliamentary canvassing is not a pleasant occupation. Perhaps nothing more disagreeable, more squalid, more revolting to the senses, more opposed to personal dignity, can be conceived. The same words have to be repeated over and over again in the cottages, hovels, and lodgings of poor men and women who only understand that the time has come round in which they are to be flattered instead of being the flatterers ... [Ultimately the candidate] comes to hate the poor creatures to whom he is forced to address himself. ... To have to go through this is enough to take away all the pride which a man might otherwise take from becoming a member of Parliament. But to go through it and then not to become a member is base indeed! To go through it and to feel that you are probably paying at the rate of a hundred pounds a day for the privilege is most disheartening. (II, 148–50, *passim.*)

Years later the memories still rankled. The descriptions of elections in the later political novels always express bitter cynicism about the motives and methods of some candidates, and, at the same time, utter contempt for the "poor creatures" who vote for them. But after Beverley there is often too a note of commiseration with the much-harassed candidate – especially the losing candidate.

At the end of the *Autobiography* chapter on Beverley, Trollope strikes a chord heard often in the political novels. One of the chief lessons of Beverley for him was the unblushing way in which a seat in Parliament was considered by a sitting member an appendage of his own – to be used for whatever personal purposes might be convenient – and the willing complicity of the voters in this egotistical scheme. Speaking specifically of Sir Henry Edwards and his supporters, Trollope refers (*Autobiography*, p. 262) wonderingly to "the time, the money, the mental energy, which had been expended in making the borough a secure seat for a gentleman who had realised the idea that it would become him to be a member of Parliament! This use of the borough seemed to be realised and approved in the borough generally. The inhabitants had taught themselves to think that it was for such purposes that boroughs were intended!" As we know, Trollope hated the idea of a man using a seat to help secure for himself financial or social status. He felt that such men as Edwards, a manufacturer of railway cars, too often looked upon Parliament as a means to non-political ends rather than as an end in itself — i.e., to serve the country — and that such men had their priorities hopelessly jumbled. At Beverley "politics were appreciated because they might subserve electoral purposes," Trollope concludes; it was not understood there, as it should have been, that "electoral purposes, which are in themselves a nuisance, should be endured in order that they may subserve politics" (*Autobiography*, p. 261).

When the dust had settled around Beverley, Trollope must have sadly, and perhaps bitterly, realized one other thing. He would now "never be made free of the admirable little door reserved for members" of Parliament, so eloquently invoked in *Can You Forgive Her?*. He had, it is true, thought at first that he might try again. On election night at Beverley he had told a meeting: "It may be that I shall appear before you again"; and in his farewell address, dated from Waltham House, 18 November 1868, he had said: "should the occasion arise I trust that you will allow me to be seen among you again."[24] But, like his own Phineas Finn at the end of *Phineas Redux*, Trollope came (much more quickly) to feel that a seat in Parliament was after all like an alluring toy in a store-window — appealing from the outside, but discovered to be unsatisfactory when brought home and examined carefully. In *Ralph the Heir* (II, 16) Sir Thomas Underwood also sees the seat he has won as only a "new toy" to enjoy for a while — and not quite so nice as he had thought.

II

In *Ralph the Heir* — written mostly in 1869, published serially in *St. Paul's* January 1870—July 1871 and in three volumes in April 1871—Trollope takes immediate revenge upon Beverley. While the Tankerville election in *Phineas Redux* also has obvious connections with Beverley, Trollope's most detailed account of his experiences as a candidate are written into *Ralph the Heir*: "Percycross and Beverley were, of course, one and the same place," he admits readily enough in the *Autobiography* (p. 295). This simple assertion is doubted by some of those who see Trollope's political stories as being wholly separate from real life; others have accepted Trollope's declaration.[25]

Over the years *Ralph the Heir* has been one of Trollope's most controversial novels; published opinions about it have diverged widely and violently. The author himself called it "one of the worst novels I have written." Indeed, he goes on in the *Autobiography* (p. 295) to say that the novel's main plot "is not good," that the two Ralphs and the ladies are lifeless, and that everything about the novel's heroine, including her name, "has passed utterly out of my mind without leaving a trace of remembrance behind" (he wrote this only half a dozen years after the novel's appearance). In sum, *Ralph the Heir*, says Trollope, has "justified that dictum that a novelist after fifty should not write love stories." He does go on to say that the political sub-plot and "the electioneering experiences of the candidates at Percycross" are well done; and he likes his Neefit family, and Moggs. The rest he condemns.

The interesting history of the novel's reputation begins with an odd case of literary plagiarism, making *Ralph the Heir*, from the moment of its appearance, controversial in an unexpected way. As soon as he had read it, the often sticky-fingered Charles Reade appropriated parts of its plot into a play he was writing called *Shilly-Shally*. Trollope was merely annoyed at the obvious plagiarism, but soon afterward he had reason to be incensed; the play was called indecent by the *Morning Advertiser*. Having, like Henry James, always coveted a dramatic success himself and been disappointed in this respect, Trollope also was angry that another writer should have made a play out of his novel and gotten it onto the boards. However, *Shilly-Shally* closed quickly; afterwards Trollope and Reade played whist at the Garrick Club for over three years without speaking to one another.[26] In the *Autobiography* (p. 295), Trollope contents himself by remarking of the incident that *Ralph the Heir* "was the novel of which Charles Reade afterwards took the plot and made it into a play."

The reviewers, with whom Trollope so often disagreed, gave him the shock of his life by pronouncing what he thought one of his worst novels an unqualified success. The *Athenaeum* told readers they would be "amply rewarded" by giving their attention to *Ralph the Heir*, "a masterpiece [of realism] in its way." The laudatory notice in *The Times* singled out for special praise the electioneering sequences and the story of the Neefit courtship: "no man alive, now that Charles Dickens has departed, can write on such subjects so humourously and so truthfully as Mr. Trollope." The *British Quarterly Review* thought the novel "equal to his best work. Sir Thomas and old Neefit are not surpassed by Mrs. Proudie and Archdeacon Grantley [*sic*] . . . There are few things in fiction finer than . . . Sir Thomas . . . Old Neefit is . . . as distinctive in drawing and indelible in impression as Pickwick." The notice concluded: " '*Ralph the Heir*' is . . . likely to live when many things that Mr. Trollope has done are dead and forgotten." The *Saturday Review* paid particular tribute to the Neefit family, and summed up: "we may with especial confidence recommend *Ralph the Heir* . . . a marvel of freshness when we consider the prodigious number of its predecessors." The *Examiner's* review was more patronizing, using the occasion to attempt to explain why Trollope was, in its words, "the most widely popular . . . of living English novelists." It suggested, shrewdly, that Trollope was typical of his audience in not being intellectually engaged in his own work: thus his "novels exactly suit the capacity of the bulk of the novel-reading public, and hence their well-merited success." In Boston, the *North American Review* compared Trollope to Jane Austen in his grasp and delineation of character (an incisive comparison in light of the novel's several echoes of Jane Austen) and pronounced him "the most representative, if not the best, specimen of the living English novelist."[27]

As was so often the case among reviews of Trollope's novels, the longest and most thoughtful notice of *Ralph the Heir* appeared in the pages of the *Spectator*.[28] Sir Thomas and Neefit, once again, are singled out for praise here. The former "is one of Mr. Trollope's finest and best" characters; "it is impossible to conceive a more carefully-finished picture." Neefit "is absolutely perfect." The *Spectator* found the Percycross election superb: "no episode of Mr. Trollope's ever surpassed [it] in ability." And the reviewer concluded: "We might write on for another page or two, without exhausting the criticisms (almost all of appreciation) which a novel so full of life as this naturally suggests."

Twentieth-century critics have been about as divided as critics can be over a novel. The spectrum runs from ecstatic comments by Sadleir and Briggs — "vivid and humourous," said Sadleir, and the election episodes are "unsurpassed in English fiction"; the novel contains "the best election episodes in English fiction," declared Briggs — to antipathetic comments by Booth and Escott: the plot is absurd, even "perversely complicated," said Booth, and the characters, once the story "wheezes and sputters to its halting conclusion," are mostly seen to be "either ridiculous or comatose"; as regards the "baffling" plot, Escott complained, *Ralph the Heir* is "as complicated and confusing as those parts of the Scriptural narrative dealing with the kings of Israel and Judah called by the same name." Everyone, however, has liked both Sir Thomas ("one of the best studies in nineteenth-century fiction of paradoxical middle-class psychology," said Polhemus) and Ontario Moggs (the "loveliest character" in the book, declared Walpole; the "truest character" in the book, declared Booth), who have received general praise as, respectively, one of Trollope's most sympathetic protagonists and one of his best minor characters.[29]

We are concerned here only with that small part of the novel that touches specifically upon political themes; most of the rest of *Ralph the Heir* is not only confusing but utterly forgettable. The political sections, however, are among Trollope's most interesting writings on the subject, and in some instances among his most revealing.

There can be no doubt that Percycross is Beverley. But there is also the question of Sir Thomas Underwood. Escott did not perceive anything autobiographical in Sir Thomas. Booth saw him, the would-be biographer of Bacon, only as "the sensitive, intelligent scholar . . . a familiar type in academic and literary circles, always engaged in taking notes and shuffling papers but never producing completed work."[30] Polhemus paired Sir Thomas as scholar with George Eliot's Casaubon, finding the latter "almost crude" by comparison; and he went on to suggest that there is much of Trollope's father, the compiler of the never-to-be-completed ecclesiastical dictionary, in Sir Thomas. (This is very wide of the mark; Polhemus wisely does not press it.) On the contrary — Sir Thomas Underwood at Percycross is Anthony Trollope at Beverley; and his roles as widower-father and frustrated scholar are utterly minor and even insignificant in comparison with this other function.

Sir Thomas at Percycross, like Trollope at Beverley, is a rebel against unscrupulousness and insincerity. Like Trollope too he is ultimately a victim of "political wire-pullers." Sir Thomas's reaction to the invitation to stand for Parliament, like Trollope's, is to feel that he would not get in, that it would cost money he ought not to spend, and that he would probably look a fool for his pains. Once on the scene he is, like Trollope at Beverley, introduced by an agent he dislikes to influential supporters he comes to detest — "Sir Thomas had not only not seen a human being with whom he could sympathise, but had been constrained to associate with people who were detestable to him" (II, 15). Like the novelist, Sir Thomas feels a prisoner to the demands of his agent and uneasy when he must say tactful things to his working-class supporters. Sir Thomas acting the member of various denominations (Wesleyan, Anglican, etc.) among different men reflects a demand continuously made upon Trollope at Beverley. Like Trollope, Sir Thomas sees his supporters turn a deaf or scornful ear when he comes out for electoral purity (indeed, Sir Thomas's supporters are portrayed as shocked, sickened, and demoralized by such pronouncements). The weariness and boredom with which Sir Thomas goes canvassing from door to door at Percycross, feeling self-conscious about intruding upon people he does not know — and constantly betraying his feeling — perfectly describe Trollope's sentiments (and his usual door-to-door performance) at Beverley. Like Trollope, Sir Thomas has no pleasure in the campaign and is thoroughly depressed by the squalid corruption he encounters at firsthand. Like Trollope, Sir Thomas is at one point asked to drop his candidacy so that the Tories and Liberals can make a deal to split the two seats between them; like Trollope, he refuses. At the end of the campaign the candidates address a rowdy crowd in the midst of public disturbances, on which occasion Sir Thomas's arm is broken by a rock hurled at him. Election night at Beverley was described by the *Hull & Eastern Counties Herald* (19 November 1868) as follows:

fights were continually occurring in the streets. At the close of the poll a terrific row began, and a strong barrier in front of the hustings was

pulled down. . . . In the *mêlée* large beams of wood were thrown by
exasperated people into the crowd. Cobbles, splinters of wood, and
other missiles were thrown into the hustings, and Sir H. Edwards and
Capt. Kennard, finding it impossible to get a hearing left the hustings.
Mr Maxwell and Mr Trollope made a few remarks, but they could
scarcely be heard. The Mayor read the declaration of the poll, but those
even below him could not hear it on account of the disturbance. Several
gentlemen of the hustings were struck by the stones and sticks, and the
ladies were obliged to retire.

When it is all over Sir Thomas is delighted to shake "off from his feet . . .
the dust of that most iniquitous borough." And later he has, if nothing
else, "the satisfaction of knowing that [he has] been the means of
exposing corruption, and of helping to turn such a man as Griffenbottom
[his Tory colleague] out of the House. Upon my word, I think it has been
worth while," says Ralph the heir (II, 234). Trollope's feelings about the
results at Beverley and the ultimate fate of Sir Henry Edwards were
essentially the same, as we have seen.

Sir Thomas's sentiments in the aftermath, described at some length by
Trollope, surely reflect those of the novelist after Beverley.

This . . . attempt of his to enter the world and to go among men that he
might do a man's work, had resulted in the loss of a great many
hundred pounds, in absolute failure, and, as he wrongly told himself, in
personal disgrace. . . . He had raised himself to public repute by his
intellect and industry, and had then, almost at once, allowed himself to
be hustled out of the throng simply because others had been rougher
than he, – because other men had pushed and shouldered while he had
been quiet and unpretending . . . But there will ever be present to the
mind of the ambitious man the idea of something to be done over and
above the mere earning of his bread; – and the ambition may be very
strong, though the fibre be lacking . . . The work . . . had been . . .
disagreeable, and . . . he had failed . . . egregiously. During his canvass,
and in all of his intercourse with the Griffenbottomites, he had told
himself, falsely, how pleasant . . . it would be to return to his
books; – how much better for him would be a sedentary life.

(II, 275–6 and 278, *passim.*)

The connections here are obvious. Trollope felt publicly disgraced after his
shattering defeat – felt that the image of respectability and worth he had
worked so long and hard to construct might have been damaged by his
humiliation. Like Underwood, he wanted to use "his intellect and
industry" to do more for England than merely earn his bread; he felt that
such ambitions were "manly" and always praiseworthy if genuine. His
sense of failure initially was strong after the election. And surely Trollope

told himself as he slogged through the filth of Beverley how much better it would be had he stayed quietly at home with his books and papers; when it was all over he came to see that it would indeed have been better.

The novelist makes, as we shall see, a few alterations of factual detail which have thrown some off the scent; but there can be no doubt that Sir Thomas Underwood at Percycross is Anthony Trollope at Beverley aspiring to a seat in Parliament.[31]

Beyond these connections between Trollope and Underwood, there are some interesting philosophical ones — more tenuous, perhaps, but suggestive and striking — that have been altogether ignored by earlier critics of the novel. *Ralph the Heir* has an autobiographical content beyond the mere recounting of the election campaign.

Sir Thomas is a man who often speaks of "consulting" others "but in truth he very rarely consulted any human being as to what he would do. ... If he went straight, he went straight without other human light than such as was given to him by his own intellect, his own heart, and his own conscience" (I, 13). Anthony Trollope was just such a man. And yet all his life, while exuding certainty, Trollope was indecisive, or at least undecided, on some questions. On that of faith, for example, the novelist's description of Underwood may be a description of himself: "He had intended to settle for himself a belief on subjects which are, of all, to all men the most important; and, having still postponed the work of inquiry, had never attained the security of a faith. He was for ever doubting, for ever intending, and for ever despising himself for his doubts and unaccomplished intentions" (II, 139). In a subsequent passage, Trollope refers musingly to Sir Thomas's "incapacity for belief." On some issues Trollope was equivocal; on religious matters he often seemed ferociously positive. And yet his ecumenicism suggests vague and unarticulated doubt beneath the assertions. Discussing Trollope's religious convictions, apRoberts emphasizes his "relativism": "If he had gone in for divinity, he would have qualified as a comparative religionist, both intellectually and emotionally." The great appeal of the Anglican Church for Trollope lay in its being "so blessedly non-committal."[32] Like George Eliot and other mid-Victorians who had had suddenly to assimilate conclusions of the new sciences, Trollope was clearly puzzled by what to do with such large concepts as "God" and "Immortality," which no longer seemed indestructibly tenable. Like Sir Thomas Underwood, he was probably aware of his own failure to think through — systematically and in depth — his religious and philosophical beliefs, or surmises.

Most interesting is a long chapter near the end of the novel in which Sir Thomas simply sits and reflects.

There come upon us all as we grow up in years, hours in which it is impossible to keep down the conviction that everything is vanity, that the life past has been vain from folly, and that the life to come must be

vain from impotence. It is the presence of thoughts such as these that
needs the assurance of a heaven to save the thinker from madness or
from suicide. It is when the feeling of this pervading vanity is strongest
on him, that he who doubts of heaven most regrets his incapacity for
belief. If there be nothing better than this on to the grave, – and
nothing worse beyond the grave, why should I bear such fardels?

(II, 284)

Thus Sir Thomas muses – in a vein that more than suggests Trollope's own
disillusionment with life in 1870. He had failed to get into Parliament – a
lifelong ambition – and saw around him the debris of what had once been
a glorious political establishment. The death of his hero Palmerston,
constitutional upheaval, rapid changes in society and in its fundamental
assumptions – by 1870 some things must have seemed pretty bewildering
to Trollope, born in the year of Waterloo. He had become comfortable
with what he thought was the pervading spirit of the age, its characteristic
order; these were now slipping away. In society, as in politics, the new
breed seemed to have no manners or principles; Trollope found the
younger generation unappealing. He had retired from the Post Office to
live on his income as a writer, but just lately his novels had been less
popular with readers and less marketable with publishers. His sons
Frederick and Henry – especially the former – needed constant financial
help. His edition of Caesar's *Commentaries* was being roundly attacked in
the press as incompetent scholarship as *Ralph the Heir* began to appear.
And the novelist found himself attached to Miss Field in a way that
surprised him – he thought he was happily married. He was 55 and
beginning to wonder what, if anything, he had accomplished or had to
look forward to. Thus Sir Thomas meditates.

What good had come to him of his life, – to him or to others? And
what further good did he dare to promise to himself? Had it not all
been vanity? Was it not all vain to him now at the present? Was not life
becoming to him vainer and still vainer every day? He had promised
himself once that books should be the solace of his age, and he was
beginning to hate his books, because he knew that he did no more than
trifle with them. He had found himself driven to attempt to escape
from them ... into public life; but had failed, and had been inexpressibly dismayed at the failure. (II, 285)

Trollope is not the first writer to feel, in his mid-fifties, that his life's work
may be vanity. When we hear that Sir Thomas "was beginning to hate his
books, because he knew that he did no more than trifle with them," we
must also be reminded of Trollope's assertion in the *Autobiography* that
he will not be known or read in the twentieth century – this was his
considered opinion of himself as a novelist. Sir Thomas, of course, is

referring to his embryo work on Bacon and not to anything he has actually written (he has written nothing) — but the novelist's self-reflexive tone seeps through. Like Sir Thomas, Trollope wished to distinguish himself through work, and like him too he had the middle-class obsession with failure — "its phobias, its guilt, and its touchy defensiveness."[33] Underwood demonstrates among other things Trollope's own fears of inadequacy in these years — and also the appeal which social convention always had for him. Both men want to "write a book that should live," and each feels that he has failed. Thus both attempt to escape from books into public life and are "inexpressibly dismayed at the failure" of the attempt.

At the end of his reverie Sir Thomas's thoughts are these:

> To walk as he saw other men walking around him, — because he was one of the many; to believe that to be good which the teachers appointed for him declared to be good; to do prescribed duties without much personal inquiry into the causes which had made them duties; to listen patiently, and to be content without excitement; that was the mode of living to which he should have known himself to be fit. But he had not known it, and had strayed away, and had ventured to think that he could think, — and had been ambitious. And now he found himself stranded in the mud of personal condemnation, — and that so late in life, that there remained to him no hope of escape. (II, 286)

Everyone knows that Trollope grew more and more pessimistic as the years went by and that this was reflected in his novels. In 1870 he apparently saw himself as a man who had conformed to general standards and to conceptions of duty widely accepted without either examining or attempting to understand them. Clearly he also questioned at this time his own capacity as a man "to be content without excitement" — his parliamentary adventure and his outpourings to Kate Field testify to that. He felt restless and dissatisfied, and this made him uneasy. Having briefly "ventured to think that he could think," as he bitterly writes of Sir Thomas here — having "been ambitious" — Trollope and his hero both settle back instead into a more knowledgeable, and a more cynical, late middle age. Nowhere else in his fiction does the novelist draw so detailed a self-portrait; by comparison there is almost nothing of Trollope in Dr Wortle.

Typically, Trollope altered a few details to make such identifications more difficult. Ingeniously — and bitterly, too — he uses as a sketch of himself in *Ralph the Heir* a man who for years has been trying to write one book and has yet to set pen to paper. Feeling that perhaps, as some of the reviewers were saying, he had written too much too quickly and thus "trifled" as a writer, Trollope — whose abrasive mother published 113 miscellaneous volumes between the ages of 52 and 76 — creates as his *alter*

ego here a man with a writing block, a characteristically ironic obfuscation. Sir Thomas is also made a Conservative, a typical Trollopian ploy
to distort ever so slightly autobiographical/historical connections. But the
novelist also gives himself in this way a richer opportunity to anatomize in
his novel the hated Sir Henry Edwards, who is Sir Thomas's Tory
running-mate Griffenbottom in *Ralph the Heir*. The many conferences
between the two candidates provide Trollope with ample means to attack
Sir Henry, which would have been more difficult had he made Sir Thomas
a Liberal like himself and thus not privy to Griffenbottom's talk.

Griffenbottom — not Griffenbotham, as Cockshut spells it — is a Conservative who has represented Percycross for years and is chiefly interested
in the share of the social spoils such a position gives him. A professional
politician, realistic and hard-nosed, Griffenbottom, like Edwards, has
always paid his way like a gentleman and never petitioned. He scorns the
ideas of purity and principle in politics. And he has been successful in
Percycross for a long time. Griffenbottom's favorite canvassing tactic —
like Edwards's — is to ask everyone if after all they do not dislike "that
fellow" (Gladstone) and never to talk of policy or substantive matters, but
to pay up when the time comes. Without political theories, mute in
Parliament, paying heavily for his seat each time he runs, Griffenbottom,
like Edwards, enjoys the life, knows no other, and finds his only real
existence in the House of Commons and in the homes of his political
masters. Like Sir Henry once again, Griffenbottom loses his seat as a result
of the petition but is himself acquitted of bribery. Undoubtedly Griffenbottom and Sir Henry Edwards of Beverley are the same man. Trollope
draws upon the Beverley campaign in all its facets in his account of the
Percycross election.

The connections and similarities are, indeed, myriad. At Percycross, as
at Beverley, two Conservatives battle two Liberals for two seats; at
Percycross, as at Beverley, the two Tories win, are unseated on petition,
and later acquitted of personal wrongdoing; as at Beverley, a commission
ultimately disfranchises the borough altogether. Like Beverley, Percycross
has had a long history of corruption and voided elections, having somehow
managed to survive the Reform Bill of 1832. Like Beverley, Percycross has
a particularly loathesome Tory agent. The voters of Percycross, like those
of Beverley, are incensed and sickened at the spectre (held up to them by
Sir Thomas) of an election without bribery. As at Beverley, at Percycross
the Liberals win on a show of hands on election eve and then lose
decisively on the "real" day itself when the voters discover that their
pocketbooks weigh more than their convictions. At Percycross, as at
Beverley, the Liberals take an early lead in the election-day poll and are
later caught and passed by the Tory candidates, whose agents are
busy bribing the voters.[34] At Percycross, as at Beverley, there is a good
deal of rowdyism on election night. Percycross is Beverley in almost every
detail just as surely as Underwood is Trollope himself.

III

The Percycross election itself still needs to be considered, as *fiction*, in its role as part of Trollope's continuing political commentary of these years. The ensuing discussion will inevitably recall points of comparison between Percycross and Beverley, now that we are able to perceive the connections between them; but of primary importance here are the ways in which the story of the election contributes to themes we have been tracing in the Palliser novels. It should be clear from what has already been said that any tendency — such as Booth's — to view the Percycross election simply as burlesque does it inadequate justice and ignores the very personal nature of its origins.[35] However, Percycross must also be examined as one of a series of events in the "political" novels — an event that helped to define the political perspectives of the novelist as well as those of the unsuccessful candidate.

Percycross enters into the story of *Ralph the Heir* late in the first volume when Sir Thomas without ceremony hands to one of his daughters his election address, which she reads "with more enthusiasm than did any of the free and independent electors to whom it was addressed" — as the bitter loser at Beverley puts it. We discover that Percycross, like Beverley, has known bribery and petitions in the past; "some men marvelled that the borough should have escaped so long." There being now abroad "a spirit of assumed virtue in regard to such matters," the political men of Percycross have decided, "just for the present," to lie low if possible until "the new broom which was to sweep up the dirt of corruption was not quite so new" — and then to return safely "to the old game, — which was, in truth, a game very much liked in . . . Percycross" (I, 234; the "old game," of course, is bribery). Immediately we are plunged into autobiography as the novelist repeats the prophecy made by a "very learned pundit" to "one of the proposed candidates": "You'll spend a thousand pounds in the election. You won't get in, of course, but you'll petition. That'll be another thousand. You'll succeed there, and disfranchise the borough" (I, 235).

We are introduced to Sir Thomas's Tory running-mate Griffenbottom, who "had been very generous with his purse, and was beloved," therefore, in the borough. Though he has spent "a treasure" in Percycross, Griffenbottom has been satisfied to do so (I, 236–7): "Did he not owe all his position in the world, all his friends, to the fact that he was to be seen on the staircases of Cabinet Ministers, and that he was called 'honourable friend' by the sons of dukes, — did he not owe it all to the borough of Percycross?" He has poured money into Percycross to maintain himself in Parliament — but (like Browborough in *Phineas Redux*, another and later version of Sir Henry Edwards) Griffenbottom "never complained. He [knew] what . . . he wanted, and what . . . he must pay for it. He had paid for it, and had got it, and was . . . contented" (I, 304). He is not such a fool as to think he can have it for nothing. Like Sir Henry Edwards,

Griffenbottom as an M.P. "rarely spoke, and when he did no one listened
to him. He was anxious for no political measures. He was a favourite with
no section of a party." But he does his job as a party hack, and for this, as
we have seen, he is satisfied to be rewarded by rubbing "his shoulders
against the shoulders of great men, and occasionally [standing] upon their
staircases." Also like Browborough, he finds "that accursed system of
petitioning . . . un-English, ungentlemanlike, and unpatriotic" (I, 304—5).
Stand up and fight, and if you're licked take it like a man: this is his
philosophy. Being, like Sir Henry Edwards and his running-mate at
Beverley, an employer of labor, Griffenbottom at Percycross is the
beneficiary of "a complete understanding . . . between . . . employers and
employed . . . the Percycross artizan [voted] as his master voted." Sir
Thomas Underwood is told by the Tory agent Trigger: "if ere a man of
[Griffenbottom's] didn't vote as he bade 'em, he wouldn't keep 'em, not a
day" (I, 238 and 242; in one of his election speeches, remember, Trollope
looked forward to the time when this sort of intimidation could no longer
be possible).

In his initial interview with Trigger, Sir Thomas had inquired if
Griffenbottom and he himself could run an honest campaign in Percycross;
he is assured that their hands will remain clean. The Tory agent simply lies,
feeling that Sir Thomas is "interfering in things beyond his province." Sir
Thomas says he will not bribe; the Conservatives, desperate for a strong
candidate, take him on anyway, believing that he is simply mouthing
platitudes. But whenever he is asked by a voter what he plans to do for the
man's own particular trade if he gets in, Sir Thomas, being honest, replies
that he can do nothing, and attempts to lecture on the virtues of electoral
purity. This does not endear him to the town's Conservative voters. Chief
among these is old Mr Pile, for whom the glory of England is eclipsed and
besmirched by the new passion for purity. A descendant of Grimes the
publican in *Can You Forgive Her?*, Pile is of that type of "citizen,"
mentioned in the *Autobiography*, which finds "politican cleanliness . . .
odious." He feels that a poor man should be paid for his vote by a rich
man; this is simple justice. The very "idea of purity of election at
Percycross . . . [made] him feel . . . sick. It was an idea which he hated
with his whole heart. There was to him something absolutely mean and
ignoble in the idea of a man coming forward to represent a borough in
Parliament without paying the regular fees" (I, 243—4). The candidate
should pay his way like a gentleman; the voter should be paid for his vote.
The system is simple and traditional. Pile, "almost weeping," finds the new
hypocrisy unintelligible; any "talk about purity . . . was a thing abominable to him . . . that a stranger should come to the borough and want the
seat without paying for it was to him so distasteful" that, in his sickness,
he actually tells Sir Thomas to go home (I, 244). "Why should a poor man
lose his day's wages for the sake of making you a Parliament man?" he
asks him; "What have you done for [us]?" Sir Thomas soon enough is

"ashamed" of and "disgusted" by the mercenary attitude of these people. Like Trollope at Beverley, he finds himself "out of his element" and "among people with whom he had no sympathies . . . He felt . . . that he [was] unfitted for [canvassing] by the [bookish] life which he had led for the last few years" (I, 248). Like Trollope too he comes to resent the interference of canvassing with his own amusements and pleasures, and almost begins to hope that he will be "lucky enough to be rejected."

Pile, Trigger, Griffenbottom and company may be outrageous symbols of the old politics, but, as is usual in the political novels Trollope wrote from 1869 on, the Liberals offer no alternative. Moggs (of whom more later) is induced by the Liberals to run as a Radical not because his views are respected (they are barely known) but rather because he happens to have a well-heeled father to pay his election expenses. Like Sir Thomas, he begins the campaign with high ideals and the best of intentions – also hating bribery and having such an inflated reverence for the theoretical independence of the voter that, comically enough, he will not even canvass. He lectures against so much as drinking a glass of beer at election time without paying for it. He dreams of becoming a Cobden or a Bright, a beloved representative of working men and a spokesman for their ideas. But they have no ideas; and he is only a cat's paw designed to give the other candidates a harder time of it (as Trollope himself, so he said, was brought to Beverley to inconvenience Sir Henry Edwards). Yet for a while Moggs entertains the pleasing illusion that he is wanted for himself. Westmacott, his Liberal running-mate, is thoroughly corrupt.

As the campaign heats up, Trigger is more and more appalled by the tactics of Sir Thomas and Moggs; their lectures on purity are bad enough, but in delivering them to the voters themselves they demonstrate a stupidity beyond belief. Trigger tries to muzzle Sir Thomas by reminding him pointedly that "In electioneering . . . it's mostly the same as in other matters. Nothing's to be had for nothing" (I, 300). Sir Thomas, like Trollope at Beverley, says what he pleases to whom he pleases – and detests the intimacy with agents and supporters of his campaign forced upon him in the present circumstances. Griffenbottom – like Browborough, and Edwards himself, "a heavy hale man" (I, 303) – does not particularly enjoy canvassing, either, but over the years he has become expert at it, and we are treated by Trollope to an over-the-shoulder view of one such outing. Listening to the voters is a waste of the candidate's time; conversation is unprofitable. Griffenbottom goes from house to house asking plainly for votes, refusing to be drawn into discussion, avoiding the question of "purity" altogether, and covering as much physical ground as possible every hour. Those who say they are unable to make up their minds are noted down in Trigger's book for particularly generous bribes later.

The last of Percycross in the novel's first volume is a conversation between those two old Tories, Pile and Trigger. Seeing that two of the four candidates continue to denounce bribery and proclaim their allegiance to purity, Pile makes a speech to his old friend. Purity, he says again, makes him "sick"; like Archdeacon Grantly in *The Last Chronicle of Barset* (in a different context, to be sure), Pile views adherents of purity and pick-pockets as "about the same. When I'm among 'em I buttons up my breeches-pockets." And he goes on to proclaim his values in one of the most bitterly ironic passages Trollope ever wrote: "the country soon won't be fit for a man to live in . . . folks wants what they wants without paying for it. I hate Purity, I do. I hate the very smell of it. It stinks . . . nothing ain't to be as it used to be. Nobody is to trust no one. There ain't to be nothing warm, nor friendly, nor comfortable any more . . . Why isn't a poor man, as can't hardly live, to have his [money] . . . for voting for a stranger?" (I, 314–5). And Pile weeps for his lost borough and the advent of purity.

His tears, however, are premature; the old game is not yet extinct at Percycross, as the election itself makes clear. The personal popularity of the candidates has nothing to do with voting habits; the "old ways of manipulation" carry the day. As Moggs "would give them no beer, and they had always been accustomed to their three half-crowns a head in consideration for the day's work" (II, 1), the prospects of the Radical candidate look bleak. The borough's new householder voters – armed with the franchise for the first time – do, however, provide a particular quandary for the veteran organizers. Can they be trusted to vote properly after being paid? Might some of them wait to vote until the last moment, throwing the result in doubt and thus increasing the price of their votes? Surveying these problems, Trigger declares in disgust that "things had got into so vile a form" since the recent Reform Bill that elections were no longer so comfortably predictable as they used to be.

The "Griffenbottomites" and the "Underwooders" remain at odds, Sir Thomas lecturing on purity to the end. Pile continues to suffer terribly: "He loved bribery in his very heart . . . It was the old-fashioned privilege of a poor man to receive some small consideration for his vote in Percycross, and Mr. Pile could not endure to think that the poor man should be robbed of his little comforts" (II, 4). Sir Thomas, meanwhile, has seen his desire to sit in Parliament again die out amidst the "misery" of Percycross and his hatred of his Tory colleagues, by whom he is constantly "snubbed and contradicted." When he makes a valedictory protest against bribery he is accused by Griffenbottom of conspiring to "foul his own nest."

The final speeches are mostly inaudible to everyone because the crowd, like that at Beverley on the last night, is so rowdy and loud. As Sir Thomas speaks once again against bribery, someone throws a rock at him which breaks his arm. Moggs alone is listened to and cheered. He tops the poll when a show of hands is called for – which leads him naively to assume that he will be elected the next day. He has reckoned without the power of money. As at Beverley, election day itself at Percycross provides results which directly contradict the more informal ones of the previous evening. The voters put up their hands for the Liberals; but they open their pocketbooks for the Conservatives, and the latter carry the day — the "real" day, as Trollope calls it. All illusions are finally dispelled on this day. It is, appropriately, "a foul, rainy, muddy, sloppy" day, "without a glimmer of sun," a day suggesting in its "atmosphere" that "nothing is worth anything" (II, 11). The Griffenbottomites consider throwing Sir Thomas over and making a deal to elect their man and Westmacott; but the plan is abandoned when Griffenbottom reminds them that a little extra money spent could easily bring in both Conservatives. The Liberal candidates take an early lead in the poll, as at Beverley; as the poll nears its conclusion, however, it is clear that Griffenbottom will be at the top of it and Moggs at the bottom. In the battle between Underwood and Westmacott for the second seat "things were done in the desperation of the moment" by the party agents "as to which it might be . . . difficult to give an account, should any subsequent account be required." There is no Watergate raid, but the Liberals watch the Tories closely. The Conservative agent at Percycross, like his real-life counterpart at Beverley, sits in a little room near the polling-place and pays "fifteen shillings a head" for votes. The two Tories are returned, Sir Thomas little suspecting how thoroughly his doctrine of purity has been subverted by his followers.

As at Beverley, there is a petition. In a chapter entitled "Horseleeches" (XXXIX), Trollope recounts the requests the beleaguered Sir Thomas receives from the voters of Percycross after the election and before the petition — attempts by them to sell their good-will for the purposes of the forthcoming investigation, during which many of them will be examined by the commissioners. He is asked to subscribe to churches, schools, funds for the elderly, and to bring in bills immediately for the protection of all of the borough's various industries. Griffenbottom refusing to share these expenses (he has paid all the election bribes), Sir Thomas discovers that if he accedes to them "he must sign cheques to the extent of his whole fortune, during his first session." Trigger presses Sir Thomas to be generous, reminding him that "there was no knowing as yet what might be done about the petition" and that payment of these claims "might be conducive" to its withdrawal; "a little money about the borough" would be a good thing at the moment. But Sir Thomas vows that he will not "ruin" himself "for the sake of a seat in Parliament," and he begins to wish, like Trollope after Beverley, that he "had never heard the name of" the borough. Undecimus Scott in *The Three Clerks* knew well enough that "a man cannot have luxuries without paying for them; and this special luxury of serving one's country in Parliament is one for which a man has so often to pay, without the fruition of the thing paid for, that a successful candidate should never grumble, however much he may have been mulcted" (p. 350). True as these precepts may be, Sir Thomas Underwood and Undecimus Scott are different sorts of men — and Sir

Thomas does "grumble." He confides to his clerk that he went to Percycross determined to keep his hands clean; "When we put our hands into other people's business, they won't come out clean" is the "judicious" reply (II, 123).

Sir Thomas continues to receive requests for patronage from Percycross; his correspondents are given by Trollope such names as Givantake, O'Blather, Cavity, and Peter Piper. At a conference of Percycross Conservatives, Griffenbottom announces that what money was spent during the election was spent primarily for the second seat, and that he does not intend to spend any more. Sir Thomas immediately asks if "votes were bought on my behalf . . . I wish I might be allowed to hear the truth." Everyone grins, wondering how "a man silly enough to ask such a question as that" ever got among them (II, 127–8). Griffenbottom replies: "I've spent my money, and got my article. If others want the article, they must spend theirs." When Sir Thomas says he understands such things as post-office clerkships – which he has been asked by one of the electors to arrange – "are given by merit" and not by influence, everyone in the room "laughed outright." Sir Thomas is then asked for £1,500 to bribe both sides – "for both will have to be paid" if the petition is to be defeated. When he refuses there is another attempt to make a deal so as to allow the seats to be split between the two parties. The Liberals will drop the petition if Sir Thomas will give up his seat to Westmacott. He is asked to resign his seat for the sake of party loyalty, love of the borough, and fear of disfranchisement; his Tory colleagues favor the plan. Sir Thomas, like Trollope at Beverley (before the poll), refuses to resign. He has been through too much; he remembers "that fortnight of labour and infinite vexation in the borough" and what he has already paid for the privilege of standing. His sentiments at this point surely draw their inspiration from the candidacy of the novelist: "He knew that he was being ill-used. From the first moment of his entering Percycross he had felt that the place was not fit for him, that it required a method of canvassing of which he was not only ignorant, but desirous to remain ignorant, – that at Percycross he would only be a catspaw in the hands of other men . . . He had found that there could be no sympathy between himself and any one of those who constituted his own party in the borough" (II, 132). And Sir Thomas reflects that such men as he and Moggs "were unable to open their mouths in such a borough as Percycross without having their teeth picked out of their jaws . . . neither Moggs nor he should have come to Percycross" (II, 132–3). An honest man in an election is like a sheep among wolves. (It is significant that here, for perhaps the first time in his fiction, Trollope, now an initiate, depicts honesty and dishonesty as being pretty much evenly divided between the Liberals and Conservatives – Underwood, a Tory, and Moggs, a Radical, are clean, while Westmacott, a Liberal, and Griffenbottom, a Tory, are not; no longer are the Liberals seen as significantly more detached from chicanery than the Conservatives.) As for giving way to protect the borough from disfranchisement — Sir Thomas's feelings on the matter are uncomplicated: "In his heart he desired that Mr. Griffenbottom might be made to retire into private life, and he knew that it would be well that the borough should be disfranchised" (II, 133; Trollope, remember, was to rejoice in the *Autobiography* that he had had a part in forcing Sir Henry Edwards into retirement and disfranchising Beverley). Sir Thomas tells his "horrid" Conservative colleagues that he will not retire and that he does not care what happens either to Griffenbottom or Percycross. "This comes of bringing a gentleman learned in the law down into the borough," laments Griffenbottom. His final speech to Sir Thomas touches upon the absurdity of thinking one can have a seat in Parliament "without any trouble and without any money." His sentiments in the matter, from all accounts, could easily have been those of Sir Henry Edwards: "I have sat for Percycross for many years, and have spent a treasure, and have worked myself off my legs. I don't know that I care much for anything except for keeping my place in the House. The House is everything to me, — meat and drink; enjoyment and recreation; and . . . I'm not going to lose my seat if I can help it." And Griffenbottom tells Sir Thomas he would have done better to let "others who knew what they were about manage matters for you" (II, 135).

Worse to Sir Thomas's mind than the loss of the £900 he has already paid for his election is the prospect, after lecturing one and all on the evils of bribery, of ignominiously losing his seat on petition. He knows that he alone on the Conservative side "had been just . . . he alone had been truthful, and he alone straightforward!" And yet, whether he resigns, defends the petition, or is unseated (II, 141), "there would be disgrace, and contumely, and hours of the agony of self-reproach in store for him!" Because he has wished to serve his country, Sir Thomas — like Trollope after Beverley — is rewarded with "the agony of self-reproach." He ponders at some length the fruits of honesty in the system he has sought to become part of:

> What excuse had he for placing himself in contact with such filth? Of what childishness had he not been the victim when he allowed himself to dream that he, a pure and scrupulous man, could go among such impurity as he had found at Percycross, and come out, still clean and yet triumphant? Then he thought of . . . [that system to] which Griffenbottoms were thought to be essentially necessary. That there are always many such men in the House he had always known. He had sat there and had seen them . . . But now that he was brought into personal contact with such an one, his very soul was aghast. The Griffenbottoms never do anything in politics. They are men of whom in the lump it may be surmised that they take up this or that side in politics, not from any instructed conviction, not from faith in measures or even in men, nor from adherence either through reason or prejudice to this or that

set of political theories, — but simply because on this side or on that
there is an opening. That gradually they do grow into some shape of
conviction from the moulds in which they are forced to live, must be
believed of them; but these convictions are convictions as to divisions,
convictions as to patronage, convictions as to success, convictions as to
Parliamentary management; but not convictions as to the political
needs of the people (II, 141–2)

There is much of substance here; again we can see how much of Trollope
there is in Sir Thomas Underwood. We perceive Trollope in the guise of
Underwood regretting his contact with the polluted electoral system,
reminding himself once more that one cannot touch pitch and not be
defiled. Again we are told how inimical scruples and purity are to the
system; to be both "clean and yet triumphant" is an impossibility. The
system itself belongs to the Griffenbottoms and Edwardses because it is
chiefly populated by them. Such men are pure opportunists, desiring only
to promote their own welfare; mere partisan animals, they are utterly
impervious to "the political needs of the people." This theme, by no
means anomalous in Trollope's political novels, is expressed here with that
peculiar sort of immediacy which suggests close personal involvement.
Sir Thomas's long reverie comes at last to an end:

> In former days he had told himself that a pudding cannot be made
> without suet or dough, and that Griffenbottoms were necessary if only
> for the due adherence of the plums . . . but no such apology . . . for the
> Griffenbottoms in the House . . . satisfied him now. This log of a man,
> this lump of suet, this diluting quantity of most impure water . . . this
> politician, whose only real political feeling consisted in a positive love
> of corruption for itself, had . . . used him as a puppet, and had
> compelled him to do dirty work. Oh, — that he should have been so lost
> to his own self-respect as to have allowed himself to be dragged through
> the dirt of Percycross! (II, 142)

One imagines the disillusioned Trollope making some such declaration to
himself when shaking off the dust of Beverley and returning to his usual
pursuits. It is significant that Sir Thomas, who bears so many resemblances
to the novelist, in his post-lapsarian phase can no longer find excuses for
such political mediocrity and corruption as he had willingly encountered
in earlier stages of his political career. Also noteworthy here is the fact
that Underwood-Trollope, groping for unflattering epithets to apply to
Griffenbottom-Edwards, finally hits upon one — "this *politician*"! —
which a few years earlier would not have seemed particularly unflattering
to the novelist without a pejorative modifier of some sort.
Sir Thomas determines neither to bribe away a petition nor to resign his
seat; he simply stands his ground. The petition follows as a matter of

course. Sir Thomas has been advised by one and all to treat it with contempt; on the contrary, he looks forward to giving evidence on the matter, as Trollope did. Griffenbottom has been hinting to everyone, in an attempt to save himself, that "any unfair practices which ... prevailed during the ... election ... had all been adopted on behalf of Sir Thomas, and in conformity with Sir Thomas's views" (II, 177). There are last-minute appeals nonetheless — "The thing could still be saved if enough money were spent."

The trial itself bears some resemblances to that of Sir Henry Edwards in 1870 (Trollope, remember, was still writing the novel in that year). On the question of undue influence used to obtain votes — the judges find that of course "there had ... been plenty. It was not likely that masters paying thousands a year in wages were going to let their men vote against themselves. But this influence was so much a matter of course that it could not be proved to the injury of the sitting members" (II, 182). However, it is clear that "there had been treating of the most pernicious and corrupt description ... That votes had been bought during the day of the election there was no doubt on earth" (II, 182–3). The man who actually handed over money to at least a hundred electors on behalf of the Conservative cause — one Glump — is nowhere to be found during the trial; Trigger has put him out of view. But treating can be proved without him. Trigger's attitude on the matter seems to represent popular feeling in the borough:

> The idea of conducting an election at Percycross without beer seemed to be absurd ... any interference with so ancient a practice was not only un-English, but unjust also ... It was beyond the power of Parliament to enforce any law so abominable and unnatural ... Though there had been a great deal of beer, no attempt [could] be made to prove that votes has been influenced by treating. There had been beer on both sides, and [Percycrossians] hoped sincerely that there might always be beer on both sides as long as Percycross was a borough.
>
> (II, 184)

Percycrossians in this respect resemble their brethren at Tankerville, as we shall see. To Sir Thomas, as to Trollope after Beverley, "It was all dirt from beginning to end ... he [believed] that nothing short of disfranchise-ment would meet the merits of the case."

The employers of labor had sworn themselves blue that the men they dismissed were dismissed because of their work and not because of their politics — this is found to be rank perjury. Treating of beer is proven easily, though Trigger had told the court that "all the beer consumed in Percycross during the election had not, to the best of his belief, affected a vote. The Percycrossians were not men to vote this way or that because of beer! ... It might be so in other boroughs" (II, 186), and so on. The funds for treating are traced to a general Conservative election fund subscribed to by the candidates. Though Glump remains invisible, a score of men testify that on election day they received ten shillings "with instructions to vote for Griffenbottom and Underwood." They declare further that such methods have always obtained during Percycross elections. Others testify they were given a sovereign apiece "with instructions," and they too voted for the Conservative candidates. And so it goes. Glump, it turns out, performed the same task for the Liberals in the preceding election, and for the Conservatives again in the election before that.

Since Glump cannot be absolutely connected with Griffenbottom, Griffenbottom himself, like Sir Henry Edwards, is exonerated. Indeed, as in the Browborough case, "Nobody seemed even to wish to [incriminate Griffenbottom]. The judge ... did not contemplate any result so grave and terrible as that" (II, 191). The counsel at the trial, as well as the judge, "abstained from their prey because he was a member of Parliament"; as in the Browborough trial, there is in this aspect at least a gross miscarriage of justice: "It was notorious ... that Griffenbottom had debased the borough; had so used its venal tendencies as to make that systematic which had before been ... frequent ... but not yet systematized; that he had trained the rising generation of Percycross politicians to believe in political corruption; — and yet he escaped" (II, 192). This is Trollope's final judgment of his Beverley opponent, Sir Henry Edwards.

Using tactics all too familiar to us, Griffenbottom at the trial claims he knew nothing of bribery or other wrongdoing; he assumed all along that his subordinates were behaving properly. He was unacquainted with Glump; perhaps Glump had been acting for Sir Thomas, who seemed as a candidate to be in need of such assistance. And so Griffenbottom — who appears to Sir Thomas "to have the hide of a rhinoceros"[36] in this crisis — escapes. Sir Thomas is also examined. No one in the court really suspects him of corrupt practices — as none of the commissioners at Beverley suspected Trollope of any wrongdoing. Indeed, everybody actually knows the truth, substantiated or not: "Griffenbottom was corrupt, and ... Sir Thomas was not ... The borough was rotten as a six-months-old egg ... Glump had acted under ... Trigger ... Intimidation was the law of the borough ... Beer was used. ... All this was known to everybody," proved or not. And yet "to the last, it was thought by many ... that corruption, acknowledged, transparent, egregious corruption, would prevail even in the presence of a judge. Mr. Trigger believed it to the last" (II, 193—4).

The verdict is "that Percycross was unfit to return representatives to Parliament," though the two Tory candidates are held to be legally innocent; disfranchisement is recommended. This is not quite the end of the "most iniquitous borough," however. Parliament appoints a royal commission to look into electoral practices at Percycross; it ultimately reports "such a tale of continual corruption" that disfranchisement follows as a matter of course, which exactly repeats the fate of Beverley. It is reported also that Griffenbottom has often been guilty of bribery during elections – and yet the commissioners are not hard upon Griffenbottom personally in their report. He has admitted that the borough "had made a poor man of him" but said that he spent money in "continued innocence"; he hoped for pure elections, and gave instructions to his agents to that effect. But he discovered at last "that he was not a sufficient Hercules to cleanse so foul a stable." This is the last we hear of Griffenbottom, who departs from Percycross forever after his unseating still a popular man there, pursued only by Trollope's hope "that the days of the Griffenbottoms are nearly at an end" (II, 274). Sir Thomas, who "had gone down to the borough with the most steadfast purpose to avoid corruption; and had done his best in that direction," is held by the electors to have "betrayed the borough" in the evidence he gives to the commission; and so, in marked contrast to the reception given Griffenbottom, he is "hooted out of the town" (II, 275).

The electors of Percycross, ultimately, are no better than their worst candidate, and in some cases – such as that of Pile, for example – they are worse. Griffenbottom is merely corrupt; the townspeople, capable of choice, have preferred corruption to cleanliness time and again. Griffenbottom could not exist without them. Trollope never placed his hopes for the future with the democracy.

IV

Another issue raised by the political sections of *Ralph the Heir* is that of Trollope's attitude toward the Radicals. There has been some argument about the character of Ontario Moggs. Critics agree that he is well-drawn; they part company, however, over the question of what Trollope thinks of him as a politician – whether he is conceived with affection or irony, whether or not his speeches and his political values are to be taken seriously.

As has been noted, Moggs himself could today be the Labour representative for a place like Percycross without being much of a Radical; in Trollope's time the Labour candidate had not yet captured the power and vogue he enjoys in the twentieth century. Escott, admitting that Moggs is "something of a prig, with a solemnity of manner and pompous pithiness of artificial phrase making him a little absurd," suggested nevertheless that he is of the sort of "idealised Industrials" made fashionable by George Eliot and Mrs Lynn Linton and an early study "of those captains of Northumbrian industry" some of whom were soon to win their way to Westminster and political power.[37] Walpole found him wholly sympathetic – as did Briggs and, as we saw, a galaxy of other critics. Once again perceiving only Trollope's humor, Booth saw Moggs as little more than "a never-failing source of amusement." But no one discusses his political speeches – which are utterly repudiated by Trollope. Moggs is depicted as sincere and honest, yes; but he is also depicted as a fool.[38] Trollope always disliked the Radicals, particularly such doctrinaire, prosperous Radicals as Turnbull-Bright. The only other Radicals we have encountered thus far in the political novels, remember, are George Vavasor and Bott in *Can You Forgive Her?*.

Moggs is not idealized, nor is he simply burlesqued. We are meant to admire him for his honesty, his goals, and the purity of his intentions; and at the same time we are led to see his pomposity and the naivety of his political yearnings and of his conduct as a practicing politician. Since the novelist had little sympathy with the poor, there is in his novels no special pleading for the working classes; on the contrary, they are much satirized, more so than the aristocracy. Trollope saw them as greedy and unprincipled in their own ways as those members of the commercial middle classes who wish to use their professions to enhance their financial and social positions. So why should anyone expect a very moderate Gladstonian Liberal like Trollope to endorse the political sentiments of even such a "well-behaved fire-eater" as Ontario Moggs?[39]

It is necessary, then, to distinguish Moggs the man from Moggs the political philosopher. When apRoberts says that Trollope's "sympathy for liberals . . . is perfectly evident in his portrayal of characters like Ontario Moggs," she fails to perceive that Trollope's "sympathy" envelops Moggs the lover but is withheld from Moggs the "liberal." So many hardened political philosophers occupy the pages of Trollope's political novels that it may seem refreshing at first to find a politician who believes that canvassing for votes, actually asking people to vote for him, is "iniquitous," a "demoralising practice tending to falsehood, intimidation, and corruption." He will campaign from a higher ground: "Let the men of Percycross hear him, question him in public, learn from his spoken words what were his political principles, — and then vote for him if they pleased" (I, 313). The electors of Percycross, however, do not hear, question or learn; they only take. Moggs's rivals filch votes from him right and left; he himself is "too noble for such work as that." Utterly inept as a campaigner, given the nature of the electoral process and the efforts required of anyone who would succeed in it, Moggs, in his ivory tower, at least has the satisfaction of peace of mind. He enjoys, if nothing else, "that supreme delight which a man feels when he thoroughly believes his own doctrine" (I, 316). This, perhaps, was also one of Trollope's only sources of solace after Beverley; he had spoken some words he did not believe, but not many. Like a proper Trollopian political hero, Moggs regards the "honourable prospect of having a seat in the British House of Parliament . . . as the highest dignity that a Briton can enjoy" (I, 317). Hoping to "move the very world," Moggs sees before him "a career such as had graced the lives of the men whom he had most loved and admired, — of men who had dared to be independent, patriotic, and philanthropical, through all the temptations of political life" (II, 10).

This is pleasant and admirable, and of course independence, patriotism, and philanthropy are prime Trollopian political virtues, but it has nothing to do with reality. Sir Thomas, remember, reflects that "such men as he and Moggs were unable to open their mouths in such a borough as Percycross without having their teeth picked out of their jaws"; and he concludes that "neither Moggs nor he should have come to Percycross" (II, 132—3). One might think, then, that Moggs should be classed along with Sir Thomas under the umbrella of the author's sympathy for plucked chickens. But one has to take into account Moggs's speeches; as soon as he starts speaking the umbrella snaps shut. As a political philosopher he is not only naive — he is, in Trollope's view, altogether wrong-headed; and so what Moggs the candidate says in *Ralph the Heir* is always treated contemptuously. Ontario's notions "about co-operative associations, the rights of labour, and the welfare of the masses," for example, Trollope calls "horrible ideas" (I, 90) even before the candidate opens his mouth. When Moggs begins to talk about "that millennium of political virtue" which could so easily be brought about if only "Purity and the Rights of Labour" would become paramount — and about making the country "the Paradise of the labourer, an Elysium of industry, an Eden of artizans" with "the aid of strikes" (II, 236 and I, 198) — he completely extrudes himself from Trollope's shielding sympathy. The capital letters signal the novelist's irony; his description of Moggs's usual audience does the rest. Among these "there was not . . . one who had reached a higher grade in commerce than that of an artisan working for weekly wages," Trollope specifies; being tremendous snobs, these people like Moggs primarily because he is not, with his rich father, one of them: "Mr. Moggs was especially endeared to them because he was not an artisan working for weekly wages, but . . . a capitalist. . . . The demagogue who is of all demagogues the most popular, is the demagogue who is a demagogue in opposition to his apparent nature" (I, 194—5). The key word here is "apparent," and the obvious example is John Bright, the millionaire Radical whom Trollope so despised. But even on this small scale Moggs earns the opprobrious epithet "demagogue." Throughout he speaks honestly but foolishly, and Trollope refuses to take him seriously as a political thinker. He will not repeat much of what his character says, the novelist tells us at one point, because "the reader might be fatigued were the full flood of Mr. Moggs's oratory to be let loose upon him." But the "oratory" of the "dirty-looking" workers who do take Moggs seriously is reported in full. " 'Hyde Park!' screamed the little wizen man with the gin and water. 'That's the ticket; — and down with them gold railings' " (I, 198—9).

Trollope at least could always recollect with satisfaction, if he desired to do so, that such support was never his.

V

Ralph the Heir is not properly speaking a "political" novel. Neither of its two heroes, the Ralph Newtons, is a politician; and Sir Thomas

Underwood returns to his old profession only briefly in what, in terms of pages, represents a fraction of the novel. The story of Percycross is one of several subplots. Yet Trollope's feelings at this time about politics come through clearly, and sometimes in ways other than those provided by the Percycross election.

Referring to Sir Thomas's political career when a much younger man (he is an ex-Solicitor General and a former Tory M.P.), the novelist announces that one of Sir Thomas's earliest learned lessons was that the "highest legal offices in the country are not to be attained by any amount of professional excellence, unless the candidate shall have added to such excellence the power of supporting a Ministry and a party in the House of Commons" (I, 3–4). Sir Thomas's career came to an end only when he was unable to perform the latter task; and he was replaced by a man "four years his junior in age, whom he despised, and who . . . had obtained his place in Parliament by gross bribery." Sir Thomas's career was also impeded by the fact that "he had made no friend, he had not learned to talk" to his political colleagues (the importance of "little words" and the dangers of diffidence in a political career are themes of the later political novels).

Another recognizable Trollopian motif concerns expressed opinions (e.g., I, 130 and 176) of various Tory country gentlemen that England is going to the dogs because their leader had induced them to support and enact such "Radical" measures as a household suffrage bill (as Disraeli so led the Conservatives in 1867); in *Phineas Redux* and *The Duke's Children* the rank and file mistrust the Disraeli-figures of Daubeny and Sir Timothy Beeswax in much the same way.

More importantly, the lesson of the manifold connections between money, politics, and society is a familiar aspect of the political story. It is stated baldly at the beginning of *Ralph the Heir* (I, 9) that the source of Sir Thomas's unpopularity with his former constituents and the direct cause of their failure to re-elect him to Parliament was their discovery "that he would never dine with the leading townsmen, or call on their wives in London, or assist them in their little private views" – he is thought less "respectable" because he won't do these things. His own views on the issues of course do not enter into the question. A paramount theme of the *Phineas* novels is also articulated here in abbreviated form by the "good" Ralph to Mary Bonner: "Nobody ought to go into the House without money," he tells her; and she understands readily enough that "Parliament was meant for men having estates" (I, 265). Neefit is seen throughout as a sort of commercial politician – depending upon who happens to be in his shop at any particular moment, he could on the same day "be a Radical and a Conservative, devoted to the Church and a scoffer at parsons, animated on behalf of staghounds and a loud censurer of aught in the way of hunting other than the orthodox fox" (I, 53). In the same way Miss Horsball, sister of the proprietor of the Moonbeam, bestows her favors only upon those who ring up a large bill; "Love and commerce with her ran together."

Then there is the Moggs-Neefit marriage. Penetrating beneath his unprepossessing surface, Polly perceives that in love, as in politics, Ontario "had some meaning in him." The two realms are juxtaposed often in their story. Ontario tells Polly several times that he would "sooner have a kiss from her than be Prime Minister" (e.g., II, 200 and 241). Like Lady Laura's for Phineas Finn, Polly's love for Ontario began to kindle, she tells him, when she heard of his intention to run for Parliament. In that case, he replies, running "has done ten times more for me than it would have done, had it simply made me a member of Parliament." He adds that he is happier with Polly "than he could have been had fortune made him a Prime Minister" (II, 246). There is a great deal of this sort of talk in their scenes. Also — like Palliser in *Can You Forgive Her?*, Finn in *Phineas Finn*, and Fawn in *The Eustace Diamonds* — Ontario typically gets his love-making and his politics mixed up with one another. He courts his future wife, for example, "with a treatise on political economy . . . in his pocket, thinking of Polly while he strove to confine his thoughts to the great subject of man's productive industry" (II, 243). Moggs's speaking career at the Cheshire Cheese also owes its inception to an entanglement of motives — his political goals are vague, while his restlessness as an employee of his father is acute and drives him to seek the company of others. Polly's ultimate triumph over her father's opposition to the Moggs alliance is likened, in political and military terms, to the triumph of "an Alexander or a Caesar"; in the same way Sir Thomas's daughters, on behalf of Gregory Newton, employ strategy like budding Daubenys and Beeswaxes. "She who can manoeuvre on . . . a field without displaying her manoeuvres is indeed a general!" Trollope comments here. Moggs's victory over *his* refractory parent stems in part from Moggs Senior's admiration of his son's pluck in love and politics, which he sees as the same things: "A young man ought to be allowed to attend trades' unions, or any other meetings, if he will marry a girl with twenty thousand pounds" (II, 239). Typically, the old man perceives Ontario's desire to sit in the House of Commons as a boon to his business; the pride he expresses when he thinks such a possibility may become a reality is much less paternal than commercial: "To have . . . a member of the firm in Parliament would [be] . . . glorious" (e.g., I, 252 and II, 237). Moggs Senior is a bookmaker.

Finally, among the familiar echoes one hears in *Ralph the Heir* are those of Jane Austen. We know that Trollope was reading and commenting upon *Emma* as he was creating his own version of an independent woman in *Can You Forgive Her?*. In 1869–70 he was still laboring under her influence, apparently. The relationship between the Underwood sisters and the "bad" Ralph bears some similarities to that of the Dashwood sisters and Willoughby in *Sense and Sensibility* (e.g., *Ralph the Heir*, I, 34 and II, 21–2). The Sir Thomases of both *Ralph the Heir* and *Mansfield Park* have penniless wards whom they lecture on the necessity of making financially advantageous marriages; "How was it possible," Sir Thomas Underwood asks himself, as Sir Thomas Bertram asks himself in connection with Fanny Price and Henry Crawford, "that a girl like Mary [Bonner], who has nothing of her own, should fail to like a lover [Ralph Newton the heir] who had everything to recommend him, — good looks, good character, good temper, and good fortune?" (II, 41). Gregory Newton, like Frank Churchill in *Emma*, travels upon one occasion (II, 169) from his country home to London just to get his hair cut. "Since the writing of Pepys' Diary," says Trollope in *The New Zealander* (the essay on "Society"), "Miss Austen has perhaps gone the nearest towards giving us a true insight into the houses of the people of her day."[40] And thus he drew on her often.

There is a little of everything in *Ralph the Heir* — not a great novel, certainly, but a primary source indispensable to any serious student of Anthony Trollope.

6 Social Politics: *The Eustace Diamonds*

> If only the good were clever,
> And if only the clever were good . . . .
> Elizabeth Wordsworth

> 'How infinitely greater are truth and honesty than any talent, however brilliant!'
> *The Three Clerks*

> 'You should not suppose that words always mean what they seem to mean.'
> *Is He Popenjoy?*

Trollope always maintained that *The Eustace Diamonds* (1871–3)[1], one of his most popular novels, was not one of his best. The novel received considerable attention in the reviews, and reactions were mostly favorable. Exceptions were the *Athenaeum*, only lukewarm in its praise; the *Spectator*, which found Lizzie unbelievable and unsympathetic, the other characters (with the exception of Lord Fawn – a general favorite) loathesome, base, sordid, and unreal, and the novel generally depressing; and the *Nation* (New York), which complained of the novelist's "familiar manneri .us" and "formal slowness." The *Examiner*, and *Harper's Magazine* (New York), both said *The Eustace Diamonds* was Trollope's greatest novel; while *The Times*, calling it one of his best, added that in it Trollope "has done one of the most difficult things in the world – he has made a respectable man [Fawn] interesting." The *Saturday Review* satisfied itself by announcing that "Trollope is himself again" and that Lizzie would live forever.[2]

With the notable exception of Booth, who called Lizzie Eustace "the poor man's Becky Sharp," most of the novel's twentieth-century readers have included *The Eustace Diamonds* among their favorite Trollope volumes. Walpole pronounced it "one of the first comedies in the ranks of the English novel," and Sadleir and others commented on the novel's superior construction.[3] What has not been sufficiently noted is the novel's political content, especially the way in which Trollope weaves politics through the story of Lizzie Eustace and her diamond necklace.

In *Can You Forgive Her?* we do not see much of the political world beyond the aspirations of the unscrupulous George Vasasor. *Phineas Finn* gives us the parliamentary world in much greater detail. Yet while both novels demonstrate how important it is for a rising young politician to have good connections and financial backing, to bend to party discipline and avoid having — or at least expressing — views of his own, the picture of the political process is not nearly so black as in *Ralph the Heir*, *Phineas Redux*, and *The Prime Minister*. The political stage of *Phineas Redux* is dominated by the amoral parliamentary magician Daubeny, who maintains himself and his Tory party in power by virtue of having no principles to fall by. In *The Prime Minister* Plantagenet Palliser, now Duke of Omnium, falls from power because he is too honest to become involved in the social and political insincerities required of a Premier who would stay in office. Here *The Eustace Diamonds*, written just after *Ralph the Heir*, is transitional; it is neither so relatively good-humored as *Phineas Finn* nor so bitterly satirical as the later Palliser novels. Along with *Ralph the Heir*, *The Eustace Diamonds* represents a watershed time in the progression of Trollope's long perspective on Victorian politics and society.

Surely the explanation for this tonal difference is the experience at Beverley. The novelist's confrontation in the flesh with English democracy was, as we have seen, an enlightening experience. Its effect may be seen in the glumly satirical way in which he subsequently describes elections in *Phineas Redux*, *The Way We Live Now*, *The Prime Minister*, and *The Duke's Children*. In these novels the difficulties encountered by impecunious non-professionals such as George Vasasor and Phineas Finn in the earlier novels are multiplied tenfold; the candidates are pictured as having to stump through a pig-sty to sit at Westminster. Trollope's unpleasant time at Beverley resulted in a deeper cynicism and an unequivocal perspective upon political unscrupulousness and adventuring; from *The Eustace Diamonds* on, the Palliser novels begin to articulate a more jaundiced view of the political process. Thus a character like Daubeny, the archfiend of the later Palliser novels, can ultimately be defeated only by his own brand of cynical opportunism. *The Eustace Diamonds*, as fully as *Phineas Finn* though less "political," prepares us to understand such a climate, and in doing so it embodies a political commentary of its own.

II

Although we see Lord Fawn and Frank Greystock in social more often than political contexts, they are undoubtedly the novel's leading men and they are professional politicians. Fawn, a Liberal, is a member of the sitting government with duties in the Colonial Office. Greystock, a barrister, is a member of the vocal Conservative opposition in the House of Commons. Between them they account for the two major marriage interests of the novel's ubiquitous anti-heroine. *The Eustace Diamonds* resembles the other five Palliser novels by virtue of the fact that some of its leading characters are politicians, even if politics is not always the paramount focus.

Lord Fawn's story is perhaps the more entertaining of the two. An Under-Secretary of State and member of the India Board, Fawn is equally timorous as lover and politician. Indeed, like Ontario Moggs and Phineas Finn, he sometimes fails to distinguish between the two roles. Having "suffered a disappointment in love [Violet Effingham] ... he ... consoled himself with bluebooks, and mastered his passion by incessant attendance at the India Board" (p. 23). His characteristic way of making love – like Palliser's as a young husband – is to lecture on "the nature and condition of the British Parliament." He is fond of "submitting his opinion in writing" on matters matrimonial as well as political. And his courtship of Lizzie Eustace finally comes to an end when she "accepts his resignation" from the affair. Indeed, one of the precipitating reasons for the termination of the relationship is his suggestion that Lizzie " 'place the diamonds in neutral hands' – Lord Fawn was often called upon to be neutral in reference to the condition of outlying Indian principalities" (p. 604). His letter to her on the subject reads like "an Act of Parliament." In him, social and political activities merge and become indistinguishable.

A peer without capital, Fawn "must marry money"; this, however, is a difficult undertaking, for he is "pompous, slow, dull, and careful." His political career, unspectacular and unexciting, suddenly becomes more controversial when he is persuaded by the family governess, Lucy Morris, to interest himself in the fate of the Sawab of Mygawb, a subject being debated in the House of Commons. Fawn, who does not understand India or its political problems, submits the government reports on the question to Lucy for her opinion, and would form his own from hers were he allowed by his political superiors to do so. As the debate on the Sawab takes a more partisan turn, Fawn, as a member of the India Board, is accused by Frank Greystock of being an administrator of tyranny. Quite clearly Fawn understands little of what goes on in his office, and nothing beyond it. And yet it is said at one point that "the whole of our vast Indian empire ... [hangs] upon him" (p. 123). This indispensable administrator, however, has a serious problem: "he ... could not think and hear at the same time" (p. 92). Despite his fairly responsible political position, Fawn possesses "no outward index of mind." He is considered by Lizzie Eustace stupid enough to be easily entrapped in marriage – a plan which nearly succeeds through Fawn's social obliviousness and his interest in Lizzie's income (about which he is frequently cross-examined by his mother). Despite Lizzie's amorality and Fawn's comparative honesty, he is not exculpated by Trollope. On the contrary: "the one was as mercenary as the other" (p. 89). Fawn, further, is described by Trollope as being a moral coward – without "strength of character" and "as weak as water"; indeed, in politics, his position notwithstanding, he "almost disgraced

[any] cause by the accidence of his adherence to it" (p. 250). And yet this man is almost a junior Cabinet minister. When, inevitably, he has a falling out with his political adviser, the Tory governess, and she says some hard things to him, Lord Fawn, "like a great child, [went] at once . . . and [told] his mother."

We first encountered Fawn in *Phineas Finn* (II, 38), where he was described as "an unmarried peer of something over thirty years of age, with an unrivalled pair of whiskers, a small estate, and a rising political reputation." In the same novel he was called by Madame Max Goesler an "oaf" and by Lord Baldock "the greatest ass in all London!" (II, 43 and 45; in *Phineas Redux* we see him utterly shattered by a grey raincoat). The final reference to him in *The Eustace Diamonds* is articulated succinctly by Lizzie Eustace: "Lord Fawn is an idiot" (p. 666). So much for the Empire.

Lizzie herself is characterized by Lady Linlithgow as "about as bad as anybody ever was . . . false, dishonest, heartless, cruel, irreligious, ungrateful, mean, ignorant, greedy, and vile!" (p. 308) and by Mrs Hittaway as "a nasty, low, scheming, ill-conducted, dishonest little wretch" (p. 602). Despite the essential truth of these assessments, Lizzie, because she is rich, is considered by her cousin Frank Greystock's relatives and some of his friends a more suitable wife for him than Lucy Morris, who is virtuous but poor (e.g., p. 287). Indeed, Mrs Greystock feels that if her son "would only marry his cousin one might say that the woolsack was won" (p. 319). The path to political glory is not obscure: a public man, as we know, needs a bank account. And so Lizzie is attended throughout much of the novel by the impoverished M.P., who does not let his engagement to Lucy stand in the way of an amorous adventure or two. Fawn, though stupid, nevertheless fears scandal enough to back away from Lizzie before she is able to catch him. No such scruples govern the behavior of Greystock, who is simply dazzled by her beauty and covetous of her wealth. "From the very commencement of his intimacy with her," Trollope reminds us, "he had known that she was a liar" (p. 642). Ultimately Lizzie is revealed as too bad even for Frank's sympathy, and so he returns at last to the forgiving Lucy. But he is in many ways a less appealing character than Fawn, as Trollope's Tories are so often less appealing than his Whigs; and his story, perhaps even more than Fawn's, contributes to the grim commentary on contemporary politics. The government may be dim-witted, but the opposition, in its amorality, is probably worse. Fawn is never sure, until she is finally exposed, whether or not Lizzie is actually a thief, and so he is cautious; Greystock has fewer illusions about her, yet wedges his foot in the door each time she opens it a crack to peek out at him. That is the way to the woolsack.

Greystock had run for Parliament hoping that election would improve his law practice — the sort of motive Trollope so abhorred. Once elected, great glory is predicted for Frank — so long as he "abstains from marrying a poor wife." The great threat, of course, is Lucy. Greystock has no political principles except those of opportunism, and no particular political allies. Such a man must seek a wealthy wife — and so he does, despite his old commitment to Lucy. In love as in politics, principles are encumbrances. Lucy is only "a log round his leg"; were he to honor his commitment to her he must "abandon Parliament altogether" — for to succeed a politician in this world must either be rich, or seem to be. Where political advancement is tied to social *éclat*, the appearance of wealth is essential. We are reminded again and again that although Frank is doing well for himself, "he could hardly continue to prosper unless he married money"; though he is well on his way to becoming a great man, he "cannot become [one] without an income"; and so on. Lizzie has no trouble understanding what is at stake: "what she offered him would be the making of him. With his position, his seat in Parliament, such a country house as Portray Castle, and the income which she would give him, there was nothing that he might not reach!" (p. 690). The qualities of the man mean nothing, his possessions, everything. When Lizzie is found to have behaved too treacherously even for Frank Greystock, he returns to Lucy — thus ruining forever, so we are told, his prospects of becoming Lord Chancellor. Lady Glencora likens his decision to marry Lucy to deliberate and calculated suicide — "To her thinking the two actions were equivalent." Conduct that is morally right is often portrayed by Trollope in the Palliser novels as politically disastrous — and such apparently is the case here. Greystock's fate in the subsequent novels is left obscure, suggesting at the very least that Lucy and the woolsack are indeed incompatible.

Trollope concludes his portrait of Greystock with the assertion that his predicament is only symptomatic of a dilemma many other such men find themselves in. He is no better or worse, the novelist argues, than "the majority of barristers and members of Parliament among whom he consorted" (p. 681). Money, social position, and moral flexibility are what, politically, it takes — and so Greystock's future, beyond any domestic happiness that may await him, is bleak.

Trollope's satire is even more pointed in his account of how the Fawn-Greystock love rivalry and the Eustace diamonds themselves are overtaken by party politics. Is Lady Eustace guilty of theft? Fawn suspects that she is, and retreats from his offer of marriage; Greystock, whatever he may really think, declares that she is not. The issue is debated in society.

It was worthy of remark that [the] Lizzieites were all of them Conservatives. Frank Greystock had probably set the party on foot; — and it was natural that political opponents should believe that a noble young Under-Secretary of State on the Liberal side, — such as Lord Fawn, — had misbehaved himself. When the matter at last became of such importance as to demand leading articles in the newspapers, those

journals which had devoted themselves to upholding the Conservative
politicians of the day were very heavy indeed upon Lord Fawn. The
whole force of the Government, however, was anti-Lizzieite; and as the
controversy advanced, every good Liberal became aware that there was
nothing so wicked, so rapacious, so bold, or so cunning but that Lady
Eustace might have done it, or caused it to be done. . . . It [was] . . . a
matter of faith with all the liberal party that Lady Eustace had had
something to do with stealing her own diamonds. That esprit de corps,
which is the glorious characteristic of English statesmen, had caused the
whole Government to support Lord Fawn. . . . The Attorney and
Solicitor-General were dead against her. . . . But they were members of
a liberal government, and of course anti-Lizzieite. Gentlemen who were
equal to them in learning, who had held offices equally high, were
distinctly of a different opinion . . . And . . . these gentlemen . . . were
Lizzieites and of course Conservatives in politics.

(pp. 423, 487, and 445, passim.)

There are many instances in the Palliser novels in which, political and social
considerations being always so closely related, political associations are
governed by influences essentially non-political, or social relationships are
affected by politics. In *The Vicar of Bullhampton* — written, along with
Ralph the Heir, just before *The Eustace Diamonds* — the high-church
Liberals and the low-church Conservatives square off over the murder
charge against Sam Brattle, and the arguments on each side are made
entirely along "party" lines. There is a similar "division" in *Phineas
Redux*, as we shall see. Here, clearly, independent judgment and objectivity are in abeyance where politics is concerned — even in trivial matters.
Indeed, the importance the Eustace controversy assumes in the political
world is a direct commentary on the absurdity of the other ersatz issues of
the day (such as the Sawab, and the Palliser penny) that have been engaging
the attention of the partisans. Whatever the question, the party line must
be followed and defended — except, perhaps, by those who are beyond
such considerations by reason of wealth or influence.

Such a one is Lady Glencora, wife of the Chancellor of the Exchequer
and future Duchess of Omnium, who causes political shock waves by
bucking the Liberal party line and defending Lady Eustace. Here a
different sort of political comedy is enacted — for Glencora's energetic
apostasy makes clear, among other things, how dependent political
underlings such as Fawn and Mr Bonteen are upon the good-will of their
social and political masters. When Glencora, perversely and irrationally,
takes Lizzie's side, "all the . . . Mr. Bonteens found themselves compelled
to agree with her. She stood too high among her set to be subject to that
obedience which restrained others, — too high, also, for others to resist her
leading . . . When she declared that poor Lady Eustace was a victim, others
were obliged to say so too" (p. 488). Among these "others," inevitably, is

Fawn, who is "more afraid of the leaders of his own party than of any other tribunal upon earth, — or, perhaps, elsewhere" (p. 559). For poor Fawn, Glencora's interference is terrifying. He wishes to tell her to mind her own business, as indeed she should — "But Lady Glencora was the social queen of the party to which he belonged, and Mr. Palliser was Chancellor of the Exchequer, and would some day be Duke of Omnium" (p. 508). In such circumstances settled conviction goes for nothing; and so the whim of one influential woman forces Fawn, no specimen of moral bravery, to adhere to his well-known suit for Lizzie's hand, lest he "give his political enemies an opportunity for calumny" beyond their present means. Fawn is shortly thereafter saved, of course, by the revelation of Lizzie's guilt — but only by that.

To recognize the part politics plays in determining the outcomes of the novel's several love stories is to see how ubiquitous the political theme is in *The Eustace Diamonds* — just as it is in *Can You Forgive Her?* and *Phineas Finn*, in both of which the connections between romantic and political endeavor are kept constantly before us.

Trollope's sardonic light penetrates everywhere. The silly debate in the House of Commons over the position of the Sawab of Mygawb gives him still another opportunity to illuminate his subject. Greystock attacks the government's position on the Sawab; Fawn's chief defends it. "We all know the meaning of such speeches," Trollope remarks. "Had not Frank belonged to the party that was out, and had not resistance to the Sawab's claim come from the party that was in, Frank would not probably have cared much about the prince . . . But what exertion will not a politician make with the view of getting the point of his lance within the joints of his enemies' harness?" (p. 60). Fawn later observes, correctly indeed, that Greystock "chose to attack me because there was an opportunity" — because, that is, the situation offered him a chance to claim "some future reward from his party"; but Lady Fawn, the Under-Secretary's mother, silences the family's indignation by reminding one and all that "everything is considered fair in Parliament" (pp. 60–2, *passim.*).

Again this is no anomaly. The Palliser novels are populated largely by men who consistently ignore their own convictions — if indeed they have any — under the yoke of party discipline, the defiance of which will usually bring down upon them exclusion from place when the party is in power. Unless he is financially independent, the political aspirant, forced to live among men richer than he and dependent on their patronage when in power for his own livelihood, inevitably finds himself in an equivocal, not to say helpless, position. "There is . . . no man who becomes naturally so hard in regard to money," *The Eustace Diamonds* tells us. Thus "A peasant can marry whom he pleases" (p. 101) and retain his political beliefs — but men like Greystock and Fawn, poor men with political aspirations, cannot afford such luxuries. Indeed, "Love is a luxury which none but the rich or the poor can afford," Trollope declares in *The Three*

Clerks (p. 194); "middle-class paupers, who are born with good coats on [their] backs, but empty purses, can have nothing to do with it." The middle classes are subject to temptations unknown to their richer and poorer brethren, and this is largely why they are considered by Trollope unfit for political service. He pounds away at this theme again and again in these novels. We saw how it operates in *Can You Forgive Her?* and *Phineas Finn.* In the latter political opposition becomes, finally, only another form of self-aggrandizement — its object being not the preservation of democracy but rather the exchange of those who are out for those who are in. To be in means solvency, and abuse leads to being in. "Most of the young men rise now by making themselves thoroughly disagreeable," says Lord Brentford in *Phineas Redux* (I, 414); "abuse a Minister every night for half a session, and you may be sure to be in office the other half." Only "make a Minister afraid of you" and "it becomes worth his while to buy you up." Under such conditions the so-called loyal opposition has as its chief goal not the safeguarding of liberty and good government but only the same mediocrity dispensed by other hands — its own. In *The New Zealander* Trollope says: "fear and not love teaches the minister where to look for support . . . the very citadel of the fortress may . . . be stormed, and the Cabinet achieved in one leap by a bitter tongue joined to a bitterer pen . . . All men through the Kingdom are taught to look upon political support as an affair of expediency, and of course all confidence in the leading principles of our leading men is lost."[4] "Giving satisfactory replies to ill-natured questions is . . . the constitutional work of such gentlemen" as sit on the Treasury Bench, Trollope says in *The Three Clerks* (p. 333). These gentlemen "have generally learned how to do so, and earned their present places by asking the selfsame questions themselves, when seated as younger men in other parts of the House." Such men, he concludes in the *Autobiography* (p. 307), get to be "leading" by being willing to "submit themselves to be shaped and fashioned, and to be formed into tools, which are used either for building up or pulling down, and can generally bear to be changed from this box into the other, without . . . the appearance of much personal suffering." The political theme of *The Eustace Diamonds* emphasizes how unappealing are the special attributes necessarily in the possession of the successful politician. He must be able to disregard criticism and eschew a "too thin-skinned sensitiveness"; he must accept the fact that "nobody . . . can be somebody without having to pay for that honour" (p. 290); and he must understand that a public man "has so many things to think of . . . that he could hardly be expected to act at all times with truth and sincerity" (p. 415). He must not, in a word, be subject to attacks of conscience. Indeed, it will be better for him in his chosen profession if he is thoroughly dishonest. For in this profession, as in so many others, nice guys finish last.

Lizzie Eustace is the novel's central character, but by weaving so many others in and out of her story Trollope means us to see that she is only, like Becky Sharp, a product of her time – and not much worse than it is. In a passage near the end of *The Eustace Diamonds*, he explicitly links her immorality with the milieu she adorns and suggests that private peculation and public opportunism are merely symptoms of one another. Is Lizzie any worse than those who court her? The eminent Mr Dove puts it this way: "She has hankered after her bauble, and has told falsehoods in her efforts to keep it. Have you never heard of older persons, and more learned persons, and persons nearer to ourselves, who have done the same?" (p. 651). And there follows an account of political intrigues sweeping the legal profession at this time with regard to "various positions of high honour and emolument, vacant or expected to be vacant." Trollope makes it clear that Mr Dove "was referring to these circumstances when he spoke of baubles and falsehoods" and that Lizzie's crimes are no worse than those committed for political motives. In politics and society both "there existed jealousy, and some statements had been made which were not ... strictly founded on fact" (p. 651). The "hankering after baubles" disease is as rife among embryo Lord Chancellors, Attorneys-General, and Chief Justices as among others. Lizzie Eustace has no monopoly on mendaciousness and greed. She is merely acting out in her own sphere the charade being performed around her by those in more responsible positions. If she is a social politician, they are political Lizzies.

We glimpse Lizzie only briefly in *The Prime Minister*, but we do get a more substantial look at her in *Phineas Redux*, in which we find her unchanged. Still socially visible, Lizzie, we are told there (II, 351), "would still continue to play her game as before, would still scheme, would still lie; and might still, at last, land herself in that Elysium of which she had always been dreaming." There is no reason for Lizzie to change her spots; they blend perfectly with her surroundings.

III

A word must be said about the man Lizzie eventually marries. Emilius, one of Trollope's least appealing and least realized villains, has nevertheless at least one interesting connection with the other Palliser novels. His portrait, brief as it is, suggests indirectly that some of Trollope's hatred of Disraeli had its origin in anti-Semitism.

It would be inappropriate here to anticipate the argument of the next chapter (on *Phineas Redux*) by quoting at length what Trollope says in the *Autobiography* about Disraeli. Briefly, however, Trollope there refers to "the wit of hairdressers" and "the enterprise of mountebanks" in connection with Disraeli's novels and novel-heroes. And he suggests that a Disraeli performance has through it all "a smell of hair-oil, an aspect of buhl, a remembrance of tailors." Emilius is a "greasy" Jew pretending to be a Protestant who marries a rich widow and achieves for a while a certain fashion; is this another swipe at Disraeli? Emilius's greasiness is insisted

upon again and again; there are two references to "hair-oil" in the relevant
section of the *Autobiography*. And Emilius, though not deep, is
glib – which is how Trollope rated Disraeli. Like Emilius of obscure (at
the time) European origins, Disraeli was born a Jew; but his
temperamental father, after a falling out with local Jewish leaders, had his
children baptized into the Protestant faith, an accident which enabled the
young man to pursue a parliamentary career. After years of financial
insecurity and embarrassment, Disraeli married a rich widow. There is no
need to pursue this further; what matter here are the vague anti-Semitism
and the Disraeliesque hints lingering around the person of Emilius, for
these things may help us to understand the violence of the attack on the
Disraeli-figures of Daubeny in *Phineas Redux* and Sir Timothy Beeswax in
The Duke's Children.

Trollope, certainly, was not immune to the resentment of the sixties and
seventies directed against the Jews, who more and more were taking over
some control of the British financial world. Melmotte, the audacious
swindler of *The Way We Live Now*, is pointedly made a Jew (again of
obscure European extraction), and his shady associate Cohenlupe is also a
Jew. Trollope as a young man had been in debt to London moneylenders,
and he undoubtedly had his visions of "Disraeli deceit and Rothschild
rascality." (Indeed, the novels are full of obnoxious and greedy Jews –
most of them moneylenders – from *The Three Clerks* to *Mr Scarborough's Family*.) As we shall see, Lopez, the dishonest stockbroker of
The Prime Minister, vaguely resembles Disraeli too in his Jewishness and
his foreign extraction. This does not mean that either Emilius, Melmotte,
or Lopez is a portrait of Disraeli; but the particular strain of "conjuring"
adventurer in these novels does much to help define Trollope's prejudice.
"People cannot suddenly be made great and good by the wisdom of a
Jew," Trollope wrote in *The New Zealander*, in the essay on "The People
and Their Rulers"[5]; this is an obvious reference to Disraeli, whose chief
political call to arms was the slogan "Dare to be great," but whom
Trollope always associated with things untrustworthy, misleading, and
precarious (let us recall too that contemptuous reference in *The Bertrams*
to "Jew senators"). Madame Max, it is true, is both Jewish and sympathetic;
but then she is neither a politician nor a novelist nor a moneylender nor a
capitalist. Had she been any of these things, Trollope's bigotry – not
virulent, but recognizable – might well have diminished her too.

IV

The political theme in *The Eustace Diamonds* is articulated in one other
way. There is a sub-plot of mock-heroic proportions which details the
vicissitudes of England's embattled Chancellor of the Exchequer. Palliser, a
genuinely heroic figure as Prime Minister in *The Prime Minister* and again
as private citizen in *The Duke's Children*, is seen here, in less flattering
terms, as the victim of an eccentric fixation. The subject is decimal

coinage. Palliser is energetic, patriotic, and honest, but his battle in behalf of currency reform is seen ironically by Trollope as a manifestation of political monomania and absurdity. A House of Commons forced to spend its time debating the penny and the Sawab of Mygawb can hardly be taken seriously, and Trollope refuses so to take it in *The Eustace Diamonds*. Everyone plays his own game in this parliamentary world; actually to be committed to something, no matter how trivial, inevitably invites the ridicule — a defense mechanism — of others. Palliser is committed, but his cause is trivial. Once again the welfare of the citizenry takes a back seat to a hobby-horse of the moment.

Trollope's language, as he recounts the heroic struggle of the Chancellor of the Exchequer, invites us to see the issue of currency reform from a comic perspective — one man's folly and a joke indeed. One wonders, however, who is watching over the economic affairs of the country while Palliser wrestles with his farthings.

> Mr. Palliser . . . was intending to alter the value of the penny. Unless the work should be too much for him, and he should die before he had accomplished the self-imposed task . . . the arithmetic of the whole world would be so simplified that henceforward the name of Palliser would be blessed by all schoolboys, clerks, shopkeepers, and financiers. But the difficulties were so great that Mr. Palliser's hair was already grey from toil, and his shoulders bent. . . . Mr. Bonteen, with two private secretaries from the Treasury . . . were near to madness under the pressure of the five-farthing penny. Mr. Bonteen had remarked . . . that those two extra farthings that could not be made to go into the shilling would put him into his cold grave before the world would know what he had done. . . . On the 13th of February Mr. Palliser made his first great statement in Parliament . . . and pledged himself to do his very best to carry [his] stupendous measure . . . in the present session. The City men who were in the House that night . . . agreed in declaring that the job in hand was too much for any one member or any one session . . . It was . . . probable, many said, that [Mr. Palliser] might kill himself by labour which would be herculean in all but success, and that no financier after him would venture to face the task . . . The halcyon penny, which would make all future pecuniary calculations easy to the meanest British capacity, could never become the law of the land. (pp. 424–5 and 485–6, *passim*.)

The absurdity of Palliser's labors is further underlined by a letter from Lady Glencora to the Duke of Omnium which describes the five-farthing-penny speech made by her husband as having been delivered, in the course of four hours, to a sleeping House: "Plantagenet says nothing about it, but there is a do-or-die manner with him which is quite tragical." Having thoroughly bored everyone (even Gresham, the Liberal Prime Minister,

slept through the address) with his new penny, Palliser's next challenge is
to find a suitable name for it: "Should he stick by the farthing; or should
he call it a fifthing, a quint, or a semi-tenth? 'There's the "Fortnightly
Review" comes out but once a month,' he said to . . . Mr. Bonteen, 'and
I'm told that it does very well' " (p. 495). Gresham suggests that the new
coin be called a "squint." Glencora fears that it might be named after her
husband: "I shouldn't like to hear that . . . two lollypops were to cost
three Palls."

In the novel's last chapter, Palliser is still at his herculean labor:

> his mind was . . . deep in quints and semitenths. His great measure was
> even now in committee. His hundred and second clause had been
> carried, with only nine divisions against him of any consequence. Seven
> of the most material clauses had . . . been postponed, and the great
> bone of contention as to the two superfluous farthings still remained
> before him . . . He now had with him a whole bevy of secretaries,
> private secretaries, chief clerks, and accountants. . . . Mr. Bonteen was
> there . . . repeatedly declaring to all his friends that England would
> achieve the glories of decimal coinage by his blood and over his grave.
> (pp. 721–2).

Despite this civil-service mobilization in behalf of the penny, the great
measure never gets passed; Palliser is called to the House of Lords before
he can complete his work. When he is Prime Minister some years later,
Palliser — by then Duke of Omnium — looks back to these days of struggle
in the House of Commons as the happiest of his life, the one period of his
career when he was constantly occupied. In the later Palliser novels he is a
more complicated figure – and a more admirable one too as we see,
especially in *The Prime Minister*, the kinds of degrading political pressure
he is strong enough to resist. Here, however, he has not yet grown into full
statesmanship, serving as he does as another reminder that the world of
politics is populated not only by the shallow and the unscrupulous but
also, sometimes, by the obsessed.

(Trollope uses decimal coinage outside the political novels too to
denote obsession and monomania. In *The Three Clerks*, p. 2, he asks
ironically: "Are we not disgraced by the twelve pennies in our shilling, by
the four farthings in our penny?" And he tells of an under-secretary, a
very worthy man, who "has already grown pale beneath the weight of this
question. But he has sworn . . . with all the heroism of a Nelson, that he
will either do or die. He will destroy the shilling or the shilling will destroy
him.")

For the first time in these novels there is no particular standard of
excellence, no "good" politician, by which to measure the badness of the
bad. Palliser is too eccentric to play that role here; Monk is invisible; there
is no one else. Trollope's first "political" novel after Beverley, *The Eustace*

Diamonds is indicative of many things to come. Palliser, of course, is soon cured of his odd solipsism; but the world around him from this point onwards continues to darken.

7 Parliament Regained: *Phineas Redux*

| Lady Basildon. | I don't know how the unfortunate men in the House stand these long debates. |
| Lord Goring. | By never listening. |

Wilde, *An Ideal Husband* (1895)

'The House of Commons would have been just the right thing for him. He would have worked on committees and grown practical.'

Disraeli, *Tancred* (1847)

'What does it matter who sits in Parliament?'

Phineas Redux

The tact of women excels the skill of men.

The Claverings

"Parliamentary debates, Cabinet meetings, murders, trials, political in-fighting, private obsession, and public tyranny" are some of the things *Phineas Redux* is about. It is, especially in its first volume, undoubtedly the most political of Trollope's political novels — even more so than *Phineas Finn*, of which it is a continuation. From its opening sentence — "The circumstances of the general election of 18— will be well remembered by all those who take an interest in the political matters of the country" — until its conclusion, *Phineas Redux* is more singlemindedly concerned with politics, politics both real and imaginary, than any other novel Trollope wrote.[1]

Phineas Redux was written in 1870–1 (as *Ralph the Heir* was appearing). Trollope put it away in a strongbox (along with *An Eye for An Eye*) during a trip to Australia; and indeed he did not find "room" for it amidst his heavy publishing schedule until 1873, when it appeared in the pages of the *Graphic*. It was published in two volumes in 1874. *Phineas Redux* is often casually dated 1874, but of course this is incorrect. Though appearing four years after *Phineas Finn* it takes up the story of Phineas after a lapse of only two years (*Phineas Redux*, I, 5); for some unintelligible reason there has been a good deal of confusion over these relatively simple facts.[2]

Trollope says little about *Phineas Redux* in the *Autobiography*. He tells us there that the editor of the *Graphic* took an instant dislike to the novel's title: he assured "me that the public would take Redux for the gentleman's surname," Trollope says, "and was dissatisfied with me when I replied that I had no objection to them doing so" (p. 296). He also tells us here that *Phineas Redux* "enjoyed the same popularity as the former part, and among the same class of readers" (p. 275). Indeed, *Phineas Redux* was somewhat more popular – with the reviewers at least – than *Phineas Finn*. Nor need Trollope have worried about continuity, for *Phineas Redux* reads well even without *Phineas Finn* in mind.

By far the longest and most enthusiastic notice of the novel was published by the *Spectator*. Using such adjectives as "delightful" and "marvellous," the reviewer found *Phineas Redux* eminently more entertaining than its predecessor – the story is better, though Phineas himself remains a feeble and unendearing hero. If it has a weakness, the reviewer said, it is in the many dull political speeches and the emphasis on patronage as part of the political story. The parliamentary sketches, however, are generally excellent. The reviewer reserved special praise for Chaffanbrass ("pure genius"), Lady Glencora, Kennedy, Lady Laura, and Madame Max (he hopes there will be more of the latter "in some future story"; Trollope obliged in *The Duke's Children*). While expressing the feeling that novels should not deal so fully with Disestablishment and the poisoning of foxes, and objecting to the lack of plot and the dearth of characters on the sunny side of 30, the *Saturday Review* nevertheless praised the characterizations of *Phineas Redux*, taking special delight in Lady Glencora ("a general favourite") and giving Trollope high marks in general for his delineation of the upper classes. The *Athenaeum*, as usual, was more lukewarm – concluding, somewhat languidly, that if in *Phineas Redux* "there is little to stimulate the imagination, or suggest topics for reflection . . . there is abundance of the light kind of intellectual gratification which may be drawn from seeing life-like portraits of commonplace people." *Phineas Redux* did call forth one venomous review, published in America. It appeared in the *Nation*, which used the occasion for a long assessment of Trollope's works and charged, incredibly enough, that the novelist had forever failed to draw one memorable character or amuse his audience. Having voiced his prejudice, the reviewer went on to assert that Trollope's picture of politics is deliberately pessimistic in order to render his political world comprehensible to readers, who will always respond to the simple-minded suggestion that "every man is actuated by motives of the basest self-interest." Yet Trollope somehow is also guilty of "easy optimism." The reviewer concluded with this provocative – though absurdly inaccurate – summary of the novelist's views:

> [He] sees in English society, as it now exists, the best of all possible arrangements in the best of all possible worlds . . . That it is a good

thing to be well off, that it is well to act honorably, that it is about the best of all things to be a well-to-do English gentleman, and that it is quite the best of all things to be at once a well-to-do English gentleman and a master of fox-hounds, are the sort of maxims which Mr. Trollope . . . presents for the acceptance of his admirers. The creed he holds is in fact that the life of an English gentleman is the most satisfactory kind of life which any man can spend.[3]

We know well enough what Trollope thought of idle men of means and talent who took no part in the governing of their country, who resisted work, who had no idea of patriotism or personal usefulness. The reviewer cannot have known much about Plantagenet Palliser (a well-to-do English gentleman who has no use for foxes or hounds) – nor can he have read *Can You Forgive Her?* very carefully, if at all.

In our century only a few critics have taken any particular notice of *Phineas Redux*. Walpole found the political content of the novel vague and disliked the intrusion of the murder trial, which he says Trollope threw in when he got tired of telling the political story. Booth thought *Phineas Redux* the most politically convincing of the series; the behind-closed-doors scenes seem real, he said, and the debates do appear to catch the tone of the House of Commons: nevertheless, "the political atmosphere remains hazy." The trial and Chaffanbrass are "magnificent," Kennedy is again well-done, Phineas "is a very human hero," and the hunting scenes are diverting; and he concluded, rather unenthusiastically, that these things (not, of course, the political content) "are enough to save a story that has a few soft spots and more than a few *longueurs*." For Polhemus, *Phineas Redux* extends the growing skepticism of *The Eustace Diamonds* to a darker pessimism; there is nothing in it, at least, to match the optimism of Monk in *Phineas Finn*. For apRoberts, *Phineas Redux* inhabits a large canvas upon which the nature of man as political animal is explored and the impact of partisan loyalties upon personal integrity is scrutinized – thus making it of crucial importance in the series.[4]

II

If *Phineas Finn* recounts actual political events of the mid-1860s culminating in the Second Reform Bill of 1866–7, *Phineas Redux*, written in 1870–1, demonstrably focuses upon the period 1868–71, the crisis years for the long debate in Parliament over Irish Church Disestablishment. Drawing on real events of the three years, the novel is actually set in only one of them – 1868 (as usual we must work to find this out; Trollope will not help us). This is the year in which the ailing Derby gave up leadership of the Conservatives to Disraeli, until then Tory leader in the Commons. Disraeli's brief first ministry ran from February to December 1868; and his eleven months as Prime Minister provide the chief political context for Trollope's story. Throughout the first volume of the novel the Tories are in power; the Prime Minister is now Mr Daubeny, who when last seen was leader of the Tory opposition in the Commons. Just as Derby retired to make way for Disraeli in 1868, so Trollope in *Phineas Redux* has Lord de Terrier, the old Conservative chief, retire from the scene and hand over the party leadership to Daubeny. We have had some weighty evidence in preceding novels as to the identity of Daubeny and some of his colleagues, but now Trollope drops any last vestiges of camouflage and we see Disraeli as Daubeny involved in issues and situations patently adapted from historical ones.

The historical facts, much simplified, come to this. Disraeli, as leader of the party that traditionally defended the Church Establishment, opposed Irish Disestablishment because he thought – wrongly – that it would be unpopular with the voters of the late sixties. On 4 April 1868, Gladstone rallied the Liberals to beat Disraeli by 60 votes in the Commons on the issue. Despite this humiliating setback, the Prime Minister refused to resign and resolved instead "to stick it out." He threatened to dissolve the House and call new elections, which no one wanted – there had been a hard-fought general election the previous year. Gladstone and the Liberals were furious; "a series of accusations and counter-accusations followed Disraeli's announcement." The ministry staggered on until November, when Disraeli – unable to command majorities, yet still refusing to resign – dissolved the House instead. He lost heavily in the general election, fought largely on the issue of Irish Disestablishment. Still Disraeli refused to resign. The ministry went on. In December Gladstone carried another resolution to disestablish. Then, and only then, Disraeli resigned. During the next few years the successful new Liberal-Radical alliance led by Gladstone carried through many of the great reforms which helped to bring England into the modern world. Gladstone's first great operation – performed in 1869 – was the disestablishment and partial disendowment of the Protestant Episcopal Church in Ireland. Gladstone himself wrote the bill – and "an ecclesiastical revolution, the largest since Tudor times," was thus proposed and enacted by one of the most devoted of England's churchmen.[5]

All of this should make perfect sense to the reader of *Phineas Redux* once it is understood that Trollope, while for the most part copying contemporary history into his novel, switched the parties around in one respect – a characteristic tactic. The idea bruited about in *Phineas Redux* that the dismemberment of the Church if carried out at all should be carried out by reverent, loving hands instead of rough ones is a reference not to the Tories but to the pro-clerical Gladstone's Disestablishment bill. The theme is one Trollope touches upon in several places. If "ancient usages" have to go, he says in his essay in *The New Zealander* on the House of Lords, then let them wear themselves out slowly and gradually – and "let no sacrilegious [*sic*] hand touch . . . them."[6] In *The Prime Minister* (I, 378–9) he says: "A Conservative in Parliament is . . .

obliged to promote a great many things which he does not really approve
. . . But as [he helps to make] the glorious institutions of the country . . .
perish, one after the other . . . [he continues to believe] it is better that
they should receive the coup de grâce tenderly from loving hands than be
roughly throttled by Radicals."

Disraeli, though leader of the Conservatives, was in fact "the least
suited by temperament and background of all contemporary statesmen to
deal with the problem [of the Church] . . . It is probably hopeless to
extract a coherent body of doctrine from his observations on religion,"
Blake has observed. "He believed different things at different times."
Trollope wrote articles in 1865 and 1866 attacking the Irish Church
Establishment and, as we have seen, proclaimed his animosity to it in his
1868 election address at Beverley, in which he staunchly supported
Gladstone's bill.[7] In *Phineas Redux* he depicts the Conservatives, led by
Disraeli and faced by likely political defeat, adopting the cry of Disestablishment to sow dissent among opponents and maintain themselves in
power — a marvellous satirical stroke. The assault on the Church, in
contravention of all the principles of the Conservative party, is made
simply to retain political power. The Liberals, who as a party believe in
Disestablishment, can foil Daubeny only by voting against the bill. As in
the battle over Tenant-Right in *Phineas Finn*, almost everyone here has to
vote against what he apparently believes in order to support his party and
his own position. That a Tory Prime Minister should bring in a bill for
Disestablishment "exaggerates only a *little* the audacity of Disraeli, and the
ironic fact that the most radical reforms of the nineteenth century were
effected under Conservative administrations." Even more to the
point is the fact that, at Beverley, Trollope in one of his speeches declared
that if the Tories came to power, their leader, on the issue of Irish
Disestablishment, would probably "go over the most beautiful conjuring
trick. It will be hocus pocus, square round, fly away, come again, up and
down, turn a somersault, come down on his feet, and present you with a
most beautiful bill to disestablish and disendow the Irish Church, and very
likely to abolish Protestantism generally."[8] That Trollope at Beverley also
accused Disraeli of being capable of disestablishing the Anglican Church as
a means of "dishing the Whigs," stealing their clothes, and the rest of it,
should be taken into account in any assessment of *Phineas Redux*, whose
political plot centers around the Disestablishment question and the various
paths of expediency by which it is approached by contemporary politicians. Certainly Trollope's language in the passage quoted above ("conjuring trick," "hocus pocus") helps us further to see who Daubeny really
is. The *Spectator*'s reviewer understood what Trollope was up to:

> Mr. Daubeny's speech to his constituents, giving the first hint of . . .
> disestablishment . . . and the way he brings his reluctant Cabinet . . .
> round to his view of the case, may be a little exaggerated, but if it be, it

is an exaggeration of Mr. Disraeli's political tactique painted with so much humour as to be the better for the exaggeration. Nor is Mr. Gresham, – of course mainly intended for Mr. Gladstone, – less skilfully painted in the chief scene of the Parliamentary struggle.

This gets us back to personalities. No one at the time questioned the identities of Daubeny and Gresham, even though Trollope, for form's sake and satire's, reversed their positions on Disestablishment (Gresham does not actually oppose Disestablishment; he simply opposes Daubeny). Disraeli "must have chuckled as he recognized the likeness. It is impossible . . . that he should not have done so, in spite of the long line of critics who have denied that Trollope drew any of these figures from life."[9]

If Disraeli "afflicted Trollope with the fascination of horror," that "horror" – in part a residue of the novelist's anti-Semitism – is expressed primarily in Daubeny, and Sir Timothy Beeswax in *The Duke's Children*. We would do well now to look closely at what Trollope says in the *Autobiography* (written mostly in 1875–6, when Disraeli was again Prime Minister and at the height of his influence) of Disraeli's novels: "An audacious conjurer has generally been his hero, – some youth who, by wonderful cleverness, can obtain success by every intrigue that comes to his hand. Through it all there is a feeling of stage properties, a smell of hair-oil, an aspect of buhl, a remembrance of tailors, and that pricking of the conscience which must be the general accompaniment of paste diamonds" (p. 223; he goes on here to talk about "the wit of hairdressers" and "the enterprise of mountebanks"). This is an important passage, especially in its opening words. Trollope consistently saw the real Disraeli as one of his own novel-heroes; if Disraeli's heroes are "audacious conjurers," Trollope's political villains are often Disraelian heroes.

There is nothing very ambivalent in the picture of Disraeli the politician that has come down to us – a picture worth examining again briefly in connection with the Daubeny of *Phineas Redux*. Greville likened Disraeli to "a perfect will-o'-the-wisp, flitting about from one opinion to another." The third Marquis of Salisbury called him a "mere political gamester," declared in the House of Commons that "he would as soon predict which way a weathercock would be pointing as prophesy Disraeli's attitude toward the great questions" of the day, and on the Church question said in an article in the *Quarterly Review* in 1869 that if "drastic legislation upon Ireland or upon the Established Church" were required, the present Tory leadership would shamelessly provide it.[10] In the midst of Disraeli's tumultuous first ministry (May 1868), Salisbury (then Viscount Cranborne) wrote in a private letter that the Prime Minister was "an adventurer . . . without principles and honesty . . . Mr. Disraeli's great talent and singular power of intrigue make him practically master of the movements of his party . . . For the time being at least [he] is the Conservative Party. . . . And in an age of singularly reckless statesmen he is I think beyond

question the one who is least restrained by fear or scruple." The man who
wrote this was himself a Tory, and an influential one; these are no mere
partisan sentiments. The picture of Disraeli as a reckless adventurer who
unscrupulously uses his partisan talents for "intrigue" and his knowledge
of parliamentary forms to achieve his ends was current in both parties for
some years. Long after Disraeli's death Gladstone remarked of him that he
"never wanted courage but his daring [was] elastic and capable of any
extension with the servility of the times ... In [the] past ... the Tory
party had principles by which it would and did stand for bad and for good.
All this Dizzy destroyed."[11] (These, of course, *are* partisan sentiments.)

Blake's splendid biography paints Disraeli, unabashedly opportunistic in
politics, as a man whose only consistent purpose was to obtain — and once
obtained, to keep — power. A politician of genius, a superb improviser, a
parliamentarian of unrivalled skill, an extraordinary manipulator of men
for whom the only "great thing was to go on winning" and "dish the
Whigs" — especially Gladstone — Disraeli "thought of politics as a matter of
'management' and 'influence' in the old-fashioned sense." A professional
"always in his place, always alert, a master of the rules of procedure and
debate," for Disraeli "politics avowedly was 'the great game,' " and a game
he loved; for him "it was the very breath of life." Disraeli excelled "in the
art of presentation. He was an impresario and an actor manager ... He
knew how much depends upon impression, style, colour ... [and that]
form can at times be more important than content."[12] His understanding
of the contemporary mood contributed largely to his political successes
over the years.

> That which is mystic in its aims; that which is occult in its mode of
> action, that which is brilliant to the eye; that which is seen vividly for a
> moment, and then is seen no more; that which is hidden and unhidden;
> that which is specious, and yet interesting, palpable in its seeming, and
> yet professing to be more than palpable in its results; this, howsoever its
> form may change, or however we may define it or describe it, is the sort
> of thing — the only sort — which yet comes home to the mass of men.

Bagehot wrote this in the sixties.[13]

Disraeli was never ashamed of being a partisan. In a letter to Sir John
Pakington (a Lord of the Admiralty) written in December 1858 he lectures
on the political facts of life: "It is not becoming in any Minister to decry
party who has risen by party. We should always remember that if we were
not partisans we should not be Ministers." When, as Chancellor of the
Exchequer in Derby's first ministry (February-December 1852), Disraeli
found himself embroiled in the difficult task of preparing a budget for
presentation to a critical Commons (rejection of this budget subsequently
caused the fall of the ministry), he received the following advice from his

chief – quoting in part from Frederick the Great: "Put a good face on it
... and we shall pull through ... L'audace – l'audace – toujours
l'audace." (*Toujours l'audace* might have been Disraeli's professional
motto; Trollope's favorite adjective for Daubeny – "audacious" –
acknowledges this.) Blake has described Disraeli's feelings on going out of
power after such a brief first taste of it in 1852:

> The prospect of defeat was most unwelcome. He thoroughly enjoyed
> the prestige, the deference, the sense of power which come to the
> holder of high office. He never even paid lip service to the convention
> that ministers accept their tasks reluctantly out of a sense of public
> duty and lay them down with a sigh of relief, returning gladly once
> again to country pursuits and the perusal of the classics. Politics had ...
> become his passion. He was prepared to try almost any expedient in
> order to prolong his uncertain tenure.[14]

The last sentence bears particular relevance to the portrait of Daubeny in
Phineas Redux.

When in opposition, as he was throughout most of his political life,
Disraeli would subordinate everything to the defeat of the government; so
tenacious was he that it was considered by some next to impossible to
govern if he were in opposition. When in office such a man naturally
would use any means to stay there. A master at "concealing behind a
façade of rigid adherence to immutable principle those deviations or
reversals which events and responsibility so often force upon governments," Disraeli in later life always claimed that he had never yielded to circumstances but had been actuated throughout by consistent policy – when
in fact "he lived from crisis to crisis, improvising, guessing, responding to the
mood of the moment."[15] A case in point was his prolonged flirtation with
the Radicals in his constant battle against the stronger Liberals, a flirtation
we glimpsed in *Phineas Finn* in connection with the story of the Second
Reform Bill. Viewing parliamentary matters almost always "in the light of
political expediency," Disraeli, as Salisbury said in 1868, was often "under
a temptation to Radical measures ... because he can only remain in power
by [courting] stragglers from his adversary's army ... [thus he] can
forward Radical changes in a way that no other Minister could do –
because he alone can silence and paralyze the forces of Conservatism." A
Disestablishment measure carried out by such a statesman is thus not so
far-fetched as it may seem; no wonder the Tories never quite accepted or
fully trusted their dashing leader. Some insight into the Conservative
malaise may be gleaned from part of a letter written by Henry Drummond
in 1859 to Sir William Joliffe – both prominent Tories. Drummond says:
"Lord Derby and Mr. Disraeli have led the Conservative Party to adopt
every measure which they opposed as Radical ten years ago. They have
made that party the tool of their ambition & sacrificed everybody's private

& public interest . . . I do not think it creditable to the intelligence or to the honour of the country gentlemen of England to vote black to be white or white to be black at their bidding."[16]

This last may remind us of passages already quoted from *The New Zealander* and *Phineas Finn*. Now of course Trollope had no access to the private papers cited here, nor did he have an insider's perspective on the Conservative party during this period. But his account undoubtedly reflects much that was true or seemed at the time to be true. Like Disraeli, Daubeny in *Phineas Redux* is not entirely trusted by his party; like Disraeli he is thought by the Tory "country gentlemen" to have sold them out on Disestablishment; like Disraeli he is an adroit parliamentarian with few scruples; like Disraeli he is capable of revising established policy whenever necessary for immediate political gain; like Disraeli he is ravenous for power and will not give it up easily, even after being badly beaten on an important matter of confidence in the Commons; and like Disraeli, Daubeny is considered by his fellow Conservatives "mysterious, unintelligible, dangerous, and given to feats of conjuring" (*Phineas Redux*, I, 56).

Which brings us back to Trollope's "audacious conjurer." In *Phineas Redux* Daubeny always seems to have at hand or in his head "some sharp trick of political conjuring, some 'hocus-pocus presto' sleight of hand, by which he might be able to retain power, let the elections go as they would" (I, 4). Throughout the novel he is characterized as a slick, unscrupulous magician. We know how Trollope hated sham, and that he often saw the Tories, particularly under Disraeli's leadership, as less sincere than the Liberals (no beacon-lights of virtue either). The reader of *Phineas Redux*, armed with such information, need not puzzle for long over Trollope's Mr Daubeny. We are reintroduced to him just after he has "been disgracefully out-voted in the House of Commons on various subjects" and it is "known to be impossible that he should find himself supported by a majority after a fresh election" (I, 3–4). His refusal to resign the Premiership is deemed by his political opponents to be "factious, dishonest, and unconstitutional"; and indeed even some of his followers regard him "with an enmity that was almost ferocious." But they, and indeed his opponents too, are kept at bay by his Disraelian threat to dissolve the House rather than resign if he is beaten again; and since "it was very well understood that there were Liberal [as well as Tory] members in the House who would prefer . . . the success of Mr. Daubeny to a speedy reappearance before their constituents" (I, 361–2), he is able to extort some support for a while longer. Like Disraeli in the autumn of 1868, however, Daubeny is eventually forced to dissolve and seek a new majority. At the eleventh hour he makes an election speech suggesting in the most subtle way that the Conservatives may soon be called upon to bring in a bill for Disestablishment of the English Church. The speech is ambiguous, eloquent, musical, and orotund; in it Daubeny explains to his constituents "that he had discovered a new, or rather hitherto unknown, Conservative element in the character of his countrymen, which he could best utilise by changing everything in the Constitution ... He manipulated his words with such grace, was so profound, so broad and so exalted, was so brilliant in mingling a deep philosophy with the ordinary politics of the day," that the voters can only admire him without understanding anything he has said (I, 48). Here is a witty description of various elements of a Disraeli speech. The Liberals are outraged (I, 49–50): "Could it really be the case that the man intended to perform so audacious a trick of legerdemain as this for the preservation of his power, and ... have the power to carry it through?" They remember, some of them, that Conservatives were in power during Catholic Emancipation, and when the Corn Laws were repealed, and when household suffrage was adopted. Mr Bonteen is "disposed to think that the trick was beyond the conjuring power even of Mr. Daubeny." But Lord Cantrip knows that Daubeny will lead his party wherever he likes, and Mr Gresham himself understands that in the past his opponent "has ... been very audacious, and ... succeeded." The Tories, meanwhile, are equally restless: "Wonderful feats of conjuring they had endured, understanding nothing of the manner in which they were performed ... but this feat of conjuring they would not endure"; and: "the audacity displayed [by Mr Daubeny was] more wonderful than" ever before (I, 56). Having woven through these references to Daubeny some of the very words he was soon to use in the *Autobiography* in connection with Disraeli's novel-heroes, Trollope goes on to describe the dissatisfaction of the Conservatives with their leader in terms that even more unmistakably suggest Disraeli:

[Mr Daubeny] was now the recognised parliamentary leader of the party to which the Church ... was essentially dear. He had achieved his place by skill, rather than principle, – by the conviction on men's minds that he was necessary rather than that he was fit. But still, there he was; and, though he had alarmed many [of] ... those who followed him by his eccentric and dangerous mode of carrying on the battle; though no Conservative regarded him as safe; yet on this question of the Church it had been believed that he was sound ... His utterances had been confusing, mysterious, and perhaps purposely unintelligible. ... He spoke those words without consulting a single friend, or ... a single supporter. And he knew what he was doing. (I, 56–7)

This is a revealing passage. Like Sir Timothy Beeswax in *The Duke's Children*, Daubeny is not really trusted by his Tory colleagues – to whom, however, he is "necessary" (rather than "fit") as parliamentary leader. Daubeny is considered eccentric, dangerous, and mysterious; like Disraeli he can be "purposely unintelligible" when he likes. Like Disraeli he operates unilaterally as a leader, expecting his party simply to follow. And like Disraeli he is considered "sound" on questions touching the Church, though often incomprehensible. (Perhaps because of his own ambiguous religious origins, origins which as a public man he did not want examined, Disraeli all his life – despite his confusion and inconsistency in religious matters – was considered very "sound" indeed on Church questions; in public he repressed his religious romanticism and supported the dowdy Evangelical party.) In *Phineas Redux* (I, 55) Daubeny is described by some of his chagrined fellow Conservatives as "the bulwark of the Church, to whom they had trusted. . . . the hero who had been so sound and so firm respecting the Irish Establishment, when evil counsels had been allowed to prevail" (Disraeli, as we have seen, opposed Irish Disestablishment; he saw Irish Protestantism as a great low-church barrier to the influence of Catholicism in Ireland and supported it against Gladstone's assault in 1868).

In a climactic speech, Daubeny lectures the House of Commons to show it that "audacity in Reform was the very backbone of Conservatism"; later he becomes "more than usually vague" (I, 359–60). For months he stays in office by alluding to a Disestablishment bill in the works without actually bringing one forward (Disraeli, remember, stayed in power after April 1868 simply by refusing to resign after Gladstone carried the first of his Disestablishment resolutions). Finally he can hold out no longer; a bill is brought in. Before the crucial vote on the issue – which he is sure to lose – it is thought by some that the outnumbered Daubeny nevertheless must have "some scheme in his head by which to confute . . . his enemies. There was nothing to which the audacity of the man was not equal." Indeed, it is feared that even if he is badly beaten again "he would simply resolve not to vacate his place, – thus defying the majority of the House and all the ministerial traditions of the country" (I, 371–2). Should this happen Parliament and the country must rise up and pull him down.

> But then, – such was the temper of the man, – it was thought that [even] these horrors would not deter him. There would be a blaze and a confusion in which timid men would doubt whether the constitution would be burned to tinder or only illuminated; but that blaze and that confusion would be dear to Mr. Daubeny if he could stand as the centre figure, – the great pyrotechnist who did it all, red from head to foot with the glare. (I, 372)

Here Trollope reveals Daubeny's egoism – as well as his own propensity to see Disraeli as a Satanic emanation ("red from head to foot"; Bonteen calls Daubeny "the Arch-enemy"), a manifestation of the "horror" which so fascinated him. His picture of Disraeli also expresses the man's mysteriousness, that element in him which causes others constantly to speculate on his motives. Disraeli, like a good novel-hero (Faulkner's Flem Snopes comes to mind), was feared, hated, never quite understood, his origins and his goals puzzled over, his doings enigmatic.

Trollope puts the finishing touches on his portrait at the end of the first volume of *Phineas Redux*. Here he describes Daubeny's hatred of Gresham (which is reciprocated) upon the latter's triumph — "he did not forget . . . nor did he forgive" — and the manner in which, after being beaten by a majority of 72 (despite the support of Turnbull and his Radical contingent — again Daubeny and Turnbull are allies here), he finally announces his resignation: "his audacity equalled his insolence . . . He . . . spoke only of his own doings, — of his own efforts to save the country." The rest of the speech is "profound, prophetic, and unintelligible"; it apparently intimates that "had the nation . . . consented to take him . . . health might not only have been re-established, but a new juvenescence absolutely created" (I, 424 and 426). Afterwards Monk describes Daubeny as "a political Cagliostro," and adds: "Now a conjuror is . . . a very pleasant fellow to have among us, if we know that he is a conjuror; — but a conjuror who is believed to do his tricks without sleight of hand is a dangerous man. It is essential that such a one should be found out and known to be a conjuror" (I, 428). In *The Duke's Children* it is Sir Timothy's failure to do his conjuring without detection that leads to his downfall. But, like Sir Timothy and Disraeli too, even in defeat Daubeny is said by opponents as well as allies to be necessary to his party. "They can't do without him. They haven't got anybody else," remarks Mr. Ratler. The first volume of *Phineas Redux* comes to an end with Bonteen's picture of Daubeny's probable doings at home on the tumultuous night of his defeat and resignation: "Had some gruel and went to bed. . . . They say these scenes in the House never disturb him" (I, 428).

"A man who entertains in his mind any political doctrine, except as a means of improving the condition of his fellows, I regard as a political intriguer, a charlatan, and a conjurer," Trollope declares, remember, in his *Autobiography*. Can there be any doubt about who is the real political villain of these novels?

III

The manner in which Daubeny is beaten on Disestablishment brings no particular credit to the political process. For if Daubeny is all opportunism, so is his opposition. Trollope's picture of partisan politics here, leaving little to choose between the parties, is a shade darker than before.

The leader of the opposition, Gresham, is a further extension of Gladstone. We actually see little of him in *Phineas Redux*; like Gladstone himself, Gresham is much less interesting than his diabolical antagonist. We see enough, however, to carry on the identification from *Phineas Finn*. Said to be "rather misty but very profound" on the subject of the Church, Gresham, "the present leader of the opposition and late Premier" (Gladstone in 1868 was leader of the opposition but not as yet a "late Premier" — when Trollope was writing the novel Gladstone actually was

Premier, however), is "generally respected by his party for earnestness and sincerity" though regarded with no particular affection by his "individual adherents in the House" (I, 355). This is an accurate picture of Gladstone's position in the Liberal party throughout much of his political life; he was respected rather than liked. Monk describes Gresham at one point in words that could be applied easily only to Gladstone among nineteenth-century English political leaders:

> 'with a finer intellect than either [Brock or Mildmay — that is, Palmerston or Russell], and a sense of patriotism quite as keen, he has a self-consciousness which makes him sore at every point. He knows the frailty of his temper, and yet cannot control it. And he does not understand men as did these others. Every word from an enemy is a wound to him. Every slight from a friend is a dagger in his side. But . . . self-accusations make the cross on which he is really crucified.' (II, 409)

Despite Trollope's early admiration for Gladstone and his preference until later in life for the Liberals over the Tories, Gresham's party in *Phineas Redux* is no more scrupulous or patriotic than Daubeny's. The few good politicians in the book are, again, Liberals; but in the darkening landscape of the Palliser novels there is less and less to choose between the two parties. In *The Eustace Diamonds* Trollope had created a picture of a society almost totally corrupt; he was soon to repeat the performance even more savagely in *The Way We Live Now*. His increasing pessimism — accelerated, as we have seen, by his experiences at Beverley — ultimately got the better of his earlier relative exuberance and led to what Polhemus has called the "quiet desperation of greater comprehension." The "glory and glamor" of politics thus disappear in these novels in the wake of growing disillusionment. Losing at Beverley gave Trollope a knowledge of the rough and tumble of political life he could never have approached as a private citizen; if *Phineas Redux* is more "political" than preceding novels in the series it is because of "the itch and sting of Beverley." Undoubtedly there is a "sting" in *Phineas Redux* one did not feel in *Phineas Finn*. Several critics have commented on the increased bitterness of *Phineas Redux* when compared with its predecessors. In his post-lapsarian (after Beverley) phase, as the two parties came to seem to Trollope more and more indistinguishable, his partisan prejudices — and thus his old political enthusiasms as well — were increasingly blunted. He had never thought, after all, that the Liberals or anybody else had a monopoly on political virtue. In *The New Zealander* he suggests that parliamentary jockeying on all sides is motivated primarily by self-interest, the result a meaningless jumble of words whose only significance is the extent to which it betrays the insincerity of the speaker. The government maintains itself in office by lying about its competence; the opposition's only motive is to substitute itself for the government. And any man unwilling to indulge in these partisan games faces a bleak political future. "Rapidly, willingly, and with courtesy" must men like Daubeny and Gresham when in office answer questions by the opposition in the House of Commons —

> but, alas, not with truth. That were too much for a man so questioned. The vessel of the state must be kept on its track. If every little leak be owned and confessed to, all hands would be required at the pump. The opponents of the minister oppose him on the high principle that nothing imperfect should be admitted in the state's governance. That much must be imperfect the minister knows well, and his adversaries as well . . . but the minister is lost if he owns to the smallest peccadillo that human infallibility can commit. It is the trade of the opponent to attack . . . it is the trade of the minister to defend; and the world looks on believing [neither] of them.

The political situation within the House of Commons being delicately balanced throughout much of the fifties and sixties, often the reform bills brought in by ministers during these years "were less triumphant vindications of principle than useful political maneuvers which had the special advantage of being very unlikely to come off," Briggs has reminded us.[17] Trollope was aware of this, and it contributed to his growing conviction that one politician was pretty much like another. Thus in *Phineas Redux*, in the midst of the Disestablishment controversy, there is this significant authorial aside:

> When some small measure of reform has thoroughly recommended itself to the country . . . then the question arises whether its details shall be arranged by the political party which calls itself Liberal, — or by that which is termed Conservative. The men are so near to each other in all their convictions and theories of life that nothing is left to them but personal competition for the doing of the thing that is to be done. (I, 358–9)

Trollope has ceased to see any significant doctrinal differences between the parties; what characterizes them now in his estimation is "personal competition" for place. Men have replaced measures as political objectives.

The party that drives "the Arch-enemy" from power typically does so, then, only because it wants power itself, and is better organized and represented in Parliament for the purpose of obtaining and keeping it. The first time Daubeny is beaten on a vote in the House it is on an issue (decimal coinage!) "allowed by the whole party to be as good as anything else for the purpose." The Liberals, hungering for office, resolve that the Tories must go not because their policies are abhorrent but rather "on the score of general incompetence. They were to be made to go, because they

could not command majorities" (I, 3—4). Giving little thought to
questions of policy, the Liberals simply obey the old herd instinct in this
crisis: "not to be loyal ... to their leader ... was ... treachery."
Gresham, who in *Phineas Redux* is at times almost indistinguishable from
his opponents in his methods as a partisan, describes himself to Lord
Cantrip as "the last man in the world to contest the possibility, or even the
expediency, of changes in political opinion." The two Liberal leaders
converse:

> 'If [Disestablishment] would come softer from [Daubeny's] hands
> than from ours, with less of a feeling of injury to those who dearly love
> the Church, should we not be glad that he should undertake the task?'
> 'Then you will not oppose him?'
> 'Ah; — there is much to be considered before we can say that.
> Though he may not be bound by his friends, we may be bound by ours.
> And then, though I can hint to you at a certain condition of mind ... I
> cannot say that I should act upon it as an established conviction.'
>
> (I, 53—5, *passim*.)

Gresham here admits that political leaders cannot act at will according to
their own "established convictions," if they have any; there are always
one's "friends" to consider, a euphemistic reference to party loyalties and
the appetite of the rank and file for office.

Some years earlier, in *The Three Clerks* (p. 355), Trollope had written
that "Every great man, who gains a great end by dishonest means, does
more to deteriorate his country and lower the standards of his countrymen
than legions of vulgar thieves, or nameless unaspiring rogues"; and to this
he added: "Expediency is the dangerous wind by which so many of us
have wrecked our little boats." Trollope had Peel in mind when he wrote
this. But his progressive disillusionment in the seventies with the
Liberals — his ostentatious disinclination to share in "the Gladstonian
enthusiasm" — was largely due to his feeling that their methods and values
had become so like those of the despised Conservatives as to render them
at last undeserving of support. Presumably he also saw Gladstone as a
former "great man" deteriorating with age. Such a picture of Gladstone
would have been less and less anomalous as the years went by.[18]

Daubeny continues to perform his conjuring feats upon the sensibilities
of his fellow Tories. "If there must be a bill, would you rather that it
should be modelled by us who love the Church, or by those who hate it?"
he asks a reluctant colleague (I, 58), thus posing the old question; and he
suggests in his usual prophetic way that in this unexpected but "divine"
contingency "a mighty hand had been stretched out to take away the
remaining incubus of superstition, priestcraft, and bigotry under which
England had ... been labouring" (I, 81). His own party "to a man, —
without a single exception, — were ... opposed to the [Disestablishment]

measure. . . . But such private opinions . . . need not, and probably would not, guide the body." So much for "private opinions" in a political crisis. Indeed, says Trollope, "the Conservatives had learned to acknowledge the folly of clinging to their own convictions. . . . Every man . . . took the measure up. . . . [They could stay in power only] by carrying measures which they themselves believed to be ruinous . . . But a party cannot afford to hide its face in its toga. A party must be practical . . . Though the country were ruined, the party must be supported" (I, 82–3).[19] Convictions are "folly"; a party must be "practical." Given a choice between (1) supporting the party, staying in power, and ruining the country, or (2) abandoning the party, going out of office, and saving the country, the Tories obviously lean to the former course. Nowhere in Trollope's novels is the selfishness of party politics described with so little subtlety and such bare contempt.

The response of the Liberals is predictable. Just as the Tories plan to vote in opposition to a lifelong conviction, so the Liberals, who almost to a man favor Disestablishment, move to oppose it now. Ratler, a representative of the Liberal rank and file, "was for opposing Mr. Daubeny with all their force, without touching the merits of the case . . . even though they themselves should disestablish everything before the Session were over" (I, 85). A hack of the most common variety, Ratler, as it turns out, articulates what becomes official Liberal policy. The Liberals will oppose the measure because it has taken them by surprise and because the other side has been in power long enough. If Daubeny is cynical, Gresham and his followers are utterly hypocritical. The Liberal line is developed as follows (I, 134–6). Daubeny has carried his people along to oppose "their own cherished convictions." In continuing to "keep his clutch fastened on power," however, he is flouting the Constitution, his own party, and the entire country. The "real majority" is being kept "out in the cold" by this wicked scheme. Church reform is "the legitimate property of the Liberals" and they are not yet ready to propose a program. No one would wish to see the Church attacked for purposes as partisan as Daubeny's or by such "rude hands. With grave and slow and sober earnestness, with loving touches and soft caressing manipulation let the beautiful old Church be laid to its rest." Thus the Liberal line (the language here suggests Gladstone). Comically, Ratler thinks the Tories are "mean" to support Daubeny "simply with a view to power and patronage, without any regard to their own consistency or to the welfare of the country" — also an apt characterization, obviously, of the Liberals' support of Gresham on the question. The Tories are actually less mean than simply "led." While they feel it is their duty to defend the Church, "so also was it a duty to support [the] party. And each one could see his way to the one duty, whereas the other was vague, and too probably ultimately impossible." It would be too much to ask of political parties, Trollope says here, "to throw off the incubus of their conqueror's authority." As for the Tories: "Of whom did the party consist? – Of honest, chivalrous, and enthusiastic men, but mainly of men who were idle, and unable to take upon their own shoulders the responsibility of real work. Their leaders had been selected from the outside, – clever, eager, pushing men, but of late had been hardly selected from among themselves" (I, 137). Trollope makes some interesting distinctions here. Tories are unlikely to be capable of "real work"; his political hard-workers are always Liberals, and we know the exalted place a capacity for work occupies in the Trollopian system. And the Tory leaders are not venerable party men but, so to speak, professional outside organizers; the novelist extends this discussion later in *Phineas Redux* when he pauses to survey the pedigree of the Liberal chiefs, as we saw in Chapter 1.

Trollope goes on here to describe the state of mind of the Liberals. The leaders feel that "Whatever may be the merits of the Bill, it must be regarded as an unconstitutional effort to retain power in the hands of the minority" (I, 213). There is no opposition on the Liberal side to Disestablishment itself; indeed, there is no opposition on principle to anything. Erle speaks for many Liberals when he says that he is "bound to follow" Gresham no matter what he does: "If he proposes Church Reform . . . or anything else, I shall support him." Political men, he reminds Phineas, must always follow their leaders; this is the only way in which "things can be made to work. Were it not [so] . . . any government in this country would be impossible" (I, 214). The majority view, he goes on to argue, being a member of a majority, should always prevail – even if it is wrong. And he adds: "A man so burthened with scruples as to be unable to act [with his party] should keep himself aloof from public life." Scruples are a burden; it is better to be in than to be right. Independent members of Parliament are deemed "insane men who never ought to have seats in the House" (I, 215). But who is insane? Phineas is made to understand that he is utterly lost to his party if he does not reverse the position he took in his last election address and oppose Disestablishment. The question arises – won't his constituents rise up against him "after manifest apostasy to his pledge"? Ratler solves the problem easily: "They won't remember." Phineas is to give in this time.

As the issue nears resolution in the House, partisan loyalties are exacerbated. Having decided to throw over their convictions in an orgy of "duty to the party" – which translates into fear for their places in the government – the Tories stick hysterically to their leader. "Mr. Gresham was accused of a degrading lust for power. No other feeling," they say, "could prompt him to oppose with a factious acrimony never before exhibited in that House . . . a measure which he himself would only be too willing to carry were he allowed the privilege of passing over to the other side of the House for the purpose" (I, 296). Gresham's views on the matter are given in detail when he speaks his mind to a meeting of Liberal colleagues at Palliser's house. Here is part of Trollope's long account:

Mr. Gresham . . . repeated his reasons for opposing Mr. Daubeny's Bill; and declared that even while doing so he would . . . pledge himself to bring in a [similar] Bill . . . should he ever again find himself in power. And . . . he would do this solely with the view of showing how strong was his opinion that such a measure should not be left in the hands of the Conservative party. It was doubted whether such a political proposition had ever before been made in England. It was a simple avowal that on this occasion men were to be regarded and not measures. No doubt such is the case, and ever has been the case, with the majority of active politicians. The double pleasure of pulling down an opponent and of raising oneself, is the charm of a politician's life . . . Men and not measures are . . . the very life of politics. But then it is not the fashion to say so in public places . . . [The worst aspect of Mr. Daubeny's Bill, Mr. Gresham concluded], consisted in this, – that it was to be passed, if passed at all, by the aid of men who would sin against their consciences by each vote they gave in its favour. What but treachery could be expected from an army in which every officer, and every private, was called upon to fight against his convictions? . . . It was agreed that the House of Commons should be called upon to reject the Church Bill simply because it was proposed from that side of the House on which the minority was sitting. (I, 333–4)

Being the majority party in the Commons, the Liberals feel it is time they got something for it. They do not dislike the bill – they look forward to bringing in a similar one of their own. But the "double pleasure" of pulling their opponents down and raising themselves up cannot be renounced. There is bitter comedy too in the spectacle of the Liberals attempting to save the Tories from sinning against their consciences by voting against their convictions.

The final sections of the novel's first volume are devoted to the debate, the last-minute maneuvering, and the final vote on Disestablishment. Daubeny speaks first. "As long as he would abuse Mr. Gresham, men could listen with pleasure"; let him get on to the philosophical merits of the case, however, and attention wanders. Understanding this old principle well enough, Daubeny devotes most of his speech to the nature of his opposition. Never till now, he says, equalling Gresham for sheer hypocrisy, "had he known a statesman proclaim his intention of depending upon faction, and upon faction alone, for the result which he desired to achieve." Let Gresham speak to the issues; otherwise his conduct must be considered "unconstitutional, revolutionary, and tyrannical" (I, 361). Gresham's response is less rhetorical but no less partisan. His opponents could not claim that their measure "was brought forward in consonance with [their] own long-cherished political conviction" and he would save them from voting against it; as for the leader of the Conservatives, "he would appeal to his followers opposite to say whether the right honourable gentleman was possessed of any one strong political conviction" (I, 364); and he concludes by lecturing the House on the virutes of majority rule. The prognosis afterwards is for a triumph of partisanship – a vote along strict party lines and thus a Conservative defeat. Gresham "would be backed by a majority of votes, and it might have been very doubtful whether such would have been the case had he attempted to throw out the Bill on its merits . . . There were very few Liberals in the House who were not anxious to declare by their votes that they had no confidence in Mr. Daubeny" (I, 366–7). A party has to be practical; the "merits" of a bill are less important than the size of its sponsoring and opposing parties. So Gresham makes the issue a matter of "confidence" rather than substance. The Tories cry "Faction!" and throw back at him his declaration that members "were to regard men and not measures." On the night of the vote, with more verbal fireworks expected, the House is full: "the prospect of an explanation, – or otherwise of a fight, – between two leading politicians will fill the House; and any allusion to our Eastern Empire will certainly empty it," Trollope remarks (I, 389). "And so the row was renewed and prolonged, and the gentlemen assembled, members and strangers together, passed a pleasant evening." The most abusive and insolent personal assaults are of course the most successful.

In the aftermath of Daubeny's resounding defeat come the post-mortems. The Tories "had accepted the treachery and bowed their heads beneath it, by means of their votes," feeling after all that the other side was also bowing "to the dominion of . . . unscrupulous and greedy faction"; while on the Liberal benches "there was undoubtedly something of a rabid desire for immediate triumph, which almost deserved that epithet of greedy." Gresham's decision "to attack his opponent simply on the ground of his being the leader only of a minority in the House of Commons" arose, ironically, from "A sound political instinct"; "from among Mr. Gresham's friends there had arisen a noise which sounded very like a clamour for place" (I, 421 and 424). So in his summing up Trollope is as hard on the Liberals as on the Conservatives. Gresham opposed Daubeny on Disestablishment even though "he himself [was] in favour of [it] . . . He had opposed Mr. Daubeny's Bill without any reference to its merits, – solely on the ground that such a measure should not be accepted from such a quarter" (II, 355). There is little to choose between them. Lady Glencora knows well enough "what Cabinet Ministers are. If they could get a majority" by doing something, that is what they will do, she says. Low asks her if she is speaking of one party or the other. "There isn't twopence to choose between them in that respect" is the tart reply (II, 154).

A postscript must be added here. By rights, chronologically speaking, it should have come earlier, but it takes its significance only from the foregoing account of the division over Disestablishment. On 9 November

1868, in a speech to the Working Men's Liberal Association of Beverley, Trollope addressed himself specifically to the question of majority rule in the Commons. At the time, remember, Disraeli was Prime Minister without a majority — having maintained himself in power for the past seven months, after being beaten for the first time on Irish Disestablishment, by the methods Trollope describes so vividly in *Phineas Redux*. "The electors are aware," said the novelist in his speech, "that the government of this country is at the present time in the hands of the Tories, and I think I need scarcely explain to them the manner in which that Government has been kept in power." Contemptuously characterizing Disraeli as the "Tory maid-of-all-work," Trollope went on to declare that the Prime Minister "has acted unconstitutionally, and has no right to maintain his position in the House of Commons except by the support and approval of the majority of its members." And he added that if Disraeli, "after the defeat he has suffered on the Irish Church question, had immediately dissolved the House he would have acted in a constitutional manner; but instead he has clung to office from which he will not be driven until he is absolutely compelled to appeal to the country." A week later, on 16 November, Trollope in a speech referred to "a majority in the House of Commons" as "the mainstay of our liberty in Great Britain."[20] Like the fleeting praise of Bright (delivered to the same Radical audience), these may fairly be seen as required partisan declarations of the moment. A Liberal in an uphill campaign against an entrenched Tory incumbent, Trollope had to make one or two compromises at Beverley. The anger of *Phineas Redux* (written just three years after Beverley) may stem in part from the novelist's memory of what candidate Trollope occasionally said when he was not saying exactly what he pleased. More to the point — he would have been sitting in that safe Essex seat had Disraeli dissolved earlier (as theoretically he should have), instead of which Disraeli's party defeated him. However, we should not underestimate the lingering distrust and hatred of Disraeli on wider grounds — either in Trollope's Beverley speeches or in *Phineas Redux*. And undoubtedly the novelist believed in majority rule (especially when the Tories were the minority). Trollope's resentment of Gladstone also dates from the years just after Beverley, where he was publicly humiliated in the great man's cause. So it is not surprising that the Gresham of *Phineas Redux* is a significantly less admirable figure than the Gresham of *Phineas Finn*.

IV

The picture of party politics *Phineas Redux* gives us emerges too from its account of some other careers. Bonteen, for example, is "a hack among the hacks" a "useful, dull, unscrupulous politician . . . acquainted with the . . . back doors of official life." Never having "entertained any high political theory of his own," he has been "a very useful man" to the Liberal party (I, 344, 376, and 395). Men such as Monk, Cantrip, and

Phineas Finn think less of the Bonteens of their party than of any other type. And yet Bonteen is the Liberal shadow Chancellor of the Exchequer after Palliser becomes Duke of Omnium. Bonteen is prevented from taking office — but only through the intervention of Lady Glencora, as we shall see; and Phineas, caring "but little for honesty . . . which is at the disposal of those who are dishonest," as he says at the time, is later to turn down office offered by "a Minister who could allow himself to be led by" a Bonteen (II, 409). That such a man should rise so high is of course a commentary on the political process, which so often weeds out individuals in its search for reliable company men. Indeed, the Liberals are dominated by "second-rate" men such as Erle, who "delights in little party successes . . . and . . . loves to get the better of the Opposition by keeping it in the dark" (II, 415). Again we see Lord Mount Thistle waiting patiently in the wings — "one of those terrible political burdens, engendered originally by private friendship or family considerations, which one Minister leaves to another" (I, 343; in this case he has been bequeathed by Mildmay to Gresham). There is again Lord Fawn, still a colonial secretary though now a viscount, described as "a muddle-headed fellow [who] can get himself to believe anything" and a "blundering fool" (though the British Empire depends upon him to so great an extent). His friends fear "that he would altogether sink under his miseries" (II, 346) during the trial at which he must testify; and indeed, "absolutely broken down by repeated examinations respecting the man in the grey coat," at last "his mind gave way; — and he disappeared." So much for Lord Fawn. And there is poor Laurence Fitzgibbon, who, as a junior minister, finds himself compelled by the Chancellor of the Exchequer to speak in the House against a financial measure that he himself has researched, prepared, and recommended for adoption to his party (II, 423–4); having done himself a good turn by his obliging deference, however, he stays in office for some time afterwards. All of these men are Liberals.

There are a number of familiar corollary themes. Again we hear of the political virtues of doing as little as possible. "It is the necessary nature of a political party in this country," Trollope tells us, "to avoid, as long as it can be avoided, the consideration of any question which involves a great change" (I, 40). Again it is made clear that parliamentary debates, staged primarily for audiences, have no effect whatever on their participants — "it was not probable that any member's intention . . . would . . . be altered by anything he might hear" during the debate on Disestablishment (I, 368–9); Phineas speaks to aid his own career understanding that what he says "would influence no human being." And there is a successor in *Phineas Redux* to poor old Lord Middlesex of *Can You Forgive Her?*. The man is not named; all we learn of him is that he has made a long study of the relationship between the adulteration of beer and the mortality rate, gathered his statistics with much care, and "been at work for the last twelve months on his effort to prolong the lives of his fellow-countrymen." When he rises to speak, however, "there was such a rush of members to the door that not a word [he] said could be heard." The beer scholar is "almost broken-hearted. But he knew the world too well to complain" — knew, that is, that "quarrels of rival Ministers were dear to the House, and as long as they could be continued the benches [would be] crowded by gentlemen enthralled by the interest of the occasion" (II, 357–8). Show, not substance, keeps the House going; attempts at real legislation empty it. The sham nature of the proceedings is also reflected in the asides (I, 347 and 382) on prospective orators catching the Speaker's eye to be recognized (they don't — such things as who will speak on an issue are arranged by the parties in advance, and in any case "some preliminary assistance [is] . . . given to the travelling of the Speaker's eye"); and in the elaborately hypocritical modes of address used by members to one another (such as when Gresham, in response to an attack made upon him by Daubeny, retorts: "I deny utterly, not only the accuracy, but every detail of the statement made by the right honourable gentleman opposite": by such standard terminology as this it is acknowledged that if the gentleman is a Member apparently he can lie and yet remain "right honourable").

In keeping with the continuing theme of political "conjuring," there are the usual — indeed, in *Phineas Redux* more than the usual — games metaphors used in connection with politics. Bribing the voters at Tankerville is twice called playing "the old game"; also Phineas characterizes his attempt to get back into Parliament as "trying my hand at the old game," while it is said of Daubeny at one point that he "had played his game with consummate skill." The beginning of the Disestablishment debate is called "open[ing] the ball." As it goes on a colleague of Daubeny's says to him of his strategy (I, 59): "It is a bold throw, but I'm afraid it won't come up sixes." "Let it come up fives, then," retorts the Prime Minister, falling in with the metaphor from dice (indeed, an unflattering comparison of the politician and the gambler — and the drunkard — is made explicitly at one point: "A drunkard or a gambler may be weaned from his ways . . . but not a politician"). Daubeny's snatch of the Disestablishment issue is likened to the winning player in a chess game appropriating "to his own use the castles and the queen of the . . . vanquished one"; the Liberals have always thought of the issue as a "valuable . . . piece of ordnance" of their own. The duel between Daubeny and Gresham, like that between Daubeny and Mildmay in *Phineas Finn*, is called a gladiatorial contest and the opponents themselves are described as "parliamentary gladiators . . . ever striving to give maddening little wounds through the joints of the harness." Like all gladiators in well-arranged public spectacles, the two antagonists have very different styles, making the contest interesting: "whereas Mr. Daubeny hit always as hard as he knew how to hit, having premeditated each blow, and weighed its results beforehand, having calculated his power even to the effect of a blow repeated on a wound already given, Mr.

Gresham struck right and left and straight-forward with a readiness
engendered by practice, and in his fury might have murdered his antagonist before he was aware that he had drawn blood" (I, 363). Elsewhere the
party battle is likened to a different sort of gladiatorial contest — a fencing
match, with both sides "flying at each other's throats, thrusting and
parrying . . . [and forgetting] that they are expected to be great. Little
tricks of sword-play engage all their skill" (II, 334). "Little tricks" are the
order of the day. And, as in *Phineas Finn* (and *The Duke's Children*), there
are in *Phineas Redux* a great many equestrian and other horsey images
used in reference to politics. Recommencing his political career, Phineas
early in the novel compares himself to an old "warhorse out at grass"
remembering "the sound of the battle and the noise of trumpets." The
imagery of *Phineas Finn* reappears here in several references to politicians
as horses in drag: "The best . . . are those which can most steadily hold
back against the coach as it trundles down the hill"; once "outside the
traces" Phineas "won't get oats [until] he works steady between the
traces" again; Phineas is known as a man who "on one occasion had taken
to kicking in harness, and running a course of his own"; it is feared by
some that even Palliser, when he becomes Duke of Omnium, may enjoy
being "released from the crack of the whip" — but Erle knows he will soon
"go into harness again." Other images relate politicians to men on
horseback. Daubeny's early successes as Prime Minister have encouraged
him, it is said, to get careless: "A man rides at some outrageous fence, and
by the wonderful activity and obedient zeal of his horse is carried over it
in safety. It does not follow that his horse will carry him over a house, or
that he should be fool enough to ask the beast to do so" (I, 53–4); the
effects of Gresham's ungovernable temper are evoked in these terms — "In
a matter of horseflesh of what use is it to have all manner of good gifts if
your horse won't go whither you want him, and refuses to stop when you
bid him? Mr. Gresham had been very indiscreet" (I, 90); Phineas prefers "a
day's canvass at Tankerville" to riding a particularly difficult horse at
Copperhouse Cross. (Trollope at Beverley said in one of his campaign
addresses: "Should I tumble at the fence or not, it is my intention to ride
boldly at it."[21]) Other images relate politics to hunting. The failure of the
old Duke of Omnium to provide foxes for the Brake hunt is said to be "as
bad as voting against the Church establishment"; and Lady Chiltern, who
doesn't see much difference between the professions, tells Phineas that her
husband "was born to be a master of hounds, and you were born to be a
Secretary of State. He works the hardest and gets the least pay for it; but
then . . . he does not run so great a risk of being turned out" (I,
18) — similarly, she wonders if her first-born will be "a master of hounds
or a Cabinet Minister." (The analogy was always one of Trollope's
favorites. Years earlier in *The Kellys and the O'Kellys* he described thus
the old hounds waiting for the hunt to begin: "there they sat, as grave as
so many senators, with their large heads raised, their heavy lips hanging

from each side of their jaws, and their deep, strong chests expanded so as to show fully their bone, muscle, and breeding" — p. 279.) Once again, in the plethora of metaphors from games and sporting events, Trollope characterizes politics as sham spectacle, entertaining but essentially meaningless — though often morally dangerous.

V

Inextricably tied to Trollope's study of partisanship in *Phineas Redux* is his scrutiny of patronage. We saw a little of the issue in *Phineas Finn*; in *Phineas Redux* patronage is the unseen mover of events again and again. The novel presents in its very first paragraph the spectacle of "Mr. Daubeny . . . distributing the good things of the Crown amidst Conservative birdlings, with beaks wide open and craving maws," while the Liberals yearn for "some equity of division in the bestowal of crumbs of comfort"; and then it goes immediately on to deal with patronage in these unsubtle terms:

> Mr. Daubeny and his merry men [had had their] chance [and] . . . had not neglected [it] . . . They made their hay while the sun shone with an energy that had never been surpassed, improving upon Fortune. . . . [But to] the Liberals, this cutting up of the Whitehall cake by the Conservatives was spoliation [*sic*]. . . . Were not they, the Liberals, the real representatives of the people, and, therefore, did not the cake in truth appertain to them? . . . They [had] given up the cake for a while . . . with a feeling that a moderate slicing on the other side would . . . be advantageous. . . . But when the cake came to be mauled like that — oh, heavens! . . . Then came a great fight, in the last agonies of which the cake was sliced manfully. (I, 1–2)

The Tories, figured here as a band of thieves, have done so well with the rare chance given them that the greedy Liberals, after only a year in opposition, are restless enough to resolve to end all "quarrels," "mismanagement," and "idleness" among themselves to get back into power. Seeing this, the Conservatives make a last flurry of appointments; suddenly there are hordes of new Tory officials: Attorney-Generals, Chief Justices, Lords of Appeal, vice-royal Governors, ambassadors, Lord Lieutenants, judges, bishops, private secretaries, even Knights of the Garter — "great places were filled by tens, and little places by twenties . . . and the hay was still made even after the sun had gone down." The image of birds fighting over the crumbs of an old cake extends through the novel's opening chapter; we hear how the Liberals fear "the cake had been left in [Mr Daubeny's] hands" for too long: "Was it to be borne that [a] . . . Conservative Prime Minister should go on slicing the cake after a fashion as that lately adopted?" (I, 3–5). When Daubeny comes up with his Disestablishment ploy many Liberals see it as a move merely to prevent them from getting their share of the crumbs (which it is). "By G——! he's going to take the bread out of our mouths again," says Ratler (I, 48). Bonteen suggests that the Tories may still, after all, care enough about the Church to refuse to go along with their chief. But Ratler knows the breed too well, being a member of it himself: "There's something they like a great deal better than the Church. . . . Indeed, there's only one thing they care about at all now . . . they like getting the counties, and the Garters, and the promotion in the army. They like their brothers to be made bishops, and their sisters like the Wardrobe and the Bedchamber. There isn't one of them that doesn't hang on somewhere" (I, 51). This is plain enough; but Ratler, Bonteen and their colleagues, in their hurry to get the cake back, betray the same single-minded greed. The Tories are in no hurry to go back "out in the cold," having come to understand that "A party can only live by having its share of Garters, lord-lieutenants, bishops, and attorney-generals . . . Latterly [the party had] enjoyed almost its share of stars and Garters, — thanks to the individual skill and strategy of that great English political Von Moltke, Mr. Daubeny" (I, 82–3). Like a great military leader, Daubeny has used cunning to confound his enemies.

It is quite true, of course, that during the nineteenth century (and most of the eighteenth as well), especially up to the time Trollope was writing *Phineas Redux* (1870–1), the Liberals — or Whigs, as they had been known earlier — were in power for a disproportionately large amount of the time (this helps explain the lopsided majority of Whig peers in the House of Lords, where the Tories were woefully outnumbered throughout the century). Occasionally, due to internal squabbling or disunity of some sort, they would fall briefly from power. The Conservatives, better organized though smaller in numbers, are thus understandably pictured here as wanting to make hay while the sun shines (and even after it has set), while the Liberals chafe at the unexpected bad luck of being out of office — the "fictional" political situation, in this as in so many instances, has some connections to political reality. "The pay, the patronage, the powers, and the pleasures of Government were all due to the Liberals," they themselves feel. If the Tories do not leave office, having a majority against them in the House, "There's nothing of honesty left in politics," says — of all men — Bonteen, in an ironic burst of pique. He wishes Gresham were a more energetic partisan but refrains from saying so "lest, when the house door should at last be opened, he might not be invited to enter with the others" (I, 85). When Gresham does bestir himself in the manner we have seen, his argument is reduced to its essentials by Daubeny in a speech to the House. What Gresham is really proposing, says Daubeny, quite rightly, is "That this House does think that I ought to be Prime Minister now." As the session drags on and Daubeny remains in office, it is clear that his strategy has had at least one successful issue. "His Church Bill has given him a six months' run, and six months is something," admits the ravenous Ratler (I, 369; remember that Disraeli, beaten on Irish

Disestablishment in April 1868, managed to get a "run" until November simply by refusing to go out). Daubeny escalates the attack on Gresham by referring to "the rabid haste" with which the Liberals "were attempting, he would not say to climb, but to rush into office, by opposing a great measure ... the wisdom of which, as was notorious to all the world, they themselves did not deny" (I, 382).

In a valedictory speech after his defeat, Daubeny blames his forced departure from office not on the issue of Disestablishment but rather on that of patronage. In it he characterizes his opponents as "gentlemen who could not keep their fingers from poker and tongs," and he concludes in this vein:

'A spirit of personal ambition, a wretched thirst for office, a hankering after the powers and privileges of ruling, [have] not only actuated men ... but [have] been openly avowed and put forward as an adequate and sufficient reason for opposing a measure in disapprobation of which no single argument [has] been used! The right honourable gentleman's proposition to the House ... [is] simply this; — "I shall oppose this measure, be it good or bad, because I desire, myself, to be Prime Minister, and I call upon those whom I lead in politics to assist me in doing so, in order that they may share the good things on which we may thus be enabled to lay our hands!" ' (I, 425)

True enough. But we should not forget that what has actuated Daubeny and *his* friends in the controversy over Disestablishment is the desire to stay in office — where they have been enabled to remain by stealing an issue from the Liberals. Adapting for his own use Disraeli's well-known characterization of Peel's policies in the forties, Trollope in *Lord Palmerston* speaks of "the story of the Tory finding the Whig bathing and running away with his clothes. Of course the Conservative wishes to prevent the Liberal from being successful and finds that he can best do so by carrying out the measures which the Liberal has proposed."[22] Given the chance, the Liberal would do the same to the Tory.

In a letter to Phineas late in the novel, Lady Laura, always a shrewd observer of the political scene, urges him on in these words: "You have to assert yourself, to make your own way, to use your own opportunities, and to fight your own battle without reference to the feelings of individuals. Men act together in office constantly, and with constancy, who are known to hate each other. When there are so many to get what is going, and so little to be given, of course there will be struggling and trampling" (II, 402). The "feelings of individuals" inevitably become subordinated to group goals, to the grabbing off of whatever there is to grab; the struggle for goodies, while not an edifying spectacle, is a comprehensible fact of life, and a man who wants to enjoy a career in politics must be prepared to scramble. By the end of *Phineas Redux*, however, it is precisely this destruction of feeling that has turned Phineas off to political life.

In an article entitled "Mr. Disraeli and the Mint," published in *St. Paul's Magazine* in May 1869 (just five months after Disraeli's fall from power), Trollope condemns the removal of career civil servants to make room for patronage appointees and warmly welcomes such improvements in the manner of making these appointments as have come to pass. His concluding paragraph should be particularly interesting to readers of *Phineas Redux*: "the position of our Prime Minister is so stained with the necessities of that support which patronage is used to obtain, that it is beyond the effort of the greatest and the honestest of mankind to keep a hand altogether clean amidst the pollution which practice has engendered."[23]

VI

Trollope's growing despondency over the political process is seen in other ways in *Phineas Redux*. The "pollution" extends into related spheres — among them that of the popular political press. In *Phineas Redux* and *The Prime Minister* its representative is Mr Quintus Slide of the *People's Banner*, whose choice of political sides seems always to result from its editor's momentary sense of personal advantage or umbrage. The infection of the House of Commons has spread so far outward that some of those men who report the doings of Parliament have come to absorb its lessons. Due to its editor's hope of getting into society and associating with important people, Slide's paper usually supports the government of the day. When Mildmay is in, Slide is a Liberal. With Daubeny as Prime Minister, Slide feels "called upon . . . to be the organ of Mr. Daubeny"; and thus it becomes "Mr. Slide's duty to speak of men as heaven-born patriots whom he had designated a month or two since as bloated aristocrats and leeches" (I, 234). No less than Ratler, Erle, or Bonteen, he is in his own sphere a hack "indefatigable, unscrupulous, and devoted" to his cause, which is himself. He attacks other newspapers and their editors — even their editors' wives — in ways reminiscent of parliamentary onslaughts. An editor, after all, is "about the same as a Cabinet Minister. You've got to keep your place." Indeed, since an M.P. must struggle mightily "for an opportunity of speaking; and could then only speak to benches half deserted; or to a few Members half asleep" (I, 291), Slide fancies his power even greater.

The account of the Tankerville election is also revealing. We have seen already a string of dishonest elections in the Palliser novels, and we will see more. What is distinctive about the election at Tankerville (Durham) and its aftermath is the virulence of its conception when compared with elections in preceding Palliser novels. After Beverley, Trollope was unable to conceive of an election even remotely honest; the dishonesty at Tankerville is presented as a routine matter. But the new violence of the description is clearly a product of Trollope's recent disillusionment: having seen at firsthand the worst aspects of political life in his own bitterly disappointing race for Parliament, he makes unsparing use of this new knowledge,[24] as he had done once before in *Ralph the Heir*. The Tankerville election has obvious autobiographical overtones. The story of the Beverley election is given in *Ralph the Heir*, yes; but it needs saying that the Tankerville election in *Phineas Redux* is still another version of Beverley. Just as Trollope, in Daubeny and Beeswax, painted at least two portraits of the hated Disraeli, so he gave himself two opportunities to work off all the irritations of Beverley — including that of Sir Henry Edwards; for Edwards-Griffenbottom is lampooned again in *Phineas Redux* as Browborough, the Tory member for Tankerville. Browborough, like Griffenbottom, is a "hulking, heavy, speechless fellow" who never says anything in the House but always votes with his party. Like Edwards-Griffenbottom, Browborough has been the town's member for decades and has spent a lot of money there. Like Griffenbottom's, Browborough's seat is everything to him — even though he knows nothing and cares little about politics. Like both Griffenbottom and Edwards, Browborough instigates his agents to pay cash for votes, is caught, unseated by petition, acquitted of bribery in a trial, and becomes a sort of hero in his town at the end of his political career. The similarities are patent.

Phineas at Tankerville also resembles Trollope at Beverley and Underwood at Percycross. In the *Autobiography* (pp. 257–8), the novelist gives this account of the conversation he had with the Liberal agent at Beverley upon his arrival there:

'So,' said he, 'you are going to stand for Beverley?' I replied gravely that I was thinking of doing so. 'You don't expect to get in?' he said. Again I was grave. I would not, I said, be sanguine, but nevertheless I was disposed to hope the best. 'Oh no!' continued he, with good-humoured raillery, 'you won't get in. I don't suppose you really expect it. But there is a fine career open to you. You will spend £1,000, and lose the election. Then you will petition, and spend another £1,000. You will throw out the elected members. There will be a commission, and the borough will be disfranchised. For a beginner . . . that will be a great success.'

The account (I, 15) of Phineas's conference with the Liberal agent Molescroft upon his arrival at Tankerville is almost identical in substance — and, in at least one instance, in language: Molescroft tells Phineas, "It's a fine career, but expensive." Sir Thomas Underwood at Percycross, remember, was the recipient of similarly dire (and prophetic) warnings. Phineas at Tankerville, like Sir Thomas at Percycross, and Trollope himself at Beverley, undergoes "ten days of unmitigated vexation and misery" in the course of completing his canvass. He dislikes Tankerville, as Trollope disliked Beverley and Sir Thomas disliked Percycross: "It would not, however, in any event be his duty to live at Tankerville, and he had believed from the first moment of his entrance into the town that he would depart from it, and know it no more" (I, 37). Phineas's change of feeling late in the novel about the virtues of a seat in the House of Commons (an alluring "toy" that doesn't work when it is brought home, is the image invoked) recalls both Sir Thomas's ultimate perception of *his* hard-won place in Parliament as little better than a "new toy" of diminishing interest and Trollope's reference in the *Autobiography* to his "insane desire," as he came to see it, to sit in the House of Commons.

The story of the election itself, briefly told, embodies familiar themes. Like the electors of Polpenno in *The Duke's Children*, those of Tankerville, never having encountered true eloquence, are easily impressed by the speeches they hear. Even Browborough – a cretinous hack unable "to string a few words together" or to "learn half-a-dozen sentences by rote" – is thought to be eloquent (e.g., I, 41–2); inarticulateness has not hampered his parliamentary career. He understands nothing of what he is asked and nothing of what he is told to say, and yet he has sat comfortably in Parliament for years.

Phineas had been told by Erle that the Tankerville campaign should cost him only about £500. "Browborough has spent a fortune there . . . I am told that [they] won't vote for [him] unless he spends money," Erle had said, but "I fancy he will be afraid to do it heavily" in these Reform-minded times, when bribery petitions have become fashionable. Once in Tankerville, however, Phineas discovers that his opponent, "that lump of a legislator," will indeed "play the old game . . . He doesn't know any other. . . . All the purists in England wouldn't teach him to think that a poor man ought not to sell his vote, and that a rich man oughtn't to buy it," says Molescroft, alluding to a point of view which may remind us of Pile's in *Ralph the Heir*. "You mean to go in for purity?" he asks Phineas. Purity, it seems, has its perils at Tankerville, as at Percycross. Phineas, like Sir Thomas, is told that if he won't bribe he will be badly thought of in the borough. The voters will feel deprived; and Browborough "will hate you because he'll think you are trying to rob him of what he has honestly bought . . . he doesn't want his seat for nothing, any more than he wants his house or his carriage-horses for nothing," says Molescroft (I, 15). For Browborough, as for Griffenbottom, a seat in Parliament is something you can buy just as "honestly" as a house or a horse. Phineas at Tankerville, like Underwood at Percycross, is "disgusted . . . to find that the people of the town would treat him as though he were rolling in wealth." Candidates, after all, exist so that votes can be purchased; and the elector is delighted to sell his vote, like his house or his horse, to the highest bidder. So the lessons of *Ralph the Heir* come home to Phineas. Browborough will not be easy to unseat: "Money is no object to him, and he doesn't care a straw what anybody says of him." Like Griffenbottom, Browborough is known to be willing to do *anything* to keep his seat; he is without shame. Like Beverley, Tankerville stays in the news long after the election. When a petition is brought, the Crown is obliged by a recent law to prosecute Browborough for bribery, and the occasion gives Trollope a chance to pen some of the novel's most satirical passages. Years earlier, in *The Kellys and the O'Kellys*, he had written, in connection with O'Connell's conspiracy trial, of "the great difficulty of coming to a legal decision on a political question, in a criminal court" (p. 16); Browborough's trial, certainly "political," is flagrantly un-legal.

Having after all won the election, Browborough, like Griffenbottom, is amazed and disgusted that there should be a trial at all. "He thought that a battle when once won should be regarded as over till the occasion should come for another battle. He had spent his money like a gentleman, and hated these mean ways. No one could ever say that he had ever petitioned" (I, 140). The trial comes on; Trollope sets the scene. Like Griffenbottom, Browborough "never spoke, [was] constant in his attendance ... wanted nothing ... had plenty of money ... gave dinners" (II, 32) – and being such "a model member of Parliament," feeling about him in the House is rather sentimental. This is due in part to prevailing attitudes toward the new laws governing bribery and its punishment, which strike many members as "cruel." The whole world knew "as a matter of course ... that at every election Mr. Browborough had bought his seat. How else should a Browborough get a seat ... a man who could not say ten words," who has no family, no following, no political zeal, no special convictions? Again we are in the presence of Edwards-Griffenbottom. Having spent his money "like a gentleman," Browborough wants his gentleman's perquisites. And though "the House of Commons had determined to put down bribery ... and certain members ... had expressed themselves with almost burning indignation against the crime," nevertheless throughout the process by which the new laws came into being "there had been a slight undercurrent of ridicule attaching itself to the question of which only they who were behind the scenes were conscious" (II, 33). As in the controversy in *Phineas Finn* over rotten boroughs, members of the House in this emergency feel "bound to let the outside world know that all corrupt practices at elections were held to be abominable by the House; but Members ... as individuals, knew very well what had taken place at their own elections, and were aware of the cheques which they had drawn" (II, 33–4). And as in *Ralph the Heir* – in which the "spirit of assumed virtue in regard to such matters" is discernible, but not the virtue itself – everything below the polished surface of profession is very ugly indeed. The House of Commons, Trollope says in *The New Zealander*, "delights in the display of a false purism before the eyes of the public, and delights no less in the fruition of lax principles within inner and closed circles." And it will continue to be weakened from within, he declares here, "as long as pretence and show are among the recognised tactics of Parliamentary life; as long as purism prevails to the exclusion of honesty, and men allow themselves to profess one code of morals for the public, and a far different code for their private circles."[25]

The utter hypocrisy, corruption, and degradation of the electoral process is figured in the Browborough trial, at which the defendant is prosecuted by a man who himself has been guilty of flagrant bribery in his own constituency, though he is Attorney-General. The prosecution, in keeping with the sentiments of the Attorney-General and his parliamentary colleagues, is deliberately incompetent. "When it came to be a matter of individual prosecution against one whom they had all known, and who, as a member, had been inconspicuous and therefore inoffensive, against a heavy, rich, useful man who had been in nobody's way, many thought that it would amount to persecution. The idea of putting old Browborough into prison for conduct which habit had made second nature to a large proportion of the House was distressing to Members." It is the old question of whose ox is being gored. Browborough eventually becomes something of a martyr — tenderly characterized in Parliament, for example, as "a poor, faithful creature, who had always been willing to accept as his natural leader any one whom his party might select" (II, 34). He has been a marvellous hack, and his fellow hacks become alarmed for themselves in his plight. But the moral infection has not been contained in the House of Commons; "the sympathies of the public generally were with Mr. Browborough, though there was ... little doubt that he was guilty." The loyal partisan is guilty of bribery; Phineas — who once voted against his party as a matter of conscience — has bought no votes. The comparison is illuminating. Partisan zeal and criminal behavior are not strangers; political independence keeps its hands relatively clean.

The trial takes a predictable course. The defendant's "safety lay in the indifference of his prosecutors, — certainly not in his innocence ... The [crime] might be condoned" (II, 36). As the trial wears on Browborough becomes "quite a hero at Tankerville ... Could he have stood for the seat again ... he might have been returned without bribery ... During no portion of his Parliamentary life had Mr. Browborough's name been treated with so much respect ... as now" (II, 36–7); Phineas, who refused to pay bribes, is abused. Browborough is much petted in the courtroom and wined and dined between sessions by the ecclesiastical hierarchy of the local diocese. The corruption is so complete that even the judge, "who had himself sat for a borough in his younger days, and who knew well how things were done ... could not but have thought of the old days" during the trial and looks sympathetically upon the plight of the defendant (II, 37). At the end of the trial the judge's summing-up "was very short, and seemed to have been given almost with indolence." Though the evidence against Browborough has not been contradicted, a verdict of acquittal is returned "without one moment's delay . . . and the affair was over, to the manifest contentment of every one there present" – including the Attorney-General, who is considered by members of both parties to have "done his duty very well." No one, says Trollope, could have been surprised by the outcome except "some poor innocents . . . who had been induced to believe that bribery and corruption were in truth to be banished from the purlieus of Westminster" (II, 40).

Of course this is in part a fairy-tale trial, but Trollope's metaphor of spiritual corruption becomes even more forceful later in *Phineas Redux* when, in a subsequent trial, Browborough's honest political opponent is energetically prosecuted by the same Attorney-General for a more serious crime of which he is innocent. Moral values in this world have been turned upside down; and at the heart of the corruption are those gothic buildings at Westminster.

There is some choric prattle at the end of the trial. Roby and Ratler agree that "no good could have come from a conviction" of Browborough. "Nobody dislikes bribery more than I do . . . But if a man loses his seat, surely that is punishment enough," says one of them. "It's better to have to draw a cheque sometimes than to be out in the cold," says the other. On a higher level, sentiments in the matter are more or less the same. Gresham tells Cantrip that a conviction in the Browborough case would have been "a great misfortune . . . it would have created ill blood; and our hands in this matter are not a bit cleaner than those of our adversaries. We can't afford to pull their houses to pieces before we have put our own in order." And he adds, candidly: "No member of Parliament will ever be punished for bribery . . . till members . . . generally look upon bribery as a crime." Monk tries to console Phineas by reminding him once again that "In political matters it is very hard for a man in office to be purer than his neighbours, – and when he is so, he becomes troublesome." But Phineas is not so easily consoled: "I am sick of the whole thing. There is no honesty in the life we lead" (II, 41–5).

The rottenness of things in general in *Phineas Redux* – the pronouncement, "There is no honesty in the life we lead" can be readily applied to any number of "lives" in the novel – is reflected in Trollope's terrible cold anger, his unamused mock-heroic treatment of despicable people and things. Thus his account, for example, of the career of Bonteen, that hack of hacks. When it seems as if Bonteen might become Chancellor of the Exchequer the prospective change in his life is described as that of an ascent "from demi-godhead to the perfect divinity of the Cabinet . . . a leap which would make him high even among first-class gods" (I, 373). When it is clear that he won't be Chancellor he is described as remaining tied to the realm of the "demigod" after all.[26] And when he is murdered he manages even in death to spawn a renewed bout of public hypocrisy among his late colleagues. Gresham tells the House that the country has had an impossibly great loss, and there is much said about Bonteen's

merits. In private, however, many members think "that upon the whole
Phineas Finn ... [did] rather a good thing in putting poor Mr. Bonteen
out of the way." "What a godsend for Gresham," declares one of them,
while another says the Liberals "are better without him." "The poor
fellow would never have got on with us," admits one of his Liberal
colleagues. The public eulogies go on.

Perhaps it is Mr Chaffanbrass, the wily barrister, who most trenchantly
defines the spirit of the age. "It's the temper of the time to resent
nothing, — to be mealy-mouthed and mealy-hearted," he says. And he goes
on to speak of "mealy-mouthed" law-courts and their failings in a way a
modern audience might find congenial: "mealy-mouthed verdicts [tend]
to equalise crime and innocence, and to make men think that after all it
may be a question whether fraud is violence, which, after all, is manly, and
to feel that we cannot afford to hate dishonesty ... You can't punish
dishonest trading [any more]. *Caveat emptor* is the only motto going. ...
With such a matter as that to guide us no man dare trust his brother. *Caveat
lex*, — and let the man who cheats cheat at his peril" (II, 210–11). The
doctrine of "*caveat lex*," after a great battle, eventually got a small
measure of comeuppance in *The Eustace Diamonds*. In a world in which
such a trial as Browborough's can be held, fewer signs of its ultimate
defeat are visible.

VII

There are, however, a few. Of that Trollopian double-vision which reveres
as it satirizes it is fair to say that the reverence grows dimmer and the
satire more bitter as the years pass. *Phineas Redux* still contains a few
elements of affirmation. Lady Chiltern, for all her joking, in a serious
moment tells Phineas that she hopes her child "will be a great statesman.
After all ... that is the best thing that a man can be" (I, 25). Of
parliamentary life itself Trollope says that once adopted it makes "contentment in any other circumstances almost an impossibility ... no other
life is worth having after it" (I, 7 and 122). He can even find it in
him — once, briefly — to have something of a defensive nature said about
political partisanship: "all [party] loyalty," muses the wise old Duke of St
Bungay, "must be built on a basis of self-advantage. Patriotism may exist
without it, but ... loyalty in politics [is] simply devotion to the side
which a man conceives to be his side, and which he cannot leave without
danger to himself" (I, 47). It simply is not possible to exclude the
self-aggrandizing drive from any democratic political system — any system
with parties.

There are other positive (and familiar) themes in *Phineas Redux*. Chief
among these is a spirited defense of the hereditary aristocracy as the
country's ruling class. This issue becomes more prominent in the last two
Palliser novels, especially *The Duke's Children*; but here too it commands
considerable attention. The old Duke of St Bungay tells the new Duke of

Omnium that "Much of the welfare of [the] country depends on the manner in which you bear yourself as the Duke of Omnium" (II, 188). A major theme of *The Duke's Children* – the leadership responsibilities of the aristocracy – is touched on here. Such men as dukes are born to lead, and therefore must do so.

Trollope grafts his prejudice into the public attitude he describes as greeting the death of the old Duke of Omnium, Palliser's uncle. Though he has led an idle and dissipated life and done nothing whatsoever for his country – still, "in no club and in no drawing-room was a verdict given against the [old] man. It was acknowledged everywhere that he had played his part in a noble and even in a princely manner, that he had used with a becoming grace the rich things that had been given to him, and that he had deserved well of his country" (I, 260). The Duke of St Bungay's assessment follows the same lines: "he was a man who understood his position and the requirements of his order very thoroughly." His manner of living, concludes the old Duke, "secured for him the respect of the nation" – no mean or irrelevant consideration. In *The Duke's Children* Palliser himself comes to feel, as his uncle had long felt, that he is obliged to act so as to maintain that respect – even when the doing so may be personally distasteful or unpleasant.

Trollope's model politician is again Plantagenet Palliser, the new Duke of Omnium, who is idealized in a number of ways in *Phineas Redux*. Ousted by his uncle's death from that world "which he had best liked" – the world of the House of Commons, where he can do real, and not just ceremonial, work – the new Duke chooses to labor at a relatively menial level of government in preference to doing nothing. His compulsiveness results in part from a vague sort of guilt about his uncle's irresponsible life; but the major motive in almost everything he does in *Phineas Redux* is to make "the process of government work."[27] Unlike most of his political colleagues, he is always willing to forgo personal prestige amidst his labors.

In a world in which social *éclat* is of utmost importance to politicians, Palliser is one of the few who prefers to rely on his own real powers rather than society's deference; he chooses, that is, to work hard rather than to be passively great. Thus "To him his uncle's death would be a great blow ... to be Chancellor of the Exchequer was much more than to be Duke of Omnium" (I, 268). No one else in Trollope's political world could – or at any rate ever does – express this sort of feeling. Though he seems at times to be a complex mechanism, the sensibilities of Trollope's hero are uncomplicated upon his translation to "the very top of the tree":

He was made master of almost unlimited wealth, Garters, lord-lieutenancies. ... But he was [unmoved] by these things ... He could never sit again in the House of Commons. It was in that light ... that he regarded the matter. To his uncle it had been everything to be Duke of Omnium. To Plantagenet Palliser it was less than nothing ... One

man walked out of a room before another man; and he as Chancellor
... had ... walked out of most rooms before most men. But he cared
not at all whether he walked out first or last. ... This thing ... that
had happened had absolutely crushed him. He had won for himself by
his own aptitudes and his own industry one special position in the
empire, — and that position, and that alone, was incompatible with the
rank which he was obliged to assume! His case was very hard, and he
felt it; — but he made no complaint to human ears. (I, 274–5).

Later on — in *The Prime Minister* and *The Duke's Children*, when the
shock of his new life has worn off — Palliser welcomes his rank and wealth
as assets in his own and his heirs' political careers, additional means of
being of service to his country; but for the moment he is "crushed." His
own "aptitudes" and "industry" — not his rank or money — have won him
his place, and so he has valued it the more. No other politician in the
novel, going in or out of office, has such purity of motives. As Lady
Glencora puts it, "My husband ... thinks a good deal of himself as a
statesman and a clever politician ... but he has not the slightest reverence
for himself as a nobleman ... Plantagenet never feels any pride of place
unless he is sitting on the Treasury Bench" (I, 277–8). Not knowing "how
to endure worship," the new Duke is thought to be "stern and proud, and
more haughty even than his uncle" — a failure in public relations that is to
plague him later as Prime Minister; "At every 'Grace' ... he winced and
was miserable" (I, 278). Indeed, the new honors turn Palliser "so shy, he
hardly knows how to speak to you. ... [But] I don't think you'll find
much difference in him when he has got over the annoyance," Erle tells
Ratler; "He can hold his own against all comers, and always could. Quiet
as he seemed, he knew who he was, and who other people were" (I,
330–1). And yet, as Trollope also says, there is about his hero "an absence
of all self-consciousness, he was so little given to think of his own personal
demeanour and outward trappings" (II, 27). He can be confident of his
powers and know their extent in spite of his lack of personal vanity; he has
self-assurance without self-conceit, ambition without greed, and is thus a
valuable toiler in the political vineyards. In this he is clearly unlike his
fellow workers. When Gresham bestows the late Duke's Garter upon Lord
Cantrip and Glencora tells her husband that he should have demanded it
for himself, his reply is characteristic: "There are things that men do not
ask for." "Don't tell me, Plantagenet, about not asking," she replies.
"Everybody asks for everything nowadays." "Your everybody is not
correct, Glencora. I never yet asked for anything, — and never shall. No
honour has any value in my eyes unless it comes unasked" (II, 182).

Immediately thereafter he does ask for something, but it is the request
of a humble man doing a favor rather than a grasping man taking
advantage. In the interests of continuity and efficiency after the Bonteen
murder, Palliser offers to take the place of his late assistant as President of

the Board of Trade. His offer is gratefully accepted by Gresham. "I am the last man to interfere as to place or the disposition of power," says the new Duke; but, as Lord Privy Seal, caring "nothing for status," "intent on his work," and having "a morbid dislike to pretences," he has been unhappy in the largely ceremonial role. "It was a great misfortune to me that I should have been obliged to leave the House of Commons . . . My whole life was there" (II, 186–7), he tells the Duke of St Bungay. The elder duke, feeling that the younger has lowered himself unnecessarily, preaches to him a short sermon. The circumstances of his birth, St Bungay tells Palliser, "have imposed duties quite as high . . . as any which a career in the House of Commons can put within the reach of a man" — he refers to the preservation of their class and of the public esteem for it. And he concludes: "you need not . . . take your place in the arena of politics as though you were still Plantagenet Palliser, with no other duties than those of a politician." Palliser replies: "I have but one ambition . . . To be the serviceable slave of my country." The elder duke tells him that a man is more "serviceable" than a slave. "No, no; I deny it . . . The politician who becomes the master of his country sinks from the statesman to the tyrant" (II, 187–90, *passim.*). Needless to say, this is not the party line. The Duke of St Bungay urges him, finally, to cultivate some of that haughtiness at the command of his late uncle. The new Duke of Omnium says: "not even you can make me other than I am. My uncle's life was to me always a problem which I could not understand . . . I do not feel the disgrace of following Mr. Bonteen." But others wonder at him; and finally "the transfer . . . did have the effect of lowering [him] in the estimation of the political world" (II, 190–2) — a world, however, with whose values we are amply familiar. Such a world could scarcely understand why such a man should want to expiate in hard work the imagined sins of an uncle — and that uncle a duke.

At the end of the novel, Palliser is still unhappy as Duke of Omnium but delighted to have again some political work to do. Phineas says of him, in words very much like those Trollope was to use in the *Autobiography*, that "No Englishman whom I have met is so broadly and intuitively and unceremoniously imbued with the simplicity of the character of a gentleman. He could no more lie than he could eat grass" (II, 368–9). We see him finally settling the Trumpeton Wood feud — though as Trollope says (using a favorite analogy), Palliser sees no more reason to the demand that he should produce foxes than that "a bear [should] be baited, or a badger . . . drawn, in . . . his London dining room." And he is summed up for us as a man "devoted to work and to Parliament, an unselfish, friendly, wise man, who . . . recreated himself with Blue Books, and speculations on Adam Smith . . . but . . . knew that he was himself peculiar, and . . . respected the habits of others" (II, 374–5). He has come a long way from those spoony days of *The Small House at Allington* — and he is to go much further. He is indeed "peculiar" in the world of the Palliser novels.

"You can trace the lines of lingering regret upon his countenance when people be-Grace him," Phineas tells Lady Laura. "There was always about him a simple dignity which made it impossible that any one should slap him on the back. . . . [But he] is the same Planty Pall" (II, 414). The novel's last paragraph describes him as being "on the very eve of success with the decimal coinage. But his hair is becoming grey, and his back is becoming bent; and men say that he will never live as long as his uncle. But then he will have done a great thing, – and his uncle did only little things." In *Phineas Finn* (II, 296) it was said of Palliser that he "works as hard as any man in the country. Will he not maintain [the dukedom] better? What did the present man [the old Duke] ever do?" Rich aristocrats have no license to dawdle. They owe the country hard work, and Palliser is paying his debt – and his uncle's. To the end of *Phineas Redux* – even in his coinage fixation, and far beyond it – the compulsive Palliser represents the moral attractiveness of the Liberal aristocracy. Honest, diligent, and patriotic, he is both anomalous and necessary in the world he inhabits.

Phineas himself is not as attractive a figure as in *Phineas Finn* – some of the gloss has worn off – but he represents the rest of what is, if not specially admirable, at least not corrupt in the world of politics. His story continues to be morally instructive. We are reintroduced to him at Tankerville as a man who "retired from office because he found himself compelled to support a measure which had since been carried by those very men from whom he had been obliged on this account to divide himself . . . He had been twelve months in advance of his party, and had consequently been driven out into the cold" (I, 5). Fitzgibbon says of him, almost in awe: "Phinny can stick to a desk from twelve to seven, and wish to come back again after dinner." He too is "a different sort of man" in this political world. Having "given up everything . . . with the view of getting into office," he has learned early that "for such a one as he, truth to a principle was political annihilation" (I, 393 and 397). This is brought home to him again when, upon getting in, the Liberals refuse him office; having voted against them once, he is considered altogether unsafe: "he would weaken any Government that would give him office," says Bonteen (I, 410).

Like a good picaresque hero, Phineas has all manner of things happen to him. There is the Tankerville election; his exclusion from office; the Browborough trial; and of course his own trial for murder.

Even in prison Phineas is "a different sort of man." He tells Chaffanbrass that if he could be sure the world would learn its mistake, he would sooner be wrongly convicted and hanged "than be acquitted and afterwards be looked upon as a murderer." He will tolerate "No subterfuges, no escaping by a side wind, no advantage taken of little forms, no objection taken to this and that as though delay would avail us anything" (II, 218). He emerges from this ordeal much shaken, and also with fewer illusions about the nature of the life he has chosen to lead: being close to death has sharpened his vision of his fellow men. "Things seem to be so different now from what they did," he tells Laura. He sees his chosen profession in a less flattering light: "I don't care for the seat. It all seems to be a bore and a trouble. What does it matter who sits in Parliament? The fight goes on just the same. The same falsehoods are acted. The same mock truths are spoken. The same wrong reasons are given. The same personal motives are at work" (II, 306). Phineas's disillusionment brings him down a long path from his early idealisms and enthusiasms; but his brief career, like Trollope's briefer one, has revealed to him – in its unveiling of "falsehoods," "mock truths," "wrong reasons," and "personal motives" – some further measure of truth and of true values. In the novel's remaining pages he is less concerned with "place" than with putting his private life in order. He becomes a more sympathetic character as he becomes more cynical – as he more closely approaches, that is, Trollope's own perspective on his created world. Polhemus has called it "cynicism born of trauma": presumably he is thinking of Beverley. Phineas grows more pessimistic as his moral sense develops and he perceives "the brutality and insensitivity of political life, the weakness of self, the strength of obsession, and the flimsiness of reputation."[28] In particular the cool reaction to his troubles from the public figures of his world have revealed to him the principle that the "feelings of individuals," as Laura had warned him, become secondary considerations in the political scramble – the destruction of feeling itself often being the price paid by those who scramble successfully. Politicians cannot be concerned with individuals; the interest of the single man must always be sacrificed to the broader interest of acquiring or retaining power.[29] Phineas had once heard Barrington Erle declare that "Heart should never have anything to do with politics" (*Phineas Finn*, I, 258); he has come now to understand the meaning and the results of this philosophy. The pursuit of power does make men heartless; only their women are (sometimes) concerned with the problems of individuals. Having grasped this melancholy truth, fed up with the heartlessness and insincerity of men without feelings or convictions, Phineas grows reluctant to return to the House of Commons. He writes to Laura:

'I shall hate to go back to the House, and have . . . learned to dislike and distrust all those things that used to be so fine and lively to me. I don't think that I believe any more in the party; or rather in the men who lead it. I used to have a faith that now seems to me to be marvellous . . . I believed that on our side the men were patriotic angels, and that Daubeny and his friends were all fiends or idiots. . . . It has all come now to one common level of poor human interests. I doubt whether patriotism can stand the wear and tear and temptation of the front benches in the House of Commons. Men are flying at each other's throats, thrusting and parrying, making false accusations and defences equally false, lying and slandering, — sometimes picking and stealing, — till they themselves become unaware of the magnificence of their own position. . . . Little tricks of sword-play engage all their skill. And the consequence is that there is no reverence now for any man in the House. . . . I did long . . . for office. . . . But I meant to earn my bread honestly. . . . The conviction remains with me that parliamentary interests are not those battles of gods and giants which I used to regard them.' (II, 334–45)

Like the Liberal candidate at Beverley, Phineas joined the battle when he thought it was important enough to have devoted to it the energies of an honest man; now he has become so disillusioned as to dislike his own party as much as the other one: "It has all come . . . to one common level of poor human interests." This is the end of "faith," and the beginning of the end of "reverence." Some of Trollope's lingered on for a few years longer, discernible in sections of *The Prime Minister* and the *Autobiography*. But the picture of the House of Commons — the reality beyond that romantic door invoked in *Can You Forgive Her?* — as the shameless scene of "lying and slandering, — sometimes picking and stealing," had already become the dominant one for him. In the hysterical self-aggrandizing scramble for place, patriotism, he decided, has no chance — except in the rare man, as recounted in the next Palliser novel. Even Gresham comes to seem common to Phineas, just as Trollope's admiration for Gladstone faded. The novelist and his hero ceased simultaneously to believe in "the party" and in "the men who lead it." So Phineas refuses office when it is at last offered "because the chicaneries and intrigues of office had become distasteful to him" (II, 412; later he will accept office when invited to do so by Palliser — but Palliser is not Gresham, who once offered a Cabinet post to Bonteen). Political leaders, Phineas realizes, must lie to live; their "words never savour of truth" (II, 359). Having seen such men occupy high places, he has learned to value the places themselves more justly, as well as the men. "To sit in the Cabinet" becomes no very wonderful thing after all; and the lower offices also are more justly appraised. Politics is defined at last as that which makes liars out of gentlemen.

Phineas's act of rejection is a deeply symbolic and important one in the dramatic development of the Palliser novels — in a sense it is the climax to which the first four of them lead. The two to come, in the narrower focus upon Palliser himself, are less broadly satirical and savage, though undoubtedly somber in mood. Phineas's renunciation expresses Trollope's final perception of his own frustrated political ambition as having been, sadly enough, little more than an "insane desire" in a world as alien as the one described here. Like Underwood after Percycross and Trollope himself after Beverley, Phineas feels at the end that what he thought he wanted all along was only "one of those toys which look to be so very desirable in the shop-window, but ... give no satisfaction when they are brought home" (II, 423). And he declares — again as Trollope surely declared to himself — that "That which I desired so ardently ... has now become ... distasteful to me. ... There is an amount of hustling on the Treasury Bench which makes a seat there almost ignominious" (II, 417).

Phineas adds a postscript to this comment (made in a letter to Laura), the tenor of which characterizes the nature of the story Trollope is telling in *Phineas Redux* — which is not, after all, completely black. "I do not say that it need be ignominious," Phineas adds. "To such a one as was Mr. Palliser it certainly is not so." After all, Phineas does get the seat at Tankerville, and Browborough is kicked out of it — there is some justice. But Phineas has come to feel that the wrong men have become too strong for justice now, so that there is not enough of it to go around. Still, he himself can live happily ever after — especially when his financial problems are solved, his marriage to Madame Max making him independent at last. Having no financial problems makes it easier for "such a one as was Mr. Palliser" to avoid the moral pitfalls of politics; being a rich man makes a difference. The reader of the Palliser novels may already know this — but it will not prevent him from being told again in *Phineas Redux*.

VIII

It has been fashionable, as we know, to say that Trollope's political novels are not "really" political — that, despite surfaces, there is no politics in them to speak of. It has also been usual for critics to separate the political and social worlds they find in the Palliser novels and to miss or ignore the important ways in which these worlds are connected. "Trollope never took his politics more seriously than as a means of creating another background for the portrayal of human beings," said Speare; and he went on to justify this by arguing that in the Palliser novels "political cabinets feed ... always upon small talk and small ideas" (he did not live to read the Watergate transcripts). Disraeli's biographer compares Trollope's political novels with Disraeli's and sees them as the novels of an outsider against those of an insider. Being concerned in any case "with the social background of politicians" rather "than with politics as an end in itself," says Blake, Trollope "misses the thrills and the suspense of that strange closed world which inhabits the great gothic palace of Westminster, the absorption with victory or defeat." Anyone who has read the political novels of Disraeli and Trollope knows how wrong this is. Disraeli's novels give a very imprecise impression of the House of Commons and the political clubs; Trollope's portray them vividly. Political ideas and methods are best discussed by half a dozen people in a back room, and that's where Disraeli usually puts them. But Parliament and the clubs provide the best background for the profession, the game, the day-to-day experience of politics; and thus "Trollope's pages smell of the House of Commons" itself,[30] while Disraeli's smell of theory and personal rancor. Trollope's novels gain strength from their relative objectivity and detachment; Disraeli's, in their passionate propagandizing, their satire, and their sentimental romanticism, tell us almost nothing specific about political processes, though they are lively social documents. As for "the thrills and the suspense" of official political life — "the absorption with victory or defeat" — nowhere in English political fiction do we find these things so extensively before us as in the *Phineas* novels, especially *Phineas Redux*. Placed next to them, Disraeli's novels, diverting as they are, seem inert tracts. They are the novels of a romantic and a polemicist; Trollope's are those of a realist and a scientist.

To say this is not to contradict the argument that Trollope's political novels connect social and political life, private and public life, so closely as to render them often almost indistinguishable. One can see these connections, as Trollope did, without having to relegate politics to a supporting role. Indeed, seeing them in this way helps make these novels rather more than less authentic.

Of all the ways in which the two spheres are related in *Phineas Redux* perhaps none is so instructive as the two-edged controversy over Bonteen's expected appointment to Gresham's Cabinet and Phineas's expected exclusion on the grounds of past disloyalty. It is a controversy only because Glencora makes it one — she and her circle lobbying passionately (and with modern efficiency) against Bonteen and for Phineas. Being rich, socially powerful as Duchess of Omnium, and the wife of an important politician, she can have substantial local impact on political issues when she chooses, social position and political power being so closely related. It is said in *Phineas Redux* (I, 329) that no ministry can go out or come in without Glencora's "assistance." This is only partly ironic; indeed, her hatred of Bonteen keeps him out of a Cabinet and even prevents, briefly, a ministry from being formed.

The story is quickly told. Wishing to help Phineas get an appointment in the Gresham government, Madame Max says "a few judicious words to her friend, the Duchess." Glencora owes Madame Max a debt of gratitude for her behavior respecting the late Duke; and anyway she likes Phineas and hates Bonteen, a pompous fool with social pretensions she wishes to deflate. When she discovers that it is by Bonteen's influence that Phineas is to be excluded from office, she declares war: "the Duchess swore that she wasn't going to be beaten by Mr. Bonteen." She rallies her forces: Lady Glencora, Lady Cantrip, Lady Chiltern, Lady Laura Kennedy, and Madame Max Goesler — their energies combined — represent a social and political influence virtually irresistible among Liberal politicians. Glencora also speaks to her husband, who speaks to the Duke of St Bungay — and the two Dukes are powerful with Gresham. Erle, Ratler, Lords Cantrip, Fawn, Brentford, and Mount Thistle are courted by the other ladies. Glencora — "there is not a better engineer going," says Madame Max — is especially resolved that of all things Bonteen is not to owe any advancement "to her husband's favour ... he made himself so disagreeable at Matching." So are enemies made; a successful politician must list the social graces among his weapons. With Erle, at least, Glencora does not bother to be subtle: "If [Phineas is] passed over I'll make such a row that some of you shall hear it." "How fond all you women are of Phineas Finn," is the reply (I, 407). As in *Phineas Finn*, a chief source of what political success Phineas has is the admiration of women; he owes his career to the influence of women — relatives who wish to help him, society women who find him attractive. Women also virtually save his life by supporting him during his trial for murder — it is notable that, as Glencora says afterwards, "nobody but women [saw] it clearly" from the start. By the end of the story Phineas owes everything he has — including, finally, his very life — to the influence of women. Women launched his political career, women kept it going, and women ultimately make it possible for him to find his long-desired independence.

Glencora with her husband is more supplicating but no less effective in the Bonteen-Finn affair. "If you can't manage this for me, Plantagenet, I shall take it very ill. It's a little thing, and I'm sure you could have it done. I don't very often trouble you by asking for anything" (I, 409). Like Bishop Proudie, Palliser values the tranquility of domestic life, sufficiently untroublesome to allow him to do as he likes most of the time; and he also knows from past experience how untranquil his wife can make things for him at home when she chooses. He speaks to the Duke of St Bungay; they decide to refuse to serve in the new Cabinet if Bonteen is to be included. Glencora, who has "sworn an oath inimical to Mr. Bonteen," therefore becomes directly responsible for Gresham's difficulty in forming a Cabinet; indeed, she is "at the bottom of it all." Her negotiating position is quite simple: "If Phineas Finn might find acceptance, then Mr. Bonteen might be allowed to enter Elysium" (I, 430). When Bonteen's stock seems to rise again momentarily, Glencora goes "sedulously to work, and before a couple of days were over she did make her husband believe that Mr. Bonteen was not fit to be Chancellor of the Exchequer ... Before the two days were over, the Duke of St. Bungay [also] had a very low opinion of Mr. Bonteen" (I, 431). Most effective of all is the way she carefully draws out her victim in company so as to make him offend the elder Duke. Bonteen, who "could not save himself from talking about himself when he was encouraged," makes a complete ass of himself with Glencora's lead:

> he offended all those feelings of official discretion and personal reticence which had been endeared to the old Duke by the lessons which he had learned from former statesmen and by the experience of his own life. To be quiet, unassuming ... modest in any mention of himself, low-voiced ... had been his aim ... He would never have ventured to speak of his own services as necessary to any Government. That he had really been indispensable to many he must have known,

but not to his closest friend would he have said so. . . . To such a man
the arrogance of Mr. Bonteen was intolerable. (I, 432)

We should note the distinction made here between the aristocrat and the
pushing *bourgeois* — as always, Trollope's sympathies are with the former.
The Duke of St Bungay is the spirit of the grand old Whigs; Bonteen is the
incarnation of the vulgar modern Liberal.

Refusing to come into the new ministry, the two Dukes are joined by
other men; Gresham, stymied, gives in. "At last Mr. Bonteen was
absolutely told that he could not be Chancellor of the Exchequer [though
there was] . . . no other man ready and fit" for the job. Erle, as patronage
secretary, suggests to Gresham that matters would go more quietly if
Phineas were given a place in the new government — but Gresham refuses
to be so driven, and this part of Glencora's campaign is not successful. "I
haven't done with Mr. Bonteen yet," she says when the news comes of
Phineas's exclusion. Trollope sums up: "There could be no doubt that Mr.
Bonteen's high ambition had foundered, and that he had been degraded
through the secret enmity of the Duchess of Omnium. It was equally
certain that his secret enmity to Phineas Finn had brought this punishment
on his head" (I, 437). Issues, aptitudes, strengths, weaknesses — these
things seem to have little to do with important political appointments.

Afterwards society makes much of Phineas, especially when it is
rumored that Bonteen's opposition to him was in part a response to the
notorious love of a married woman (Lady Laura) for him: "many ladies
. . . could not understand why he should be shut out of office . . . and by
no means . . . [approved] the stern virtue of the Prime Minister. It was an
interference with things which did not belong to him" — though where the
one world ends and the other begins it is difficult to say. Lady Cantrip and
the Duchess of St Bungay continue to pursue Bonteen with their anger:
"The young Duchess was a woman very strong in getting up a party; and
the old Duchess, with many other matrons of high rank, was made to
believe that it was incumbent on her to be a Phineas Finnite." (The elder
Duchess doesn't understand anything of the affair, but "once fancied
[herself] to be rudely treated by Mrs. Bonteen" — this is enough.) The
result of all this for Phineas is "that though [he] was excluded from the
Liberal Government, all Liberal drawing-rooms were open to him, and that
he was a lion" (II, 26). The drawing-room, as we know, can be as powerful
as the Cabinet-room, such influences being simply part of the political
process. That political success is usually impossible without social approval
is sometimes a good thing, apparently; Bonteen clearly is *not* fit to be in
the Cabinet, and so although Glencora's campaign is grounded in personal
considerations it has the ultimate effect of justice — as the voice of society
so often does in Trollope's novels. If Trollope emphasizes the importance
of dinner-parties and feminine influence in the political world, he is
revealing a reality rather than distorting one. A political novel that deals

almost exclusively with politics (Disraeli's *Coningsby* is a good example)
tells us very little indeed about the political process if it is not also careful
to place its subject in the social contexts from which, after all, it cannot
really be separated. The comparison is a revealing one. In his preface to
Coningsby (1844), Disraeli explained:

> It was not originally the intention of the writer to adopt the form of
> fiction as the instrument to scatter his suggestions, but, after reflection,
> he resolved to avail himself of a method which, in the temper of the
> times, offered the best chance of influencing opinion. . . . The main
> purpose of its writer was to vindicate the just claims of the Tory party
> to be the popular political confederation.

Coningsby fails as fiction precisely because it is so exclusively political; its
other scant materials remain unassimilated. Trollope's purposes being
different from Disraeli's, he does not write tracts.[31] Thus we read his
novels today.

We should note that Bonteen has his small party of followers too; and
that there is a social bifurcation of part of the political world into the
camps of the Bonteenites and the Finnites, as in *The Eustace Diamonds* the
Lizzieites and the Anti-Lizzieites split along political lines over matters
essentially social. Bonteen's murder and the subsequent indictment of
Phineas therefore have ramifications both social and political, emphasizing
further the proximity of the two realms. Mrs Bonteen is sure that Phineas is
guilty; Glencora is sure that he is innocent. Again the young Duchess tries
her influence in several places. She tells her husband that she will "go into
mourning" if Phineas is hanged, guilty or not: "You had better look to it"
(she assumes that judges and juries, like politicians, are easily bought — an
assumption not altogether unwarranted in the milieu which acquitted
Browborough). She and Madame Max offer to Phineas's defense "any sum
of money . . . that the case may want." While no one is actually bribed,
Phineas's rich female admirers use their resources to hire a first-class
barrister and to have some crucial detective-work done; these help get
Phineas acquitted and thus are by no means negligible contributions. One
senses, however — at least in Glencora's case — that such efforts are
undertaken more to bury what remains of the Bonteen party than to
restore Phineas Finn to the world; they represent her ultimate victory in
Phineas Redux in the realm of social politics. The feelings of others for
and against Phineas after the murder and before the acquittal are
significantly divided. The Chilterns, Laura, the Duchess of Omnium,
Madame Max, Monk, the Cantrips, and the Bunces are all more or less
certain of his innocence — and they are all Liberals. Erle, Fitzgibbon,
Gresham, and the Dukes of St Bungay and Omnium think he is innocent
but have doubts ("though the younger Duke never expressed such doubts
at home"), and they too are Liberals. Such leading Tories as Daubeny,

Roby, Boffin, and Sir Orlando Drought "were full of doubt" (Low, a Conservative, does believe in his friend, however). Mrs Bonteen, certain of Phineas's guilt, is supported by her two great friends, Lady Eustace and Mr Ratler. These three people are Liberals of various shades, but of course socially antagonistic to Phineas's cause. Lord Fawn, a Liberal, thinks he saw Phineas commit the murder, but Lord Fawn is always wrong. Mr Maule Senior is pursuing Madame Max and is therefore "quite sure" that Phineas is guilty (he also happens to be vaguely Tory). And so it goes. There is little genuine feeling expressed, except by Madame Max; people tend to divide along lines that can only be called "partisan," both politically and socially. This heartlessness among politicians even in social matters has been discussed earlier.

Ultimately the political and social aspects of such attitudes become impossible to isolate. The murder and the controversy that grows up around it have an effect upon the government, for example. Roby, the Tory patronage secretary, observes that with Bonteen out of the way there will be no spokesman for decimal coinage in the House of Commons and that the Liberals will therefore have "a good excuse" to drop it; and he tells Sir Orlando that in the present situation it is impossible that the government "should bring in any Church bill this Session." Indeed, the affair finally stops the session cold and renders both government and opposition inactive until it is resolved. "Nobody has done anything since the arrest," observes Glencora. "While Mr. Finn has been in prison legislation has come to a standstill altogether . . . When the excitement is over they'll never be able to get back to their business before the grouse . . . they'll hardly go on with the Session. . . . London will break up" (II, 278). Hearing that the Chief Justice has been "very civil" to Phineas in his trouble, she resolves to "have him down to Matching, and make ever so much of him." Her quarrel with Bonteen is finally seen to have repercussions equally political and social. When Walpole complained that the "political gentlemen" in *Phineas Redux* seemed inert because they were viewed only in political contexts, he must surely have forgotten the novel's entire second volume. The murder trial, indeed, is no mere piece of stage machinery dragged in to liven up the tedium of a dry novel about politics, as some have said.[32] It is not only dramatic and skilfully recounted; but in forcing characters to make choices, take sides, and display either the depth or paucity of their feelings, it also takes its place in the novelist's pattern of themes. And of course it is meant to be seen in counterpoint to the novel's other important trial, the trial of Browborough.

We have seen how events in "society" such as the Bonteen affair and the death of the old Duke of Omnium can have direct and substantial effects upon the political world, and we have seen how political alliances and antagonisms can invade the drawing-room. The two realms are connected in other ways too in *Phineas Redux*, perhaps more subtly. Mr Maule Senior, like Lizzie Eustace, is a knowledgeable social politician. He has a "parliamentary point of view" of his own social life – which is a continuing political campaign – understanding, for example, that there are certain "dinners ... which [he] ... cannot afford not to eat" when invited to do so. Slide's political loyalties seem to be tied to his treatment as a guest (or non-guest) in the political salons. Even that least politic of men, Lord Chiltern, finds himself compelled to use ploys of diplomacy and power politics to achieve his ends for Trumpeton Wood. That this is patently true is the point of Glencora's remark to him, after having been the target of much of his diplomatic maneuvering, that there ought to be "an officer of State, to go in and out with the Government, – with a seat in the Cabinet or not according as things go, [called] ... Foxmaster-General" (II, 379). Politics and society are also linked together when – as is often the case in *Phineas Redux* – images used throughout to characterize political life are applied also to society. Thus the social "world," like the political, is seen by Phineas as an oyster which is opened and kept open only with great difficulty (I, 13 and 63–4); and thus the same kind of equestrian and hunting imagery related to the political chase is used to characterize social life and achievement again and again (e.g., I, 76, 201, 204, 311, and II, 309).

(Perhaps the most interesting social metaphor has nothing to do with politics: the extended image used to connect engagements and marriages with boating. Lady Chiltern asks Adelaide Palliser why she has consented "to get into [Gerard Maule's] boat." The reply is: "You ask me why I got into his boat. Why does any girl get into any man's boat? Why did you get into Lord Chiltern's?" She then denies that she has committed herself: "I haven't got into this man's boat yet," but she adds: "I have a feeling that I should like to be in his boat, and I shouldn't like to be anywhere else." Lady Chiltern sums up: "You love him." It is difficult to read this exchange – II, 7 – without remembering the more famous similar passage in *The Ambassadors*; is this yet another of those political novels by Trollope that James did "not read"?)

The close connection between political and social considerations is emphasized through another familiar theme – the importance of money and its relationship to political and social success and failure. Again the chief exemplar is Phineas himself. In *Phineas Redux* he rediscovers that in order to live as part of the political and social set which dominates all other sets in England "a man should have means of his own." He once thought that as a politician he "could earn [his] bread ... as men do at other professions," but he is brought to confess later that he should not have thought so: "No man should attempt what I have attempted without means" (I, 439). As we have seen, he tells Lady Laura that while a man rich enough to be independent – a man such as Palliser – can be a politician without particular risk to his character, the "hustling on the Treasury Bench" can be "ignominious" for one "who goes there to get his bread, and has to fight his way as though for bare life" (II, 417). The nation is safer in the hands of rich men.

At the end of *Phineas Redux*, after Phineas has refused office, Madame Max puts to him a question which the *Phineas* novels were written largely to answer: "Do you think that public life then is altogether a mistake, Mr. Finn?" The reply, out of experience, is unambiguous and important: "For a poor man I think it is, in this country. A man of fortune may be independent; and because he has the power of independence those who are higher than he will not expect him to be subservient. A man who takes to parliamentary office for a living may live by it, but he will have but a dog's life of it" (II, 424). To sit in Parliament, Trollope had written many years earlier, "is a desirable position for a rich man, or a rich man's eldest son, or even for a poor man, if by getting . . . in he can put himself in the way of improving his income."[33] Trollope makes Phineas go through fire to learn that "For a poor man . . . in this country" politics without money is morally dangerous. Phineas undergoes an educative process in these novels not unlike Trollope's own between 1866 and 1871 — years during which he began writing *Phineas Finn* and finished writing *Phineas Redux*, and in between stood for Parliament.

The money theme is emphasized in one or two other ways. Laura, after her husband's death, thinks of starting a sort of political salon to "get people around me by feeding and flattering them, and by little intrigues"; she understands well enough that "It is money that is chiefly needed for that work, and of money I have enough now" (II, 403). We have seen what political power well-connected women with money may exercise when they choose to do so. And there is our old friend Fitzgibbon, who finally finds a wealthy lady willing to marry him — "by which it was hoped that the member for Mayo might be placed steadily upon his legs for ever." Erle wonders if the annuity of £2,000 a year she has settled on him for his life is sufficient consolation for marriage, and he goes on to compare marriage to the House of Commons with marriage to a wife — perhaps the closest pairing of all of the public and the private lives. "Office isn't very permanent," Erle the bachelor concludes (II, 370), "but one has not to attend the House above six months a year, while you can't get away from a wife much above a week at a time."

8   The Top of the Greasy Pole: Prime Ministers and *The Prime Minister*

'It is all nothing unless one can go to the very top.'

Phineas Finn

To be popular one must be a mediocrity.

Oscar Wilde

Men with large aims cannot afford to be scrupulous in small details.

Gissing, *Demos* (1886)

The Duke . . . is the T. E. Lawrence of Trollope's political scene.

A. O. J. Cockshut

After the failure of *The Way We Live Now* — which remained out of print from 1879 until 1941, so violent was the reaction against it — Trollope turned back to more familiar, and to what he hoped would be more congenial, scenes. But instead the result was more controversy; rather than restoring him to the good graces of the reading public, *The Prime Minister* (published serially November 1875–June 1876 and in four volumes in May 1876) received an explosive reception and gave Trollope the worst press he had ever had for a major work. As in the case of *The Way We Live Now*, however, modern opinion has reversed that of the 1870s; *The Prime Minister* has become a favorite subject (if not always a favorite novel) of the Pallisers' modern critics and one of Trollope's most written-about works. True, only two decades ago it could be said of *The Prime Minister* that, as Trollope's contemporaries had refused to read the novel, so in recent years it had been read "only by those few enthusiasts who will settle for nothing less than *all* of Trollope."[1] But every major study of Trollope published in the last ten years has devoted considerable space to *The Prime Minister*; it has become, like *The Last Chronicle of Barset*, *The Eustace Diamonds*, and *The Way We Live Now*, one of those novels critics feel they cannot pass over — it is too rich, too full, too interesting.

Trollope, who pinned his hopes for a popular comeback on *The Prime Minister* — and who of course felt he had a personal stake in the fortunes of his favorite people, subjects of four previous novels — was especially hurt and baffled by the poisonous reviews which greeted the publication of this most cherished story. (His bafflement was to deepen when his next two novels, *The American Senator* and *Is He Popenjoy?*, were more kindly received.) Indeed, his confidence in his own literary judgment was so badly shaken that he wondered if he ought to stop writing altogether. Among notices of *The Prime Minister* he was "specially hurt," he says in the *Autobiography* (which he was finishing as the first reviews of the novel began to appear), by that of the usually friendly *Spectator* — written by Meredith White Townsend but erroneously attributed by Trollope to his friend R. H. Hutton (and thus one possible cause of his special "hurt").[2] The *Spectator*'s review was not pleasant. It found the novel and its major characters unbelievable; especially galling to Trollope was its pronouncement that his beloved Pallisers — most particularly his favorite, the Duke of Omnium — had been smirched and degraded into "vulgarity" along with everyone and everything else in *The Prime Minister*. Palliser, it said, had become insolent, overbearing, unjust, and even ungentlemanly (since Trollope wrote in the *Autobiography*, before reviews of the novel began to appear, that Palliser "is a perfect gentleman. If he be not, then I am unable to describe a gentleman" — p. 310 — his outrage can be imagined); and Lady Glencora had been transformed into a pushing, perspiring, ill-bred parvenue. The review also accused Trollope of failing "to perceive what relations are and are not possible among English political men"; it found the "political sketches" — except for the portrait of the Duke of St Bungay — generally unsatisfactory. The notice concluded by declaring that Trollope's powers were declining. This became a major theme of the *Saturday Review*, which also accused the novel of vulgarizing its chief characters. Trollope, "faltering," had published a volume of tame "political gossip," it concluded. The bad notices piled up. The *Examiner* and the *Athenaeum* pronounced themselves bored by Trollope's politicians, while the *Illustrated London News* — incredibly — rated the political chapters of *The Prime Minister* the "weakest" in the book. In America, the *Nation* called the novel "monotonous," while *Harper's* rated it "commonplace." Predating Henry James's comment about Trollope's "complete appreciation of the usual," F. R. Littledale wrote in the *Academy* that the author of *The Prime Minister* was the only novelist since Jane Austen "to fathom the resources of the entirely commonplace"; though he found the novel "sub-par," at least he admired its portrait of Palliser. The only critical praise appeared in the pages of *The Times*, which had also applauded *The Way We Live Now*. The editor of *The Times*, John Delane — author of the so-called Printing House Square Manifesto, which had in part inspired Trollope in *The Way We Live Now* to attack the "commercial profligacy of the age" — was a close personal friend of the novelist. The *Times* critic — who obviously had been watching Palliser's development through the series — discussed his growth as a character from *Can You Forgive Her?* on. Finding Trollope's hero utterly convincing, he pronounced himself surprised that the novelist should be able, in *The Prime Minister*, to "make us know . . . and like" Palliser better than ever before. Lady Glencora he also found to be very real; but "The rest of the story hardly seems up to Mr. Trollope's usual mark." The *Times* reviewer concluded: " 'The Prime Minister' . . . will be greatly enjoyed by people who can take an interest in its public personages, and who appreciate clever studies of political character; but . . . it will [never] be numbered among the favourites of those who delight in Mr. Trollope for his love stories."[3]

One other contemporary response to *The Prime Minister* should be mentioned. Tolstoy pronounced it "a beautiful book," one of the most remarkable of all novels. (His other well-known comment about Trollope, "Trollope kills me, kills me with his mastery" − or "excellence," as in one translation − was made not about *The Prime Minister*, as Snow has asserted, but about *The Bertrams*, written earlier.)[4]

Escott said that Trollope relied on the Wharton-Lopez-Fletcher plot "to popularise the book by relieving the strain of the demand that the purely political sections made on the reader's attention"; and Trollope's own admission that "The Lopez part of the book has only been to me a shoe-horn for the other" tends to bear this out. Nobody but Polhemus has taken seriously this part of *The Prime Minister*; Booth's comment that it "is as bad as such things can be" was quite right.[5] Reactions to the Palliser sections of the novel have been mixed in recent years. Walpole, though bored by the political story ("one vast draught, scraps of political papers blowing down empty corridors before a ghostly breeze"), thought the harsh reviews "undeserved." Curtis Brown pronounced the novel one of Trollope's greatest, on a par with *The Last Chronicle of Barset* and *The Way We Live Now*. Booth found *The Prime Minister* bad, but not as bad as some of the other political novels (none of which − except, perhaps, *Phineas Finn* − he really liked) since at least "the interest of the political story is well-sustained." Polhemus called *The Prime Minister* "magnificent." Pope-Hennessy rated the political scenes "no longer stirring" and thus the whole "pretty dull." Finding, like everyone else, Emily Wharton "something of a trial," Snow nonetheless declared *The Prime Minister* "an admirable book . . . The political scenes are the best in the Palliser series, and the development of the Duke . . . is one of Trollope's subtlest triumphs."[6] So thought Trollope himself.

II

It is symptomatic of assessments of *The Prime Minister*, as of the Palliser novels generally, to belittle or ignore its political content and to discuss it as if it were either a sociological tract or a failed love story. Polhemus, in twenty trenchant and articulate pages, devotes the last half of the last page to politics in the novel. Despite its title, *The Prime Minister* has often been treated as if the political themes in it got there by accident. But it is not only a political novel — it is a very political novel, along with *Phineas Finn* and *Phineas Redux* one of the most political of the series.

The critic of *The Prime Minister* — like the critic of *Phineas Finn* and *Phineas Redux* — must deal first with questions of who and what, and especially who; for some of the vivid characterizations suggest once again figures of the contemporary scene. Over the years there has been a vague sense of this on the part of some. The *Saturday Review*, in its notice of *The Prime Minister*, declared that the novel included an "account of events that actually happened," but the reviewer did not specify or elaborate. Both the *Examiner* and *Harper's* speculated mistily that *The Prime Minister* seemed to convey some idea of what a career in Parliament was really like. Little else has been said.

It is probable that Palliser and Glencora are essentially original creations. But Trollope while writing *The Prime Minister* had other Prime Ministers running through his head and put into Palliser — consciously or not, it does not matter — a great deal of his own two favorite Liberal Premiers, Lord Palmerston and Lord John Russell. This probability becomes that much more credible when we are able to recognize in Glencora, in her role as the Prime Minister's wife, unmistakable characteristics of Lady Palmerston, the second Lady Russell, and another prominent member of the Russell clan, Lady Stanley of Alderley — all conspicuous Liberal hostesses.

Trollope's little-known memoir of *Lord Palmerston* was probably written just a year before his own death.[7] Palmerston, the central political figure of his time, was Foreign Secretary, except for one five-year interval, between 1830 and 1851, then Home Secretary for a few years, and finally Prime Minister from 1855 to 1858 and again from 1859 to 1865. During these latter years he presided over a powerful coalition of Whigs, ex-Peelites, and Radicals from which, subsequently, Gladstone's Liberal following was formed. Palmerston died in office in 1865. He is portrayed admiringly by Trollope as a man who hates self-display and immodesty, a man of principle whose stubbornness even to the point of perversity is in part what makes him a strong and effective leader, a man of courage, industry, perseverance and patriotism, and above all a man of total and uncompromising honesty who hated sham, cunning, and mystery in political affairs. "He was by no means a man of genius and was possessed of not more than ordinary gifts of talent," Trollope says, but "he was a man who from the first was determined to do the best with himself; and he did it with a healthy energy" (consciously or not, Trollope might also have been describing himself here; he shared with Palmerston some habits of mind). "Against his honesty, his industry and his courage," Trollope concludes his memoir, "we feel that no true word can be said." Palmerston is seen by Trollope, at times with less objectivity than admiration, as the English bulldog incarnate:

He was brought up in that school of politicians in which a man uses his power of speech, or used to use it, not as a woman uses her teeth, for ornament, but as a dog does, for attack and defence ... [Palmerston] clung to his work with that tenacity which in official life will get the better of all arrears ... It was the nature of the man not to be diffident, and therefore he succeeded. His courage was coarse and strong and indomitable, like that of a dog.[8]

The historical Palmerston, we may note here, was from all indications a more crafty and disingenuous man than he appears in Trollope's memoir. But what is most significant is not the idealized and often uncritical approach, nor the accuracy or inaccuracy of the novelist as political historian or biographer – but rather what his book reveals about the ways in which *he saw* Palmerston, rightly or wrongly. While only indifferent history, Trollope's study is an interesting repository of his own political ideals.

Palliser in *The Prime Minister* is certainly no English bulldog. Unlike Palmerston, he has little self-confidence and almost no combativeness. His major interest in life is decimal coinage, a subject Palmerston would have found deadly and trivial. There are many other differences between the historical and fictional Prime Ministers, but in a number of important respects there are interesting and unmistakable resemblances. Like Palmerston (as depicted by Trollope), Palliser hates self-display and immodesty; he too can be stubborn and intractable to the point of perversity; he too is patriotic; he too is a tireless worker. No genius, he too has ordinary intellectual gifts with which, through energy and perseverance, he is determined to do as much as he can. Above all, he too hates sham, dishonesty, and cunning. He would rather be thrown out of office than tell the tiniest of fibs. At the end of the novel Monk sums up Palliser's tenure as Prime Minister in much the same way as Trollope sums up Palmerston's: "History will give you credit for patriotism, patience, and courage," Monk tells Palliser (II, 468). Another interesting though more tenuous connection between them lies in Trollope's several references to Palmerston as "manly" and "masculine" and his pronouncement in *Phineas Redux* (II, 303) that manliness is by definition incompatible with affectation – a vice, as he makes clear again and again throughout the series, by which Plantagenet Palliser, the wealthy, well-born, and powerful Duke of Omnium, has been untouched.

This is a bare outline. There are other indications that Trollope had Palmerston at least partly in mind in the Prime Minister of *The Prime Minister.*

While Prime Minister, and in spite of his wife's lavish entertainments, Palliser remains simple in his tastes: "No man more easily satisfied as to what he eat [*sic*] or drank lived in London in those days," says Trollope. Of Palmerston he says: "It was characteristic of him that neither in his early or in his later life was there any love of display" – despite the fact that he too, as we shall see, was married to a woman (the sister of Lord Melbourne) who loved to give lavish political parties. Trollope also says of Palmerston that "industry and ... perseverance had come before his ambition." In *The Prime Minister*, Palliser grows particularly unhappy when he begins to feel that he is only a figurehead and that his ministers are doing all the work. Such a position might well appeal to some men, but "The absence of real work, and quantity of mock work" only irritate this man, as such a situation would have irritated Trollope himself. Like Palmerston as conceived by Trollope, Palliser loves work and hates idleness; he would rather be an industrious member of the Cabinet than the relatively idle man in charge of it.[9]

The most striking resemblance between the two, however, is in the singular brand of stubbornness Trollope depicts in each. Palliser behaves during a number of crises in *The Prime Minister* — the Silverbridge election, the Lopez affair, the bestowal of the Garter — as if he belonged neither to a party nor a government. He does what he feels is right — often with disastrous political results. Trollope saw Palmerston as such a man. When he "had found, or thought he had found, that a thing was just," says Trollope, Palmerston "would have his way," no matter what the consequences; the slaking of partisan thirsts was always secondary to him (true or not, this is the way Trollope *saw* Palmerston). No matter what the causes or the results, says the novelist, Palmerston believed that "The right thing to do must be the right thing ... an English statesman cannot dare to be other than honest ... Palmerston possessed two virtues by means of which his name will go down to posterity altogether unsullied. He was brave, and he was honest ... It is difficult indeed to defend his manner; but that which he desired to get, he desired honestly." Like Palmerston "brave" and "honest," Palliser is also condemned by others for his "manner"; good or bad, however, his manner has nothing to do with the purity of his intentions, which throughout *The Prime Minister* remain "unsullied." Indeed, some of the things Palliser does in the novel, though "right" from a purely objective point of view, border on the perverse when seen from a political or partisan point of view. But Palliser does not care for this latter perspective; he refuses to see anything from it. Citing Palmerston's "stubbornness" both in and out of office, Trollope says that when once the man found himself in a position of political authority "it was not probable that he would become more malleable than before" — a statement which also perfectly fits Palliser in *The Prime Minister*. And Trollope goes on: "This perversity was an essential part of Lord Palmerston's character, — and of his strength." The novelist also refers to Palmerston's "determination to have his own way which governed him through all his life." Any reader of *The Prime Minister* may detect here a profound temperamental similarity between Trollope's real and imaginary Prime Ministers — both of them heroes to the novelist though so different in terms of political achievement. Finally, Trollope's approving quotation of a statement made by Palmerston while Prime Minister — "I am satisfied that the interest of England is the Polar star, — the guiding principle of the conduct of the Government" — may remind us of his characterization of Palliser in *The Prime Minister*: he is, says Trollope, "the very model of an English statesman. He loved his country dearly, and wished her to be, as he believed her to be, first among nations" (I, 124).[10]

Nowhere, of course, does Trollope suggest that Palliser is Palmerston, and the evidence assembled here (as well as the resemblance of their names) is only circumstantial. Indeed, Palliser and Palmerston in many ways are very unlike one another. For example: Palmerston's "great merit as a governing man arose from his perfect sympathy with those whom he was called upon to govern," says Trollope. Nor was Palmerston's genuine zest for the rough and tumble of political affairs — "Not to be in the centre of everything . . . ready for all attacks, for all explanations, for all discussions . . . was to him not to live," says Trollope in *Lord Palmerston* — at all like Palliser.[11] Important here is not the question of how closely the two men may resemble one another at every point but rather what it is that Trollope values in each as a useful public servant. If there are differences in temperament — and of course there are — the differences in terms of courage, tenacity, and patriotism are very few indeed. Both are idealized.

At one point in *The Prime Minister* (II, 6) the Duke of St Bungay explicitly contrasts Palliser as Prime Minister with Lord Brock, the Liberal Premier of *Can You Forgive Her?*. Citing the younger Duke's thin-skinned sensitivity to the political guests he continually finds in his house, St Bungay bursts out to Lord Cantrip: "Do you remember old Brock? By heavens; — there was a covering, a hide impervious to fire or steel! He wouldn't have gone into tantrums because his wife asked too many people to his house." Brock, as we saw in Chapter 4, clearly is modelled on Palmerston. Now Glencora, like her husband, is essentially an original creation; but when Palliser assumes the mantle of Palmerston, she begins to act and sound like Palmerston's wife. Lady Palmerston, like Lady Brock, was famous — actually infamous — for her attempts to help her husband govern England through what is referred to in *The Prime Minister* as the "drawing-room influences" of mammoth parties. When Glencora, who wants to do the same, declares that she intends by her hospitality as the Premier's wife "to make Buckingham Palace second-rate" (II, 66), every sentient contemporary reader of *The Prime Minister* would have remembered Lady Palmerston. Thus there is a singular irony in St Bungay's remark to Cantrip quoted above — as there is in Phineas Finn's comment to Glencora herself that though the time for drawing-room influences has almost gone by, "They used to be very great. Old Lord Brock used them extensively" (I, 265–6). Like Glencora, Lady Palmerston entertained all shades of political opinion while passionately intriguing along partisan lines in her husband's interest. Like Glencora, she fought with journalists constantly, and often excluded them from her gatherings. Certainly she was the social center of the Liberal salons of the day, as Glencora is. Lady Palmerston's Saturday night receptions at Cambridge House were famous; the guest lists as they appeared the next morning in *The Times* or the *Morning Post* "were political barometers where politicians could literally read of the possible success or failure of some measure or some statesman" — thus the scramble, in *The Prime Minister*, to get into Glencora's parties. The account of Lady Palmerston given by the Countess of Airlie is simple-minded yet in its starkness reminiscent, perhaps, of some of Glencora's uncomplicated thinking in *The Prime Minister*: "Should Lord Palmerston need votes or support for some measure — 'Stay! we will have a party,' said Lady Palmerston."[12]

In *Ralph the Heir* (I, 234), Trollope refers to "the great Reform Bill [of 1832] which had been initiated and perfected and carried through as a whole by the almost unaided intellect and exertions of the great reformer of his age." He does not mention the great man's name, but it is a safe assumption that he is Lord John Russell; and there are also unmistakable resemblances between Palliser in *The Prime Minister* and Trollope's other chief political hero. Russell came to political prominence in the 1830s as an architect of the first Reform Bill, held the Premiership from 1846 to 1852, participated between 1852 and 1855 in the Conservative Lord Aberdeen's compromise coalition ministry of Whigs and Peelites as leader of the House of Commons, and served briefly as Prime Minister once again in 1865. Trollope was an outspoken supporter of Lord John and sometimes used his name to represent what he most admired in a statesman — nobility, honesty, and candor.[13] Like Palliser, Russell was a Whig whose family was both wealthy and aristocratic. Neither was a distinguished orator. Both were undemonstrative and shy and thus unfairly thought to be cold. Both were serious, studious men (Russell edited Moore and Fox), and both were hard workers. Both men encountered political trouble which arose directly out of their own uncongeniality. In 1848, Greville wrote that Russell was "admirable in the House of Commons, but wanting in the qualities that a Prime Minister ought to have ... he is miserably wanting in amity, and in the small arts of acquiring popularity, which are of such incalculable value to the leader of a party, still more of a government; then, while he has the reputation of being obstinate, he is wanting in firmness." The resemblances here to the personality and the political troubles of Palliser (whose Cabinet is nicknamed "the Fainéants") will be manifest to any reader of *The Prime Minister*.

Equally to the point, some of Trollope's political ideals are close to Lord John's. Both, for example, said that a democratic monarchy divested of direct political power is the best kind of government man can devise. Russell, like Trollope's Prime Minister, advocated the continuing advance of democracy, worked to widen the franchise and reduce electoral corruption, championed individual freedom, and yet opposed the complete and more radical democracy of universal suffrage. In a letter to the *Examiner* of 6 April 1850, Trollope, writing from Ireland, explicitly defended Russell's Irish policy.[14]

In *Can You Forgive Her?* (I, 351), Glencora, at the height of exasperation with her inattentive husband, remarks of Burgo Fitzgerald: "I could stoop at his feet and clean his shoes for him and think it no disgrace!" In *Phineas Finn* (II, 284), Phineas says to himself that he would "sooner clean boots for barristers" than marry a woman simply to get her money. In *Phineas Redux* (II, 193–4), Glencora complains to her husband of his excessive humility in public affairs. "You would clean Mr. Gresham's shoes for him, if — the service of your country required it," she petulantly declares (Gresham is the Prime Minister of the moment). The response is unhesitating. "I would even allow you to clean them, — if the service of the country required it," says Palliser. These passages were probably inspired by Lady Russell's celebrated remark of the fifties that her husband "would not mind being 'shoe-black to Lord Aberdeen' if it would serve the country"[15] (Russell was serving at the time in Aberdeen's ministry). There are other obvious connections between Glencora and the second Lady Russell; as Trollope put bits and pieces of both Palmerston and Russell into the Premier of *The Prime Minister*, so he put bits and pieces of their wives into the Premier's wife. Glencora and Lady Russell both came from wealthy and aristocratic Scottish families (Lady Russell was the daughter of the Earl of Minto), both were considerably younger than their husbands and required the encouragement of their families before marrying, both were lively and impulsive.[16]

Lady Russell once wrote to her husband: "My ambition is that you should be the head of the most moral and religious government the country has ever had";[17] clearly she was capable of a moral fervor in politics totally alien to Glencora, whose ambitions are more personal and less spiritual. In this Glencora is perhaps a little more like another member of the Russell family, Lady Stanley of Alderley — wife of Trollope's post-office boss and frequently the novelist's hostess — another enthusiastic political party-giver. A woman of great influence in middle and late Victorian social and political circles, her wit and power may be judged by the fact that her husband, when Liberal patronage secretary, was called by Lord Palmerston " 'joint-whip' with Mrs. Stanley," while her grandson Bertrand Russell remembered her as a woman who "had a caustic tongue, and spared neither age nor sex" and was "contemptuous of Victorian goody-goody priggery." If this reminds us of Glencora, even more striking is Lady Stanley's announcement to her family that "I have left my brain to the Royal College of Surgeons . . . because it will be so interesting for them to have a clever woman's brain to cut up"[18] — which sounds just like Glencora's characteristic irreverence. Lady Stanley, a zealous and intelligent social politician, also used her drawing-room to help her husband and his party; indeed, her "social efforts matched her husband's political ones for diligence," Bartrum has noted. Especially interesting in this connection is the fact that Trollope himself, according to Lady Stanley's engagement book, was invited to at least six of her political-social gatherings, and to at least four of those given by her daughter, Lady Amberley. A further measure of the novelist's popularity with the Stanley-Russell contingent is the fact that Trollope's sister and brother-in-law (John Tilley, a post office colleague of Trollope's) came twice to Lady Stanley's, while the great enemy of the Trollope-Tilley party, Sir Rowland Hill (advocate of competitive examinations for the Civil Service, pilloried as Sir Gregory Hardlines in *The Three Clerks* and again as Sir Raffle Buffle in *The Last Chronicle of Barset*), was never asked, despite his higher status and rank.[19]

Lest it seem too easy to match up Lady Stanley and Glencora, it should also be pointed out that Lady Stanley, who interested herself greatly in politics, was an enthusiastic partisan of several social causes, while Glencora is portrayed as equally indifferent to all of them; and that Lady Stanley, unlike Glencora, liked journalists and often had them in her house.

Trollope was not that much in demand as a guest at political soirées, and undoubtedly he got some of the doings of political hostesses from the social columns of the daily newspapers — which, as his letters make amply clear, he read regularly and carefully. Certainly his political novels tell us enough of such affairs to bear out his familiarity with them, at either first or second hand. Until the late 1860s "the Whigs held the key to society," historian John R. Vincent has written, "and their price was a political one";[20] that the Palliser novels demonstrate this is further confirmation of their substantial authenticity.

There have been, and of course there continue to be, other speculations of this sort — all of them more tenuous in the original they suggest than those offered here. Certainly Trollope's more painstaking readers have often wondered about possible real-life models, though few of them have tracked any down in convincing fashion. Hoyt thought the idealized leader of Taylor's *Statesman* was the original of Plantagenet Palliser; apRoberts has compared Trollope's character to Shakespeare's Brutus.[21] There are also two unpublished essays which argue, in the first instance, that Palliser is based on Trollope's friend Charles Buxton, and, in the second, that his career is modelled on that of the fifth Duke of Newcastle.[22] In fact it represents — outwardly, at least — neither Palmerston's nor Russell's nor Newcastle's, all of whom were professional party men; Palmerston and Russell each spent upwards of forty years in and out of office, than which nothing could be more unlike the career of Plantagenet Palliser. Indeed, if Palliser's ministry resembles any historical one, it is that of Lord Aberdeen, a Tory who joined with Whigs in 1852 to become Prime Minister in a coalition government and like Palliser held office, ineptly, for three years. It is unlikely, given what we know of Trollope's political leanings, that there are any more substantial connections between the Liberal Duke and the Conservative Aberdeen, whose ministry was largely responsible for the Crimean debacle which brought Palmerston back to power. We know, however, how fond Trollope was of reversing parties for the sake of obfuscating such connections. There is certainly one clear pattern. Palmerston began political life as a Canningite Conservative, served in several Tory governments, and ended up as a very conservative Liberal. Russell also participated in several Conservative governments; he was an old-fashioned Whig of the most moderate school. Palliser is described again and again as a moderate, a Liberal who dislikes the Radicals and does not see much difference in terms of *doctrine* between his party and the Tories (he often speculates whimsically on the accidents which lead men into one party or the other). Trollope himself, a self-described "advanced conservative liberal," was of the same general school. This may help explain why he should have chosen these men as models for his ideal politician.

But — any possible similarities between Palliser and Lord Palmerston or Lord John Russell or anyone else are less important as evidence of a connection between the men in Trollope's mind than as a demonstration of what the novelist values in the character of a public man. That is to say, Palliser in all likelihood represents not a particular Prime Minister but rather an ideal composed of several men. (In the same way Glencora as political hostess may be seen as a synthesis of Lady Palmerston, Lady Russell, and Lady Stanley — though despite her tremendous appeal she is not meant to be taken as any kind of "ideal" in *The Prime Minister*.) It is the ideal we should be most concerned to define here. What is chiefly important about Palliser is not who he is (interesting as such speculations are), but rather what he is, what he represents, what he means.

Given what we know about Trollope's political prejudices and antipathies, even a cursory reading of *The Prime Minister* should be sufficient to establish Palliser as a sort of ideal politician — ideal not in terms of political success, for he accomplishes little while in office, but in terms of the resolute resistance he offers to the potential moral corruptions of political place. Trollope felt that it was more important for a leader to remain honest and true to himself than to master the morally questionable skills or make the purely opportunistic compromises necessary to keep himself in office and at an advantage over his adversaries. The statesman's faults as a politician are often his virtues as a man. Typically, Trollope's major interest is in defining politics, showing what it consists in and what constitutes moral conduct in the political context, rather than in slyly introducing real politicians into his fiction. Insofar as Palliser resembles Palmerston or Russell at all it is in the way all three men represent to Trollope various manifestations of moral political leadership. Using as models admired political men, Trollope creates his own Prime Minister — a man who, whatever his literary origin, represents in himself the novelist's ideal statesman.

III

Let us exorcise various claims to the contrary. Some of Trollope's recent critics have failed to discern, in Palliser's political failure, a victory of another sort — and of a kind to put him closer to the novelist's heart than any political success might have done. For Polhemus, an important theme of *The Prime Minister* is that "the days of amateur political pundits like Planty Pal were numbered," that Palliser's "qualities . . . are hardly the qualities it takes to govern a modern state . . . He obviously does not have the political intelligence to cope with the new world"; thus for him the novel ends on a fatalistic note. But Trollope in *The Prime Minister* is not interested in the "modern state" or "the new world"; he is interested in old-fashioned — not amateurish — political virtue. Booth saw Palliser as a "*political* failure" due to "weakness of character." And he added: "English Prime Ministers in the nineteenth century were brilliant and exciting; the Duke of Omnium, by contrast, is a dry stick." But it is Palliser's *strength* of character, not weakness, that makes him a political failure in the novel: the difference is important. And apparently Booth never heard of Liverpool, Peel, Russell, Aberdeen, Derby, Cavendish, or Gladstone — all of whom, by contemporary accounts, were certainly unexciting characters; only Canning, Palmerston, and Disraeli among nineteenth-century British Premiers were "brilliant and exciting." And apRoberts has also contended that Palliser fails — fails "through his very goodness," but fails. Citing as an example the arbitrary bestowal of the Garter on Lord Earlybird, she reached the astonishing conclusion that "even" he — Palliser — succumbs to the perversions of power.[23] This is patently untrue.

Surely Palliser's political failure represents to Trollope a moral success of significant proportions. Let us take a closer look at the Palliser of *The Prime Minister*.

We first become reacquainted with him during a political crisis. The Conservative government has resigned, the Liberals are unable to put together a Cabinet, and confusion and uncertainty reign. Palliser — "with the simple and single object of doing some special piece of work for the nation," without "any personal ambition," and doubting whether he has "any gift for governing men" — agrees to attempt to form a coalition ministry, and succeeds in doing so. It is a weak government with a reluctant and unself-confident man at its head, and we are led to fear the worst, as Palliser himself does.

Palliser's weakness as a political leader, however, is not the result of blind ambition or greed for power. On the contrary; his wife knows him

to be full of scruples, unable to bend when aught was to be got by bending, unwilling to domineer when men might be brought to subjection only by domination. The first duty never could be taught to him. To win support by smiles when his heart was bitter within him would never be within the power of her husband. He could never be brought to buy an enemy by political gifts, — would never be prone to silence his keenest opponent by making him his right-hand supporter. (I, 61)

Here we see that Palliser is innocent of many of the crimes Trollope is so fond of attributing to the successful politicians of his day. The Duke would rather be right than Prime Minister. He comes into office lamenting the fact that he can no longer, as he used to do, sit in the House of Commons as Chancellor of the Exchequer and devote his waking hours to currency reform — "regretting the golden inanity of the coronet which in the very prime of life had expelled him from the House of Commons," as Trollope puts it (II, 27). He wishes he were not a duke so that he might still have ahead of him, at the age of 46, some real work to do. The Premiership is to him simply an awful burden — but he is willing to try it, for the sake of the country. "Politics with the Duke have been simple patriotism," Mrs Finn remarks.

Palliser's attitude toward his elevation is sharply contrasted throughout with that of his wife, who sees in her husband's translation to the Premiership an opportunity for unrivalled social display. For the Duke, however, such political aggrandizement in the name of sociability is unpleasant. He is unpretentious, humble, and self-aware, committed to a patriotic effort without partisanship and afraid only of failing to serve his country as he feels it deserves to be served.

He did doubt his ability to fill that place which it would now be his duty to occupy ... He told himself again and again that there was wanting to him a certain noble capacity for commanding support and homage from other men. With things and facts he could deal, but human beings had not opened themselves to him ... No ambition had prompted him ... Only one consideration had forced him into this great danger, and that had been the assurance of others that it was his manifest duty to encounter it. (I, 72)

Palliser is explicitly compared in these early chapters to the many political opportunists who surround him (e.g., I, 117 — "Had some inscrutable decree of fate ordained and made it certain ... that no candidate could be returned to Parliament who would not assert the earth to be triangular, there would rise immediately a clamorous assertion of triangularity among political aspirants").

The new Premier's first battle is with his wife, who wishes to promote his ministry through spectacular and sustained hospitality. Palliser loses this battle. Unable to make his road smooth through easy social bribery, content to depend on his own talents and scornful of those who will respect him only for his rank or great wealth, he generally goes off by himself during his wife's grand parties and broods, or discusses mundane matters with private friends. He continuously chafes under the collar of Glencora's lavish hospitality; finally he tells her pointedly: "I would not have you make yourself conspicuous by anything like display." He dislikes most of the people his wife, for political reasons, invites to their various houses; he is unable or unwilling to ingratiate himself with them through the small talk and superficial social intimacy so often necessary to a politically shaky government — indeed, he has "a conviction that a public man should not waste his time . . . Life had always been too serious to him to be wasted" (I, 226). When one of his ministers, the Tory Sir Orlando Drought, takes momentary advantage of a social intimacy with Palliser provided by one of Glencora's house-parties to suggest a future ministerial policy supporting free trade and parliamentary reform, the Liberal Duke can only recall, as Trollope again uses one of his favorite analogies, "how the bathers' clothes were stolen" during the Disestablishment controversy "and that Sir Orlando had been one of the most nimble-fingered of the thieves" (I, 229) — and the Duke snubs Sir Orlando. He tells Glencora later: "I have not the knack of seeming to agree with a man while I let his words pass idly by me . . . People are not dull to me, if [only] they are real" (I, 232–3).

The coalition survives its first year in office and goes on to its second, its only weakness being the chronic unhappiness of its leader, who is tortured by silly newspaper attacks and suffers continuously under the various painful self-accusations of an over-punctilious nature. What the Prime Minister does not seem fully to understand is that it is precisely his own reputation for probity and conscientiousness which enables his government to enjoy and retain the uninterrupted confidence of the House of Commons and the country.

His coalition sailing along, Palliser takes a step which proclaims his personal honesty, moral bravery, and political tactlessness — in the best tradition of Palmerston. When a parliamentary vacancy occurs in his own borough of Silverbridge he decides not to interfere. He would rather see a Conservative elected than have it said that the Prime Minister exercised the kind of unconstitutional influence which almost every other large land-owner in the country continued to exercise as a matter of course. Palliser's attitude irritates his own party, but he remains immovable. The old Duke of St Bungay observes to Glencora on this occasion: "His honesty is not like the honesty of other men. It is more downright; — more absolutely honest; less capable of nearing even the shadow which the stain from another's dishonesty might throw upon it" (I, 323). The Duchess tells her husband that his conduct in the matter of the Silverbridge election reminds her of "King Lear throwing off his clothes in the storm because his daughters turned him out" (I, 365); and Palliser, who will not change his mind, finds that he most lacks sympathy at home and reminds himself "that a grievous calamity had befallen him when circumstances compelled him to become the Queen's Prime Minister" (I, 367). "I ought never to have been where I am," he muses. Ultimately he publishes a statement of formal neutrality in the election, thus pulling the rug out from under Glencora's Liberal candidate, Ferdinand Lopez. And so the Tory Fletcher wins, much to the dissatisfaction of everyone in the Liberal Party except Palliser himself.

Believing that "nothing can justify a direct falsehood," the Duke goes on refusing at every turn to make concessions to political expediency, averring that he would rather fall from power than compromise. He is still, we are told, all the while "sighing for some sweet parliamentary task, and regretting the days in which he was privileged to sit in the House of Commons till two o'clock in the morning" (I, 427).

Palliser commits another of his honest but politically inexpedient acts by honoring Lopez's request to be reimbursed for his election expenses. Feeling that his wife has led the man on to run, he gives him money — knowing that this might make it appear that Lopez had been his candidate and that he had taken a covert interest in the Silverbridge election despite his public disclaimer. Shortly thereafter a newspaper gets hold of the reimbursement story; Palliser thinks he must resign from office — for though he knows he is innocent of wrongdoing, he will not publicly blame his wife, nor will he condescend to defend his own conduct. It never occurs to him that his reputation for "patriotism, intelligence, devotion, and honesty" is so widespread and solidly based that few will pay attention to the newspaper story. The Duke refuses to have his conduct explained; no public response to the newspaper is made. But the newspaper — Slide's *People's Banner* — continues its abuse, broadening its attack to include a condemnation of Palliser's ministry as a whole. The Duke reads everything written about him, and the nastier it is the more likely he is to believe it. He fears not so much that people will accept as true what is written about his alleged failures as Prime Minister, but rather that it is in fact true — that he is indeed a failure. Glencora chides him: "I sometimes think, Plantagenet, that I should have been the man, my skin is so thick; and that you should have been the woman, yours is so tender" (II, 24). The Prime Minister cannot endure the attacks, neither can he ignore them; he is more miserable than ever.

All through the parliamentary novels Trollope demonstrates that one of the requisite weapons of an ambitious politician is a thick skin. "A man destined to sit conspicuously on our Treasury Bench, or on the seat opposite to it, should ask the Gods for a thick skin as a first gift," he says in *Phineas Redux* (I, 358). Criticism must be either ignored or scornfully counterattacked. Here once again Palliser is seen to be under-supplied in comparison with his more professional colleagues (Lord Brock, remember, sported "a hide impervious to fire or steel!"). But there is no question that for Trollope the moral advantage lies in thin-skinnedness. "A thick skin is a fault not to be forgiven in a man or a nation," he says in *North America* "whereas a thin skin is in itself a merit, if only the wearer of it will be master and not the slave of his skin." Palliser's "slavery" in this respect, though an impediment to the leader, is attractive in the man. Speaking in *The New Zealander* of the necessary restraints a free press imposes on a Prime Minister, Trollope suggests that they merely push politicians toward further insincerities: "can [the Prime Minister] be called free to speak or free to act, being driven as he is to weigh every word and deed, not by its innate propriety but by its probable acceptation with the public press?"[24] But Palliser is no ordinary Prime Minister; he will not let the press drive him to obfuscation, nor will he have his wife accused. And so he suffers in silence while his journalistic opponents continue to goad him. Glencora, while impatient with her husband's suffering, sees once again that in his determination to keep silent "He is all trust. . . . He is honour complete from head to foot . . . He wants always to be doing something that shall be really useful. . . . He never wants to say anything unless he has got something to say" (II, 185 and 187). For Trollope, whose Duke sometimes (as in this description of him) reminds one of Tennyson's King Arthur, stubbornness in a course one feels to be right — one of Palmerston's great virtues — deserves to be applauded; it is a sign, at least, of sincerity. In the Lopez affair the Prime Minister's stubbornness finally results in a mild (and planted) question being asked and an effective answer given in the House of Commons. And the third year of the Omnium ministry begins in a relatively peaceful way.

Palliser's personal troubles, however, are compounded by Lopez's suicide and further newspaper attacks upon himself. The absurdity of these are patent, but the thin-skinned and morbidly sensitive Prime Minister continues to suffer under them. In the midst of this "crisis" other signs of his weakening political position begin at last to appear. It is not until he contemplates going out that he discovers the growth in him of some attachment to office. Some criticis have thought he becomes power-mad, or at least personally ambitious. But "He is a man . . . entirely devoted to his country . . . He only wants to be useful . . . If he were to die to-morrow as the penalty of doing something useful to-night, he wouldn't think twice about it" (II, 256, 264, and 266, *passim.*). Although he still "envies Mr. Monk, because Mr. Monk is Chancellor of the Exchequer," Palliser begins to feel that to be cast out of office now would be to write "failure" across the last three years' efforts. For this reason he wishes to stay.

It is at this point in the story, however, that he has the fatal opportunity of bestowing a Garter. Garters up to this time were usually given, in return for political influence and support, to wealthy men of rank in the party of the Prime Minister of the day (only recently have they reverted to the personal gift of the Sovereign). But Palliser will not bestow the Garter on any of the three obvious choices — himself ("No man of high character is desirous of securing decorations which he may bestow upon others"), the Marquis of Mount Fidgett, heir of the late Whig K. G. ("He has done nothing for his country, and nothing for his Sovereign"), or his Cabinet colleague Lord Drummond ("I do not think that we ought to pay an increased price for [his] support"). Palliser ultimately makes an astonishing decision (II, 277—80): he selects a man who is both a Tory and actually deserving of official recognition – the Earl of Earlybird, an obscure old peer who for many years has quietly "devoted himself to the improvement of the labouring classes." The Duke's reason for this un-heard-of choice is simple and cogent: "He is a man of great heart and of many virtues." The Duke of St Bungay lectures the Prime Minister severely on party loyalty and patronage: "You will offend all your own friends, and only incur the ridicule of your opponents." Palliser replies simply: "It is well that I know the penalty," and the Garter is given to Lord Earlybird. It is immediately said that the Prime Minister has done this to show his supporters how little he owes or needs them; Palliser as usual refuses to justify himself, and so begins a Cabinet revolt which ultimately leads to his fall from power. Of course it is politics and not disagreement on issues that causes the disaffection and division in the Cabinet; greedy men are personally aggrieved. And so the coalition's third year in office comes to an ominous end.

Before Palliser is parted from his job, however, we encounter an interesting chapter entitled "The Prime Minister's Political Creed." In conversation with Phineas Finn (at last a member of the Cabinet as Secretary of State for Ireland), Palliser says of his own ministry:

'If it has been of service to the country, that is everything . . . With the statesman to whom it is not everything there must be something wrong . . . I suppose what we all desire is to improve the condition of the people by whom we are employed, and to advance our country, or at any rate to save it from retrogression . . . The idea that political virtue is all on one side is both mischievous and absurd. We allow ourselves to talk in that way because indignation, scorn, and sometimes, I fear, vituperation, are the fuel with which the necessary heat of debate is maintained.' (II, 316 and 319, *passim*.).

Before Beverley Trollope was not so sure that "political virtue" was not indeed "all on one side." But this is 1875, by which time he had come to see Tories and Whigs as indistinguishable elements of the same mixed bag. The feeling that politicians should want above all "to improve the condition of the people" is one Trollope had all of his life. It is this theme that leads Palliser to expand the discussion with Finn into the realm of the possible philosophical differences between Conservatives and Liberals.

'The Conservative who has any idea of the meaning of the name which he carries, wishes, I suppose, to maintain the differences and the distances which separate the highly placed from their lower brethren. He thinks that God has divided the world as he finds it divided, and that he may best do his duty by making the inferior man happy and contented in his position, teaching him that the place he holds is his by God's ordinance ... that is the great Conservative lesson. That lesson seems to me to be hardly compatible with continual improvement in the condition of the lower man. But with the Conservative all such improvement is to be based on the idea of the maintenance of those distances... That is my idea of Conservatism. The doctrine of Liberalism, is, of course, the reverse. The Liberal ... must I think have conceived the idea of lessening distances.' (II, 319–21, *passim*.)

We know that the philosophical differences actually dividing Liberals from Conservatives had been narrowing more and more in Trollope's view from the late sixties on; but one of the most interesting things about this statement is the limited nature of the criteria Palliser uses to distinguish between the parties. There is no mention here of Ireland or the Church, of Empire or foreign policy, of education or women's rights, of universal suffrage or the ballot. In the *Autobiography*, written mostly while *The Prime Minister* was appearing, the novelist on this subject of "distances" sounds very much like his favorite character:

The so-called Conservative ... being surely convinced that ... inequalities are of divine origin, tells himself that it is his duty to preserve them. He thinks that the preservation of the welfare of the world depends on the maintenance of those distances between the prince and the peasant by which he finds himself to be surrounded. ... Such, I think, are Conservatives. ... [The] Liberal ... is alive to the fact that these distances are day by day becoming less, and he regards this continual diminution as a series of steps towards that human millennium of which he dreams. (pp. 252–3)

Some years earlier, in 1868, Trollope had written in *St. Paul's*:

It is the object of the Tories to maintain the inequalities between various ranks of men, as though such inequality was in itself a thing good. ... It is the object of the Liberals to lessen these inequalities, believing such inequality to be in itself a thing bad ... [Let] all legislation go to reduce the existing inequalities between man and man; — let the man below be assisted to tread on the heels of the man above him, rather than deterred from doing so; — that thus by degrees there may be none who cannot read, none who cannot learn what it is to be civilized. The Tory would always wish to be bountiful to those below him; whereas the Liberal would fain give nothing in bounty, but would enable him who wants to earn all in justice.

Before this, he had written into *Phineas Finn* (I, 154–5), during the political gathering at Loughlinter, a discussion of the same subject. Glencora, somewhat iconoclastically as usual, speaks out first. "You are no Liberal," she tells Mrs Bonteen, unless you believe in "equality . . . unless that is the basis of your political aspirations . . . Do you not wish to make the lower orders comfortable . . . [and] educated, and happy and good?" But she confides to Kennedy: "I am not saying that people are equal; but that the tendency of all law-making and of all governing should be to reduce the inequalities." This sentiment clearly has been picked up from her husband. Monk says to Phineas afterwards: "Lady Glencora was not so far wrong. . . . Equality is an ugly word and shouldn't be used. It misleads, and frightens, and is a bugbear. And she . . . had not perhaps a clearly defined meaning for it in her own mind. But the wish of every honest man should be to assist in lifting up those below him, till they be something nearer his own level than he finds them" (I, 156). Equality is chimerical; but whereas the Liberal wishes to reduce the distance between the top and bottom rungs of the ladder, the Conservative wishes to preserve the distance. And going back a little farther – as early as 1862, assessing in *North America* the American system of public education, Trollope had said: "I . . . like the political feeling . . . which induces every educated American to lend a hand to the education of his fellow citizens. It shows, if nothing else does so, a germ of truth in that doctrine of equality. It is a doctrine to be forgiven when he who preaches it is in truth striving to raise others to his own level – though utterly unpardonable when the preacher would pull down others to his own level."[25] Equality preached by levelling demagogues is a joke; but those who are "at the top of the tree" and yet "desirous of giving all an opportunity of raising themselves," those who wish to improve rather than to degrade further the lives of those below them, are to be encouraged and admired. Trollope always believed this.

Like the novelist and his heroes Palmerston and Russell, Palliser is a moderately progressive and egalitarian-minded man, but no Radical (we know what Trollope thought of *them*). He may dream of social equality in some future heaven ("Equality would be a heaven, if we could attain it," he tells Phineas in *The Prime Minister*, II, 321), but, like Trollope, he hates the idea of revolution and accepts distinctions of rank and class as inevitable. He values his rank and wishes it to be respected insofar as it represents a tradition which he loves. He believes in men more than in measures, and is never very interested, either in or out of office, in sweeping reform of any kind (except in the currency). But the Duke is no snob. He is an honest and industrious man who respects these same virtues and detests their antitheses in others regardless of rank. He would have all men, aristocrats and commoners alike, love work, eschew idleness, and wish to serve others before themselves. To the extent that these things are emphasized, Palliser is seen throughout the novel as a just man among rogues, which also aptly describes the way in which Trollope saw Palmerston. The great man may be baited, he may be tempted, he may even make errors of judgment – but he remains sincere and unflinchingly true to his principles, which are seen to be more worth preserving than any political success or parliamentary legislation of the moment. Nominally a Liberal, Trollope believed less in parties than in men. He never trusted ideologues of any variety; in both *Lord Palmerston* and *The Prime Minister* what is valued in the man is a practical honesty which wisely avoids the many dangers of the partisan, the metaphysical, or even the theoretical. Trollope said of Palmerston that "He was a statesman for the moment. Whatever was not wanted now, whatever was not practicable now, he drove quite out of his mind"; clearly this side of Palmerston appealed to him. Briggs's comment on Palmerston could apply as well to Trollope: "He was more interested . . . in his own age than in the past or the future . . . In his distaste for theory . . . he reflected his age."[26]

Even before Palliser's government falls on the issue of a county suffrage bill, the few people in the novel whose judgment we trust justify in no uncertain terms his tenure of office. The ministry "has been of great service to the country," says Monk. "His purity is the same as ever," says Mrs Finn. As the Duke's period of service comes to an end, "Patriotism with him was a fever, and the public service an exacting mistress." The Duke of St Bungay tells the Prime Minister that his Cabinet has "carried on the Queen's Government prosperously for three years . . . We have done what Parliament and the country expected us to do, and to my poor judgment we have done it well" (II, 372). But Palliser, though he knew the moment must come, senses failure in going out of office – not only because his ministry will be at an end, but more than anything else because he fears he will have nothing to do: "What was now to come of himself? How should he use his future life? . . . What was he to do with himself when called upon to resign?" (II, 373–4). Unlike the Duke of St Bungay, he does not look forward to a vacation and solitude: "There could be nothing for him now till the insipidity of life should gradually fade away into the grave." He knows he may eventually come back into a Cabinet, but he feels, despite subsequent offers from his successors in office, that it should not be for some time. And yet (invoking the old fear): "I do not like to think that I shall be without work" (II, 375).

"Political coalitions are never firm," Trollope tells us in *Lord Palmerston*, "because they are formed of individual men, and each man has a heart in his bosom in which he carries memories of the past as well as his hopes for the future."[27] Palliser's government illustrates this political principle. At last he must go from office, abandoned in the House of Commons by many of his former supporters – to most of whom, it is said, "he has not spoken a word . . . since he became Prime Minister." The

Duke's obvious impatience with sociable small talk, combined with his natural reserve, is made to account in large measure for his fall from power. Palliser's ministry ends not because he has lost the confidence of the country, but because his failure to play the usual political games has finally offended his colleagues. They are bored by his rectitude. They resent him because he cannot be superficial or gregarious. In an interesting aside, Trollope explains why the Duke, though a prince among knaves, is unable to retain political power:

> If one were asked in these days what gift should a Prime Minister ask first from the fairies, one would name the power of attracting personal friends. Eloquence, if it be too easy, may become almost a curse. Patriotism is suspected, and sometimes sinks almost to pedantry. A Joveborn intellect is hardly wanted, and clashes with the inferiorities. Industry is exacting. Honesty is unpractical. Truth is easily offended. Dignity will not bend. But the man who can be all things to all men, who has ever a kind word to speak, a pleasant joke to crack, who can forgive all sins, who is ever prepared for friend or foe but never very bitter to the latter, who forgets not men's names, and is always ready with little words, — he is the man who will be supported at a crisis such as this. (II, 382–3)

Like Palmerston and Russell, Palliser is not known as an orator; like them, he is patriotic, studious, industrious, honest and dignified. But Palmerston succeeded again and again precisely where the Duke (and Lord John) failed – in attracting supporters through easy friendships and "little words." Trollope, remember, says of Palmerston: "It was the nature of the man not to be diffident, and therefore he succeeded." The politicians of this world being alienated more by diffidence than by stupidity or dishonesty, Palliser finally fails. Clearly, however, Trollope loves the Duke for his "failure," just as he admired Palmerston for his success. The immovable integrity and conscientiousness of both are cut from the same cloth. Although "men may be alienated by silence and a cold demeanour" (II, 385), Palliser has been true to himself and to his principles. He can only say things that mean something; he cannot pretend to be interested in the idle chatter of political intriguers. He will not play the game of partisan politics. And so, being too good for this political life, he must go.

Next to the passage quoted above on the required talents of fledgling prime ministers, notable among other things for its bitter irony, it is instructive to put a passage Trollope wrote at the end of the *Autobiography*. In it he discusses the character of his favorite fictional personage:

> I had ... conceived the character of a statesman ... of a man who should be ... superior. ... The statesman of whom I was thinking ...

should have rank, and intellect, and parliamentary habits, by which to
bind him to the service of the country; and he should also have
unblemished, unextinguishable, inexhaustible love of country . . . This
man should have it as the ruling principle of his life; and it should so
rule him that all other things should be made to give way to it. But he
should be scrupulous, and, as being scrupulous, weak. (pp. 308–9)

The Duke of St Bungay, a wise man, tells Lord Cantrip at the end of *The
Prime Minister* that Palliser "has but one fault, — he is a little too
conscientious, a little too scrupulous" (II, 441). In a would-be successful
politician, scrupulosity is weakness, a fault. Trollope says it twice:
scrupulosity is weakness. It is an important part of his idea of politics —
and indeed helps to define that idea.

> Whatever men do they should do honestly. Speaking broadly one may
> say that the rule applies to nations as strongly as to individuals, and
> should be observed in politics as accurately as in other matters. We
> must, however, confess that men who are scrupulous in their private
> dealings do too constantly drop these scruples when they handle public
> affairs . . . When men have political ends to gain they regard their
> opponents as adversaries, and then that old rule of war is brought to
> bear. Deceit or valour — either may be used against a foe. Would it were
> not so! . . . We all understand . . . how [strongly personal a man's bias]
> may become when the man is not specially scrupulous.[28]

Thus Trollope in *North America*. *Phineas Redux*, after all, presented a
frightening picture of what the politics of selfishness may do to men's
minds and personalities. Scruples are burdensome to most politicians,
while shameless ruthlessness is a great virtue — surely this is one of the
things *Phineas Redux* told us. It follows that the men who become leaders
of political factions must have special attributes. Obviously moral flexibility is one of these. Another is an equable temper in the midst of violent
verbal altercations with one's "enemies" in the House and one's "friends"
in the Cabinet-room. After all, what is wanted is "practical results rather
than truth. A clear head is worth more than an honest heart" (*Phineas
Redux*, I, 90). The preference for "results" over "truth" is the cornerstone
of this pragmatic world; it is what keeps it going. This is also why Trollope
despises it. Nor does the secondary importance of the "honest heart"
recommend this world to Trollope; like many of his Victorian contemporaries, he decried in his books the decline of *feeling* in a world that came
increasingly to admire the kind of "results" that could be produced only
by an enterprising "clear head." We saw this too at the end of *Phineas
Redux*.

Interestingly enough, Disraeli sketches in one of his novels not the ideal
but the most likely sort of man to become a political leader.

Find a man who, totally destitute of genius, possesses nevertheless considerable talents; who has official aptitude, a volubility of routine rhetoric, great perseverance, a love of affairs; who, embarrassed neither by the principles of the philosopher nor by the prejudices of the bigot, can assume, with a cautious facility, the prevalent tone, and disembarrass himself of it, with a dexterous ambiguity, the moment it ceases to be predominant; recommending himself to the innovator by his approbation of change 'in the abstract,' and to the conservative by his prudential and practical respect for that which is established; such a man, though he be one of essentially small mind, though his intellectual qualities be less than moderate, with feeble powers of thought, no imagination, contracted sympathies, and a most loose public morality; such a man is the individual whom kings and parliaments would select to govern the State. ... Instead of statesmen they desire shufflers; and compromise in conduct and ambiguity in speech are ... the public qualities now most in vogue.[29]

The political leader ultimately must make so many "compromises in conduct" as to become a kind of moral chameleon; on this, at least, Trollope and Disraeli were in agreement — even if Trollope saw Disraeli as having become the sort of man Disraeli himself disdainfully describes here.

In his *Life of Cicero* — begun three years after he finished writing *The Prime Minister* — Trollope complains bitterly about posterity's tendency to idealize Caesar and condemn Cicero. Caesar "has been lauded because he was unscrupulous," he says here, while Cicero "has incurred reproach because, at every turn in his life, scruples dominated him." And he adds that one cannot admire the success produced by the worship of expediency. A man who succeeds in this way, he concludes, echoing sentiments expressed in *The Three Clerks*, "let him be ever so great ... will in the end do more harm than good."[30] In the *Autobiography* Trollope tells us that the successful politicians are precisely those who are willing to compromise, to bend, and to become useful in this way. But this of course does not make them better men; and it is the moral quality of the politician rather than his political success or failure at the game he plays that most interests Trollope. In *Phineas Redux* there is obviously a direct relationship between the depth of Daubeny's amorality and the length of his tenure in office. By throwing his principles overboard in the midst of a tricky parliamentary situation, Daubeny maintains his power in a manner which obviously would have been unthinkable in a man such as Palliser, who is manifestly unused to "conjuring." To succeed politically, a man must be morally flexible; he must be — unscrupulous. Throughout, the Duke opposes the various arguments in favor of *Realpolitik* put to him by others (including Glencora) with a quiet wisdom and uprightness that hold our sympathy. There can be little doubt that Trollope prefers the weak but scrupulous man he describes here and in the *Autobiography* to the more flexible and successful politicians he describes everywhere else.

In the final pages of the novel we see Palliser, lonely and depressed, reviewing his bittersweet memories: "Surely it was a great thing to have been Prime Minister of England for three years. . . . Surely he had done something of which he might be proud. And so he tried to console himself" (II, 389). When Glencora wishes that he had been "less scrupulous and more persistent," he can only reply: "my honour is everything." He mopes around, refusing as beneath his just-resigned dignity a subordinate place in the new Liberal Cabinet. He feels that "There was nothing now which he could do, which another might not do as well." Again he longs to be back in the House of Commons. He has, Glencora tells him accusingly, "no idea of the personal grandeur" of position; and indeed she is right. "There is a peculiar safety in [the] method of separating power from grandeur, the power of the ruler from the grandeur of the sovereign," says Trollope in his essay in *The New Zealander* on "The Crown."[31] Palliser is not a sovereign; but the principle of separation and its benefits rightfully prevent him from assuming any "grandeur" of a personal kind.

At the end, as we have seen, Monk tells the Duke that "History will give you credit for patriotism, patience, and courage. No man could have done it better than you did; — probably no other man of the day as well" (II, 468). The country prospered under Palliser's stewardship, and his only regret, Monk concludes, is the Duke's own self-imposed retirement from political life. Trollope allows the novel to close with Palliser's words, characteristically modest and patriotic and pointedly at odds in sentiment with the gamesmanship of political expediency so rampant around him. "I shall certainly never desire to be at the head of a Government again," says the Duke. "For a few years I would prefer to remain out of office. But I will endeavour to look forward to a time when I may again perhaps be of some humble use" (II, 470).

IV

We know about Trollope's preference for the aristocracy as political rulers. In *The Duke's Children* the theme is taken up again in earnest; here it is important too, but more by implication than direct argument.

The political rule of the aristocracy was so often a fact of life in nineteenth-century England that, to begin with, a duke's Premiership would not have seemed extraordinary to Trollope's audience. We have heard the novelist lecture on the great families and the superiority of the old Whigs to the Tories; the Pallisers represent exactly what Trollope loved best — a great old aristocratic Whig family. As we have seen, the novelist wrote in his *Autobiography* that such a man as Palliser "justifies to the nation the seeming anomaly of an hereditary peerage and of primogeniture." And yet one of Palliser's charms in *The Prime Minister*, surely, is lack of personal vanity. "It had never occurred to him to be proud of being a duke, or to think of his wealth otherwise than a chance accident of his life, advantageous indeed, but by no means a source of honour" (II, 389); he has no sense of personal "grandeur." Certainly Trollope's stockbrokers and railway magnates think about their wealth and social status with more complacency and single-mindedness than his Duke of Omnium. For Palliser, "honour" comes from what a man actually does during his life and not from who he is at birth or what he is lucky enough to inherit from others. In this respect the novelist is much less progressive in his ideas than his own hero — for he is not at all hesitant about seeing a duke's rank as an *a priori* emblem of his right to lead. The novelist *always* favored government by aristocracy. His chief political hero, Palmerston, was a lord (though as an Irish viscount a member of the House of Commons all his life; but in Palmerston's last Cabinet, 1859—65, sat three dukes and six peers or sons of peers). "There is probably more of the flavour of political aristocracy to be found still remaining among our Liberal leading statesmen than among their opponents," Trollope wrote, remember, in *Phineas Redux*. "They still entertain a pride in their Cabinets." One of the few Disraelian phrases Trollope was fond of quoting was a reference to "the free patrician life" of England — which always produced, he felt, the best possible rulers for the nation. "Of that dispensation, in his patriotism, his sympathies, at once popular and aristocratic, in home affairs, and in his championship of oppressed nationalities abroad, Palmerston struck him as the best type of the time," said Escott of Trollope.[32] Like Palmerston, Lord John Russell, despite the courtesy title, was a commoner until late in life; but he was made an earl in 1861 — three years before Trollope began his political series; and his father was the sixth Duke of Bedford. A man born and raised at Woburn Abbey could hardly fail to be an aristocrat.

Trollope had some hard things to say of aristocrats, and he sometimes satirizes them as a class. His novels do contain, after all, vain, snobbish, unscrupulous, licentious, lazy, dishonest, and bovine aristocrats. In his essay in *The New Zealander* on the House of Lords he expresses the opinion that there are no more than five competent peers in Parliament, and in *The Prime Minister* itself he refers in a well-known phrase to the jaded men who are "weighed down at last by their own incapacity and sink into peerages" (II, 443). Despite this, he never ceased to regard the aristocracy as the only class capable of political leadership. It is true that although Trollope was "distrustful, even cynical, about society, he was curious and optimistically sympathetic about individual people."[33] Thus while he might laugh at the hollow pretensions of some aristocrats, Trollope could also feel that the country was safest with one of them in charge of it. Who else was there? His bias is everywhere obvious.

In his portrait of Palliser, then, Trollope demonstrates his preference for an aristocrat — even one "weakened" by scrupulousness — over other men made strong by the audacity of opportunism; his Duke is a vivid example of the moral beauty, to him, of such weakness. Certainly Trollope does not think it is better for the country that a Prime Minister be weak, even if such weakness be spiritually better for the man himself; but he does think that moral leadership is better than amoral leadership, and that in its purest form such leadership is more likely to be found in the aristocracy than anywhere else (this makes nonsense of Polhemus's unfathomable assertion that Trollope hated "the whole degenerate aristocracy"³⁴). Palmerston, though only an Irish viscount, was a viscount nonetheless, and Lord John Russell, though like Palliser he preferred the House of Commons to the House of Lords, was ultimately, like Palliser again, a peer. "Lords have been made lords in nine cases out of ten for good work done by them for the benefit of their country," declares Sir William Patterson in Lady Anna (p. 365). Trollope believed this all of his life.

V

As in Can You Forgive Her?, there is in The Prime Minister in counterpoint to Palliser a villainous stockbroker who, purely for social and financial gain, tries to get into Parliament. George Vavasor made it, briefly; Ferdinand Lopez does not make it at all. A measure of Trollope's growing impatience with such men is the fate he assigns to Lopez — a violent death under the wheels of a train. Lopez is one of the few in Trollope's novels to die "on stage," and of these one of the only ones to die violently. George got off to America, but Lopez kills himself; there are eleven souring years between the two episodes. Unlike George, Lopez is — as Mr Meagles might say — "not English." Like Melmotte and Emilius, he is a European wanderer, and a Jew. But he is specifically of Portugese extraction. It is impossible not to suspect that, in Lopez, Trollope was still working off his "horror" of Disraeli — the Portugese-Italian Jew who was Prime Minister of England as The Prime Minister was being written. At any rate Lopez is yet another of Trollope's treacherous "greasy" European Jew-adventurers who covets political place.

Like most of Trollope's politician villains, Lopez wants a seat in the House for purely selfish reasons: it "would be of the greatest possible advantage to me. It enables a man to do a great many things which he could not touch without it" (I, 330). Old Mr Wharton sees clearly enough what it is his son-in-law is after: "Men go into Parliament [today] because it gives them fashion, position, and power" (I, 331). A man without a single patriotic impulse, Lopez is another of those amoral financial manipulators Trollope so detested. In this novel Palliser himself alludes to the dangers to the system represented by such men. When Glencora takes up Lopez's cause in the Silverbridge election, Palliser preaches to her a sermon "showing the utter corruption which must come from the mixing up of politics and trade" (II, 18) — a sermon continuously preached in Trollope's political novels.

Critics of The Prime Minister have from time to time tried to make more than there is out of the Silverbridge election, in which Lopez's

political aspirations are annihilated; but in fact it is one of the most feeble
and least realized of all the election sequences among Trollope's novels.[35]
Having put his very soul into the elections at Percycross and Tankerville in
Ralph the Heir and *Phineas Redux*, Trollope in his account of the elections
at Silverbridge in *The Prime Minister* and *The Duke's Children* — and that
at Westminster in *The Way We Live Now* — performed more languidly.
Polpenno in *The Duke's Children* is the last of his elections to be described
with any vividness.

VI

One of Lady Stanley of Alderley's lavish receptions was reported in the
columns of a newspaper the next day under the heading "Political and
Fashionable Entertainments."[36] The worlds of politics and social fashion,
fused as they were in the Victorian political milieu, are portrayed once
again in *The Prime Minister* as functioning symbiotically.

Lady Stanley's social efforts, remember, are said to have matched her
husband's political ones for diligence. In *The Prime Minister*, Lady
Glencora once again gets deeply into politics and political intriguing — so
effectively, indeed, that Palliser begins to wonder if it is his wife, who
appears to be working so much harder than he is, who is really keeping the
political coalition together. Could it be, muses the Duke, that she, not he,
is the real Prime Minister?

> It might . . . be . . . that she with her dinner parties and receptions, with
> her crowded saloons, her music, her picnics, and social temptations, was
> Prime Minister rather than he himself. It might be that this had been
> understood by the coalesced parties, — by everybody . . . except him-
> self. It had, perhaps, been found that in the state of things then
> existing, a ministry could be best kept together, not by parliamentary
> capacity, but by social arrangements, such as his Duchess . . . alone,
> could carry out. She and she only would have the spirit and the money
> and the sort of cleverness required. In such a state of things he of
> course, as her husband, must be the nominal Prime Minister. (I, 195)

In the world of *The Prime Minister*, in which there is so little political
consensus, "social arrangements" are in danger of replacing — perhaps to
some extent have already replaced — "parliamentary capacity." Even the
remote, unsocial Palliser recognizes the supreme importance to this milieu
of social relations.

It would be easy to accuse the Duke of paranoia here, and some critics
have done so. But they have missed the point. Glencora's zeal in her
husband's behalf *is* in large part a result of her own love of power, of her
desire and capacity to manipulate people to achieve social — and thus
political — ends. She *is* an efficacious and an ambitious "politician"; and it
may in fact be a fair question "whether on the whole the Duchess did not

work harder" than her husband, as Trollope himself says (I, 87). Indeed, at
a climactic moment Glencora tells Mrs Finn how much more effective
than her husband she could be as a political character were she ever given a
proper chance. Her expertise as a social in-fighter has helped to provide her
with most of the political education required; her husband's career has
done the rest.

> 'They should have made me Prime Minister, and have let him be
> Chancellor of the Exchequer. I begin to see the ways of Government
> now. I could have done all the dirty work. I could have given away
> garters and ribbons, and made my bargains while giving them. I could
> select sleek, easy bishops who wouldn't be troublesome. I could give
> pensions or withhold them, and make the stupid men peers. I could
> have the big noblemen at my feet, praying to be Lieutenants of
> Counties. I could dole out secretaryships and lordships, and never a one
> without getting something in return. I could brazen out a job and let
> the "People's Banners" and the Slides make their worst of it. And I
> think I could make myself popular with my party, and do the
> high-flowing patriotic talk for the benefit of the Provinces . . . A Prime
> Minister should never go beyond generalities about commerce, agri-
> culture, peace, and general philanthropy. Of course he should have the
> gift of the gab, and that Plantagent hasn't got. He never wants to say
> anything unless he has got something to say. I could do a Mansion
> House dinner to a marvel!' (II, 186–7)

Her education in Society has enabled Glencora to "see the ways of
Government," which are not very different from social "ways." Both
involve power plays, bargaining, bribery, blackmail, and a certain strain of
rhetoric. Not being herself a reader of the Palliser novels, it has taken the
Duchess some time to find all of this out; she knows the game now, and is
willing to play it. Perhaps she *would* have made a more successful Prime
Minister than her husband (his suspicion of this marks him as less paranoid
than shrewd). But the novelist is interested less in political success than in
moral imperviousness to the kinds of influences Glencora welcomes here.
She tells Palliser at one point, remember, that she "should have been the
man, my skin is so thick; and . . . you should have been the woman, yours
is so tender." In this context Trollope is concerned with weakness rather
than strength; and so, while the Duchess is one of his favorite characters, it
is the thin-skinned husband, not the impervious wife, who is closest to his
heart.

That Glencora's game is political at the same time that it is social — that
the two realms in fact are again the same realm — is emphasized everywhere in *The Prime Minister*. Men rather than measures — personnel rather
than doctrine — being primarily at issue, the Duchess works to maintain
her own "set" in office, and initiates strategies tougher and often more

effective than her husband's to keep the other side out. At the start she sets up her own "Cabinet." "I mean to have a cabinet of my own," she tells the foreign-born Mrs Finn, "and I mean that you shall do the foreign affairs." Mrs Finn, being "very good at accounts," requests the exchequer instead. "I'll do that myself," is the reply. "And I mean to be my own home-secretary. . . . I think a small cabinet gets on best" (I, 66). Soon "solemn cabinets" are held "at which she presided. . . . In this cabinet the Duchess always had her own way." After one argument with her husband, Glencora threatens to "send in her resignation"; and indeed she refuses forever afterward to invite to their home Sir Orlando Drought, one of her husband's important Cabinet colleagues — a social rupture which helps to undermine Palliser's political position. After yet another argument with him she declares that she cannot be dismissed and "won't resign." When the coalition finally falls apart, Glencora — who, as she says herself, hates "being beat. I'd sooner be cut in pieces" — outlines pungently the strategy she would have employed as Premier to preserve her position. The main ingredient of her bid for power would have been the bestowal of peerages and baronetcies where they would have done the most good: "When a man has power he ought to use it. It makes people respect him. Mr. Daubeny made a duke, and people think more of that than anything he did" (II, 422). This is very shrewd of Glencora; Palliser's failure to use such perquisites of his office in fact has hastened his fall from power.

When at last it is over, the Duchess admits readily enough what she had wanted: "she had almost thought that she could rule England by giving dinner and supper parties." Indeed, she actually made some political headway and created a feeling abroad that " 'Glencora' was a 'good sort of fellow' and ought to be supported" (I, 422). She has worked hard at it, her object throughout being utterly clear to her: "In London there should not be a Member of Parliament whom she would not herself know and influence by her flattery and grace, — or if there were men whom she could not influence, they should live as men tabooed and unfortunate" (I, 62). Such is the career of social and political bullying open to a rich woman who is both a duchess and a Premier's wife. No wonder, then, that the Premier himself — no paranoiac — should "in his heart . . . [suspect] her of a design of managing the Government in her own way, with her own particular friend, Mrs. Finn, for her Prime Minister" (I, 369).

At the end of the novel Glencora speaks to her husband of their household as if it were his political constituency. What, she asks him, will he find to do with himself in political retirement? "It's all very well to talk of me and the children, but you can't bring in a Bill for reforming us. You can't make us go by decimals. You can't increase our consumption by lowering our taxation. I wish you [would go] back to some Board" (II, 445). The connections between the public and the private life, it would seem, are more durable than a political coalition.

The politics of marriage — and the "marriages" of politics — are not the only avenues of such interconnection in *The Prime Minister*. Slide attacks Palliser in the *People's Banner* only because of his failure to gain an invitation to one of Glencora's parties. Arthur Fletcher stands for Parliament in part as a distraction after his disappointment in love. It is said that when such a man as Ratler, the Liberal whip, won't come to dinner at the Prime Minister's house, the Prime Minister undoubtedly will be going soon ("It is like pigs carrying straws in their mouth," says Glencora to Phineas Finn; "Mr. Ratler is my pig."). When the new Gresham ministry takes over, Monk predicts that in the present session "Nothing less strong than grouse could break up Parliament."

It had been said, in the midst of Palliser's troubles in the Lopez affair, that the possible mention in the House of Commons of his wife's name would be more likely to draw a crowd there than discussion of the most serious political issue. "Had the taxation of the whole country for the next year been in dispute ... [or had] the welfare of the Indian Empire occupied the House, the House would have been empty. But the hope that a certain woman's name would have to be mentioned" when a question is asked "crammed it from the floor to the ceiling" (II, 197). When Sir Orlando Drought decides to leave the Cabinet – largely because he has been snubbed by Palliser at one reception and uninvited to its successors – the Duke of St Bungay advises the Prime Minister to take "no more notice ... than if your footman was going." Indeed, the odd ways in which men who are socially uncongenial often find themselves connected politically – and vice versa – are alluded to at one point by Glencora. "Political enemies are often the best friends in the world," she tells Emily Wharton, while "I can assure you from my own experience that political friends are often the bitterest enemies. I never hated any people so much as some of our supporters." And she adds: "There's an old saying that misfortune makes strange bedfellows, but political friendship makes stranger alliances than misfortune" (II, 432).

In all of these ways too, then, society and politics are seen to be inextricably linked. Indeed, in *The Prime Minister* we see the novel's leading politician – Palliser – more often at home than at the office. Much of the political action of the novel springs from social or domestic causes, Trollope shows us, and many private actions have political causes; so the Duke's most revealing moments come not during altercations in the Cabinet-room but rather during those tempestuous scenes at home with the Duchess – the best scenes in the book. The Pallisers at home demonstrate many of the ways in which the political and personal lives are inseparable. Their marriage itself, Polhemus has noted, is shown throughout as "process," like history or politics. A power-struggle that never really ends, even in the drawing-room, private life among these people can be intensely political – as we saw, for example, in the "struggle" between the man and his wife for "control" of the Cabinet. Every private act is in a sense political because it has some effect on the "balance of power" between people; distinctions between public and private become artificial in this context, there being no escape possible from politics – from political motivation and political acts. Conversely, public policies often are the offspring of the private, the psychological, idiosyncrasies of public men (e.g., decimal coinage). If personal life is largely governed by political considerations, political life is also largely a phenomenon of personality, or personalities. *The Prime Minister* invites us to see life itself as "a series of coalitions – personal, social, and political – doomed to failure":

> [Trollope] organized the book around the word and concept of *coalition*: Palliser presides over a coalition government; he and Glencora live together . . . in uneasy coalition; and the marriage of Emily . . . to the Portugese Jew . . . forms a coalition. . . . Since for Trollope man is a social animal, and society is an organic whole, a good life always depends on the possibilities of coalition of some kind. . . . All the parts of *The Prime Minister* reinforce and comment on each other in showing the misunderstanding and aggression that break up coalition. Different points of view cannot be reconciled, and selfish party spirit prevails.[37]

VII

The Prime Minister, finally, embodies some other familiar themes. There is the usual partisanship, as in the fierce hatred of the Duke of St Bungay for Daubeny: "To keep Mr. Daubeny out was the very essence of the Duke of St Bungay's life, – the turning-point of his political creed, the one grand duty the idea of which was always present to him" (II, 114). Even such a good man as St Bungay has a narrow and rather silly motivating "political creed." As in *Phineas Redux*, a ministry is made to fall not because its principles or acts are disliked but rather because people simply get tired of having it around; the coalition, it is said at last, has "served [its] turn, and . . . ought to go." Again we are told how the invective of the political aspirant may open unto him the door of patronage he makes it his business so contemptuously to besiege:

> perhaps the most wonderful ministerial phenomenon . . . is he who rises high in power and place by having made himself thoroughly detested and also . . thoroughly feared. Given sufficient audacity, a thick skin, and power to bear for a few years the evil looks and cold shoulders of his comrades, and that is the man most sure to make his way to some high seat . . . To the man who will once shrink . . . the career is impossible. But let him be obdurate, and the bid will come. (II, 443–4)

Trollope probably refers here to Disraeli once again – then Prime Minister yet still considered by long-time political foes an adventurer who had been incredibly lucky. The novelist goes on to remind us what it takes to crash the sacrosanct portal: " 'Not because I want him, do I ask for him,' says some groaning chief of a party . . . 'but because he stings me and goads me, and will drive me to madness as a foe.' Then the pachydermatous one enters into the other's heaven, probably with the resolution already formed of ousting that unhappy angel" (II, 444). In his essay in *The New Zealander* on the House of Commons, Trollope tells us that whenever national political goals are lost sight of "in individual antagonism and party contests, the assembly . . . is neglectful of its higher duties." Most debates in the House, he says here, arise "from some party accusation" and are carried on "with gladiatorial skill and internecine malignity." Rarely if ever is there a real debate; what is of interest to M.P.s is the reputation of others and of themselves rather than truth or policy. Fortunately such men are unable to "induce others to believe any of the evil things which fall from" their mouths, and in fact they believe none of them themselves. Yet "it is by sedulously asserting in such debates, and by manfully taking a part in such battles, that would-be statesmen get themselves lifted up into the Elysium of government places." And the novelist concludes – bluntly: "to become one of a ministry it [is] necessary to attack it . . . As long as men are better treated for indiscriminate abuse than indiscriminate support, the cleverer of our rising politicians will naturally begin life by opposing the ministers under whom they hope ultimately to act."[38] Again among these familiar Trollopian sentiments there is an obvious reference to Disraeli, a "rising" man when *The New Zealander* was being written – and a "clever" man who made his reputation in opposition (what Trollope refers to as "indiscriminate abuse" is his account of Disraeli's principle of always opposing, no matter what the merits of the proposition, when not a member of the government). Indeed, Disraeli's first major operation was against Peel, a fellow Tory under whom, certainly, as a young man he hoped to act. The "ministerial phenomenon" *The Prime Minister* so pointedly evokes here is once again the hated Disraeli – a man who did indeed "sting" and "goad" his political foes and drive them to "madness."

In this connection Trollope reminds us how easy it would be for Palliser to get his foot back into the Cabinet door if he were given to partisan invective. But when, after his fall from power, his wife urges him to "pitch into them, all round, like a true ex-minister and independent member of Parliament" (II, 446–7), he demurs. He will not, says Trollope, be tempted down this "audacious" path. Monk defines accurately enough the spirit of opposition prevailing at the moment: "Politicians now look for grievances, not because the grievances are heavy, but trusting that the honour of abolishing them may be great. It is the old story of the needy knife-grinder who, if left to himself, would have no grievance of which to complain" (II, 469).

Again the hold of party is so tenacious that parliamentary debates have no effect on the voting habits of M.P.s: "it was hardly on the cards that a

single vote should be turned this way or that by any violence of speaking"
when Sir Orlando attempts to carry a no-confidence resolution against the
coalition (II, 384). And again, in this penultimate volume of the Palliser
series, we hear how close the two major parties are to one another. "The
country goes its own way, either for better or for worse, whichever of
them is in," says Glencora to Mrs Finn. "I don't think it makes any
difference as to what sort of laws are passed. But among ourselves, in our
set, it makes a deal of difference who gets the garters, and the counties,
who are made barons and then earls, and whose name stands at the head of
everything" (I, 64). This is perhaps the shrewdest assessment of the
political world of *The Prime Minister* we are likely to find anywhere. Most
politicians want to get in not to pass particular laws or promulgate favorite
policies – the laws and policies of each side are likely to be similar
anyway – but rather to swallow as many crumbs as possible of the
political cake.

   The language of games is another familiar element of *The Prime
Minister*. The Duke of St Bungay sees the comings and goings of ministries
in terms of the shifting partnerships of a game of whist: "As a man cuts in
and out at a whist table, and enjoys both the game and the rest from the
game, so had the Duke . . . been well pleased in either position" (II, 367).
Palliser himself refers to the men of his chosen profession as "meddlers in
the game of politics." But the novel's most persistent games metaphor is
that of baiting. Trollope, remember, saw Palmerston as the English
bulldog, and his invocations of the man are full of this kind of imagery –
he used his power of speech the way a dog uses its teeth, his courage was
like that of a dog, and so on. Palliser's characterization of his job as
Premier depends upon the same kind of imagery: "When they used to bait
a bear tied to a stake, every one around would cheer the dogs and help to
torment the helpless animal. It is much the same now, only they have a
man instead of a bear for their pleasure" (II, 297). One of the only men in
the political world of *The Prime Minister* who does not want to play
games, the Duke is deadly serious; but even he cannot change the rules.
When it is clear that he is going from office, Glencora, fiercely competitive
as she is, expresses her relief for him in similar language: "Rough people
. . . trod upon you, and worried you with their teeth and wounded you
everywhere. I could have turned at them again with my teeth, and given
them worry for worry; – but you could not. Now you will be saved from
them" (II, 376; an example is Slide, who in his newspaper attacks on
Palliser over the Lopez affair finds it difficult "to draw his badger"). Once
again Glencora is seen as having more of the requisite political equipment
than her husband.

   Trollope thought so much of the badger-baiting contest as a metaphor
for government that he used it in *The New Zealander* and then copied the
same passage verbatim into *The Three Clerks*. Here is the passage he was so
taken with:

So it is that the sport [of badger-baiting] is played in Hampshire; and so also at Westminster — with a difference, however. In Hampshire the two brutes retain ever their appointed natures. The badger is always a badger, and the bull-dog never other than a bull-dog. At Westminster there is a juster reciprocity of position. The badger when drawn has to take his place outside the hole, and fight again for the home of his love; while the victorious bull-dog assumes a state of badgerdom, dons the skin of his enemy, and, in his turn, submits to be baited.[39]

Trollope precedes this, in both places, with a detailed description of how a bulldog actually baits and tries to draw a badger; and when in *The Three Clerks* he comes to discuss the fruitless rivalries of a wasteful parliamentary committee, he specifically connects badger-baiting and politics as above. In a subsequent passage in the novel he describes the opening of a debate in the House of Commons in the same vein: "the dogs began to whet their teeth and prepare for a tug at the great badger"; after the parliamentary critics have failed effectively to wound their adversary, "the big badger sat by and grinned, not deigning to notice the dogs around him" (pp. 550–1). Clearly in the sport of badger-baiting Trollope saw an emblem for the pointless acrimony and warfare of partisan politics. And in the image of the badger and the bulldog changing places now and then to achieve "reciprocity of position" he expressed his conception of the English party system, in which men fight like animals for the grandeur of a "home" — and then give it up in order to fight for it again. In such activity there is much movement but little advance.

And then there is that curious Trollopian double vision which can proclaim (through the Duke of St Bungay) that, after all, "Prime Ministers . . . are not very different from other men. One wants in a Prime Minister a good many things, but not very great things. He should be clever but need not be a genius; he should be conscientious but by no means strait-laced; he should be cautious but never timid, bold but never venturesome; he should have a good digestion, genial manners, and, above all, a thick skin" (II, 5) — and in the same novel declare (through Glencora) that to be Prime Minister of England "is as much as to be an Emperor in France, and much more than being President in America . . . It is to be the greatest man in the greatest country in the world" (II, 467 and 365). That to be the greatest man in the contemporary world may require "not very great things" — little more than good digestion, geniality, and thick skin — suggests Trollope's state of mind in the mid-seventies, when so much of his work, including this novel, was harshly condemned. Certainly the mere presence and the brief success in the system of such a man as Palliser is cause for some hope; but the man's ultimate withdrawal from politics despite his moral victory also represents a sad commentary on the system itself. We rejoice that such men exist, and we see how much the novelist loves them; and yet we also see what happens to them when they enter the world of other men, the "real" world of politics. The progress of Trollope's pessimism led finally to Palliser's political retirement; and so in the last of the Palliser novels politics, though still omnipresent, becomes more vicariously experienced by the great man.

9 The Last Chronicle of Palliser: *The Duke's Children*

'No man will succeed with us in politics who has not a reputation for
solid earnestness. Therefore, the more stupid a man, the better
chance he has.'

Gissing, *Thyrza* (1886)

Though the country were ruined, the party should be supported.

Phineas Redux

A majority is always the best repartée

Disraeli

In the *Autobiography*, Trollope concludes his discussion of *The Prime
Minister* with these words: "I have an idea that I shall even yet once more
have recourse to my political hero as the mainstay of another story" (p.
310). Trollope had more than simply "an idea" when he wrote these
words. *The Duke's Children* (*All the Year Round*, October 1879–July
1880; published in three volumes in 1880) was finished in 1876 but put
away for three years when *The Prime Minister* failed so dismally. The last
Palliser novel was not a popular success either (Trollope's accountants in
the venture lost £120, which the novelist offered to repay[1]), but it was
received by the critics with enthusiasm; and in recent years, though it
remains one of Trollope's more neglected novels, *The Duke's Children* has
been treated with respect and admiration by the few critics who have dealt
with it.

Contemporary reviewers proclaimed *The Duke's Children* one of
Trollope's best novels. They praised the novelist's grasp of aristocratic life
and thought, found the story carefully conceived and the plotting skilful
but unobtrusive. The *Athenaeum* and the *London Illustrated News*
especially admired *The Duke's Children* for its realism. The *Spectator* went
so far as to assert that "No novelist ... seems to possess so sane a
comprehension of the mode of life and thought of the British aristocracy
as Mr. Trollope." In New York, the *Nation* said that *The Duke's Children*
was one of Trollope's greatest novels — so "real," indeed that not a word
could be changed for the better. The novel, declared the *Westminster
Review*, demonstrated that Trollope had not "been falling off" after all.
And its reviewer wrote what was, surprisingly enough, the *only* comment

in contemporary notices on the absence of Lady Glencora: "The death of the Duchess so early in the tale will be a great shock to many worthy people, but even duchesses must die that novels may be written." Clearly there was no wringing of hands over her demise, as there had been on the occasion of Mrs Proudie's similarly abrupt leavetaking a dozen years earlier. Nor did the reviewers note, or seem to care, why the Duchess was put out of the way. Their assessments of the novel do not mention the psychological richness Trollope is able to mine in the Duke's sudden isolation.[2]

Henry James — of whom more shortly — declared in his memorial essay on Trollope that "the great faults of *The Duke's Children*, and perhaps of the entire Palliser series" — which he also says, remember, he did not read — "are a predictive inevitability in the love story and a maundering narrative manner." The little that Trollope's twentieth-century critics have said about *The Duke's Children* has generally been complimentary. Escott reported merely that he liked it better than *The Prime Minister* — a universal reaction. But Walpole ranked it, without explanation, among Trollope's six best novels. The only two relatively recent critics of Trollope who have given *The Duke's Children* extended and serious treatment — Polhemus, and John H. Hagan — found very little political content in the novel; Hagan described *The Duke's Children* as "not very political" and its parliamentary scenes as "perfunctory." He and Polhemus both emphasized something indisputable: in terms of its psychological insights *The Duke's Children* "is, of all Trollope's works, one of the most modern." One would be hard put indeed not to see the psychological depth of Palliser here, or to ignore the skilfulness of the portraits of Lord Silverbridge and Lady Mabel Grex.[3]

What must be revealed, however, is the novel's political content — certainly more substantial than previous commentators have thought. "There is virtually nothing in the way of politics" in it, Booth wrote — admiringly — and thus "the Duke comes alive at last"; lack of political content makes *The Duke's Children* the "most real" of the political novels, he declared.[4] The silliness of such a statement may suggest that it is time to say something more about this greatest of the Palliser novels.

II

First, however, it will be necessary to take up once again — but for a different reason now — the question of the possible literary relationship between Trollope and Henry James. In Chapter 3 some parallels and similarities between Alice Vavasor and Isabel Archer were identified. Now we shall examine Trollope's Isabel Boncassen and her possible predecessors and successors in the wider context of the "international" theme — the context, that is, of several novels and stories by Trollope and James written between the late sixties and early eighties. *The Duke's Children* falls in the midst of these and may be, in the way its international theme is presented, part of an exchange of views on the subject between the novelists – a literary dialogue of the late seventies, the key to which lies in the international stories of each.

James's *Daisy Miller* appeared in the *Cornhill* in June-July 1878 and his *An International Episode*, also in the *Cornhill*, in December 1878-January 1879. One may be reasonably sure that Trollope, a voracious consumer of contemporary fiction and himself a former contributor to the *Cornhill*, read them both. In June 1878 he sold *The Duke's Children* to *All the Year Round*. It did not begin its ten months' run, however, until October 1879, and James read it as he was finishing *The Portrait of A Lady*. Isabel Boncassen, the heroine of *The Duke's Children* and an American, does not appear upon the scene until a third of the way through the novel. Since Trollope had finished *The Duke's Children* as early as 1876 and had it by him during the next three years, we cannot rule out the possibility that his portrait of an American in Europe was affected in part by James's stories, even though Trollope himself had already dealt with the "international" subject – in much less depth, to be sure – in *He Knew He Was Right* and *The American Senator*. Indeed, there is much in *The Duke's Children* that suggests both *Daisy Miller* and *An International Episode*; and, equally to the point, there is much in *The Portrait of A Lady* that suggests *The Duke's Children*.

On 15 April 1874 – two years before Trollope wrote *The Duke's Children* – Lord Randolph Churchill, third son of the seventh Duke of Marlborough, and Miss Jennie Jerome of New York City were married with much fanfare and publicity at the British Embassy in Paris. The Duchess of Manchester, of an earlier generation but no less removed from the social limelight, was also an American, and there were soon to be other international marriages of this sort – culminating some years later in that of Lord Randolph's nephew, the eighth duke, to Consuela Vanderbilt. Undoubtedly the marriages of the Duke of Manchester and Lord Randolph Churchill were on Trollope's mind when, in *The Duke's Children* (II, 204), Lord Silverbridge, elder son of the Duke of Omnium, contemplates his desire to marry an American: "there were certain changes going on in the management of the world which his father did not quite understand . . . Some years ago it might have been improper that an American girl should be elevated to the rank of an English Duchess; but now all that was altered."

The marriage of Caroline Spalding, an American, to the heir of Lord Peterborough in *He Knew He was Right* (1868–9) recalls that of the Manchesters and anticipates that of the Silverbridges. When Charles Glascock, the future Lord Peterborough, virtually picks up Caroline Spalding during a trip to Florence, the themes of free association with whomever one pleases and of international differences on the subject gain substantial importance – as they were to do later in *Daisy Miller*. American women, Trollope tells us here (pp. 373—4), talk and move about with the freedom of men; and he comments: "There is a feeling, however, among pretty women in Europe that such freedom is dangerous, and it is withheld. There is such danger, and more or less of such withholding is expedient; but the American woman does not recognize the danger; and, if she [should withdraw], it is because she is not desirous of the society which is proffered to her." When Caroline's sister reminds her that "we are not in Boston" and that to have an intimacy with a male acquaintance only recently met "might be the most horrible thing in the world to do . . . in Florence," Caroline replies: "Why should that make a difference? Do you mean that one isn't to see one's friends? That must be nonsense" (p. 375). Caroline's uncle, the American minister in Florence, also has doubts about the proprieties involved: "That their young ladies should walk in public places with unmarried gentlemen is nothing to American fathers and guardians. American young ladies are accustomed to choose their own companions. But the minister was tormented by his doubts as to the ways of Englishmen, and as to the phase in which English habits might most properly exhibit themselves in Italy" (p. 517).

Surely the question of whether or not an American girl might properly walk in public in Italy with an unmarried male friend anticipates *Daisy Miller*, published a decade later. A constant supporting element in Trollope's version of the international theme — we find it in *The American Senator* and *The Duke's Children* too — is the American antipathy to English titles which, through association with English aristocrats, is transformed into admiration (Trollope, as we know, was no enemy of aristocracy). Caroline's uncle had made republican speeches at home attacking the idea of aristocracy, but when it seems that his niece is actually about to marry an aristocrat he changes his tune:

> Mr. Spalding was clearly of opinion that, let the value of republican simplicity be what it might, an alliance with the crumbling marbles of Europe would in his niece's circumstances be not inexpedient . . . He had been specially loud against that aristocracy of England which, according to a figure of speech often used by him, was always feeding on the vitals of the people. But now all this was very much changed . . . [At Caroline's wedding] he declared that the republican virtue of the New World had linked itself in a happy alliance with the aristocratic splendour of the Old. (pp. 520, 817 and 824, *passim*.)

In the same novel, remember, appears the feminist Wallachie Petrie — a tedious and masculinely assertive woman who is called "Wally" by her friends, violently opposes the marriage of her friend Caroline, and has more than a suggestion of the lesbian about her. Whether or not she helped to inspire James's treatment of the subject in *The Bostonians* (1886) is a question that might well be asked (and answered elsewhere); in any case,

Miss Petrie gives the lie to the assertion that James's novel is the first in English to address itself to this theme.

In *The American Senator* (1877), Gotobed also begins his visit to England predisposed against aristocracy; he too, soon enough, changes his mind. Praising their "ease of manner," "grace," and physical appeal, Gotobed decides that "there is a pleasure in associating with those of the highest rank," that in being among aristocrats "he was surrounded by people who claimed and made good their claims to superiority," and that it is "more easy in this country to sympathise with the rich than with the poor" (p. 263). Expressing at one point his astonishment over this and other matters to his English friend John Morton, Gotobed is told: "I suppose . . . the habits of one country are incomprehensible to another" (p. 267). At the end of the novel Trollope sums up his feelings about the international question this way: "when an American comes to us, or a Briton goes to the States . . . the differences which present themselves are so striking that neither can live six months in the country of the other without a holding up of the hands and a torrent of explanations . . . [Nevertheless] we Americans and Englishmen go on writing books about each other, sometimes with bitterness enough, but generally with good final results" (p. 401). James, no doubt, would have written his novels and stories on the international subject without such encouragement; the fact remains that *The American Senator* appeared just a year before *Daisy Miller* and *An International Episode*, and *He Knew He Was Right* a decade earlier.

In *Mr Scarborough's Family*, the great late novel published in 1882–3 – four years after *Daisy Miller* and *An International Episode* and just a year after *The Portrait of A Lady* – Trollope, in his portrayal of Florence Mountjoy, reverts to some of the themes treated in *He Knew He Was Right* (and in James's intervening stories). There is nothing "international" in Florence's engagement and subsequent marriage to Harry Annesley – they are both English – but the paramount question at issue in her story is the degree of independence an unmarried woman may have in associating with an unmarried man whom she likes and intends to marry. "In America," Trollope reminds us here, young ladies "carry latch-keys, and walk about with each other" (p. 451). Florene's mother complains that her daughter is more American than English in this respect (p. 453): "she'll go out in the streets and walk with a young man when all her friends tell her not. Is that her idea of religion?" The "walking about" business is as central an issue in *He Knew He Was Right* and *Mr Scarborough's Family* as in *Daisy Miller*. After all, we think of James as the great comparer of America and Europe; but we perhaps forget that Trollope years earlier devoted an entire two-volume work to the international question. *North America* was published back in 1862, and among other things it deals precisely with the kinds of subjects under scrutiny here. Having spent eight months in America (he went back there again in 1875) and paid much attention to American women, Trollope in this study constantly compares them to British women, and speaks often of the "different laws ... which govern ... different societies." He even devotes several paragraphs to the frequency with which he has seen — with dismay — American "young girls in the streets ... alone" at night, coming home from tea-parties and other amusements.[5]

Like Caroline Spalding and Isabel Boncassen, Bessie Alden, the heroine of *An International Episode*, is from Boston. Like Isabel, she is proposed to by a future English duke, and like Isabel Archer she turns down her aristocratic suitor — the first of James's international heroines to do so. She too respects the old-world aristocracy — even lecturing Lord Lambeth at one point on his duties as a nobleman. Lord Lambeth's family, like Lord Silverbridge's, objects to an American marriage; because of this, and also because, like Isabel Archer, Bessie has aspirations that go beyond an easy marriage, she rejects her duke — a reversal of the plot of *The Duke's Children*, though the situation is similar in other respects.

This is preface to and context for the main interest here — the similarity of Trollope's Isabel to the international heroines of James. Finished in 1876 and published in 1879–80, *The Duke's Children*, let us remember, falls in the midst of a flurry of international stories by James, who was still experimenting with his new subject.

Like Mr Spalding and Senator Gotobed, Isabel Boncassen arrives in England prepared to dislike aristocrats. Soon thereafter, though she is not materialistic, Isabel is thrilled by the prospect of marrying a man she can love who also happens to be the heir of a duke: very quickly indeed "a certain sweetness of the aroma of rank [began] to permeate her republican senses" (I, 315). More to the point, she bears a number of resemblances, beyond her name, to the heroine of *The Portrait of A Lady*. She is intelligent and quick-witted, though not intellectual or even overly bright. There is a touch of the snob in her. Independent, spirited, open to experience, she is nevertheless no paragon, and she is never sentimentalized. Prepared to laugh at English aristocrats, she ends up admiring one of them instead.[6] In all of these things she resembles her Jamesian namesake. She, of course, accepts her lord, and will presumably be happy. Isabel Archer lives in a universe less benign; to have accepted *her* lord (Warburton — the name, incidentally, of Palliser's private secretary) would have been too easy, a premature closing of the door of experience — or so it appears to her.

James may be responding in part to Trollope in *The Portrait*, the patently unhappy ending of his novel declaring that such complicated matters are not always so easily or happily resolved. Could he be speaking here directly to the author of *The Duke's Children*? James, remember, was reading Trollope's novel in *All the Year Round* as he was finishing *The Portrait*; he finished it in July 1880, the month in which *The Duke's Children* ended its serial run. (*The Portrait* then ran from October 1880 to November 1881 in *Macmillan's Magazine* in England and from November

1880 to December 1881 in the *Atlantic* in America.) Most interesting is the fact that the novelists' descriptions of their Isabels often sound strikingly similar.

> She had a very high opinion of herself and was certainly entitled to have it by the undisguised admiration of all that came near her . . . Her brain was firmer than that of most girls.

This, astonishingly enough, is not James – it is Trollope (I, 315–16). A reading of the sixth chapter of *The Portrait* will quickly show how alike James's conception of his Isabel is to Trollope's of his. James says of Isabel:

> It had been her fortune to possess a finer mind than most of the persons among whom her lot was cast . . . Whether or no she were superior, people were right in admiring her if they thought her so; for it seemed to her often that her mind moved more quickly than theirs. . . . Isabel was . . . liable to the sin of self-esteem . . . It often seemed to her that she thought too much about herself.[7]

There is also more in *The Duke's Children* about American ladies "walking about" in public. Isabel, when she takes a walk with Silverbridge shortly after they have met for the first time, is immediately aware of the problem:

> 'In our country . . . [a] young lady may walk about with a young gentleman just as she might with another young lady; but I [think it is] different here . . . judging by English ways, I believe I am behaving very improperly in walking about with you so long. Ought I not to tell you to go away? . . . I wish to behave well to English eyes . . . when the discrepancies are small, then they have to be attended to. So I shan't walk about with you any more.' (I, 268)

Trollope's Isabel, like James's Daisy, has a mind of her own in such matters, however, and often refuses to be bound by arbitrary conventions: "the daughter hardly seemed to be under control from the father. She went alone where she liked; talked to those she liked; and did what she liked" (I, 294). Some of her friends admire her sense of freedom, but Trollope himself is not so sure: "There is . . . a good deal to be said against it. All young ladies cannot be Miss Boncassens, with such an assurance of admirers as to be free from all fears of loneliness" (I, 294). Isabel, like Daisy, is warned about the conventions – Lady Clanfiddle, for example, tells her "Americans couldn't be expected to understand English manners," but on that account they should not be ignored (I, 324). Isabel suspects that "all conventional rules" of this sort "are an abomination," but, more than Daisy, she heeds the warning. Nevertheless she will not be dictated to in love: in America, "If two young people love each other they go and get married" (II, 71), she tells Silverbridge when he worries about marriage settlements. Like Bessie Alden, she is both more responsive to conventional expectations than Daisy and less stubbornly imperceptive than Isabel Archer. And so, being resident in a universe where marriages between Cinderellas and princes may felicitously take place, she can live happily ever after with her duke. The general situation is similar to those in James's international stories, even if the resolutions are different.

We need not be overly concerned here with the possible real-life counterparts of the two Isabels, though both characters seem derived from actual Platonic affections. (If Isabel Archer is another version of Minny Temple, Isabel Boncassen may be the youthful object of Trollope's well-known esteem late in life, Kate Field — also from Boston. Like Caroline Spalding and Isabel Archer, Kate went to Italy as a very young woman. From all accounts she too was "emotionally ardent and sensually cold." Kate apparently was imperious in the same pleasant way Isabel Boncassen is imperious with her admirers. The young man at a loss before a girl of spirit fiercer than his own — i.e., Silverbridge — and an older man moved by an emotion not entirely that of a decorous father-in-law — i.e., Palliser — represent, perhaps, two aspects of Trollope's own response to Kate Field.[8] *The Duke's Children*, remember, was written at the same time as the last part of the *Autobiography*, which contains — p. 262 — Trollope's famous outburst about "one of the chief pleasures which has graced my later years" and "a ray of light" encountered in the darkness of his old age. He did not know many American women, after all; there has got to be some of Kate Field in Isabel Boncassen.) However, what matters most here are the literary connections. If James had Trollope's Alice Vavasor in mind when dealing with the "thoughtful" woman theme in *The Portrait*, he may well have had Isabel Boncassen in mind when dealing with the international theme. He may also have remembered Caroline Spalding. And it is possible that James's Daisy and his Bessie had some impact upon Trollope's Isabel. The question here is not so much that of "influence" as that of the community of interests between the two novelists, the fact that their themes are often the same themes.

There are, after all, other examples of this sort — not necessarily "international" in nature yet nonetheless interesting as part of the picture. One of these is the striking similarity between Trollope's odd little novel *Sir Harry Hotspur of Humblethwaite* (1870) and James's *Washington Square* (1881). In both novels a rich father prevents a marriage between his heiress-daughter and an unprincipled but clever and attractive cousin with whom she is in love. In each case the daughter thinks the would-be lover better than he is; and in each the father tactlessly proves to the daughter that the cousin is only after her money. Each daughter comes to see that the father has been right about the lover — but loves neither the one better nor the other less for having her eyes opened; the interference in each case destroys forever the daughter's only chance for happiness. Neither daughter ever marries. The description of the one — "She suffered under a terrible feeling of ill-usage. Why was she, because she was a girl and an heiress, to be debarred from her own happiness? If she were willing to risk herself, why should others interfere?" — could easily fit both (the passage is taken from *Sir Harry Hotspur*, p. 163).

In his essay on Trollope (1883), James said that "in these matters" — international matters — Trollope did well, though he felt that Isabel Boncassen was more an Englishman's American than an American's. (Presumably he would have had to read *The Duke's Children* — another of those political novels of Trollope's he says he did not read — in order to know this.) The *Spectator*'s reviewer had also suggested that Isabel Boncassen "is as English as the Duke himself, and not American at all." Other adverse reactions to Trollope's Isabel have come more recently from the Stebbinses (Trollope, they say, did not understand American girls so well as James and Howells, and should have left the international theme alone), and Pope-Hennessy (Isabel Boncassen "is convincing without being particularly interesting").[9] One of her most "interesting" properties, however, has been almost totally ignored — the possibility of her having in part inspired James to improve upon her, to create a more domestic version of the real thing.

As Polhemus has pointed out, "A short while after he read Trollope's novel, James portrayed another American lady named Isabel who visits England and wins a proposal from a lord." True enough, but clearly there is more to say. Trollope and James in the late seventies were writing about many of the same things; and it seems likely that they were responding in some of their fictions to each other and that "influence," between them, goes in both directions. It appears at times as if a dialogue, an exchange of views, engaged them (it is known that they met one another several times[10]). What may be of most interest here is that, obviously enough, James took from Trollope as much or more than Trollope took from him — despite the fact that such influence as may have occurred has sometimes been assumed to travel in the other direction.

III

Before considering the political theme, which is connected intimately with the account of Lord Silverbridge's escapades, a word about the novel's other major plot must be said. The story of Frank Tregear and Lady Mary Palliser is what most gives psychological focus to Palliser himself in *The Duke's Children*. There is never any real doubt about his having to give way in the end and approve the marriage; indeed, it is the fate of almost all stubborn parents in Trollope's novels to be beaten down at last by persistent children. In *Sir Harry Hotspur of Humblethwaite* the point is made that "young lovers, if they be firm, can always conquer opposing parents" (p. 196). Lady Altringham in that novel tells George Hotspur: "Even in ordinary cases the fathers and mothers are beaten by the lovers nine times out of ten. It is only when the men are oafs and louts that they are driven off" (p. 67). *John Calidgate* conveys the same lesson: "In such cases it is so often the daughter who prevails with her parents after she has surrendered her own heart" (p. 124; the novel's account of Hester Bolton's marriage to Caldigate is a case in point). So the interest of this part of *The Duke's Children* is not in what Palliser will do, but rather in what he will undergo before giving in. That his objection to Tregear as a son-in-law, though seemingly arbitrary, is based on unwritten but thoroughly believed rules of rank as they are seen by him to apply to his family, is quite clear – we shall examine these ideas later. But what gives this aspect of the novel its peculiar flavor and its psychological depth is the haunting – for it is no less than that – of the Duke by his late Duchess. In spirit she is everywhere in *The Duke's Children*, and her presence is most apparent in Lady Mary's story.

Glencora's children inherited from her the tenacity and impulsivness with which, throughout the novel, Palliser has to struggle. In having sanctioned, just before her death, the engagement between Tregear and Mary, Glencora yet again becomes an obstacle to her husband's peace of mind. Most crucial is the fact that Mary's passion for Tregear recalls to Palliser his late wife's youthful passion for Burgo Fitzgerald, recounted in *Can You Forgive Her?*. No doubt it recalled the same thing to Glencora, reawakening her old nostalgia for the impossible. By attempting to make Mary give up Tregear and to substitute for the glamorous but penniless suitor the dull but respectable Lord Popplecourt, Palliser, it has been pointed out, is in effect symbolically re-enacting – or trying to re-enact – his "victory" over Fitzgerald, for he sees Tregear as Fitzgerald, Mary as Glencora, Popplecourt as himself, and a Popplecourt success as a would-be symbol of his own.[11] Once again, in this last novel of the series, Palliser must fight the battle of *Can You Forgive Her?* – this time against an adversary no less powerful in its disembodied form. The Duke's mistake here is in being blinded to the fact that Tregear (ultimately an M.P.) is a more responsible and trustworthy man than Burgo Fitzgerald.

There are some poignant moments in the novel that make clear the personal nature of Palliser's dilemma.

His own Duchess, she whose loss to him now was as though he had lost half his limbs, – had not she in the same way loved a Tregear, or worse than a Tregear, in her early days? Ah yes! And though his Cora had been so much to him, had he not often felt . . . that Fate had robbed him of the sweetest joy that is given to man, in that she had not come to him loving him with her early spring of love, as she had loved that poor n'er-do-well? (I, 66)

Palliser's marriage – its origins, its early failures, its final successes – are constantly present to him when dealing with his children's marital affairs. "Do you think that love is a passion that cannot be withstood?" he snaps at Silverbridge at one point (II, 201); and when, in conversation with Mrs Finn, he asks sardonically if a girl should be allowed to marry anyone she likes, "his mind was intent on his Glencora and on Burgo Fitzgerald." Thus he launches the abortive Popplecourt scheme, remembering vividly how his wife's relatives had separated Glencora from Burgo and thrust himself in her path: "Surely that method of bargaining to which he had owed his own wife would be [best] . . . It was thus that he had been married" (I, 109). Palliser is sensitive enough to such "bargaining" as to be thoroughly "disgusted by it. And yet it had answered so well with his wife!" "Could [Mary be] made to consent to marry someone else," the Duke reasons, "terrible as the rupture might [be], she would [reconcile] herself at last to her new life. So it had been with his Glencora, – after a time" (II, 95). The theme even touches Lord Silverbridge, who tells Tregear that Mary will some day marry a wealthy man with a good position and that their present attachment will then seem irrelevant. "It might almost have been supposed," Trollope interjects here, "that the young man had been acquainted with his mother's history" (I, 132).

Tregear and Mary are thus re-enacting a painfully sensitive phase of Palliser's youth – as for the late Duchess, encouragement of the two young people was a vicarious means of reliving one of the most diverting episodes in *her* early life.[12] Fearing perhaps that his own marriage was a failure because his wife never forgot her first love, Palliser responds to this fear with the rationalization of parental duty – to assuage his sense of failure he attempts to subdue and punish his wife once and for all in the person of his daughter, thus bringing the marriage theme full cycle in the final novel, as Hagan has said. This aspect of *The Duke's Children*, by revealing the burden of jealousy and anxious fear borne by the Duke during his marriage, gives the novel its chief psychological interest and helps illuminate retrospectively the nature of those years of the marriage chronicled in preceding volumes.[13] In finally consenting to the Tregear marriage, and to the Boncassen one as well, Palliser is able at last to reconcile himself not so much to present social conditions and ideas (an argument that is often put forward by critics of the novel) but rather to his own past – a lonely, unspectacular accomplishment, certainly, but nonetheless, for him, a comforting one. His achievement here is not, as some have argued, final understanding that all of his values and ideals are outdated, but rather, in reconciliation with his own past life, a personal reaffirmation of his own humanity. It therefore seems wrong to conclude, as Hagan did, that the Duke's children help complete the social education of their father begun by Glencora and thereby enable him by the end of the novel to achieve a victory over himself, or his past ideas; or that Palliser, as apRoberts has said, "must overcome his political prejudices" at the end of *The Duke's Children* in order ultimately to be "victorious over himself" in the matter of his children's marriages.[14] Clearly Palliser is not edified by the various kinds of irresponsible behavior of which his children are guilty; indeed, his mind is a finer one than any of theirs, his ideas better ideas than theirs. Any education going on in *The Duke's Children* proceeds in the other direction — from him to them. It also proceeds from him to us; for in pairing off against one another what the *Spectator* called "the best and highest type of the surviving aristocracy of the last generation" with "the children of progress," the novel teaches that "emancipation" from past traditions may also deprive people of dignity and self-respect.

IV

By consenting to the marriages of his children, then, Palliser is not admitting that his ideas have been wrong and theirs right. *The Duke's Children* is not the usual generation-gap story, and this is because the father is a much more admirable figure than his sons and son-in-law. Nor is this a "levelling" novel. Palliser's defense of aristocracy is made in the teeth not so much of democratizing tendencies as of irresponsibility; Trollope, distrusting the self-indulgence of the new generation, sides with his middle-aged hero instead.[15] Silverbridge is decent but gullible, slow to mature, even a little stupid; his thoughtlessness gets his younger brother rusticated from college, and (like Thackeray's Pendennis — and the heir of the fifth Duke of Newcastle, the Earl of Lincoln) he gambles away a fortune. He is not much of a hero; and his trouble with his father is the result of his own shallowness rather than differences in social theory (Hagan's notion that "Father and son have been divided by the inevitable transformations of history itself" is nonsense). The intellect of the second son, Gerald, is bovine. Tregear is deeper than either, but there is nothing he can teach Palliser. Indeed, though there is much Palliser can teach the younger generation of *The Duke's Children*, there is little he can learn from it. "Judging from what we can . . . read of the manner in which our fathers and mothers lived," Trollope says in *The New Zealander* (the essay on "Society"), "we cannot but think that we have greatly retrograded and are still quickly retrograding." And he goes on here to refer contemptuously to the generation of young men then on the way up as "curled darlings of the nation. Oh what a subject for the national pride!"; and he pities "that class of young ladies who *malgré lui* are bound to fall in love with these wooden specimens of youthful manhood."[16] Trollope wrote this passage two decades before *The Duke's Children*, but his opinion of the younger generation, if anything, grew less sanguine as the years went by.

We must ask why Palliser puts aside his relatively liberal theories about class when the question comes to concern his own family. Why should a political liberal who advocates the narrowing of class distinctions want to educate his children to the duties of their rank and teach them to help preserve the aristocracy? The easy answer is — hypocrisy. The real one, however, is consistent with all that we have learned of this man in preceding novels: Palliser, "the Victorian spirit of self-sacrifice and public spirit incarnate," ranks the *duties* of his order higher than its *privileges*.[17] There is no place for thoughtless self-indulgence in families so situated, he feels.

Let us see what the novel tells us about rank. The Duke is no snob. That is, he values his rank, as we have seen, not for itself but for what it can enable him to do. There is no inconsistency here; and as a matter of fact a number of passages in *The Duke's Children* call attention both to Palliser's social liberalism and to his desire to maintain and perpetuate his own order. "He had by no means always found that he liked best the companionship of his own order . . . He liked to remember that the son of any tradesman might, by his own merits, become a peer of Parliament . . . [But] was it not his duty to fortify and maintain that higher, smaller, more precious pinnacle of rank on which Fortune had placed him and his children?" (II, 207). Asserting that he is not "specially wedded to [rank]," the Duke nevertheless "would wish [Mary] to mate with one of her own class . . . He must be of high rank, and an eldest son, and the possessor of, or the heir to, a good estate. He did despise himself when he found that he put these things first, — as a matter of course. Nevertheless he did put them first" (I, 106–7 and 231). He can feel that Gatherum Castle, official residence of the Dukes of Omnium, is "All vanity . . . and vexation of spirit!"; and yet he can also feel that a man such as Tregear should not be "asking for the hand of one who was second only to royalty." But Palliser is no conventional snob. He tells Isabel:

> 'if a man can raise himself by his own intellect . . . no one will think of his father or his grandfather. The sons of merchants have with us been Prime Ministers more than once, and no Englishmen ever were more honoured . . . Our peerage is being continually recruited from the ranks of the people, and hence gets its strength . . . There is no greater mistake than to suppose that inferiority of birth is a barrier to success in this country.'
>
> . . . [Never] in discussing such matters generally did he ever mingle his own private feelings, his own pride of race and name, his own ideas of what was due to his ancient rank with the political creed by which his conduct in public life was governed. The peer who sat next to him in the House of Lords, whose grandmother had been a washerwoman and whose father an inn-keeper, was to him every whit as good a peer as himself. And he would as soon sit in counsel with Mr. Monk, whose father had risen from a mechanic to be a merchant, as with any nobleman who could count ancestors against himself. But there was an inner feeling in his bosom as to his own family, his own name, his own

children, and his own personal self, which was kept altogether apart from his grand political theories. It was a subject on which he never spoke; but the feeling had come to him as a part of his birthright. And he conceived that it would pass through him to his children after the same fashion. (II, 85–6)

"That one and the same man should have been in one part of himself so unlike the other part, – that he should have one set of opinions so contrary to another set" (II, 87) – is one aspect of Palliser that Trollope continually emphasizes, and always uncritically. Because his "private feeling" and his "political creed" *are* kept separate, he is able to act without bias for the public interest when called upon to serve it.

Mrs Finn, who argues Mary's cause with Palliser, is told by him: "duty is – duty; – and whatever pang it may cost should be performed." "If every foolish girl were indulged," he tells himself, "all restraint would be lost, and there would be an end to those rules as to birth and position by which he thought his world was kept straight . . . [His daughter] had no conception that there should be something in the world . . . more valuable to her than the fruition of her own desires!" (II, 95–6). He tells Silverbridge: "Whether I may be wrong or right I think it to be for the good of the country, for the good of our order, for the good of our individual families, that we should support each other by marriage. It is not as though we were a narrow class, already too closely bound together by family alliances" (II, 293). The key statement of this theme is as follows:

Anxious as he was that both his sons should be permeated by Liberal politics, studious as he had ever been to teach them that the highest duty of those high in rank was to use their authority to elevate those beneath [them], still he was hardly less anxious to make them understand that their second duty required them to maintain their own position. It was by feeling this second duty, – by feeling it and performing it, – that they would be enabled to perform the first . . . The endurance and perpetuation of [nobility] should be the peculiar care of every Palliser. (II, 240–1)

This explains a good deal. In order to be effective as a liberal politician and to be able to help "elevate those beneath them," men of Palliser's rank must "maintain their own position." The effective statesman should value rank not for its own sake but for the political and moral authority it gives him and which in turn enables him to accomplish good things. The theme is a familiar one, but nowhere is it articulated more explicitly. The class containing those most fit to lead is bound to maintain some separation from the other classes in order to function; it must preserve itself in order to perpetuate its ability to serve. Thus Palliser feels that "with bad Dukes his country would be in worse stress than though she had none at all"; he yearns for "an aristocracy that shall be of the very best! He believed himself thoroughly in his order ... An England without a Duke of Omnium, – or at any rate without any Duke, – what would it be? ... It was not by his own doing that he belonged to an aristocracy which, if all exclusiveness were banished from it, must cease to exist." But having through mere chance "been born to such privileges and such limitations, was he not bound to maintain a certain exclusiveness?" (II, 301 and 103). The nobleman's first duties must be outside of himself; in preserving his order he is preserving the country. "It was not the happiness of this or that individual which should be considered. There is a propriety in things, – and only by an adherence to that propriety on the part of individuals can the general welfare be maintained ... Such were the opinions ... of one who was as truly Liberal in his ideas as any man in England," says Trollope, who argues that such opinions are not in conflict with that ideal of the "drawing-nearer of the classes [which] was the object to which all this man's political action tended" (I, 213). As we know, Liberalism and a belief in aristocracy are not incompatible; on the contrary, they are often symbiotic in the nineteenth century. Of course the aristocrat had to understand the duty he owed in his position to his countrymen, and they had to be confident that it would continue to be performed. Precisely because it owes so much to the country, aristocracy must be preserved to go on paying that debt. Indeed, such paying keeps the country going; the privilege of rank comes only at the expense of duty, and when peers do not do their duty any justification of their order disappears. Sir William Patterson, an enlightened Liberal Solicitor-General who voted for the Great Reform Bill, puts it this way in *Lady Anna* (p. 214): "Our titles of honour bear so high a value among us, are so justly regarded as the outward emblem of splendour and noble conduct ... that we are naturally prone to watch their assumption with ... caution." Patterson is a sympathetic character in the novel, and the modifiers he uses here – "justly," "naturally" – are as much Trollope's as the sentiments themselves. So when Silverbridge in *The Duke's Children* avers that "by law" he has the same freedom to marry whom he pleases as anyone else, his father lectures him passionately:

'Is there to be no duty in such matters, no restraint, no feeling of what is due to your own name, and to others who bear it? ... To such a one as you the law can be no guide ... Does the law require patriotism, philanthropy, self-abnegation, public service, purity of purpose, devotion to the needs of others who have been placed in the world below you? ... Between you and me there should be no mention of law as the guide of conduct. Speak to me of honour, of duty, and of nobility; and tell me what they require of you!' (II, 199–200)

High rank, because of the moral authority it carries, offers to the individual who has it the greatest opportunities to be of use to others, and therefore, and only therefore, it is a thing to be cherished and preserved. Should it be misused, or used selfishly, then it had better disappear altogether. (Palliser preaches a similar lesson on money and its uses to his younger son Gerald later in the novel – II, 238–9; when Hagan suggested that wealth is seen in *The Duke's Children* as "an obstacle in the way of realizing the noble purposes of hard work and social service,"[18] he missed Trollope's point completely. On the contrary – like high rank, money in the right hands offers opportunities for political effectiveness rather than obstacles to moral action. We know how contemptuous Trollope was of honest ascetics who, through diffidence, permit the dishonest to take more than their share of the world's good things.)

It is right to attempt to reduce the distance between the classes, but to believe in the abolition of class distinctions or in the absolute equality of all men is to believe in a dream – as we also know. Tregear at one point refers to the zealots of the French Revolution "who thought they could do a deal of good by making everybody equal. A good many were made equal by having their heads cut off" (II, 144). Even Isabel declares that "There is no such mischievous nonsense in all the world as equality ... What men ought to want is liberty" (II, 83). The *Spectator*'s reviewer was one of the few – then and now – to recognize Trollope's true feelings on the subject. The conflict in *The Duke's Children* between tradition and "progress," he said, emphasizes the issue of "caste": "caste is the very root of the tree of the English political oak, and can be interfered with only at the risk of destroying the entire organism." Trollope's theme is ubiquitous. Nor is it to be regretted that Lord Silverbridge absorbs some of his father's teachings on the subject. He tells Tregear: "A fellow is not any better to me because he has got a title, nor yet because he owns half a county. But men have their ideas and feelings about it ... Money and rank and those sort of things are not particularly charming to me. But still things should go together" (I, 31 and 131). Palliser's hope that his feelings in such matters "would pass through him to his children" apparently will not be altogether vain.

The Duke's Children has not irrelevantly been called (again by the *Spectator*'s perspicacious reviewer) a "dramatic essay ... upon the aristocratic principle, in its relation to politics, society, and morality." As the *Saturday Review* pointed out,[19] Palliser "represents the struggle between the old aristocratic sentiment and modern liberalism"; Trollope approved less and less of the latter as he got older. Among other things, the *Saturday Review* said, Palliser in *The Duke's Children* personifies pride of birth, sense of nobility, long ancestry, and great historical position. This is quite true; the only confusion is in the minds of modern critics who, imposing backwards upon the novelist their own social prejudices, see him as treating the issue ironically. But his attitudes about class –

"blood" — were unchanging. As far back as *The Kellys and the O'Kellys* one can find such a passage as this: "Rank and station are in themselves tremendous benefits; but they require more rigid conduct, much more control over the feelings than is necessary in a humbler position. You should always remember . . . that much is expected from those to whom much is given" (p. 358). The "more control" and "more rigid conduct" are ideals, not jokes. One of the chief lessons of *Sir Harry Hotspur of Humblethwaite* is that "good blood" and "honesty" inevitably "assist in producing the highest order of self-denying man" (p. 197). Indeed, Sir Harry, faced with a dilemma similar to Palliser's in *The Duke's Children*, muses thus upon the problem (p. 195): "Was his higher duty due to his daughter, or to his family, — and through his family to his country, which, as he believed, owed its security and glory to the maintenance of its aristocracy? Would he be justified, — justified in any degree, — in subjecting his child to danger in the hope that his name and family pride might be maintained?" Nor should we forget the two long and important statements in *Phineas Redux* on aristocracy — Erle's declaration of belief "in the patriotism of certain families . . . [which] have for some centuries brought up their children to regard the well-being of their country as their [highest personal interest. . . . The school in which good training is most] practised will, as a rule, turn out the best scholars" (I, 216); and the Duke of St Bungay's lecture to his despondent fellow duke: "the England which we know could not be the England that she is but for the maintenance of a high-minded, proud, and self-denying nobility . . . the success of our order depends chiefly on the conduct of those whose rank is the highest and whose means are the greatest" (II, 188). If this is true then Palliser's education of his children and their response to his teachings must have consequences beyond the family circle; indeed, the welfare of the country is at stake. It is in this sense that *The Duke's Children* is old man Trollope's "future of England" novel, his *Howards End*.

V

We have seen how Palliser's attitude toward marriage is flavored with poignant memories of his own past. In agreeing to the marriages of his children he is also acknowledging that in some respects one "must live as others live around one" (II, 321). His ideas about rank and class are not changed, but they are tempered by considerations purely personal — another reminder of the constant interaction between politics and society and between the outer and the inner lives.

In the novel's opening chapter we find the bereaved Duke counting up the losses he has sustained with the passing of his wife, not least of which was her having made it possible for him, wholly devoted to politics, to live a social life: "his loving and liking had been exclusively political. He had so habituated himself to devote his mind and his heart to the service of his country, that he had almost risen above or sunk below humanity. But she, who had been essentially human, had been a link between him and the world" (I, 4). Conversely, in plotting with her daughter to effect the Tregear engagement, Glencora had used tactics essentially political: "The father had been regarded as a great outside power, which could hardly be overcome, but which might be evaded, or made inoperative by strategem" (I, 20–1). Attempting to listen to an important debate in the House of Lords, Palliser finds it impossible to concentrate on the issues "as he thought of the condition of his children."

Again love and politics are seen to affect one another. Lord Silverbridge, who does not like being in Parliament, nevertheless offers to work hard at politics if Lady Mabel wishes him to (I, 155 and 157). Later, when enamored of Isabel, he finds "the tedium of those parliamentary benches" less alluring than her company and offers to give up them – and everything else he has – to marry her (II, 269). At a party he patently prefers chasing after Isabel to talking to the "old humbug," as he calls him, who is the leader of his party; and when she disappears for a time he finds everything, and especially the House, "stupid." Personal and political considerations are intimately connected and continually influence one another. Silverbridge, who goes to the House only for his father's sake, as he tells his sister, resolves at one point "to read up parliamentary literature" in penance for Palliser's displeasure with his non-political conduct. When Silverbridge is asked by the old humbug himself (Sir Timothy Beeswax) to second the Queen's Address, both he and his father (rightly) assume the invitation has been made because, having switched from the Liberals to the Tories, such a display of Silverbridge would further embarrass the Duke, a former Liberal Premier.[20] Characteristically, Palliser advises his son to accept the invitation anyway – but Silverbridge refuses because Sir Timothy, is, he says, "such a beast" (II, 259). The Duke points out that "intimacies" must "come from politics," and so must antipathies; but feelings of a social nature often have political consequences, and vice versa. Mrs Finn, trying hard to avoid a quarrel with Palliser over the fate of Mary, knows very well that such a quarrel, though her husband has nothing to do with it, "might be prejudicial to his position as a member of his political party." Lord Popplecourt, who is a politician only because "there isn't much else to do," knows equally well that a most efficacious means of political advancement in the Liberal party is to agree with everything Palliser might say to him – "there floated before his eyes visions of under-secretaryships." Such is the relationship of political and social matters in this novel.

An important analogous theme is the apparent ease with which, for some, partisan loyalties may be revised, annihilated, or even reversed by extra-political considerations. Lady Mabel is ready instantly to desert the Toryism of her family should she marry into the Liberal Pallisers (II, 183). While she thinks that "people in politics should remain as they are born," she knows that "statesmen . . . change backwards and forwards" whenever they find it convenient to do so — which does not shock or surprise her. Of major importance here are the political convictions — or rather the lack thereof — of Silverbridge, who feels that party loyalty means "nothing more than choosing one set of companions or choosing another . . . It does seem so hard . . . to find any difference between the two" (II, 143). Silverbridge departs from the age-old Liberalism of the Pallisers on a whim and comes back to it at last only because he does not much care for the "set of companions" he has got among on the Tory side — "Sir Timothy is such a beast," and so forth. At one point before his return to the fold he thinks he might strike a bargain with his father: "he should consent to go back to the Liberal party on being allowed to marry the girl he loved . . . As far as his political feelings were concerned he did not think that he would much object to make the change" (II, 130). Tregear, who had talked Silverbridge over to the Tories, is perfectly willing to have his friend re-enlist with the Liberals when it becomes clear to him that this would be an effective way of propitiating Palliser with regard to his own hoped-for marriage with Mary (e.g., I, 40).

What gives this part of the story its chief interest is the reaction such casual zig-zagging draws from the Duke himself. In *The Prime Minister* Silverbridge's unwitting mother was heard to say that "A Palliser who was not a Whig would be held to have disgraced himself for ever" (I, 432). Blowing this way and that, apparently indifferent to questions of party, Silverbridge theoretically should draw from his father a pronouncement of odium — and this long before the son decides on his own that he has been wrong to leave the family party. "It was quite wrong," Silverbridge ultimately discovers. "What did it matter to me? . . . I've made an ass of myself . . . After all it is not very important . . . I don't think it matters on which side you sit: — but it does matter that you shouldn't have to act with those who go against the grain with you . . . I have had my little vagary" (I, 277 and 233, and II, 338–9 and 367). Palliser's response to this — "I never heard a worse political argument in my life" (II, 339) — is indicative. His son's temporary conversion to the Conservatives is less worrisome than Silverbridge's obvious indifference to his parliamentary obligations. Again, as in the case of the domestic troubles he causes (gambling, getting his brother expelled, and so on), Silverbridge's political apostasy is seen as a result of thoughtlessness rather than conviction. Domestic and political failures stem from similar causes, a theme typical of Trollope's view of politics. In the end, of course, Silverbridge, like Prince Hal, renounces his youthful follies and returns to the family fold. But this is not until he has been lectured to at some length. The political advice Silverbridge receives from his father is worth reviewing.

While Palliser asserts over and over again that his son's "apostasy from the political creed of the Pallisers" is "a blow," he is steadfast, though unenthusiastic, in maintaining that "he may be a good Member of Parliament though he has turned Conservative . . . a Conservative patriotic nobleman may serve his country even as a Conservative" (I, 77, and II, 206). Palliser never condemns Silverbridge outright for the switch – indeed, the father pays the son's expenses in the Silverbridge election. Silverbridge may be a fool, but at least he is not a criminal – so says his father (I, 71). What alarms the Duke is the absence in his son of any sense of the duties of public service. A man's political obligations, Palliser says, are such that he need only recognize that "the greatest benefit of the greatest number [is] the object to which all political studies tend" (I, 69). If the young man will only work hard for others he may think what he likes. When Silverbridge expresses to his father his feeling that choice of party only means choosing between various sets of acquaintances, Palliser responds with a lecture. Often in public life one must act with people one does not personally esteem in order that public good may be achieved. If you are a conscientious public servant, "you are concerned with others for the good of the State; and though even for the State's sake, you would not willingly be closely allied with those whom you think dishonest, the outward manners and fashions of life need create no barriers" (I, 248). A man must not "be this or that in politics according to [his] personal liking for an individual" (II, 260); in this way the public is served. And so Palliser encourages his son to "take an active and useful part on that side to which you have attached yourself . . . I shall hear you . . . with infinite satisfaction, even though I shall feel at the same time anxious to answer all your arguments and to disprove all your assertions. I should be listening no doubt to my opponent; – but I should be proud to feel that I was listening to my son" (II, 259).

Once again Trollope portrays Palliser, though now out of office, as a kind of ideal politician – arguing, as always, the paramount importance of the public good and the irrelevance of personalities in the pursuit of it. Perhaps nowhere does Palliser articulate the Trollopian political ideal so eloquently as in the letter he writes to Silverbridge upon the latter's election to Parliament:

'as you have voluntarily undertaken certain duties you are bound as an honest man to perform them, as scrupulously as though you were paid for doing them. There was no obligation in you to seek the post; – but having sought it and acquired it you cannot neglect the work attached to it without being untrue to the covenant you have made . . . I would have you always remember the purport for which there is a Parliament elected. . . . It is not that some men may shine there, that some may acquire power, or that all may plume themselves on being the elect of the nation . . . I have known gentlemen who have felt that in becoming members of Parliament they had achieved an object for themselves instead of thinking that they had put themselves in the way of achieving something for others. A member of Parliament should feel himself to be the servant of his country, – and like every other servant, he should serve . . . If the harness gall him he need not wear it. But if he takes the trappings, then he should draw the coach. You are there as the guardian of your fellow-countrymen, — that they may be safe, that they may be prosperous, that they may be well governed and lightly burdened, — and above all that they may be free. If you cannot feel this to be your duty, you should not be there at all.' (I, 148—9)

To work diligently not for oneself but for others — to "serve" — is Palliser's only real political creed from the first volume of the series to the last. It is what justifies his vocation, his class, his very existence. The letter goes on to advise Silverbridge to learn the forms of the House so as to know how he may best serve his party and his constituents; and it points out that committee work, in obscurity, is more likely to achieve these ends than speaking in session, in public view. A good M.P., the letter concludes, will vote with his party when he can, but always and only "for the measures . . . which he believes to be for the good of the country" (I, 149). Ultimately then, says the Duke, "there will come upon you the ineffable delight of having served your country to the best of your ability. It is the only pleasure in life which has been enjoyed without alloy by your . . . father" (I, 150).

Patriotism is hard work without personal benefit on behalf of others. We know the importance Trollope attached to working hard; many of his "villains" get into trouble simply by having too much time on their hands. In Trollopian tones Palliser preaches the doctrine of hard work to his son again and again:

'To feel that your hours are filled to overflowing, that you can hardly steal minutes enough for sleep, that the welfare of many is entrusted to you, that the world looks on and approves, that some good is always being done to others, — above all things some good to your country; — that is happiness. For myself I can conceive none other . . . For that feeling of self-contentment, which creates happiness — hard work, and hard work alone, can give it to you.' (I, 238—9)

We know how important it was for Trollope to stand well in his own eyes, to achieve the approval of others while maintaining his own sense of self-justification, to keep himself busy enough to avoid the idle thoughts of a melancholy temperament and the bitter memories of a humiliating youth. Palliser as politician enacts the public part of Trollope the private man; the ideal politician is often Trollope's vision of *himself* as public man.

Again we find Palliser in *The Duke's Children* wishing he could be Chancellor of the Exchequer and sit in the House of Commons, where the real work of governing the country is done. Earlier, as we know, he regretted the inanity of the golden coronet that had taken him out of the

Commons; now he tells Silverbridge that he wishes "the title could have passed over my head . . . and gone to you at once" (II, 366) so that he himself could return to his "old place." Silverbridge thinks he means the Premiership, but Palliser, who is without vanity of place as he is without vanity of rank, sets him straight: "I would return to the Exchequer where the work is hard and certain . . . A man there . . . need not be popular, need not be a partisan, need not be eloquent, need not be a courtier . . . [need not have] recourse to that parliamentary strategy for which I know that I am unfit" (II, 366). Palliser's forte is scholarship and not strategy; he prefers work to public relations. In this he is explicitly contrasted with the current Tory leader, as we shall see

Trollope's ideal politician has no personal ambition except to serve others; as in preceding volumes of the series, he is pictured as wanting only to "be useful as a legislator" even "though he was no longer a minister" (I, 2). Again we hear it said of him that "there is perhaps no other man at the same time so just and so patriotic" (I, 117); again "accusations which others made against him were as nothing to those with which he charged himself" (I, 209); again his conscience troubles him over trifles — he is "so thin-skinned that all things hurt him." And again he has to be continually propped up by the Duke of St Bungay. In this novel the old Duke writes to urge him, after Glencora has been dead for a decent interval, to re-enter politics once again. St Bungay writes to the younger Duke in a strain not unlike that in which Palliser had written to Silverbridge:

> 'Nothing is more essential to the political well-being of the country than that the leaders . . . should be prepared for their duties . . . if your country wants you, you should serve your country. It is a work as to which such a one as you has no option . . . he cannot recede without breach of a manifest duty. The work to be done is so important, the numbers to be benefited are so great, that he cannot be justified in even remembering that he has a self.' (I, 206 and 208)

Again we see that a man of high rank, great wealth, and exceptional energies is expected to return to the country, by way of hard work, that which the country has given to him as a trust. Reading the letter, Palliser finds himself most in agreement with the last sentence, seeing the requirement of selflessness as "a true thing" and "his duty": "he was called upon to serve his country by good service." In such a man as a Duke of Omnium, selfishness and laziness would be particularly treacherous crimes. It is this lesson he constantly preaches to Silverbridge: "A man can never be happy unless his first objects are outside himself. Personal self-indulgence begets a sense of meanness which sticks to a man even when he has got beyond all hope of rescue" (I, 252). The Duke defines here a moral weakness with which Trollope is concerned in *all* of his novels, political or otherwise.

When St Bungay suggests that Palliser's reluctance to re-enter public life may be due to "diffidence," he in fact misjudges the younger man – who is diffident in personal relationships, but whose reluctance here stems more from his vision of himself as a political failure: "Our Duke's friends had told him that his Ministry had been serviceable to the country; but no one had ever suggested to him that he would again be asked to fill the place which he had filled ... He felt that he had failed" (II, 365). His nostalgia for office is founded not so much on love of power as on his knowledge of the enormous opportunities office offers, under the right circumstances – "with a loyal majority, with a well-conditioned unanimous cabinet" – for spending oneself "night and day, even to death, in the midst of labours" (I, 211). At the end of *The Duke's Children* Palliser accepts the Cabinet post of President of the Council – a job more honorific than real, yet nevertheless one he feels he ought to take: "He knew that if anything could once again make him contented it would be work; he knew that if he could serve his country it was his duty to serve it; and he knew also that it was only by the adhesion of such men as himself that the traditions of his party could be maintained" (II, 365). And so he does his duty – contributing, perhaps, more by his mere presence in the Cabinet than by any substantial work, but contributing in this way nonetheless.

If the future of England is to depend in any measure upon the labors of Palliser's two sons, then *The Duke's Children* paints a rather bleak picture of that future, entirely in keeping with Trollope's opinion of the generation then on the way up. However, despite the novel's title (in the initial agreement with *All the Year Round* and Chapman & Hall in 1878, the novel is referred to as *Lord Silverbridge*; later, before he hit upon the title he was actually to use, the novelist called it *The Ex-Prime Minister*[21]), Trollope's focus is on the father rather than the children, and in the father there is much to be grateful for. The fact that he does not entirely succeed in implanting in his children his own sense of duty is less important, perhaps, than that that sense of duty exists in the father at all. Though Palliser is oppressed by a sense of failure, the very efforts he makes are a cause for hope. Especially striking is Trollope's obvious sympathy for conscientious men of Palliser's class and age – those who wish, in contravention of the commercial spirit of the age, to preserve their position for the country's benefit rather than their own. Palliser's sense of failure is therefore given a particular poignancy.

> If he could only so operate on the ... minds of both his sons, as to make them see the foolishness of folly, the ugliness of what is mean, the squalor and dint of ignoble pursuits ... if he could teach his children to accept those lessons without which no man can live as a gentleman, let his rank be the highest known, let his wealth be as the sands, his fashion unrivalled ... How completely had he failed to

indoctrinate his children with the ideas by which his own mind was fortified and controlled. ... From their young boyhood nothing had seemed so desirable to him as that they should be accustomed by early training to devote themselves to the service of their country ... What good would all his wealth or all his position do for his children if their minds could rise to nothing beyond the shooting of deer and the hunting of foxes? (II, 239–40)

That the next Duke of Omnium may be more like his great-uncle than his father is to be deplored; as Erle says in *Phineas Redux*, speaking of the great families: "there have been failures. Every child won't learn its lesson however well it may be taught." The threat of such a national misfortune throws into even greater relief the virtues of the man Trollope so admires.

VI

The political theme in *The Duke's Children*, as in the other Palliser novels, is articulated by examples both positive and negative. The positive example here is Palliser himself. But the other side is no less in evidence.

Tregear, when elected to Parliament, writes to Lady Mabel that he has "achieved that which all commoners in England think to be the greatest honour within their reach" (II, 155). Trollope may still think so too, but if so it is with less heat than ever before; Tregear's assertion is argued only perfunctorily in this last chronicle. Tregear himself is certainly no ideal politician; and the novelist shows us in particularly uncomplimentary terms how it is that this "greatest honour" may be achieved and what one may reasonably expect to find in the House of Commons after achieving it.

There are two elections in *The Duke's Children*, and they follow the usual patterns. Silverbridge gets himself returned by the family borough of Silverbridge, the electors of which are happy enough to demonstrate their fealty to the Pallisers. Since it is clear that they will elect whoever the Duke sends them — "the first and only strong feeling in the borough was the one of duty" — the contest is never in doubt. Silverbridge casually goes down to his borough "a few days before the election to make himself known," having been "told that his presence in the borough would be taken as a compliment" (I, 126–7). He speaks vaguely to some of the electors, mumbling that "order and all that sort of thing should be maintained" (I, 136). The electors care nothing for his opinions — they simply want to hear "the tone of his voice and to see his manner." These being considered satisfactory, there is "nothing else to be done ... the next day he returned to town with the understanding that on the day appointed ... he should come back again to be elected" (I, 137). The day comes, and he is elected. Such is the Silverbridge election, the story of which comprises a brief but unsubtle commentary on pocket-borough loyalties and the ease with which some few fortunate candidates may be elected.

The other election is at Polpenno, which sends Tregear to Parliament. Here there is a vague resonance of Beverley and more of the usual trappings of Trollope's fictional elections. Tregear's father says flatly at the outset that whoever spends the most money will win the seat; and since Tregear's Liberal opponent, Mr Carbottle, is a rich man, it is generally assumed in the borough that he will be elected. The Carbottle forces arrange to pay ten shillings a head for every vote; they are found out, however, by the town's Conservative tailor (himself paid £25 for the work by the Tories, the money "smuggled in among the bills for printing") and Carbottle's intended bribery is prevented. This infuriates the Liberal electors: "As Mr. Carbottle had been brought down to Polpenno on purpose that he might spend money, — as he had nothing but his money to recommend him, and as he had not spent it, — the true and independent electors of the borough did not see their way to vote for him" (II, 152). The other ingredient of Tregear's success is the supportive "eloquence" of Silverbridge, who campaigns with him in the borough. Silverbridge's eloquence may be judged from the following speech on Tregear's behalf:

> 'My friend Frank Tregear ... is a very good fellow, and I hope you'll elect him ... I have known Frank Tregear ever so long, and I don't think you could find a better member of Parliament anywhere ... I am sure you feel that he ought to be member for Polpenno ... I think you'll return Frank Tregear. I was at school with him; — and I tell you, that you can't find a better fellow anywhere than Frank Tregear.'
>
> (II, 146—7)

This is generally considered "the speech of the evening." Tregear and Silverbridge appeal to the ladies, and the men are incensed by the Liberal candidate's failure to pay up. So Tregear is elected.

One might assume that, though canvassing is apparently a lightweight affair, the House of Commons is a different matter. The House, however, provides a further disappointment. The boredom is terrible. One receives "general respect" only when he has demonstrated his capacity "to sit on a bench for six consecutive hours without appearing to go to sleep" (I, 278). Parliament seen through Silverbridge's eyes — not always unfocused — is tedious and inane. The wrong men talk forever, and in such a way as to make it appear that "the welfare of the nation depended chiefly upon sugar" or some other triviality. Everyone has an axe to grind, and grinds it inexorably. When Lady Beeswax expresses to Silverbridge the hope that he will distinguish himself in Parliament during the current session, his reply is indicative: "I don't mean to go near the place."

In fact Silverbridge's truancy is seen as a result not only of boredom but also of disgust at what is going on there, and here Trollope's continuing portrait of the House of Commons — assessed intelligently even by the lackadaisical Silverbridge – is given a final brush-stroke. In the world of the later Palliser novels most people are crooked, and a man who keeps his mouth open for long is likely to have his teeth stolen (I, 351 – the same image used in *Ralph the Heir* to describe what happens to Underwood and Moggs at Percycross). The House of Commons is a case in point. Lord Nidderdale, fairly perspicacious, says that "the most unpopular man in the House may make himself liked by owning freely that he has done something that he ought to be ashamed of . . . The fact is if you 'own up' in a genial sort of way the House will forgive anything . . . The House puts up with anything now . . . there's no earnestness about anything" (I, 338–40, *passim.*).

That the House of Commons is seen in its worst light in *The Duke's Children* is due in part to the fact that, until the very end of the novel, when Monk becomes Prime Minister, the Conservatives are in power – and they are once again a despicable lot. They have come and gone from power several times in the course of the Palliser novels – remaining in throughout much of *Phineas Redux*, as we may recall. Daubeny was certainly a bad man; he had, however, a style, a flair, and a fair degree of courage. The leading Tories here have no virtues at all. In this last of the political novels Trollope is least able to hide his contempt for political processes.

The House of Commons of *The Duke's Children* is the House of Sir Timothy Beeswax, the Tory majority leader. The Prime Minister is now Lord Drummond, who sits in the upper House. Though Daubeny in the *Phineas* novels is clearly Disraeli, there is also an uncanny resemblance between the Beeswax-Drummond leadership and that of Disraeli and Derby in the fifties. Disraeli succeeded Bentinck as Tory leader in the Commons in 1849. From this time and well on into the fifties, Disraeli, though considered untrustworthy by many, was felt by the Conservative members to be indispensable to their cause. At the time he was, Blake has written, "the only figure on his side capable of putting up the oratorical display essential for a parliamentary leader"; and yet he was also "highly unpopular . . . with a large section of the party. His position always depended on the indispensability of his talents. It owed little to personal affection." The Tories continued to distrust him for years while depending on him to fight their battles in the Commons – feeling, as Derby wrote to Malmesbury on one occasion, that "they could not do without him even if there were anyone ready and able to take his place."[22] Usually Disraeli and Derby managed to seem to act together even when their differences were prodigious – which was often. Derby, as we know, was a very private man and no energetic partisan; Disraeli was often at him to be more aggressive. The Tories of *The Duke's Children* find it "irksome to recognize Sir Timothy as a master"; though there is "no other man among them to whom the lead could be conveniently transferred," they are "uncomfortable, – and perhaps a little ashamed" of Sir Timothy, who they feel is "hardly all that the country required as leader of the county

party" (I, 203). This is an accurate distillation of the uneasiness of
Disraeli's party with its leader early in his career – the voluble leader of
the protectionist county party, Disraeli was considered by many too
flamboyant, too clever, vaguely immoral, vaguely Jewish (Mr Thorne in
Barchester Towers, published in 1857 when Disraeli was still Tory leader
in the Commons, thinks the current leader, never named, untrustworthy,
not quite right to lead "the county party"). Lord Drummond, though
generally respected, is aloof and listless – which again describes Derby as
Prime Minister. Drummond and Sir Timothy act together in public – there
being, however, little love lost between them in fact. The resemblances are
suggestive.

Sir Timothy Beeswax is Daubeny-Disraeli stripped bare, the camouflage
tossed aside. As Trollope gave himself (in *Ralph the Heir* and *Phineas
Redux*) two shots at the hated Sir Henry Edwards, so now, writing at the
height of Disraeli's power and fame, he gives himself a second shot at this
man too. His portrait of Beeswax is too scathing, too indignant, to be that
of a purely imaginary politician.

> He had no idea as to the necessity or non-necessity of any measure
> whatever in reference to the well-being of the country. It may, indeed,
> be said that all such ideas were to him absurd, and the fact that they
> should be held by his friends an inconvenience ... To him Parliament
> was a debating place, by having a majority in which, and by no other
> means, he, – or another, – might become the great man of the day.
> And this use of Parliament ... had been for so many years present to
> his mind, that there seemed to be nothing absurd in an institution
> supported for such a purpose. Parliament was a club so eligible in its
> nature that all Englishmen wished to belong to it ... He who could be
> the chief of the strongest party, and who therefore ... should have the
> power of making dukes, and bestowing garters and appointing bishops
> ... of snubbing all before him ... would have gained an Elysium ...
> not to be found [elsewhere] ... I do not think that he ever cared much
> for legislation. Parliamentary management was his forte. (I, 198–9)

The totally political being is defined here once again as one who seeks
political place for personal gratification, possessing neither ideas nor
principles. Palliser fell from power in *The Prime Minister* precisely because
he was no good at the kind of "management" so enjoyed by Sir Timothy.
Indeed, Trollope tells us that Sir Timothy had studied carefully the
examples of such men who, once in power, became so obsessed with duty
as to ignore their friends – men who did not "bend,"and so at last, "in
some great solitude, though closely surrounded by those whose love
[they] had neglected to acquire," broke their hearts (I, 199). The contrast
between Beeswax and Palliser is explicitly drawn. Sir Timothy has learned
the lesson well and will not make such mistakes as the Duke made in the
purity of his intentions. Fulfilling the cynical definition of political

ambition offered in *The Prime Minister* by Lady Glencora, Beeswax is interested in power primarily as a social lever — as a means of rewarding his "set" and punishing his enemies. In such a context political power is little more than ego-massage.

Like Daubeny-Disraeli, Sir Timothy is interested only in "a majority" — that is, in acquiring and retaining political power. Seeing that "patriotism, judgment, industry, and eloquence" are useless without a popular following, he "smiles and learns the necessary wiles" to be loved (I, 199). He helps his friends and attacks his enemies. And if an enemy becomes too strong? We know what must be done. To a dangerous adversary Sir Timothy will always "open his bosom. He will tempt into his camp with an offer of high command any foe that may be worth his purchase" (I, 200). This can also be dangerous; Trollope comments here once again on the unenduring nature of political alliances. Nevertheless, Sir Timothy's chief stratagem is to offer hope to those who are out that they may be allowed to come in, and to assure those who are already in that they must always be in — unless he should go from among them.

But the heart of Trollope's attack occurs in his account of Sir Timothy's "parliamentary doctrines," his theory of how to remain in.

> The Statesman who falls is he who does much, and thus injures many. The Statesman who stands the longest is he who does nothing and injures no one. He soon knew that the work which he had taken in hand required all the art of a great conjuror. He must be possessed of tricks so marvellous that not even they who sat nearest to him might know how they were performed.
>
> For the executive or legislative business of the country he cared little. The one should be left in the hands of men who liked work; — of the other there should be little, or, if possible, none . . . Of patriotism he did not know the meaning . . . But he invented a pseudo-patriotic conjuring philosophy which no one understood but which many admired . . . He could only be . . . the cleverest by saying and doing that which no one else could understand. If he could become master of some great hocus-pocus system . . . then would they who followed him believe in him more firmly. (I, 200—1)

"Conjuring," Trollope concludes here, "when not known to be conjuring, is very effective" (I, 202), and conjuring is Sir Timothy's game, as it was Daubeny's. The highest political art, then — or at least the one most likely to maintain an office-holder in office — is the art of the magician: to do nothing while seeming to do much (the same lesson was preached to George Vavasor back in *Can You Forgive Her?*). For this a command of "tricks," a "hocus-pocus system," is required — not patriotism, not hard work, not intellect, not honesty. Sir Timothy's great weapon, there-fore — as it was Daubeny's in *Phineas Redux* — is "a pseudo-patriotic conjuring philosophy which no one understood." Clearly we are again in the presence of Disraeli — or at least of Trollope's image of him (at Beverley, remember, the novelist accused Disraeli of using "conjuring tricks" and "hocus pocus" to achieve his ends). Though he cares and knows nothing about government, because "he had worked harder in a special direction than others around him" Sir Timothy has become the party leader: "He had shown himself to be ready at all hours to fight the battle of the party he had joined. And no man knew so well . . . how to elevate a simple legislative attempt into a good faction fight. He had so mastered his tricks of conjuring that no one could get to the bottom of them" (I, 202). There was nothing dearer to the heart of Disraeli, as we know, than "a good faction fight" which could be induced out of some ordinary "legislative attempt" — especially when he opposed a majority.

Sir Timothy Beeswax, in a sense Daubeny writ large, is Trollope's final and most devastating metaphor for the totally partisan animal — and the final degradation of the House of Commons. No man more unlike the Duke of Omnium could be imagined. Sir Timothy's talents are precisely those which Palliser lacks — those talents so conducive to successful parliamentary management. Perhaps nowhere in the Palliser novels is the lesson as clearly drawn: to succeed in politics, one must be without principle; he who succeeds as a moral being usually will not succeed as a politician. To succeed is to fool all of the people all of the time; to do less is to fail. Of course this principle depends for its effectiveness upon a constituency of fools. The hierarchy of fools in the political universe is seen by Trollope as being, in a sense, socially vertical. At the bottom, most easily fooled of all, are the voters; next — sharper than the voters but less acute than the party leaders — are those who run for office but do not lead, the middle class of the party; and at the top reign the party leaders, those whose power is based on their ability to keep fooling the party's middle. When they can no longer do so they are replaced by new leaders, who rise to power on the strength, presumably, of new and different obfuscations, and who in turn stay in as long as they are not found out.

There is a great deal more about Sir Timothy Beeswax, most of it of the same tenor. Trollope is particularly detailed about his oratorical style:

when there was nothing to be said [Sir Timothy] was possessed of . . . plenty of words. And he was gifted with that peculiar power which enables a man to have the last word in every encounter. . . . You shall meet two men of whom you shall know the one to be endowed with the brilliancy of true genius, and the other to be possessed of but moderate parts, and shall find the former never able to hold his own against the latter. In a debate, the man of moderate parts will seem to be greater than the man of genius. But this skill of tongue, this glibness of speech is hardly an affair of intellect at all. It is, — as is style to the writer, — not the wares which he has to take to market, but the vehicle in which they may be carried. (I, 243–4)

The first part of this passage repeats an old theme — quality will usually be beaten by mediocrity, which is less scrupulous. Just as the dishonest man will always get the better of the honest man when they compete for the same job — as in the parable of *The Eustace Diamonds* — so will cunning get the better of intellect in Parliament. Trollope hates verbal dissembling; in the last sentence quoted above he relates it to his own craft. What counts is substance, not clothing; the vehicle is unimportant. This may also be taken as a defense of "plain" writing, an action Trollope often felt called upon to fight. It is no accident that the lies Mrs Stantiloup tells about Dr Wortle's school are euphemistically — but also ironically, even angrily — referred to by Trollope as "figures of speech" (*Dr. Wortle's School*, p. 128). Sir Timothy's style is as baroque as Palliser's is plain; the former is most useful in politics, the latter in life. And the conscientious novelist will also do his teaching with as much clarity, as little of the rhetorical flourish, as possible. Trollope's distaste for figurative language, a departure from literal truth, can be seen in virtually every paragraph he wrote — and, in the political novels, from Palliser's theory of plain language in *Can You Forgive Her?* to the utter corruption of language by Sir Timothy Beeswax in *The Duke's Children*.

This, however, is not all there is to Sir Timothy; the novelist proceeds with the account of his parliamentary virtues:

> to parliamentary strategy he had devoted all his faculties. No one knew so well . . . how to make . . . [things] troublesome to his opponents . . . He knew how to blind the eyes of members to the truth . . . And this to him was Government! It was to these purposes that he conceived that a great Statesman should devote himself! Parliamentary management! That, in his mind, was . . . the one act essential for Government.
>
> In all this he was very great . . . [He] was never stronger than when he simulated anger. His mock indignation was perhaps his most powerful weapon. (I, 244–5)

His only interest is in strategy; his words, spoken for the gallery, are never sincere. That angry words must be spoken by "irate gentlemen," and that such words mean nothing either to the speaker of them or to his audience, is a lesson familiar to the reader of the Palliser novels. And Sir Timothy's facility for making things "troublesome to his opponents" may remind us again of Disraeli.

Even Sir Timothy's tenure, however, must come to an end. He is not immortal, and he falls. His political demise results from his crumbling alliance with Lord Drummond, a phenomenon described by Trollope as a falling-out among thieves.

> Lord Drummond . . . and Sir Timothy had, during a considerable part of the last session, and through the whole vacation, so belarded each

other with praise in all their public expressions that it was quite
manifest that they had quarrelled. When any body of statesmen make
public asseverations ... that there is no discord among them, not a
dissentient voice on any subject, people are apt to suppose that they
cannot hang together much longer ... Never had there been such
concord as of late, – and men, clubs, and newspapers now protested
that as a natural consequence there would soon be a break-up.

(II, 288–9)

Here is still another Trollopian commentary on the mendaciousness of
political rhetoric. As when Brock praised Finespun in *Can You Forgive
Her?*, one can only believe the opposite of what is said. Sir Timothy in this
crisis thinks that there might be a golden opportunity to grab the
Premiership for himself if he can find an excuse to resign as leader, thus
forcing the resignation of the ministry. But to achieve this goal he must
first achieve new heights of conjuring – he must make it appear that the
dissolution is not so much his fault as that of his Cabinet colleagues. Sir
Timothy, Trollope reminds us, has tremendous advantages with which to
compete: he is adept at partisan manipulation, thick-skinned, insincere,
and totally unprincipled: "Great gifts of eloquence are hardly wanted, or a
deep-seated patriotism which is capable of strong indignation. A party has
to be managed. ... The subordinate task of legislation and of executive
government may well fall into the hands of less astute practitioners. It was
admitted on both sides that there was no man like Sir Timothy for
managing the House or coercing a party" (II, 290; again we are confronted
with Trollope's image of Disraeli). The legislative and executive burdens of
government are seen here as both less onerous and less important than
partisan management – seen, that is, by the most shameless, and yet also
one of the most successful, political hacks in Trollope's rogue's gallery of
politicians. It is significant that such a man – all surface, no depth –
should be able so easily to "manage" his colleagues and the House itself.
One despises the wolf – and yet the sheep are hardly preferable. What
kind of congress is this in which a Sir Timothy Beeswax can reign
supreme?

It is in the hocus-pocus department, however, that Sir Timothy fails, in
"the art to underlie and protect the art; – the art that can hide the art"
(II, 340) that he is finally found wanting. His tricks ultimately are
perceived; and though tricks by such a man are expected and even
admired, he must not be detected in the actual process of tricking – just as
a successful actor should not seem to be acting. Sir Timothy finally
exposes himself. Trollope compares him to Dickens's professor of deport-
ment, the old fraud Turveydrop. "You could see a little of the paint," says
the novelist, "you could hear the crumple of the starch and the padding."
Sir Timothy now fails "to carry his buckram without showing it";
Trollope adds bitterly: "after all it may be a question whether a man be

open to reproach for not doing that well which the greatest among us . . .
would not do at all" (II, 340). A Walpole or a Pitt would have had higher
concerns; great men achieve personal dignity without effort.

> It is good to be beautiful, but it should come of God and not of the
> hairdresser. And personal dignity is a great possession; but a man should
> struggle for it no more than he would for beauty . . . A real Caesar is
> not to be found every day. . . . Of course it is all paint, – but how
> would the poor girl look before the gaslights if there were no paint?
> The House of Commons likes a little deportment on occasions. (II, 341)

Again the Commons is likened to a dramatic production which must
observe certain forms while the curtain is up. The audience does not mind
the "paint" so long as it is not seen to be paint – so long as surfaces
remain convincing.

Keeping in mind the striking distinction made here between God and
the hairdresser, let us review once again that important passage in the
Autobiography in which Trollope speaks of Disraeli's novels as having, all
of them, "the same flavour of paint and unreality":

> the glory has ever been the glory of pasteboard, and the wealth has
> been a wealth of tinsel. The wit has been the wit of hairdressers, and
> the enterprise has been the enterprise of mountebanks. An audacious
> conjurer has generally been his hero. . . . Through it all there is a feeling
> of stage properties, a smell of hair-oil, an aspect of buhl, a remembrance
> of tailors, and that pricking of the conscience which must be the
> general accompaniment of paste diamonds.

Sir Timothy, if not actually Disraeli, is at least an ironic version of a
Disraeli novel-hero, like Daubeny in *Phineas Redux* – sham from top to
bottom, a product (like Disraeli himself as perceived by Trollope) of
hairdressers' paint and ointment, adept and at home in the theater
(Disraeli was a famous dandy in his early years, and well into his seventies
used to "make up" for public appearances). The antithesis of God in the
Palliser novels is a conjuring Tory hairdresser. Beeswax and Daubeny may
be seen as a composite picture of a single man – the man who, from 1874
until 1880, was Prime Minister of England.

As is so often the case in Trollope's political world, the ministerial
shake-up which takes place in *The Duke's Children* is brought on by a
trivial issue made controversial only by private political motives. As Brock
dismissed Finespun from his Cabinet over a disagreement about French
wine tariffs, Sir Timothy now feels called upon to resign from Lord
Drummond's ministry due to a disagreement with his Cabinet colleagues
over brewers' licences. The issues are as trivial as the men themselves. Sir
Timothy manages to take with him out of the government the current

Chancellor of the Exchequer, and Drummond is forced to resign. Sir Timothy temporarily achieves his goal of seeming not to be the cause of the break-up which in fact he has occasioned: he "had been at pains to ascertain on what matters connected with the Revenue ... Lord Drummond's closest advisors ... had opinions ... strong enough not to be abandoned; and having discovered that, he also discovered arguments on which to found an exactly contrary opinion" (II, 364). Sir Timothy, however, is never sent for. In the aftermath of the government's resignation his scheming is perceived, and the next ministry is a Liberal one headed by Monk. Nevertheless, in the political world of these novels such men as Sir Timothy Beeswax have it in their power to make governments succeed and fail. That a man may be a "beast" does not disqualify him from political leadership if he be more unscrupulous, cunning, and dishonest than his colleagues. The beastliness here is again on the Tory side. When Silverbridge tells his father that, despite Sir Timothy and his cohorts, there ought in his opinion to be Conservatives as well as Liberals in the world, Palliser pointedly replies that "every carriage should have a drag to its wheels, but ... an ambitious soul would choose to be the coachman rather than the drag" (II, 154).

And again the cynical commentary on politics is articulated in part through games metaphors. "It does not often happen that an English statesman can go in and make a great score off his own bat. But not the less is he bound to play the game and go to the wicket when he finds that his time has come," says the Duke of St Bungay to the Duke of Omnium (I, 207; the analogy to cricket is particularly striking given Palmerston's frequent delight in describing brushes with political opponents in which he emerged victorious as "capital strokes ... off my own bat"[23]). There are also references to chess — "Those on the opposite side of the House could find themselves checkmated by his astuteness ... when with all their pieces on the board, there should be none which they could move" (I, 245), muses Sir Timothy during a strategy session with himself — and to the old badger-baiting business: the "Ministers had gone through their course of baiting with that equanimity and air of superiority which always belongs to a well-trained occupant of the Treasury bench" (I, 242); and again: "By-the-bye, Isabel, you must come down some day and hear Sir Timothy badgered" (II, 324), says Silverbridge to his fiancée. But the most persistent political game-metaphor in *The Duke's Children* is that of racing. Trollope uses Silverbridge's addiction to the sport as an occasion for making a series of comical puns connecting politics and the turf. Silverbridge's prize race-horse is named Prime Minister (in honor of his father!), and in the novel's early chapters there is much concern about the state of his readiness for the upcoming Derby.

'Well, Silverbridge, how's the Prime Minister?'
'How is he, Tifto?' asked the noble partner.

'I don't think there's a man in England just at present enjoying a very much better state of health.'

'Safe to run?' asked Dolly.

'Safe to run! Why shouldn't he be safe to run?'

'I mean sure to start.'

'I think we mean to start him, don't we, Silverbridge?' asked the Major. (I, 63)

Silverbridge's other horse is called Coalition — "which failed, as coalitions always do" (I, 158). Prime Minister, deliberately lamed by Tifto, also fails, but not before some pointed repartée takes place linking the Derby and imminent parliamentary elections. The following conversation between Silverbridge and Lady Mabel occurs just before Silverbridge stands for Parliament, and also just before the Derby (the two events, significantly, are scheduled to occur almost simultaneously).

'They say that the elections will be over before the Derby.'

'And which do you care for the most?'

'I should like to pull off the Derby, I own.'

'From what papa says, I should think the other event is the more probable.'

'Doesn't the Earl stand to win on Prime Minister?'

'I never know anything about his betting . . . I do so hope you'll get the seat, — and win the Derby.' (I, 93–4)

Trollope links politics and racing in two other places in the novel. When politicians combine in a party "to do much," he says, ironically echoing Sir Timothy's theory of parliamentary management, there will always be disagreements among them; when they "combine to do nothing," disagreement is less likely. "Thirty men can sit still, each as like the other as peas. But put your thirty men up to run a race, and they will soon assume different forms" (I, 197). Perhaps more to the point, Silverbridge ruminates sadly on his racing misfortunes after losing heavily on the Derby.

His father had spoken in very strong language against racing, — saying that those who went were either fools or rascals. He was sure that this was exaggerated. Half the House of Lords and two-thirds of the House of Commons were to be seen at the Derby; but no doubt there were many rascals and fools, and he could not associate with the legislators without finding himself among the fools and rascals. (I, 178)

That he cannot "associate with legislators without finding himself among the fools and rascals" is a proposition to which *The Duke's Children* addresses itself. Whether or not the Duke has "exaggerated" the case the reader of the Palliser novels may decide for himself.

10 Palliser Agonistes: A Backward Glance

But Pope, like many ironists, loves the folly he mocks.

> Reuben A. Brower

And like Pope . . . he belittles in order to magnify and magnifies to belittle.

> A. O. J. Cockshut

"No one is so critical as a lover," says Cockshut in his summary discussion of Trollope's political novels,[1] and this aptly characterizes the duality of their treatment of political themes. One satirizes to cure; loving the folly he mocks — or at the very least fascinated by it — Trollope shows how deeply he cares, how he reveres even as he slashes.

Is it still possible to think that "Trollope never took his politics . . . seriously," or that he "has no philosophy about public life, no ideas," as one critic says; or that politics "did not influence him at all," as another proclaims?[2] That Trollope's political creed would not admit of the triumph of virtue does not also mean that he was shallow or unreflective on political subjects; but it does mean that he was less likely than modern liberals — being less progressive — to view such subjects with optimism. Like most men of essentially conservative temperament, he was less prone — at least throughout his last twenty years, when the political novels were written — to see the doughnut than to see the hole. He loves the doughnut, even while he sees it being eaten away; yet as he describes what he sees we are more likely to feel loss than gain. This may be matter for disagreement, even for argument; but it is no excuse for misreading.

Perhaps we are ready now to answer the "honesty" question posed by Alaric Tudor's debate with himself in *The Three Clerks*. Alaric wondered, remember, whether most men really were honest or whether they in fact just *seemed* to be, cultivating the *impression* of honesty. "There are two kinds of honesty, I take it," says Charley Tudor, the Trollope-figure of that novel: "that which the world sees, and that which it does not see" (p. 313). Whether the two can be made one is a question to which the Palliser novels address themselves. Is it possible to succeed in politics without compromising one's integrity? Can one please others and still retain one's soul? Trollope's answer is that the preservation of moral integrity in such circumstances is both possible and impossible – possible for the exceptional man, impossible for the ordinary man. Thus it is important that exceptional men should interest themselves in political questions.

Let us recall for a moment two of Trollope's most memorable protagonists. Palliser and Melmotte represent among other things the two kinds of honesty – genuine honesty, honesty which remains itself in private when unobserved; and sham honesty, "honesty . . . which is at the disposal of those who are dishonest" (*Phineas Redux*, II, 409), honesty of which great play is made in public but which in fact does not exist at all.

The Way We Live Now contains an election of some interest. With the single exception of Polpenno in *The Duke's Children*, the election at Westminster in *The Way We Live Now* is the last in Trollope's fiction to be described in any detail[3] – making it also the last to be described outside of the Palliser novels. It is particularly appropriate that this penultimate political exercise is located by Trollope not only in the metropolis instead of in the counties – heretofore always the case – but more specifically in the borough of Westminster. For here we are finally brought onto the front porch of Parliament – the very seat of government. Small constituencies and old backwaters give way in this novel to the heart of darkness itself. In a sense this is the climax of a long process of evaluation by Trollope, who in *The Way We Live Now* takes his satire to the source of infection. Here, as in *The Eustace Diamonds* but more unequivocally, politics is seen as one product of the general evils of the age – tied more closely than ever before to social and financial corruption. And in the picture of the Westminster electors voting by ballot for the first time, Trollope – who as a candidate opposed the ballot, remember – suggests that the new method is no more rational or efficient than its predecessors. Indeed, the election story reiterates Trollope's belief that the path to the glories of parliamentary representation lies through the darkest regions of corruption and misunderstanding – the regions, that is, of the British voter.

Trollope says he wrote *The Way We Live Now* to combat "the commercial profligacy of the age."

> There seems to be reason for fearing that men and women will be taught to feel that dishonesty, if it can become splendid, will cease to be abominable. If dishonesty can live in a gorgeous palace with pictures on all its walls, and gems in all its cupboards, with marble and ivory in all its corners, and can give Apician dinners, and get into Parliament, and deal in millions, then dishonesty is not disgraceful.
>
> (*Autobiography*, p. 304)

Melmotte's public "honesty," made for the world to see, is in fact hollow to the core. His standards of conduct become those of almost everyone else in the novel – in all the professions, in all walks of life. Everything, even literature, is turned by Melmottian values into commodities of exchange; the economic savagery of this world makes a man's worth depend exclusively upon how much money he has. *The Way We Live Now* shows the most heartless aspects of Social Darwinism, pushed to their most corrupt extreme, destroying the moral fibre of England. Lady Carbury advocates a moral theory which is itself a savage caricature of Social Darwinism:

> 'You have to destroy a thousand living creatures every time you drink a glass of water, but you do not think of that when you are athirst. You cannot send a ship to sea without endangering lives. You do send ships to sea though men perish yearly. You tell me this man [Melmotte] may perhaps ruin hundreds, but then again he may create a new world in which millions will be rich and happy.' (II, 279)

"It is not of swindlers and liars that we need to live in fear, but of the fact that swindling and lying are gradually becoming not abhorrent to our minds," Trollope said in *The New Zealander*. Lady Carbury is a fulfilment of his prophecy. "The business of this world is now business"; humanity has gone upon the gold standard. A case in point is Melmotte's celebrated party for the Chinese Emperor, an episode which shows business methods permeating social life as the party tickets rise and fall in value like shares.[4]

Seizing upon what he saw as the collapsing moral standards of the time, Trollope portrays the "patterns of profligacy" emerging in the new gilded age. In doing so he anticipated the breakdown of political and business ethics which was to follow. In 1913 Escott could still call Melmotte "a grotesque and nauseating monstrosity";[5] nowadays, unfortunately, Melmotte seems less grotesque than frighteningly real. Indeed, he uses methods which, shocking as they might have appeared a century ago, would seem moderate enough now if discussed around a board. Today the book which infuriated the Victorians is considered a masterpiece.

It is significant that Melmotte runs as a Conservative; *The Way We Live Now* contains attacks both on the Tory hierarchy which puts him up and the constituency which elects him. Melmotte's committee consists of peers, bankers, and publicans — "with all that absence of class prejudice for which the party has become famous since the ballot was introduced," snarls the novelist (I, 326—7). Trollope's account of the voters' feelings is one of the book's most crucial passages:

> It was supposed that the working classes were in favour of [Melmotte], partly from their love of a man who spends a great deal of money, partly from the belief that he was being ill-used — partly, no doubt, from the occult sympathy which is felt for crime, when the crime committed is injurious to the upper classes. Masses of men will almost feel that a certain amount of injustice ought to be inflicted on their

betters, so as to make things even, and will persuade themselves that a criminal should be declared to be innocent, because the crime committed has had a tendency to oppress the rich and pull down the mighty from their seats. (II, 128)

We know about Trollope's idea that the voters are as bad as the candidates, or worse. Here we see them actually admiring a criminal, with whom they feel a spiritual identity. Their own stock of imagination is so thin that Melmotte's audacity is able to seduce them. George Vavasor, an earlier Tory criminal, ultimately fared badly with the voters, but Melmotte is triumphant. His success represents one of Trollope's most telling commentaries upon the system, and specifically upon the ways in which candidates are chosen. And he makes it plain here that the voters are accessories in the crime of Melmotte's election to Parliament. For Trollope, the voters are not only potentially dangerous manipulators in a democratic system but also actively corrupt agents in an undemocratic system — indeed, they are "far more wicked than the candidates"; thus "only the glory of the goal [itself makes] the contestants' struggle worth while."[6]

It is "the glory of the goal," not the good things that grabbing off the goal may bring, which motivates Palliser. There is not much more to say about him. But it may be appropriate to conclude with a final glance at the man who inspired Trollope to write his novels of Parliament.

In *North America* the novelist pauses briefly in his account of a visit to Mount Vernon to eulogize that "great and good man," George Washington. A man "whose patriotism was . . . an honest feeling, untinged by any personal ambition of a selfish nature," Trollope says admiringly, Washington "did not mar [his] success by arrogance, or destroy the brightness of his own name by personal aggrandisement."[7] To serve one's country unselfishly is a constant ideal; prevented from doing so himself, the novelist sublimated his passion in the person of his favorite fictional creation.

There can be no doubt that Palliser *is* Trollope's favorite character. "Taking him altogether, I think that Plantagenet Palliser stands more firmly on the ground than any other personage I have created," Trollope says in the *Autobiography* (p. 159): "I love the man." And he adds later — studiously ignoring such public favorites as Mrs Proudie, Mark and Lucy Robarts, Lady Mason, John Eames and Lily Dale, and Lizzie Eustace — that any "permanence of success" he may happen to achieve as a novelist "will probably rest on the character of Plantagenet Palliser, Lady Glencora, and the Rev. Mr. Crawley" (p. 310). It is significant that two of Trollope's three selections come from the Palliser series, which except for *Can You Forgive Her?* and *The Eustace Diamonds* was not popular during the novelist's lifetime, as we know. Of the three, Palliser is put first. Epitomizing Trollope's political and social ideal, and endowed with the vividness which only a novelist's love can give to a character in fiction, Palliser — one critic's verdict — is "as highly individuated as any character in nineteenth-century fiction." Indeed, this is so despite the fact that Trollope, as Booth observed, saw "that political characters must be colorless because they are so often called upon to submerge their identity in group action."[8] Trollope says in the *Autobiography* that a statesman must frequently "set aside his own idiosyncrasy" to work with others with whom he has nothing in common if "in no other way can [he] serve [his] country or [his] own ambition" (a cardinal lesson of *The Duke's Children*). But men who are publicly useful face the danger of becoming, through much usage, like "stones of ... strong calibre ... worn down to the shape and smoothness of rounded pebbles." He envisioned as the hero of his political novels, Trollope discloses here, a different sort of man, both superior and inferior to his fellow men — a man "who could not become a pebble, having too strong an identity of his own." And he continues:

> To rid oneself of fine scruples — to fall into the traditions of a party — to feel the need of subservience, not only in acting but in thinking — to be able to be a bit, and at first only a very little bit, — these are the necessities of a growing statesman. The time may come, the glorious time when some great self-action shall be possible, as when Peel gave up the Corn Laws; but the rising man, as he puts on his harness, should not allow himself to dream of this. (pp. 308–9)

The rough and tumble of political life experienced at first hand had enabled Trollope to see, between the writing of *The Three Clerks* in 1858 and the *Autobiography* nearly twenty years later, that a man (such as Peel) may change his mind without personal disgrace, that in politics the unconventional action is always more heroic — because unusual — than any other kind. Note too how the acceptance of party "traditions" is equated here with the abandonment of "fine scruples." If one wishes to become "a good, round, smooth ... useful pebble," Trollope says, continuing the analogy, "he must harden his skin and swallow his scruples"; "scruples" and "usefulness" are mutually exclusive in politics. Yet there are men who will bravely make the political attempt even though they "cannot get their skins to be hard," and these men "after a little while generally fall out of the ranks." But the hero he conceived of — "of whom I had long thought" — was to be "one who did not fall out of the ranks, even though his skin would not become hard ... Such was the character I endeavoured to depict in describing the triumph, the troubles, and the failure of my Prime Minister. And I think that I have succeeded" (p. 309).

Palliser is the justification for and symbol of Trollope's social conservatism. A representative of the best traditions of the English aristocracy, "the very model of an English statesman" (*The Prime Minister*, I, 124), he personifies the novelist's faith in "the free patrician life of England," the stratification of society and the leadership of the aristocracy.[9] Trollope wrote the Palliser novels to express this faith. About the social class from which his hero is drawn, Trollope says in the *Autobiography* (p. 152): "if I have not made the strength and virtues predominant over the faults and vices, I have not painted the picture I intended."

Speare characterized Palliser as "slow, plodding, unimaginative ... peculiarly conscientious ... sly, fretful, a man of stiff reserve ... too cold for friendship, uncommunicative, sensitive to the point of morbidity" — and concluded that Trollope's hero was utterly unconvincing as a politician.[10] True or not, Palliser convinces as a man; and there can be little doubt what the man represents, what he means, in the series of novels to which his name has been given. Yes, he is fretful, reserved, and morbidly sensitive. Thus in his self-imposed isolation as Prime Minister, amidst the squads of political guests in his house, Palliser becomes fond of the company of an unpolitical old maid, takes her for walks and has dull conversations with her about mundane matters. Lady Rosina de Courcy "was natural and ... wanted nothing from him. When she talked about cork soles, she meant cork soles." Sir Orlando Drought always means something else, no matter what he says. Palliser's retreat from the horrors of intrigue is Trollope's condemnation of the political world. In this retreat there is both "triumph" and "failure," as the novelist says in the *Autobiography*. Even though Palliser may suffer political defeat at the hands of this world, the novelist's double vision perceives the man as remaining morally stronger than the system — never becoming a smooth and rounded pebble.

Notes

CHAPTER 1

1   See his notice of R. H. Hutton's *Studies in Parliament* in the *Fortnightly Review*, 4 (1 April 1866) and his letter to the *Examiner* (6 April 1950, written from Ireland) defending Russell's Irish policy. See also N. John Hall, "Trollope Reading Aloud: An Unpublished Record," *N&Q* (March 1975), 117–18. And – on the comment of the *Dublin Review* – see Chapter 4, n. 4.

2   "The People and Their Rulers," in *The New Zealander*, p. 13; and *St. Paul's Magazine*, 1 (October 1866), 4. Booth, pp. 75 and 240–1n, surmises that this is the argument of Trollope's lost lecture on "The Study of Politics," which the novelist reportedly gave at Leeds in 1864.

3   Briggs, pp. 93–4.

4   E.g., Speare, p. 217. See also Escott, p. 256.

5   *The New Zealander*, p. 107 (the essay on "The House of Commons").

6   See Booth, pp. 78 and 86–7; Amery's Introduction to the Oxford edition of *The Prime Minister*; Polhemus, p. 150; and Pollard, p. 24.

7   *The New Zealander*, pp. 120–1.

8   *North America*, p. 176; and Polhemus, p. 150.

9   *The New Zealander*, p. 108.

10   *The New Zealander*, pp. 108 and 121.

11   See Burn, p. 166.

12   Quoted by Cockshut, pp. 94–5. The two previous quotations are taken from the *Beverley Recorder*, 31 October 1868, and the *Hull & Eastern Counties Herald*, 3 November 1868. Full citation for Trollope's election address and his other political speeches at Beverley will be found in Chapter 5, accompanying notes and discussion.

13   See *Letters*, p. 206.

14   Burn, p. 168. The discussion just above in the text of Mrs Trollope's books is indebted in part to Donald Smalley's informative Introduction to his paperback edition of *Domestic Manners of the Americans* (New York, 1949; repr. 1960).

15   *The New Zealander*, pp. 135, 144–5, and 13.

16   *The New Zealander*, p. 18, and Speare, p. 216.

17   Undoubtedly some of his pleasant associations with the great Whig-Liberal families came from his going so frequently to Lady Stanley of Alderley's political salon. The Stanleys – like the fictional Standishes, FitzHowards, Mildmays, etc. – were related to all the great Liberal families of the day, and Trollope surely met there many of the family members (including the Russells). See the more detailed discussions of this in Chapters 4 and 8.

18   Donald Southgate, *The Passing of the Whigs, 1832–1886* (London, 1962), p. 77. On Trollope's reference in the passage from *Phineas Redux* quoted above in the text: Fox and Sheridan led the formation in 1794 – after George III's break-up of the supremacy of the old Whig Party – of what was called the New Whig Party, which after 1820 developed into the Liberal party.

19   *Thackeray*, p. 84.

20   See Briggs, pp. 91–100, *passim.*; my argument throughout this paragraph is indebted largely to his.

21   *The New Zealander*, pp. 167 and 169. The two passages just above in the text are quoted without attribution by Burn, pp. 170–1.

22   *North America*, p. 188.

23   *North America*, p. 55; and Daniel Becquemont, "Politics in Literature, 1874–1875: *The Way We Live Now* and *Beauchamp's Career,*" in *Politics in Literature in the Nineteenth Century*, ed. Janie Teissedon (Lille and Paris, 1974), p. 141.

24   *The New Zealander*, pp. 107 and 18. See *Australia and New Zealand*, I, 487, and *The Fixed Period*, II, 87 and 96.

25   *North America*, pp. 190 and 181–2; and pp. 140 and 52.

26   *North America*, pp. 39, 196, and 63–4.

27   On Tenant-Right, see Chapter 4, notes 33 and 34; and on the Church question, see the *Beverley Recorder* for 7 November 1868 and Chapter 7, n. 7.

28   *North America*, p. 211, and *passim.*

29   James, p. 131.

30   Pollard, p. 25.

CHAPTER 2

1   Speare, p. 185.

2   Trollope Papers, II, Folio 158.

3   Escott, p. 257.

4   The letter, part of the Robert H. Taylor Collection at Princeton, is dated 26 February 1881. It was kindly made available to me by N. John Hall, who is editing the novelist's complete letters.

5   Sadleir, p. 419.

CHAPTER 3

1   See the twenty-two-year-old James's review in the *Nation*, 1 (28 September 1865), 409–10: reprinted in *Notes and Reviews* (New York, 1921); unsigned notice, *Spectator*, 38 (2 September 1865), 978–9; and unsigned notice, *Saturday Review*, 20 (19 August 1865), 240–2. Other unsigned notices appeared in the *Athenaeum* (2 September 1865), 305–6; the *Westminster Review*, 75 (July 1865), 284; and *Month*, 3 (September 1865), 319–23. I should like to thank Leon Edel for helping to unearth James's review of *Can You Forgive Her?* – so far as I can tell unreprinted since 1921.

2   The figure given for the novel under "Total Sums Received" (*Autobiography*, pp. 312–13) is £3,525. The closest competitors are *Phineas Finn* (1867–9) and *He Knew He Was Right* (1868–9), £3,200 each. Trollope's popularity reached its height in the late sixties subsequent to the appearance of *The Last Chronicle of Barset* (1867), one of his greatest popular successes. In the early seventies, however, it was already on the wane.

3   See Booth, p. 237. *Barchester Towers* is far in the lead here; in distant second place with modern readers is *The Last Chronicle of Barset*.

4   Escott, p. 186; Sadleir devotes two pages of his book to *Can You Forgive Her?* – the quotation in the text, however, is taken from an Introduction by him to *Can You Forgive Her?* (London, 1938), I, x; Walpole, p. 100; the Stebbinses, p. 219; Curtis Brown, p. 75; and Marsh's Introduction to *Can You Forgive Her?* (London, 1950) I, xiv.

5   Booth devotes four pages to the novel. Cockshut mentions it four times but never discusses it in detail. Polhemus devotes nine pages to the love-interests but ignores the political content. Pope-Hennessy deals off-handedly with it for just three pages – despite its many possible biographical connections. Ruth apRoberts mentions the novel twice in passing. Skilton surveys contemporary critical reaction to the novel, and little else, in less than three pages. The recently published essays alluded to in the text are David S. Chamberlain, "Unity and Irony in Trollope's *Can You Forgive Her?*", *SEL*, 8 (Autumn 1968), 670–7; Juliet McMaster, " 'The Meaning of Words and the Nature of Things': Trollope's *Can You Forgive Her?*", *SEL*, 14 (Autumn 1974), 603–18; and George Levine, "Can You Forgive Him? Trollope's 'Can You Forgive Her?' and the Myth of Realism," *VS*, 18 (September 1974), 5–30.

6   These cases are persuasively argued by Norris D. Hoyt in " 'Can You Forgive Her?': A Commentary," *TT*, 2 (September 1947), 57–70, and at greater length in his unpublished Yale dissertation, *The Parliamentary Novels of Anthony Trollope* (1940). Snow, pp. 46–7, is the only recent critic to discuss in any detail the novel's connections with Sir Henry Taylor and *Philip van Artevelde*.

7   Hoyt, "Commentary," 64ff.

8   The quotation is taken from James, p. 131. James was free enough in acknowledging his debt to George Eliot (he published nine essays on her) and Hawthorne (a book in 1879), but his expressed distaste for Jane Austen's novels ("The Lesson of Balzac," 1905) and his apparent ambivalence toward Dickens are belied everywhere in his work.

9   See *The Portrait of A Lady*, ed. Leon Edel (Boston, 1963), Chapter 6, pp. 52–5, *passim*. Subsequent references in the text are to this (the Riverside) edition.

10   See "On the Higher Education of Women" (1868), reprinted in *Four Lectures* and quoted in the text below.

11   *North America*, p. 117.

12   See Trollope's "The Migration of A Library," *Pall Mall Gazette*, 17 (September 1880), 1079. I am grateful to Andrew Wright for calling this to my attention.

13   See J. A. Banks, "The Way They Lived Then: Anthony Trollope and the Seventies," *VS*, 12 (December 1968), 177–200, especially 194; and *Four Lectures*, p. 77.

14   *North America*, pp. 117 and 200; and *On the Subjection of Women* (London, 1869), p. 43.

15   See Speare, p. 207; and also McMaster (n. 5, above), 609.

16   Quoted by John Butt and Kathleen Tillotson in *Dickens at Work* (London, 1957), p. 96. The article appeared in *Household Words*, No. 85 (8 November 1851).

17   Chamberlain (n. 5, above), 672–3, especially n. 14. Snow, p. 96, says that Trollope "idolized" Jane Austen but offers no proof. Certainly there are many echoes of her in some of Trollope's novels – as, for example, in *Ralph the Heir* (noted in Chapter 5).

18   Levine (n. 5, above), 15; and Polhemus, p. 229.

19   My argument here is adapted from Booth's, p. 89, and from Bartrum's in "Lady Stanley," *passim*.

20   See, in connection with the argument in this paragraph, McMaster, 609; Booth, p. 84; Escott, p. 209; and Polhemus, p. 105.

21   *Middlemarch*, ed. Gordon S. Haight (Boston, 1956; the Riverside edition), pp. 610–13, *passim*.; and *The Mill on the Floss*, VI, iii.

22   See F. R. Leavis, *The Great Tradition* (London, 1948); Q. D. Leavis, "A Note on Literary Indebtedness: Dickens, George Eliot, Henry James," *Hudson Review*, 8 (1955); Oscar Cargill, " 'The Portrait of A Lady': A Critical Reappraisal," *Modern Fiction Studies*, 3 (1957); George Levine, "Isabel, Gwendolen, and Dorothea," *ELH*, 30 (1963); Cornelia Pulsifer Kelley, *The Early Development of Henry James* (Urbana, 1965); and John Halperin, *The Language of Meditation* (Devon, 1973). See also James's unsigned review of *Middlemarch* in *The Galaxy* (March 1873), widely reprinted.

23   See Sadleir, p. 368n; Snow, p. 184n; and Chamberlain, *passim*. It seems unclear exactly what George Eliot *did* say to Mrs Linton. Sadleir

quotes her as saying in effect that she could not have written *Middlemarch* had it not been for Trollope; while according to Snow she said she could not have planned the novel on such a scale if it hadn't been for Trollope. Neither Sadleir nor Snow makes any attempt to give proper attribution.

24 *The New Zealander*, p. 168.
25 Briggs, p. 108; and Sadleir, p. 398.
26 *Cicero*, I, 50.
27 *The New Zealander*, p. 18. The quotation just below in the text is taken from *North America*, p. 82.
28 See apRoberts, p. 169.
29 My argument in this paragraph is derived from Chamberlain's, 670–9.
30 See *North America*, p. 47; and Greville, entry for 17 May 1860.
31 *The New Zealander*, p. 117.
32 *The New Zealander*, p. 106.

CHAPTER 4

1 Polhemus, p. 149; Booth, p. 90; and Skilton, p. 25 — who reports, erroneously, that the novel was more popular with critics than readers. Smalley, who says that *Phineas Finn* was more popular with readers than critics, has it right (*Critical Heritage*, p. 307).
2 *Spectator*, 42 (20 March 1869), 356–7, and *Saturday Review*, 27 (27 March 1869), 431–2.
3 When *The Kellys and the O'Kellys*, like *The Macdermots of Ballycloran*, failed, Trollope was told by the publisher of *The Kellys*, Henry Coburn, to try something else. "Readers do not like novels on Irish subjects so well as others," Coburn wrote. And he added: "Thus you will perceive, it is impossible for me to give any encouragement for you to proceed in novel writing." The letter is dated 11 November 1848; it is among the Trollope Papers, I, Folio 10. Twelve years later Trollope had not forgotten the lesson. "Irish stories are not popular with the book-sellers," he says in the opening paragraph of *Castle Richmond*. But by 1860 he could afford to try again.
4 "Trollope's Irish Novels," *Dublin Review*, 65 (October 1869), 361–7. The article is in fact a longish survey of Trollope's early Irish novels, of which *Phineas Finn* is said to be one. There is no record of any review in the same pages of *Phineas Redux*, in which the Irish part of Phineas's life is (literally) killed off.
5 Booth, pp. 87–9, and Speare, p. 217. Booth goes on here to demonstrate that Lord Chiltern is George Vavasor all over again — he even has a scar on his face which becomes inflamed when he is angry; and he traces this gentleman-savage type back to the novelist George Alfred Lawrence, whose *Guy Livingstone* may well have been Trollope's literary

model. The novelists Ouida and Rhoda Broughton also learned from Lawrence's example, Booth argues.

6   See Snow, pp. 109 and 184n.

7   The letter is dated 31 March 1869 and was published by the *Daily Telegraph* on 1 April, p. 3. See *Letters*, p. 241. Booth, the editor, adds a note here directing the reader to Chapman, who refused to accept Trollope's assertion of innocence. The reference to Sadleir just below in the text is to p. 418.

8   See *Letters*, p. 355.

9   See Cockshut, pp. 241—9, especially 241 and 245—6; Curtis Brown, p. 84; Booth, p. 100; and Sadleir, p. 418.

10   The argument of this paragraph is derived largely from Snow, pp. 66 and 83; see also Booth, pp. 119—20, Escott. p. 298, and Bradford A. Booth, "Trollope and *Little Dorrit*," *NCF*, 2 (March 1948), 237—40.

11   They were made of black silk, according to Trollope. See *Phineas Finn*, I, 196—8, for a detailed description of "Turnbull."

12   Cockshut, pp. 244—5.

13   Trevelyan, p. 345. I am indebted here to Trevelyan's account (pp. 344—6) of the events leading up to the Second Reform Bill.

14   On one of the work sheets for *The Fixed Period*, Trollope wrote this note to himself: "What should be the weight of the gun?" Obviously he acquired some expert advice. See Trollope Papers, II, Folio 125. The quotation above in the text is taken from Pollard, p. 16.

15   I am indebted to the summary given by David Skilton in "*The Fixed Period*: Anthony Trollope's Novel of 1980," *Studies in the Literary Imagination*, 6, No. 2 (Fall 1973), 39—50.

16   The speech in question is reported by the *Beverley Recorder* for 14 November 1868. I should like to thank N. John Hall for transcribing Trollope's unpublished letter to Collins and passing it on to me.

17   Published anonymously in the *Quarterly Review* for April 1860 and quoted by Blake, p. 426. The passage quoted just below is taken from Blake, p. 355.

18   E.g., Blake, p. 502. The subsequent quotation from Briggs is taken from p. 90.

19   Kenney, 281—5, argues for this identification. Much of the foregoing summary of the Mildmay-Russell connection is derived from his essay.

20   Escott, Sadleir, Booth, and apRoberts all ascribe *Lord Palmerston* to the period 1866—7, but without attribution or proof of any sort. There is nothing in Trollope's business papers to suggest that he was working on *Lord Palmerston* in the sixties. There is, however, a memorandum in the novelist's hand (Papers, II, Folio 116) dated 24 August 1881 noting his agreement "to write a volume on Lord Palmerston — 200 pages — for £200 — for W. Isbister — to be delivered in March-1882." This evidence — and the fact that the memoir did not appear until 1882 — suggests that all of these critics are wrong. Booth, in fact, admitted in an article published

several years after his monograph that there is no evidence that Trollope wrote *Lord Palmerston* in the sixties; he has come to assume, he says here, that it was "written to order in 1881." Surely this is right. See Booth's "Author to Publisher: Trollope and Isbister," *PULC*, 24, No. 1 (Winter 1962), 58n.

21 These points are made by Frank E. Robbins, "Chronology and History in Trollope's Barset and Parliamentary Novels," *NCF*, 5 (March 1951), 310–12, and J. R. Dinwiddy, "Who's Who in Trollope's Political Novels," *NCF*, 22 (June 1967), 31–46. Palmerston, incidentally, is mentioned twice by name in *Phineas Finn* (I, 195–6).

22 R. W. Chapman, "Personal Names in Trollope's Political Novels," in *Essays mainly on the Nineteenth Century presented to Sir Humphrey Milford* (London, 1948), p. 75.

23 Sadleir, p. 418.

24 See Escott, p. 258, and Speare, p. 189. Burke's feelings on the matter are available, among other places, in Boswell's account of a meeting of "The Club" on 3 April 1778, as reported in his *Life of Johnson* (1791). See also John Wain, *Samuel Johnson* (London, 1974), p. 238; it is Wain's account that suggested to me the relevance of this aspect of Burke's thought. It should also be pointed out that Monck was the name of the governor-general of Canada with whom Trollope stayed during his visit there and was on excellent terms. The novelist's usual compositional habits suggest less that this Monck and the fictional politician are identical than that Trollope may have used the name of a person he esteemed for a character he esteemed.

25 My references here are to Escott, p. 259; Sadleir, p. 418; Pope-Hennessy, p. 280; and an unpublished essay — part of an in-progress Princeton dissertation — by Barry A. Bartrum, which he has been kind enough to make available to me. Trollope himself, for whatever it is worth, always denied the identification of Chiltern with Hartington.

26 See Chapman, *passim.*, for more speculation along these lines. Chapman, incidentally, identifies the Duke of St Bungay tentatively as the third Lord Lansdowne (d. 1862).

27 Escott, p. 266; Sadleir, p. 418; Pope-Hennessy, p. 280; and Snow, p. 181n (he later says — p. 182n — that John Pope-Hennessy is a likelier model). See also *T.P.'s and Cassell's Weekly* for 5 June 1926, in which T. P. O'Connor argues for the Pope-Hennessy connection.

28 My argument in this paragraph is derived largely from information provided by Bartrum (see n. 25, above).

29 Escott, p. 37; see also Booth, pp. 87–8.

30 Snow, p. 135; the information about Trollope's social connection with Lady Stanley is drawn largely from Bartrum, "Lady Stanley," 133–46 (see also Chapter 8, notes 18 and 19).

31 Polhemus, p. 151.

32 See Snow, p. 75, on Trollope's belated promotion and his reaction to

it; my discussion is adapted from his. The quotation from *The New Zealander* is taken from p. 170 (the essay on "Society").

33   The argument of this paragraph is largely derived from an un-published essay by Janet Egleson Dunleavy entitled "Irish Politics and the Novels of Anthony Trollope"; I am grateful to Professor Dunleavy for making a draft of her essay available to me. She also suggests that Trollope, at least in retrospect, had some sympathy for the Tenant Right League. Historian Stephen Gwynn points out that while Trollope in his Irish fiction attacks injustices within the land system he never attacks the system itself and that he seems to feel that if specific Irish landlords are bad they should simply be replaced by better ones — thus he would be likely to oppose any attempt by government to regulate free enterprise. See Gwynn's "Trollope in Ireland," *Contemporary Review*, 129 (January 1926), 72–9.

34   *Four Lectures*, p. 113. Here his view of Tenant-Right might seem to be closer to Gwynn's version than to Dunleavy's, as enumerated just above; see also *Castle Richmond*, Chapter VII. The rest of what Trollope says here seems to me to be a criticism of Dickens.

35   Dinwiddy, 33. The list of Trollope's journalistic subjects given just above in the text is taken from Booth, p. 80.

36   Snow, p. 43.

37   The information in this paragraph is derived liberally from Trevelyan, pp. 356–7, and Snow, pp. 88–9 and 182n.

38   Trevelyan, p. 357.

39   That Phineas does vote against reform makes even more nonsensical apRoberts's garbled assertion (p. 51) that he stands "for a rotten borough so that he can get into Parliament so that he can effect the abolition of rotten boroughs."

40   Cockshut, p. 85.

41   *Fortnightly Review*, 3 (15 January 1866), 650; and *Cicero*, I, 270, and II, 277.

42   *The New Zealander*, pp. 110–11.

43   *The New Zealander*, pp. 122 and 140. Trollope liked this analogy and used it in several places. It crops up, for example, in *The Three Clerks* (pp. 550–1) in connection with a parliamentary debate on the Civil Service.

44   Again, this image is a favorite of the author's. E.g., Alaric Tudor in *The Three Clerks* (p. 409), urging himself to run for Parliament, judges that "the ball [is now] at his foot."

45   *The New Zealander*, pp. 123 and 129.

46   Cockshut, p. 99, makes these points in his discussion of the novel.

47   Speare, p. 200; Sadleir, p. 418; and especially Polhemus, pp. 154–5, whose incisive argument I have freely adapted to my own use here.

48   *Tancred* (1847), p. 101 (I am quoting from the second edition — London, 1877).

49   Cf. Disraeli's account, also in *Tancred* (Book II, Chapter VII), of the career of Mrs Guy Flouncey, a great "social general" and aspiring hostess. Like Madame Max Goesler, interestingly enough, Mrs Guy also (twenty years earlier) uses the tactic of *not* making love to an important and willing man in order to cultivate the gratitude, friendship, and social beneficence of his fastidious and influential female connections.

50   My argument here is adapted from Polhemus's, p. 155.

51   My discussion is derived from Polhemus's, p. 155.

52   Booth, p. 87; and Bartrum, "Lady Stanley," *passim*.

53   According to Blake (p. 568), at least, this was the usual posture of the Victorian M.P.; little has changed since then. Several critics, incidentally, have wondered how, in a supposedly realistic novel, Trollope could have allowed Phineas and Lord Chiltern to duel. But there were indeed duels in England well into the 1850s. By the 1860s, however, Prince Albert had made duelling unfashionable as well as illegal, and thus Phineas and Chiltern wish to preserve secrecy by leaving England to fight.

54   Polhemus, p. 157.

CHAPTER 5

1   See the Stebbinses, p. 258; Sadleir, p. 302; Lance O. Tingay, "Trollope and the Beverley Election," *NCF*, 5, No. 1 (June 1950), 23; Escott, p. 248; Briggs, p. 100; and Booth, p. 74. Mr Tingay, incidentally, now writes tennis reports for the *Daily Telegraph*.

2   Briggs, p. 100, and Escott, p. 251n. Among the constituencies which rejected Bagehot's candidacy were Manchester, Bridgwater, and London University. The rest of the information in this paragraph is adapted from the discussions by Escott, p. 245, Booth, p. 74, and Pope-Hennessy, p. 279. The quotation from *Thackeray* is taken from pp. 48–9.

3   Thomas Adolphus Trollope, *What I Remember* (New York, 1888), p. 362. By one of the strange coincidences that pop up now and then among literary people and their relations — especially in the nineteenth century — Frances Trollope, Tom's second wife, was the sister of Dickens's mistress, Ellen Ternan.

4   Escott, pp. 245–6; Booth, p. 75; and Briggs, p. 100.

5   Sadleir, p. 302.

6   The information in this paragraph is taken largely from Briggs, pp. 101–2. The quotation from *The Times* comes from the *Beverley Recorder* of 26 February 1870, and that from the *Manchester Examiner* is taken from Pollard, p. 3.

7   My information here and the quotations from Thackeray's letters are taken from Escott, pp. 246–7.

8   The information in this paragraph is taken largely from Escott, pp. 247–8, and the Stebbinses, pp. 258–9.

9   See the *Autobiography*, p. 260; the Stebbinses, p. 259; and Sadleir, p. 302. Trollope in the *Autobiography* recounts a conversation he had with the Liberal agent at Beverley during which he was supposedly told that his campaign would cost him £1,000 and the inevitable petition another £1,000; and in *Ralph the Heir* Sir Thomas Underwood is given the same figures by his agent at Percycross. Either or both of these passages may be the origin of Sadleir's plausible but erroneous "nearly £2,000."

10   These details are recounted by Escott, p. 246, and the Stebbinses, p. 259.

11   *Beverley Recorder*, 14 November 1868.

12   The information in this paragraph is taken largely from the Stebbinses, p. 259; Escott, p. 250; the *Autobiography*, p. 259; and Sadleir, p. 302.

13   Escott, pp. 249–50; large chunks of the speeches are reprinted in Tingay, 23–39 (Trollope's election address is also reprinted – alone but in its entirety – by Pope-Hennessy, p. 258); Booth, pp. 75 and 80; and James Bryce, *Studies in Contemporary Biography* (New York, 1927), p. 121. Trollope's speech is reprinted in the "Eastern Question Report of the National Conference at St. James's Hall, London, 8 December 1876," pp. 19–21. The phrase quoted just below in the text from Pollard appears on p. 8.

14   Tingay, 25; the latter quotation is taken from the *Hull & Eastern Counties Herald*, 3 November 1868.

15   See the Stebbinses, p. 258; Booth, p. 75; and the *Beverley Recorder*, 21 November 1868.

16   *Beverley Recorder*, 14 November 1868.

17   *Beverley Recorder*, 14 November 1868.

18   *Beverley Recorder*, 14 November 1868.

19   Booth, p. 75.

20   *Beverley Guardian*, 21 November 1868; and *Hull News*, 21 November 1868.

21   These slogans are reprinted from the *Beverley Guardian* of 14 November 1868 and an election poster in the possession of the Beverley Public Library. The Liberal poster is reprinted as the frontispiece to the printed text of Pollard's lecture-essay.

22   My account is taken from the Stebbinses, p. 259.

23   *Beverley Guardian*, 4 September 1869; and *Report of the Commissioners appointed to inquire into the Suggestion of Corrupt Practices at the last election . . . the Borough of Beverley* (London, 1870).

24   The Stebbinses, p. 260; and the *Beverley Recorder*, 21 November 1868.

25   While Cockshut (p. 106) does not actually deny the identification of Percycross with Beverley, his choice of words suggests some doubt (e.g., Trollope "says" that Percycross is Beverley – thus the reader "would be wise, if he wishes to be just, to consider these chapters carefully," and so

on). However, Pope-Hennessy declares that *Ralph the Heir* "is the book in which Trollope worked off all the irritations he had personally experienced when standing ... for Beverley" (p. 307); Sadleir says the novel "resulted directly from the election fiasco" of Beverley (p. 302); Escott calls *Ralph the Heir* a "record of its author's personal partialities or prejudices" during the "electioneering errand to Yorkshire" and says that "each detail" of the political story reflects "Trollope's Beverley conflict ... now satirised" (pp. 251 and 253–4); and Briggs simply observes that *Ralph the Heir* "recapitulated the gloomy experiences of Beverley" (p. 105).

26 The best sources of information about this incident are the Stebbinses, p. 285, whose general account of it mine chiefly depends upon; Bradford A. Booth, "Trollope, Reade, and *Shilly-Shally*," *TT*, 1 (March 1947), 45–54, and 2 (June 1947), 43–51; and letters written by Trollope to George Smith (20 May 1872, dated from Melbourne; see *Letters*, pp. 292–3) and John Hollingshead (14 March 1873; *Letters*, p. 305).

27 Unsigned notice, *Athenaeum*, 15 April 1871, p. 456; unsigned notice, *The Times*, 17 April 1871, p. 6; unsigned notice, *British Quarterly Review*, 54 (July 1871), 126–7; unsigned notice, *Saturday Review*, 31 (29 April 1871), 537–8; unsigned notice, *Examiner*, 22 April 1871, p. 419; unsigned notice, *North American Review*, 112 (April 1871), 433–7. The latter review goes on to speculate on possible reasons for the superiority of the English over the American novel and examines questions of "class" in this connection. See the *Critical Heritage*, p. 355.

28 Unsigned notice, 44 (15 April 1871), 450–3.

29 See Sadleir, p. 302; Briggs, p. 104; Booth, pp. 118–19; Escott, p. 251; Polhemus, p. 170; and Walpole, p. 105. Other published comments include those by Cockshut, who likes the novel (p. 106), and Snow, who does not (p. 95). Polhemus goes on to accuse *Ralph the Heir* of being full of philosophical inconsistencies, including "equivocal middle-class ditherings about the undeclared class war." Booth, p. 244n, points out that Reade, in *Shilly-Shally* (n. 26, above), eliminated the Ralph Newton who is not the heir, thus tightening up the plot and making it more "manageable."

30 Booth, p. 118. He also points out that at the time Trollope wrote *Ralph the Heir* he seemed to have no special interest in Bacon, the subject of Sir Thomas's never-to-be-completed biography (not Dr Johnson, as Curtis Brown says, p. 67). In 1879, however, Trollope was given by his son a new edition of Bacon's essays, which he carefully annotated. See Michael Sadleir, "Trollope and Bacon's Essays," *NCF*, 1 (Summer 1945), 21–34. Polhemus (cited in the text just below) discusses Sir Thomas on p. 171. Both Sadleir and Cockshut instinctively saw some of Trollope in Sir Thomas Underwood, though neither of them took the connection as far as I do.

31   The preceding account of the similarities of Sir Thomas's and Trollope's political experiences is taken in part from Sadleir, p. 303. Also in this connection see Cockshut, p. 106.

32   See apRoberts, p. 125.

33   Polhemus, p. 170.

34   I base these last two points on the account given by Tingay, 34.

35   Booth, p. 118, uses such adjectives as "serio-comic" and such phrases as "mock solemnity" in connection with the Percycross election. Clearly he did not see it as a particularly revealing passage in Trollope's life or fiction.

36   In *The Prime Minister* Trollope uses the phrase "pachy-dermatous one" to describe a type of politician without convictions other than a desire for self-promotion.

37   Booth, p. 118, and Escott, p. 254.

38   See Briggs, p. 105; Booth, p. 118; and, on Trollope's repudiation of Moggs the politician, Burn, p.167 (the latter mentions Daniel Caldigate in *John Caldigate* as another example of the sort of prosperous Radical Trollope disliked — but Daniel's political utterances are negligible). The only other critic to hint at Trollope's real attitude toward Moggs as politician is Booth, p. 118.

39   Polhemus, p. 170; and Booth, p. 118. The quotation from apRoberts just below in the text is taken from p. 131.

40   *The New Zealander*, p. 158.

CHAPTER 6

1   The first edition bears 1873 on its title page, though it actually appeared in three volumes late in 1872. The novel ran in the *Fortnightly* from 1 July 1871 to 1 February 1873. Inexplicably, Polhemus (p. 172) lists it as having appeared in 1869–70.

2   Unsigned notice, *Athenaeum* (26 October 1872); unsigned notice, *Spectator*, 45 (26 October 1872), 1365–6; unsigned notice, *Nation*, 15 (14 November 1872), 320; unsigned notice, *Examiner* (16 November 1872); unsigned notice, *Harper's Magazine* (December 1872); unsigned notice, *The Times* (30 October 1872), p. 4; unsigned notice, *Saturday Review*, 34 (16 November 1872), 637–8.

3   Booth, p. 91; Walpole, p. 99; and Sadleir, p. 419 — "It is one of the best constructed of all Trollope's novels."

4   *The New Zealander*, pp. 120–1.

5   Polhemus, p. 192; and *The New Zealander*, p. 27. Breghert, in *The Way We Live Now*, is somewhat more ambivalently presented; but the horror with which his proposal to Georgina Longstaffe is greeted by the members of her family — and the unnecessary violence of their language on the subject — are indicative.

CHAPTER 7

1   Critics sometimes unthinkingly assign this place to *Phineas Finn*, perhaps remembering *Phineas Redux* in part for the dramatic murder trial in its second volume. But any comparison of the two novels demonstrates that there is much more "love and intrigue" in *Phineas Finn* than in its sequel, which has fewer subplots and sticks more closely to the parliamentary scene. Booth, p. 93, and Polhemus, p. 180, have noted this, but they are exceptions. The opening quotation is taken from Polhemus, p. 185.

2   The Stebbinses, for example, say five years have elapsed between the two novels (p. 271); Winifred and James Gerould, in *A Guide to Trollope* (Princeton, 1948), say seven years have passed (see Booth, p. 242n). The current (1964) Oxford World's Classics edition of *Phineas Redux* proclaims 1874 as the date of its original appearance.

3   Unsigned notice, *Spectator*, 47 (3 January 1874), 15–17; unsigned notice, *Saturday Review*, 37 (7 February 1874), 186–7; unsigned notice, *Athenaeum* (10 January 1874), p. 53; and unsigned notice, the *Nation*, 18 (12 March 1874), 174–5 (I rely in part on Smalley's summary of the latter article's content – see the *Critical Heritage*, p. 385).

4   Walpole, pp. 108–9; Booth, pp. 93–7, *passim.*; Polhemus, pp. 178–85, *passim.*; and apRoberts, p. 50.

5   Blake, p. 501; and Trevelyan, p. 350.

6   *The New Zealander*, p. 139.

7   See Blake, p. 503. Trollope's "The Irish Church" appeared in the *Fortnightly Review* in August 1865; "The Irish Beneficed Clergyman," first published in the *Pall Mall Gazette* on 23 January 1866, was also reprinted in Trollope's *Clergymen of the Church of England* (London, 1866; repr. 1974). As the discussion in Chapter 4 (and notes) may suggest, there has been disagreement about Trollope's position on some aspects of Victorian England's Irish policies. Burn, p. 67, argues that Trollope saw no danger in the connection between church and state since he felt that the clergy had that connection "in their bones and could not be imagined as the leaders of a spiritual crusade, were they to be freed from it." But this hypothesis is difficult to defend, I think, in view of Trollope's election address and some of his other statements at Beverley (see Chapters 1 and 5). A more judicious position is taken by E. W. Wittig in "Trollope's Irish Fiction," *Eire-Ireland*, 9, No. 3 (Autumn 1974), 97–118.

8   See apRoberts, p. 49; and the *Hull & Eastern Counties Herald* for 3 November 1868.

9   Booth, p. 95 (despite his other failings as a critic of the Palliser novels, Booth at least accepts Chapman's reading of them rather than Cockshut's). The quotation just below in the text is taken from Cockshut, p. 248.

10   Greville, VI, p. 342; and Blake, pp. 498 and 516, quoting from the *Quarterly Review*. Salisbury's speech was made in 1868 as Viscount

Cranborne. It may be worth recalling here that Trollope uses the weathercock image in an important passage in *The New Zealander* (p. 117).

11   Salisbury Papers – quoted by Blake, pp. 499–500; and again Blake, p. 607.

12   Blake, pp. 477, 442, 469, 476, 567, 766, 515, and 764, *passim*.

13   Quoted from *The English Constitution* by Briggs, p. 92.

14   Hughenden Papers, Box 107, B/XX/P/44, draft, quoted by Blake, p. 389; Hughenden Papers, Box 109, B/XX/S/81, November 30, quoted by Blake, p. 338; and again Blake, pp. 341–2.

15   Blake, pp. 764, 474, and 464, *passim*.

16   Blake, p. 396; Salisbury Papers – quoted by Blake, pp. 499–500; and Hughenden Papers, Box 101, B/XX/J/73 – quoted by Blake, p. 408.

17   See, in connection with the argument of this paragraph, Polhemus, p. 179; Booth, p. 93; Sadleir, p. 304; Briggs, p. 105; *The New Zealander*, pp. 19–20; and again Briggs, p. 90.

18   Trollope became particularly angry with Gladstone in the late seventies and early eighties over Liberal Irish policies. See, for example, P. D. Edwards, "Trollope to Gladstone: An Unpublished Letter," *N&Q* (May 1968), 184–5.

19   A measure of Trollope's contempt in this passage may be gleaned from the fact that the image of hiding one's face in one's toga is often used by the corrupt Melmotte – a Tory – to urge himself on in *The Way We Live Now*.

20   *Beverley Recorder*, 14 and 21 November 1868.

21   *Beverley Recorder*, 14 November 1868 (the speech was made on 9 November).

22   *Lord Palmerston*, p. 83.

23   "Mr. Disraeli and the Mint," *St. Paul's Magazine*, 4 (May 1869), 197; the article appears on pp. 192–7. I am grateful to George Butte for calling it to my attention.

24   Polhemus, p. 178.

25   *The New Zealander*, pp. 116 and 129–30.

26   Trollope's application of mock-heroic language to political events is not confined to the Palliser novels. In *The Three Clerks* (p. 86) there is this description of the sudden summoning from his bed of a party whip on the occasion of an unexpected division: "Off flew on the wings of Hansom a youthful member . . . to the abode of the now couchant Treasury Argus. Morpheus had claimed all for his own . . . But even in his deepest slumber the quick wheels of the bounding cab struck upon the tympanum of his anxious ear. He roused himself as does a noble watch-dog when the 'suspicious tread of theft' approaches. The hurry of the jaded horse, the sudden stop, the maddened furious knock, all told a tale which his well-trained ear only knew too well."

27   Polhemus, p. 182.

28   Polhemus, pp. 179—80.

29   Polhemus, p. 181.

30   Speare, p. 219; Blake, p. 217; and Cockshut, p. 109.

31   See Booth, pp. 78—9.

32   See Walpole, p. 108 — and Pollard, who says (p. 20) that *Phineas Redux* is "marred" by the trial.

33   *The Three Clerks*, p. 407. In the same novel (p. 431) it is said of Alaric Tudor, an aspiring politician: "He is not a man of fortune, and he ought not to think of Parliament . . . He has no private fortune to back him."

CHAPTER 8

1   Booth, pp. 99 and 101.

2   *Critical Heritage*, pp. 17—18 and 418—19.

3   Unsigned notice, *Spectator*, 49 (22 July 1876), 922—3; unsigned notice, *Saturday Review*, 42 (14 October 1876), 481—2; unsigned notice, *Examiner*, (22 July 1876); unsigned notice, *Athenaeum* (1 July 1876); unsigned notice, *Illustrated London News* (8 July 1876); unsigned notice, the *Nation* (20 July 1876); unsigned notice, *Harper's Magazine* (August 1876); unsigned notice, *Academy* (29 July 1876); unsigned notice, *The Times* (18 August 1876), p. 4.

4   Nor could Tolstoy have got the idea for the suicide of Anna in *Anna Karenina* from Lopez's suicide (the chronology won't work), as Snow has also suggested — though Tolstoy was indeed fascinated by this new and horrible form of sudden death and surmised "that the English were likely to be expert about suicides on railway lines." See Snow, pp. 146—7 and 184n, and a recent (1976) review in *NCF* by N. John Hall of Snow's book. Other sources for information given in this paragraph are N. N. Glisev (or Gusev), *Chronicle of the Life and Work of L. N. Tolstoy 1818—1890* (Moscow, 1958), pp. 315 and 466 (also called *Recollections* rather than *Chronicle* in some translations); Polhemus, p. 207; and Pope-Hennessy, p. 331.

5   Escott, p. 266; *Letters*, p. 355 (letter to Mary Holmes, 15 June 1876); and Booth, p. 98.

6   Booth, pp. 97 and 101; Polhemus, p. 211; Pope-Hennessy, p. 329; and Snow, p. 146.

7   There has been some controversy over the probable date of the composition of *Lord Palmerston*. See Chapter 4, n. 20.

8   Briggs, pp. 88—9; and *Lord Palmerston*, pp. 214, 24—5, and 166, *passim.*

9   The quotations from *Lord Palmerston* in this paragraph are taken from pp. 27 and 213.

10   The quotations from *Lord Palmerston* in this paragraph are taken from pp. 118, 63, 95, 168, 31, 203, and 73, respectively.

11   *Lord Palmerston*, pp. 200 and 9.

12   The information in this paragraph is taken in part from Philip Guedalla, *Bonnet and Shawl* (London, 1928), p. 62; S. Walpole, *The Life of Lord John Russell* (London, 1892), II, 481; Bartrum, "Lady Stanley," *passim.*, especially 133; and Mabell, Countess of Airlie, *Lady Palmerston and Her Times* (London, 1922), II, 43.

13   See Trollope's review of R. H. Hutton's *Studies in Parliament* (cited in full in Chapter 1, n. 1). The rest of the information in this paragraph is taken largely from Kenney, *passim.*, especially 282; see also Greville, II, 224.

14   In connection with the ideas cited in this paragraph, see Russell's *Essay on the History of the English Government and Constitution* (London, 1823), p. 12, and Trollope's *North America*, p. 55. Again, much of my information here is derived from Kenney, *passim.*, especially 284–5.

15   Quoted by Stuart J. Reid in *Lord John Russell* (London, 1895), p. 205.

16   Kenney, *passim.*

17   Quoted by Desmond McCarthy and Agatha Russell in *Lady John Russell: A Memoir* (London, 1911), p. 72.

18   See the *Encyclopaedia Britannica* (11th ed.); *The Autobiography of Bertrand Russell 1872–1914*, Vol. I (London, 1951), pp. 29–30; and *The Amberley Papers*, ed. Bertrand and Patricia Russell (London, 1938), I, 18. Lady Stanley's announcement is recollected by Bertrand Russell.

19   Bartrum, "Lady Stanley," 140 and 137–38, *passim.*

20   John R. Vincent, *The Formation of the Liberal Party 1857–1868* (London, 1966), p. 22.

21   See Chapter 3, notes 6 and 7; and apRoberts, p. 141, who quotes from *Trollope on the Old Drama*, notes on *Julius Caesar*.

22   The two unpublished essays are each part of in-progress dissertations by George Butte (Johns Hopkins) and Barry A. Bartrum (Princeton). I should like to thank Mr Butte (on Charles Buxton) and Mr Bartrum (on the Duke of Newcastle) for having kindly made their work available to me. Newcastle was not a friend of Trollope's, but he was certainly known to the novelist; he is mentioned by Escott (p. 141), and Trollope himself devotes several paragraphs to Newcastle in *The New Zealander* (pp. 82–3). There are a few superficial resemblances between the Dukes of Newcastle and Omnium (both were morally punctilious, worked very hard, had sons who gambled and American daughters-in-law); but most other details of their lives are strikingly different.

23   Polhemus, p. 208; Booth, pp. 101 and 99; and apRoberts, pp. 145–6. The latter does perceive the important lesson in *The Prime Minister* that "the mere existence of such goodness as . . . Palliser's is enormously important. He fails as Prime Minister, but . . . he triumphs morally" (p. 147); and "his real inadequacy is his greatness" (p. 141).

24   *North America*, p. 213; and *The New Zealander*, p. 10.

25 *St. Paul's Magazine*, 1 (March 1868), 541–2; and *North America*, p. 188.
26 Briggs, pp. 89 and 93.
27 *Lord Palmerston*, p. 163.
28 *North America*, pp. 27–8.
29 Quoted from the second edition of *Tancred* (London, 1877), p. 73. *Tancred* was first published in 1847.
30 *Cicero*, II, 118. Trollope of course also published (in 1870) an edition of *The Commentaries of Caesar* – which, as Sadleir says (p. 304), "earned the scorn of scholarship and very little uninstructed praise to balance it."
31 *The New Zealander*, p. 147.
32 Escott, p. 255.
33 Briggs, p. 93.
34 Polhemus, p. 210.
35 Thus Escott says (p. 267) that Spurgeon and Sprout, the election agents at Silverbridge, are drawn from agents known to Trollope at Beverley – but they are scarcely portrayed as vividly as either Trigger in *Ralph the Heir* or Molescroft in *Phineas Redux*. And thus apRoberts says (p. 143) that Trollope's Beverley experiences are "recollected in tranquillity" in *The Prime Minister*; "tranquillity" is hardly the right word to apply to the recollections Trollope had of Beverley – but in any case after *Ralph the Heir* and *Phineas Redux* he had little more to say in his novels specifically about Beverley, and indeed said virtually nothing about it in *The Prime Minister*. The memories, of course, remained; and the nature of politics in the novel reflects this.
36 See Bartrum, "Lady Stanley," 138.
37 Polhemus, pp. 214 and 213, *passim.*, and p. 198. The argument in this paragraph is based largely on his.
38 *The New Zealander*, pp. 118–19 and 121.
39 I am quoting from *The Three Clerks*, pp. 393–4; the identical passage appears in *The New Zealander*, p. 110.

CHAPTER 9

1 See Trollope's letter to R. P. Harding (dated 13 August 1880) in *Letters*, p. 444. Here the novelist mentions that the "bargain" in question (the financial terms of publication) were "made as far back as June 1878."
2 Unsigned notice, *Athenaeum* (29 May 1880), p. 694; unsigned notice, *Illustrated London News*, 76 (26 June 1880), 622; unsigned notice, *Spectator*, 53 (12 June 1880), 754–5; unsigned notice, the *Nation*, 31 (19 August 1880), 138–9; unsigned notice, *Westminster Review*, 114 (October 1880), 574.

3   See John H. Hagan, *"The Duke's Children*: Trollope's Psychological Masterpiece," *NCF*, 12 (June 1958), 1–21, and Polhemus, pp. 219–31. The quoted phrase is taken from Hagan, 21. Snow, p. 115, calls Lady Mabel "one of the best women in fiction."

4   Booth, p. 101.

5   *North America*, pp. 102 and 42.

6   The *Spectator* review of *The Duke's Children* (n. 2, above) declared that a real American girl would have laughed at such an English family instead of being impressed by it. Trollope obviously disagreed; and all the available evidence suggests that he was right.

7   I am again quoting from the Riverside edition (see Chapter 3, n. 9), pp. 52–5, *passim*.

8   Snow, pp. 126 and 128. The phrase quoted just above in the text appears on p. 126. Much of the speculation in this paragraph about Kate Field derives from Snow's excellent discussion.

9   James, p. 121; the Stebbinses, p. 296; and Pope-Hennessy, p. 352.

10   At least twice – once aboard ship travelling from America to England in 1875, and again in 1877 at the home of Lord Houghton. My information comes from Leon Edel, *Henry James: The Conquest of London 1870–1883* (London, 1962), *passim*. The quotation in the text above from Polhemus is taken from p. 228.

11   This is brilliantly argued by Hagan (n. 3, above), 18–19.

12   Hagan, 16–17.

13   My argument here is indebted to Hagan's, 16–20, *passim*.

14   See apRoberts, p. 148.

15   Polhemus, p. 224.

16   Hagan, 6, and *The New Zealander*, p. 159.

17   Hagan, 7.

18   Hagan, 8.

19   Unsigned notice, *Saturday Review*, 49 (12 June 1880), 767–8.

20   There is a long aside in *Phineas Redux* (I, 87) on the sham nature of the Queen's Address and the seconding speeches. Among other things, Trollope comments here on the fact that the "gorgeously apparrelled speakers ... seem to have great latitude allowed them in the matter of clothing ... [but] very little in the matter of language. And then it always seems that either of the four might have made the speech of any of the others."

21   See Trollope Papers, II, Folios 76–8, for references to *Lord Silverbridge*; and II, Folios 75 and 81–3, for references to *The Ex-Prime Minister*.

22   See Blake's account of this, pp. 264–7. The quotations in the text just above are taken from Blake, pp. 247 and 368. See also Lord Malmesbury, *Memoirs of an Ex-Minister*, 2 vols. (London, 1884), II, p. 45.

23   Escott, p. 255.

CHAPTER 10

1 Cockshut, p. 105.
2 Speare, pp. 219 and 218; and Cockshut, p. 248.
3 There are the two Silverbridge elections in *The Prime Minister* and *The Duke's Children*, but Trollope's account of them is very slight — perhaps because the candidates in each case are so uninteresting.
4 *The New Zealander*, p. 188; Polhemus, p. 192; and Cockshut, p. 206.
5 Escott, p. 297.
6 Briggs, p. 104.
7 *North America*, pp. 172–3.
8 See apRoberts, p. 136; and Booth, p. 98.
9 See Booth, p. 78.
10 Speare, pp. 200–1. He thinks Slide is a better character than Palliser — and so of course likes Disraeli's fictional politicians better than Trollope's.

Select Bibliography of Secondary Sources

I BOOKS

Ruth apRoberts, *The Moral Trollope* (Athens, Ohio, 1971).

Robert Blake, *Disraeli* (London, 1966).

Bradford A. Booth, *Anthony Trollope: Aspects of His Life and Work* (Bloomington, Indiana, 1958).

James Bryce, *Studies in Contemporary Biography* (New York, 1927).

A. O. J. Cockshut, *Anthony Trollope: A Critical Study* (London, 1955).

Beatrice Curtis Brown, *Trollope* (Denver, 1950).

Leon Edel, *Henry James: The Conquest of London 1870–1883* (London, 1962).

T. H. S. Escott, *Anthony Trollope: His Public Services, Private Friends and Literary Originals* (London, 1913: repr. Port Washington, N.Y., 1967).

Winifred and James Gerould, *A Guide to Trollope* (Princeton, 1948).

Philip Guedalla, *Bonnet and Shawl* (London, 1928).

Norris D. Hoyt, *The Parliamentary Novels of Anthony Trollope* (unpublished Yale dissertation, 1940).

James Gibbon Huneker, *Steeplejack* (New York, 1920).

R. H. Hutton, *Studies in Parliament* (London, 1866).

Mabell, Countess of Airlie, *Lady Palmerston and Her Times*, 2 vols. (London, 1922).

Lord Malmesbury, *Memoirs of an Ex-Minister*, 2 vols. (London, 1884).

Desmond McCarthy and Agatha Russell, *Lady John Russell: A Memoir* (London, 1911).

Robert M. Polhemus, *The Changing World of Anthony Trollope* (Berkeley and Los Angeles, 1968).

James Pope-Hennessy, *Anthony Trollope* (London and Boston, 1971).

Stuart J. Reid, *Lord John Russell* (London, 1895).

Bertrand Russell, *The Autobiography of Bertrand Russell 1872–1914*, Vol. I (London, 1951).

Bertrand and Patricia Russell (eds.), *The Amberley Papers*, 2 vols. (London, 1938).

Michael Sadleir, *Trollope: A Commentary* (London, 1927; repr. 1961).

David Skilton, *Anthony Trollope and His Contemporaries* (London, 1972).

Donald Smalley (ed.), *Anthony Trollope: The Critical Heritage* (London and New York, 1969).

C. P. Snow, *Trollope* (London, 1975).

Donald Southgate, *The Passing of the Whigs, 1832–1886* (London and New York, 1962).

Morris E. Speare, *The Political Novel* (New York, 1924).

Lucy Poate Stebbins and Richard Poate Stebbins, *The Trollopes: The Chronicle of A Writing Family* (New York, 1945).

G. M. Trevelyan, *British History in the Nineteenth Century* (New York, 1922; repr. 1966).

Thomas Adolphus Trollope, *What I Remember* (New York, 1888).

John R. Vincent, *The Formation of the Liberal Party 1857–1868* (London, 1966).

Hugh Walpole, *Anthony Trollope* (New York, 1928).

S. Walpole, *The Life of Lord John Russell*, 2 vols. (London, 1892).

Philip Whitwell Wilson (ed.), *The Greville Diary*, 6 vols. (London, 1927).

II   ARTICLES AND ESSAYS

J. A. Banks, "The Way They Lived Then: Anthony Trollope and the Seventies," *VS*, 12 (December 1968), 177–200.

Barry A. Bartrum, "A Victorian Political Hostess: The Engagement Book of Lady Stanley of Alderley," *PULC*, 36, No. 2 (Winter 1975), 133–46.

Daniel Becquemont, "Politics in Literature, 1874–1875: *The Way We Live Now* and *Beauchamp's Career*," *Politics in Literature in the Nineteenth Century*, ed. Janie Teissedon (Lille and Paris, 1974), pp. 137–50.

Bradford A. Booth, "Author to Publisher: Trollope and Isbister," *PULC*, 24, No. 1 (Winter 1962), 51–68.

Bradford A. Booth, "Trollope and *Little Dorrit*," *NCF*, 2 (March 1948), 237–40.

Bradford A. Booth, "Trollope and the *Pall Mall Gazette*," *NCF*, 4 (June 1949), 51–69, and 4 (September 1949), 137–58.

Bradford A. Booth, "Trollope, Reade, and *Shilly-Shally*," *TT*, 1 (March 1947), 45–54, and 2 (June 1947), 43–51.

Asa Briggs, "Trollope, Bagehot and the English Constitution," in *Victorian People* (London, 1954 and Chicago, 1955), pp. 87–115.

W. L. Burn, "Anthony Trollope's Politics," *The Nineteenth Century and After*, 143 (March, 1948), 161–71.

David S. Chamberlain, "Unity and Irony in Trollope's *Can You Forgive Her?*," *SEL*, 8 (Autumn 1968), 670–7.

R. W. Chapman, "Personal Names in Trollope's Political Novels," in *Essays mainly on the Nineteenth Century presented to Sir Humphrey Milford* (London, 1948), pp. 72–81.

J. R. Dinwiddy, "Who's Who in Trollope's Political Novels," *NCF*, 22 (June 1967), 31–47.

P. D. Edwards, "Trollope to Gladstone: An Unpublished Letter," *N&Q* (May 1968), 184–5.

Janet Egleson Dunleavy, "Irish Politics and the Novels of Anthony Trollope" (unpublished).

Stephen Gwynn, "Trollope in Ireland," *Contemporary Review*, 129 (January 1926), 72–9.

John H. Hagan, "*The Duke's Children*: Trollope's Psychological Masterpiece," *NCF*, 12 (June 1958), 1–21.

N. John Hall, "Trollope Reading Aloud: An Unpublished Record," *N&Q* (March 1975), 117–18.

John Halperin, "Politics, Palmerston, and Trollope's Prime Minister," *Clio*, 3, No. 2 (February 1974), 187–218.

John Halperin, "Trollope, James, and the International Theme," *Yearbook of English Studies*, 7 (January 1977).

Norris D. Hoyt, " 'Can You Forgive Her?': A Commentary," *TT*, 2 (September 1947), 57–70.

Henry James, "Anthony Trollope," *Century Magazine* (July 1883); repr. *Partial Portraits* (New York, 1888), pp. 97–133.

Blair G. Kenney, "Trollope's Ideal Statesmen: Plantagenet Palliser and Lord John Russell," *NCF*, 20 (December 1965), 281–6.

George Levine, "Can You Forgive Him? Trollope's 'Can You Forgive Her?' and the Myth of Realism," *VS*, 18 (September 1974), 5–30.

Juliet McMaster, " 'The Meaning of Words and the Nature of Things': Trollope's *Can You Forgive Her?*," *SEL*, 14 (Autumn 1974), 603–18.

Arthur Pollard, "Trollope's Political Novels," Inaugural Lecture, University of Hull (April 1968).

Frank E. Robbins, "Chronology and History in Trollope's Barset and Parliamentary Novels," *NCF*, 5 (March 1951), 303–17.

Michael Sadleir, "Trollope and Bacon's Essays," *NCF*, 1 (Summer 1945), 21–43.

David Skilton, "*The Fixed Period*: Anthony Trollope's Novel of 1980," *Studies in the Literary Imagination*, 6, No. 2 (Fall 1973), 39–50.

David Stryker, "The Significance of Trollope's *The American Senator*," *NCF*, 5 (September 1950), 141–9.

Lance O. Tingay, "Trollope and the Beverley Election," *NCF*, 5 (June 1950), 23–39.

E. W. Wittig, "Trollope's Irish Fiction," *Eire-Ireland*, 9, No. 3 (Autumn 1974), 97–118.

General Index

Notes to Index

Italic figures in parentheses following a page number indicate a reference to a note. For example, *Athenaeum*, 31 (*3—1*) means that there is a reference to the *Athenaeum* on p. 31, and a further reference in note 1 to chapter 3

(A.T.) = Anthony Trollope

Political Novels: Fictional Characters

Key: Can You Forgive Her?   I
     Phineas Finn   II
     Ralph The Heir   III
     The Eustace Diamonds   IV
     Phineas Redux   V
     The Prime Minister   VI
     The Duke's Children   VII

Barset and Other Novels: Fictional Characters